# Four-Eyed Prince

**1**

## Wataru Mizukami

Translated and adapted by
Jamie Jacobs

Lettered by
North Market Street Graphics

DEL REY

Ballantine Books · New York

*Four-Eyed Prince* volume 1 is a work of fiction. Names, characters, places, and incidents are the products of the author's imagination or are used fictitiously. Any resemblance to actual events, locales, or persons, living or dead, is entirely coincidental.

A Del Rey Manga/Kodansha Trade Paperback Original



Published in the United States by Del Rey, an imprint of The Random House Publishing Group, a division of Random House, Inc., New York.



Publication rights arranged through Kodansha Ltd.

First published in Japan in 2007 by Kodansha Ltd., Tokyo

ISBN 978-0-345-51624-4

Printed in the United States of America

www.delreymanga.com

2 4 6 8 9 7 5 3 1

Translator/Adapter: Jamie Jacobs
Lettering: North Market Street Graphics

# Contents

# HONORIFICS EXPLAINED

Throughout the Del Rey Manga books, you will find Japanese honorifics left intact in the translations. For those not familiar with how the Japanese use honorifics and, more important, how they differ from American honorifics, we present this brief overview.

Politeness has always been a critical facet of Japanese culture. Ever since the feudal era, when Japan was a highly stratified society, use of honorifics—which can be defined as polite speech that indicates relationship or status—has played an essential role in the Japanese language. When you address someone in Japanese, an honorific usually takes the form of a suffix attached to one's name (example: "Asuna-san"), is used as a title at the end of one's name, or appears in place of the name itself (example: "Negi-sensei," or simply "Sensei!").

Honorifics can be expressions of respect or endearment. In the context of manga and anime, honorifics give insight into the nature of the relationship between characters. Many English translations leave out these important honorifics and therefore distort the feel of the original Japanese. Because Japanese honorifics contain nuances that English honorifics lack, it is our policy at Del Rey not to translate them. Here, instead, is a guide to some of the honorifics you may encounter in Del Rey Manga.

-san:   This is the most common honorific and is equivalent to Mr., Miss, Ms., or Mrs. It is the all-purpose honorific and can be used in any situation where politeness is required.

-sama:   This is one level higher than "-san" and is used to confer great respect.

-dono:   This comes from the word "tono," which means "lord." It is an even higher level than "-sama" and confers utmost respect.

*-kun:*  This suffix is used at the end of boys' names to express familiarity or endearment. It is also sometimes used by men among friends, or when addressing someone younger or of a lower station.

*-chan:*  This is used to express endearment, mostly toward girls. It is also used for little boys, pets, and even among lovers. It gives a sense of childish cuteness.

*Bozu:*  This is an informal way to refer to a boy, similar to the English terms "kid" and "squirt."

*Sempai/*
*Senpai:*  This title suggests that the addressee is one's senior in a group or organization. It is most often used in a school setting, where underclassmen refer to their upperclassmen as "sempai." It can also be used in the workplace, such as when a newer employee addresses an employee who has seniority in the company.

*Kohai:*  This is the opposite of "sempai" and is used toward underclassmen in school or newcomers in the workplace. It connotes that the addressee is of a lower station.

*Sensei:*  Literally meaning "one who has come before," this title is used for teachers, doctors, or masters of any profession or art.

*-[blank]:*  This is usually forgotten in these lists, but it is perhaps the most significant difference between Japanese and English. The lack of honorific, known as *yobisute,* means that the speaker has permission to address the person in a very intimate way. Usually, only family, spouses, or very close friends have this kind of permission. It can be gratifying when someone who has earned the intimacy starts to call one by one's name without an honorific. But when that intimacy hasn't been earned, it can be very insulting.

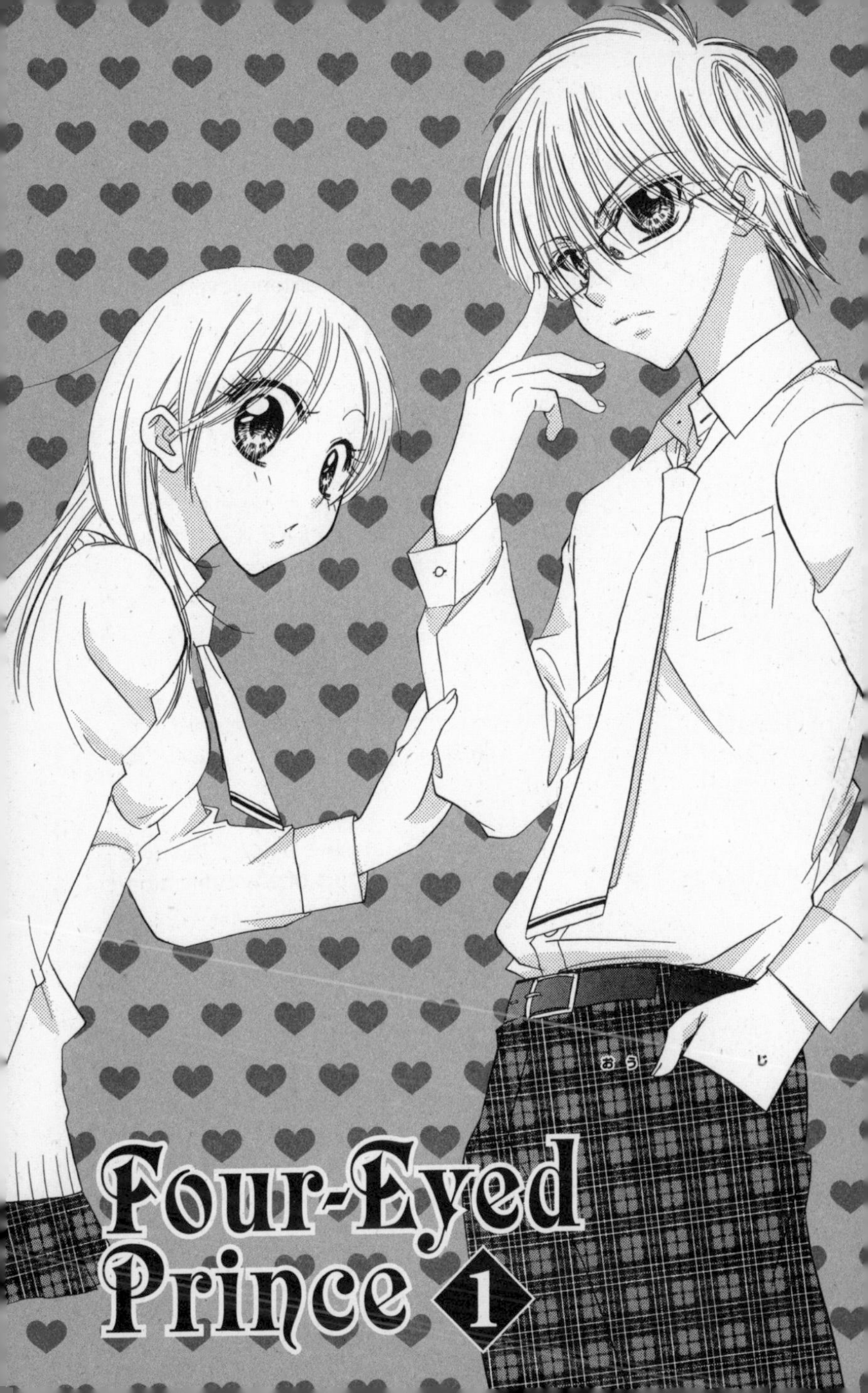
Four-Eyed
Prince 1

# Four-Eyed Prince
## ∞ Table of Contents

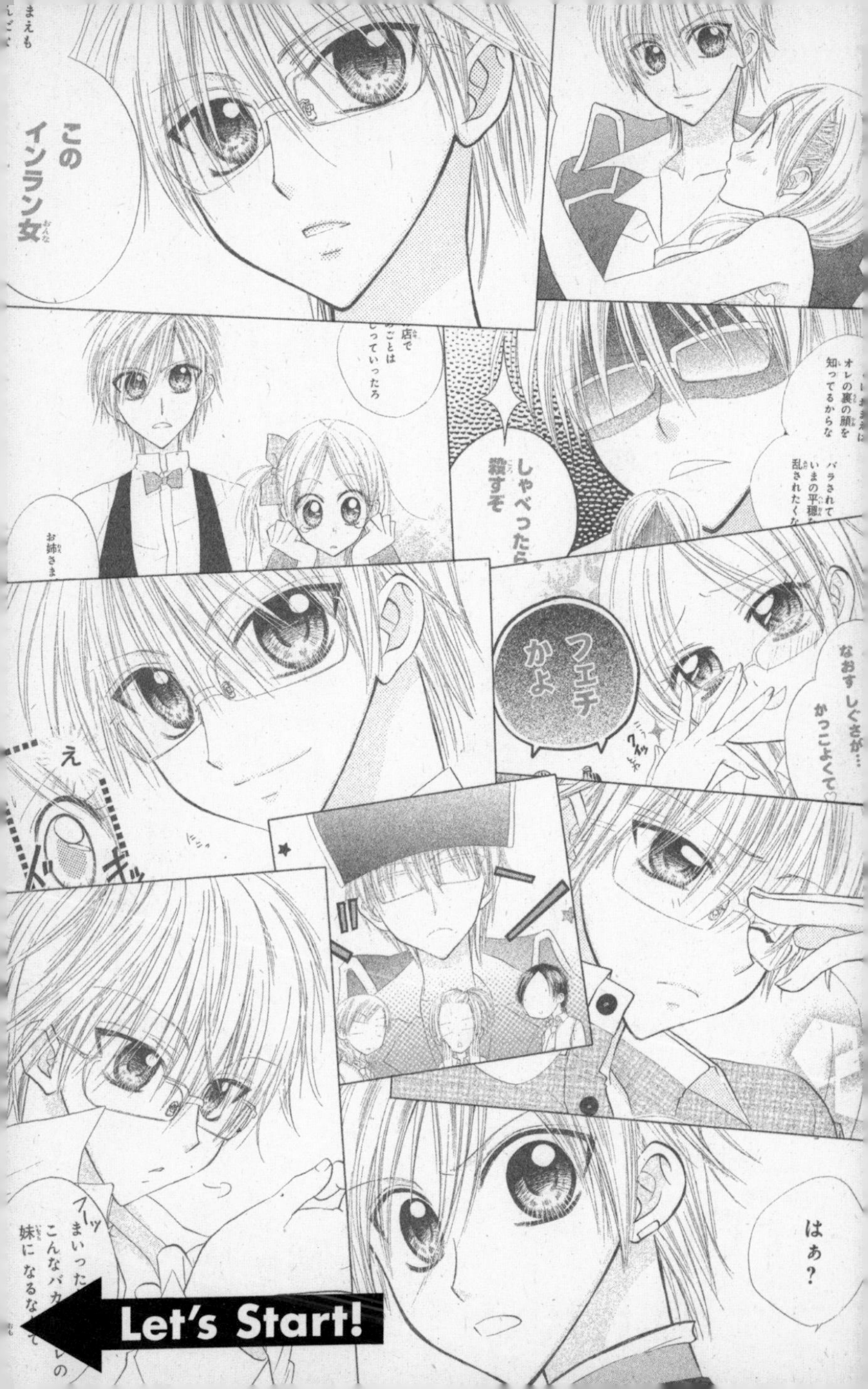

このインラン女
オレの裏の顔を知ってるからな
バラされていまの平穏を乱されたくな
しゃべったら殺すぞ
店でのごとはしっていったろ
お姉さま
なおすしぐさがかっこよくて♡
フェチかよ
え
はぁ?
フーッ
まいった
こんなバカ
妹になるなんて
Let's Start!

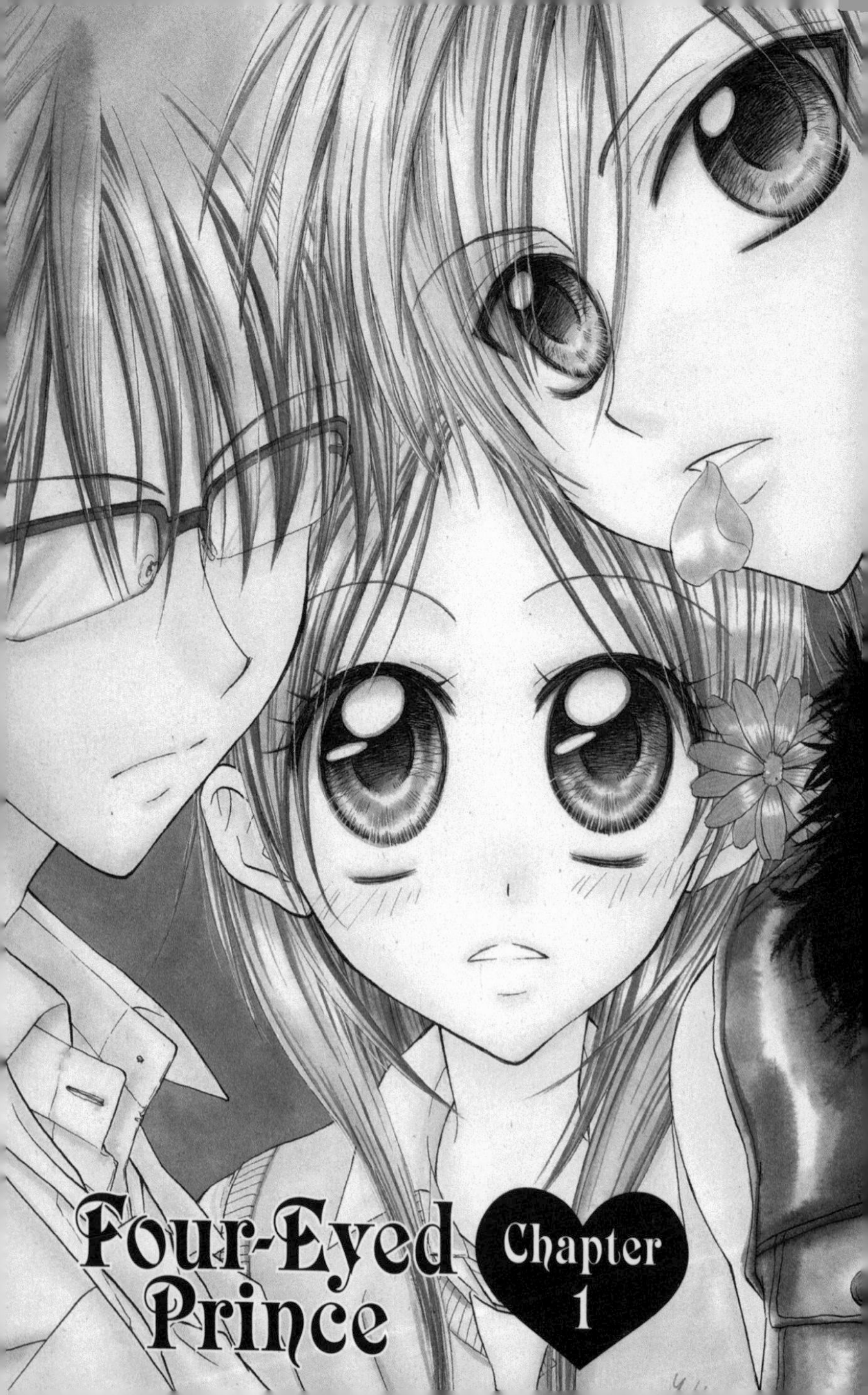
Four-Eyed Prince
Chapter 1

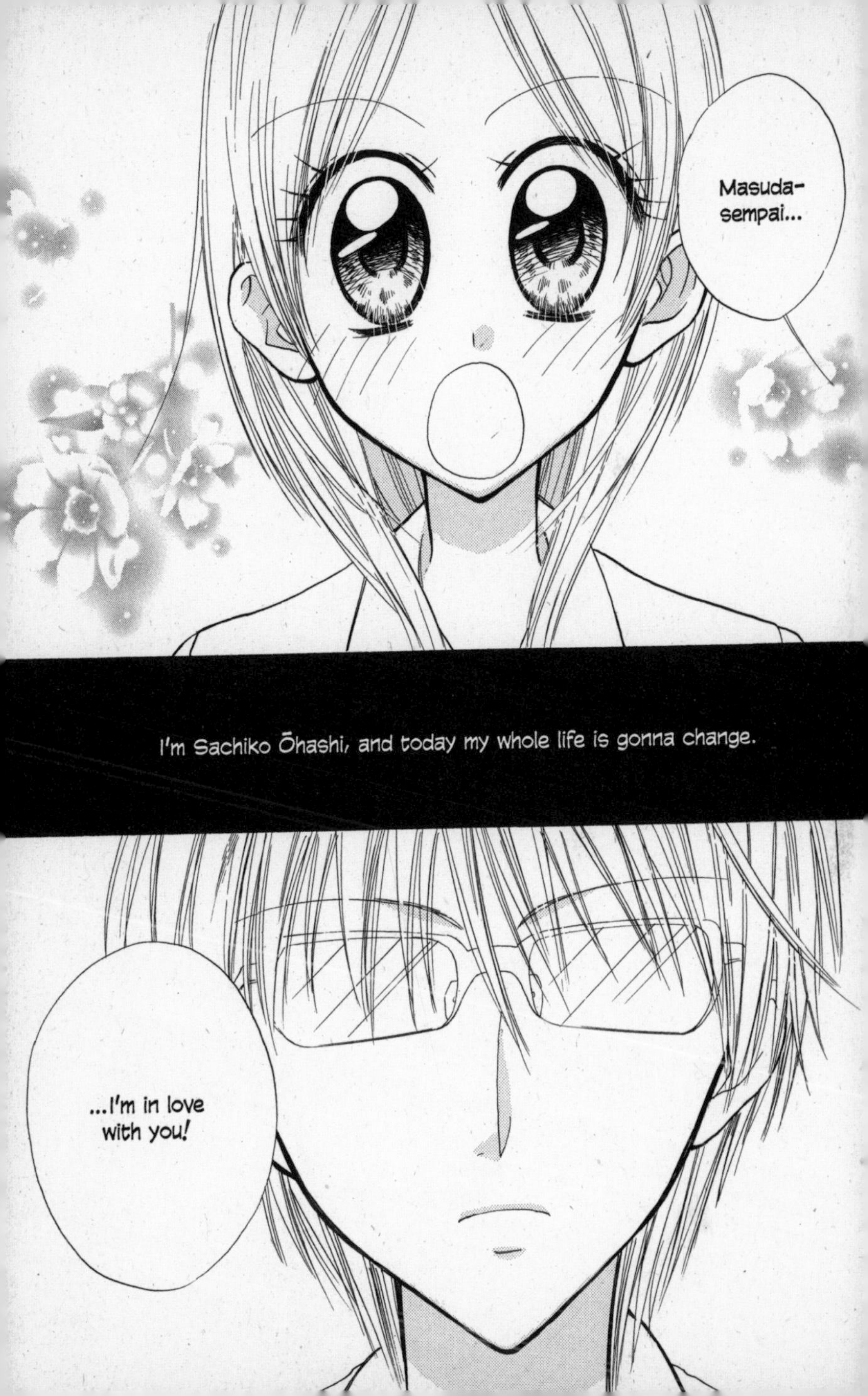
Masuda-sempai...
I'm Sachiko Ōhashi, and today my whole life is gonna change.
...I'm in love with you!

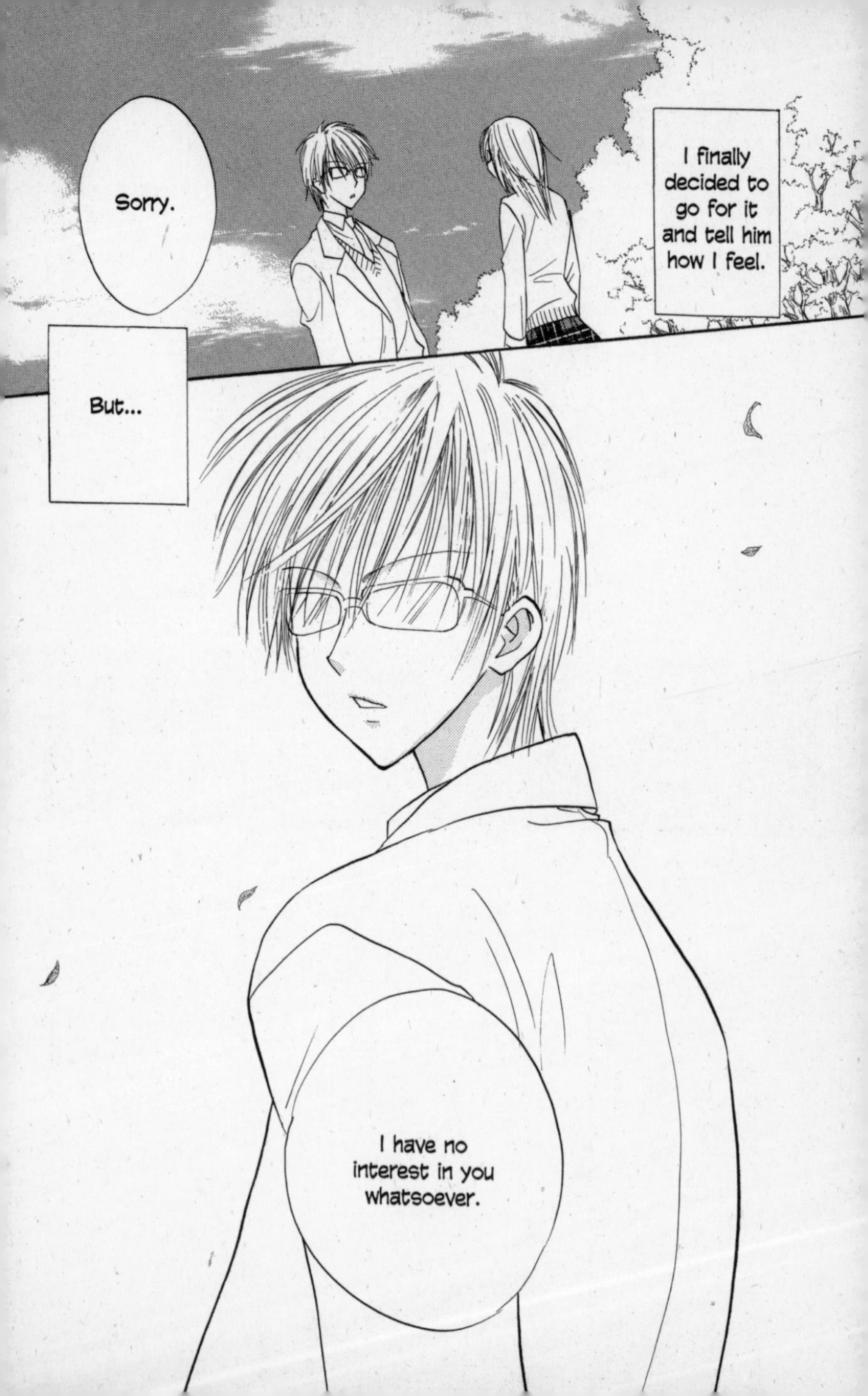
I finally decided to go for it and tell him how I feel.
Sorry.
But...
I have no interest in you whatsoever.

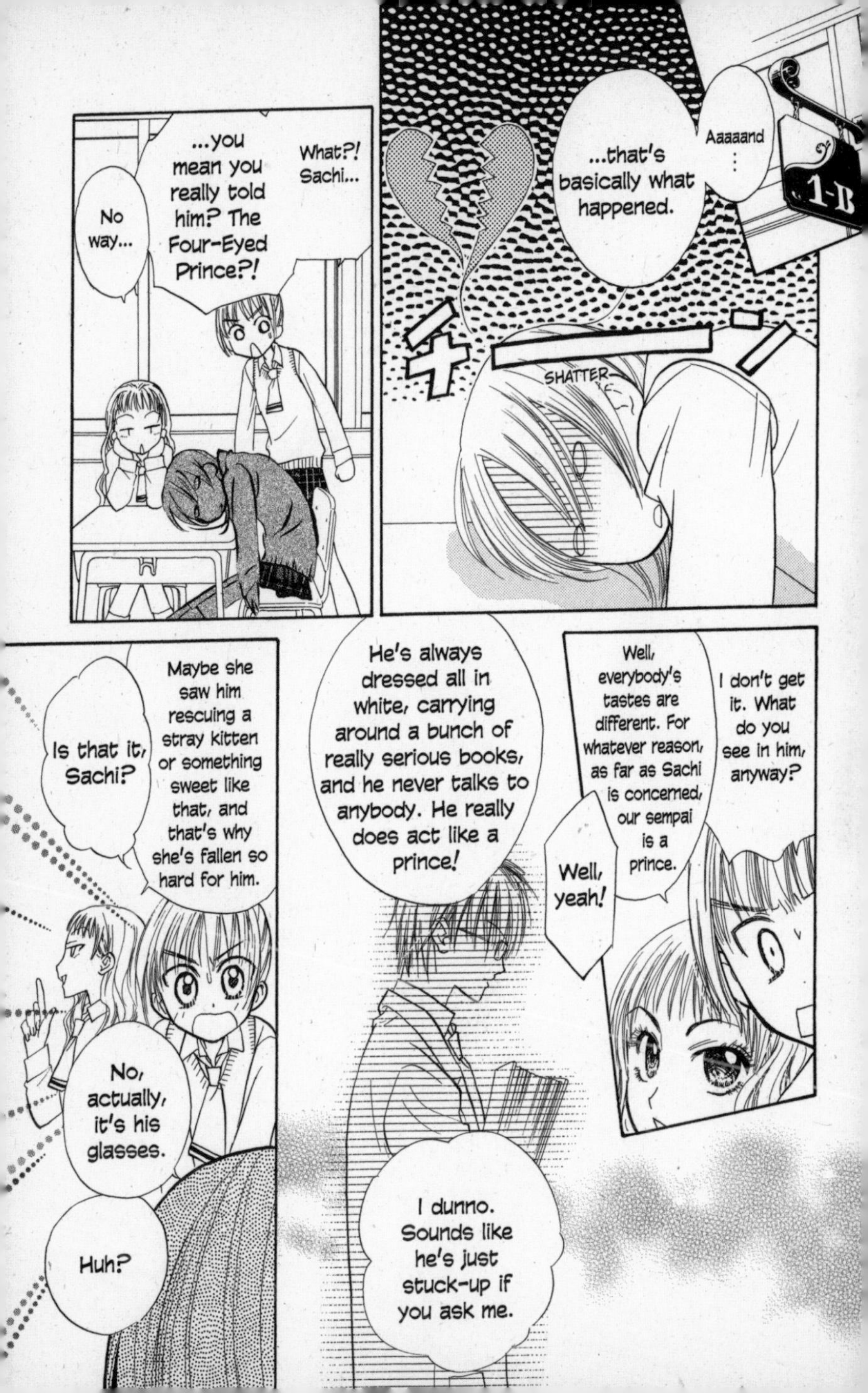
Aaaaand ...
...that's basically what happened.
SHATTER
What?! Sachi...
...you mean you really told him? The Four-Eyed Prince?!
No way...
I don't get it. What do you see in him, anyway?
Well, everybody's tastes are different. For whatever reason, as far as Sachi is concerned, our sempai is a prince.
Well, yeah!
He's always dressed all in white, carrying around a bunch of really serious books, and he never talks to anybody. He really does act like a prince!
I dunno. Sounds like he's just stuck-up if you ask me.
Maybe she saw him rescuing a stray kitten or something sweet like that, and that's why she's fallen so hard for him.
Is that it, Sachi?
No, actually, it's his glasses.
Huh?

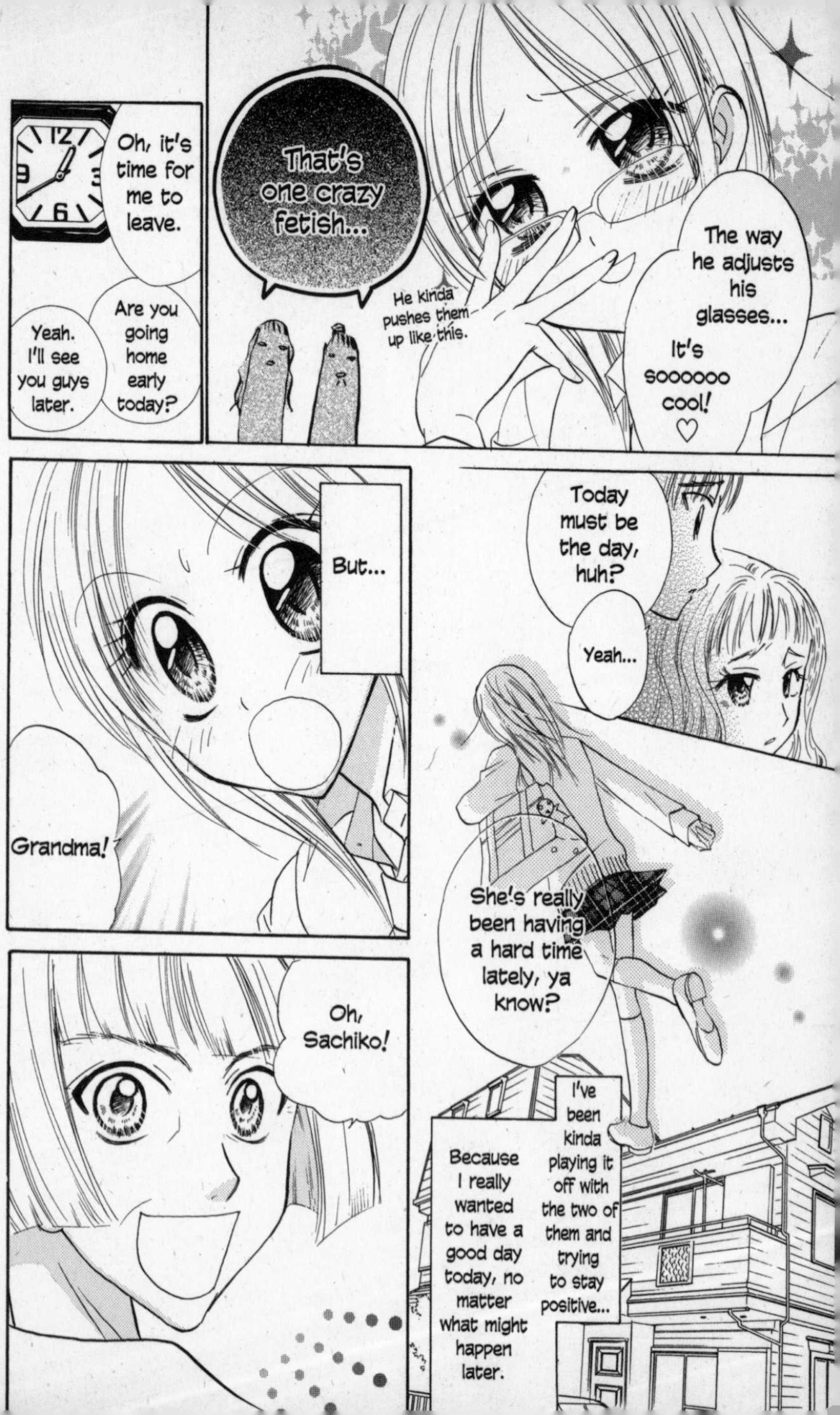

The way he adjusts his glasses... It's sooooooo cool! ♡
He kinda pushes them up like this.
That's one crazy fetish...
Oh, it's time for me to leave.
Are you going home early today?
Yeah. I'll see you guys later.
Today must be the day, huh?
Yeah...
She's really been having a hard time lately, ya know?
I've been kinda playing it off with the two of them and trying to stay positive...
Because I really wanted to have a good day today, no matter what might happen later.
But...
Grandma!
Oh, Sachiko!

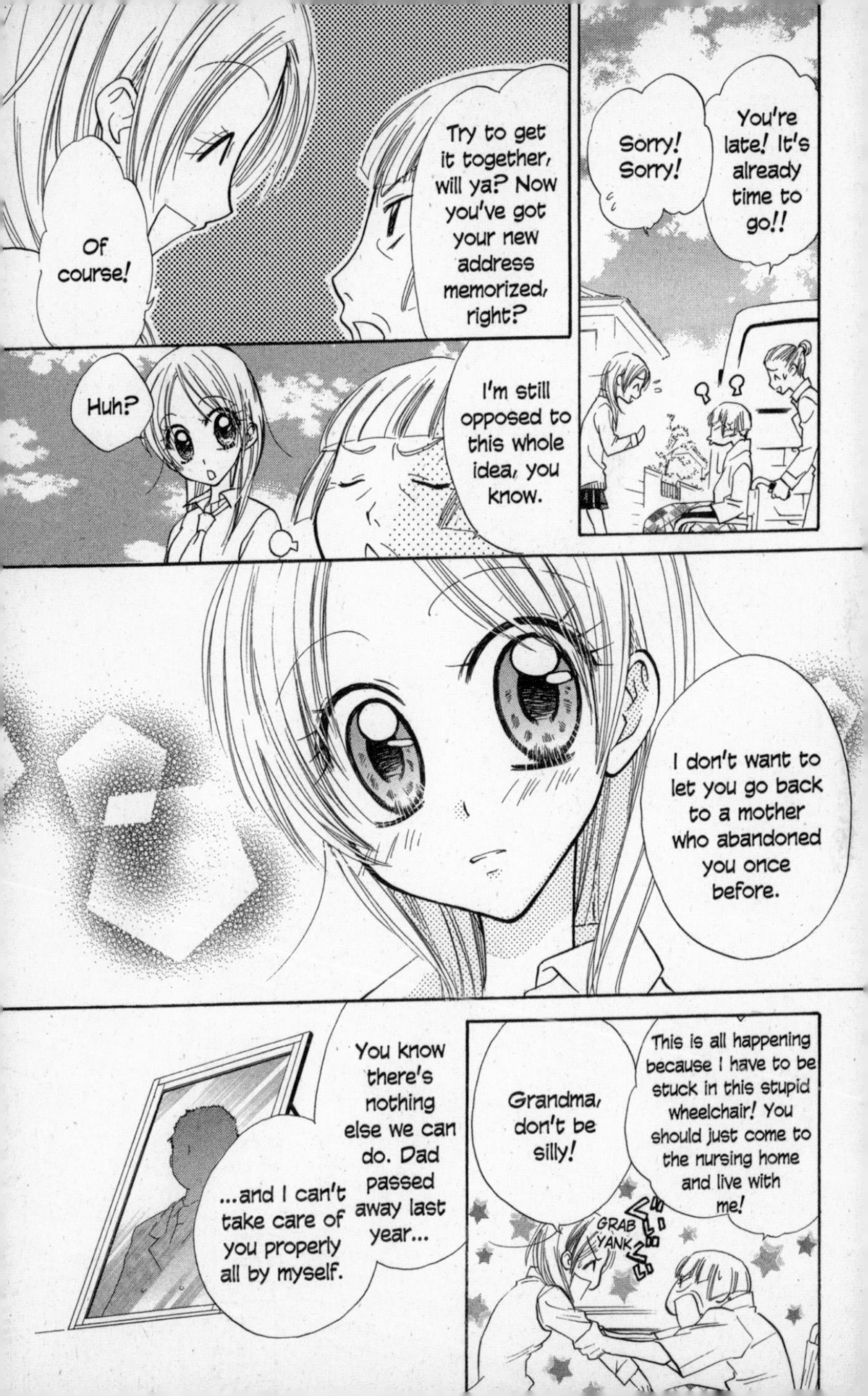
You're late! It's already time to go!!
Sorry! Sorry!
Try to get it together, will ya? Now you've got your new address memorized, right?
Of course!
I'm still opposed to this whole idea, you know.
Huh?
I don't want to let you go back to a mother who abandoned you once before.
This is all happening because I have to be stuck in this stupid wheelchair! You should just come to the nursing home and live with me!
Grandma, don't be silly!
GRAB
YANK
You know there's nothing else we can do. Dad passed away last year...
...and I can't take care of you properly all by myself.

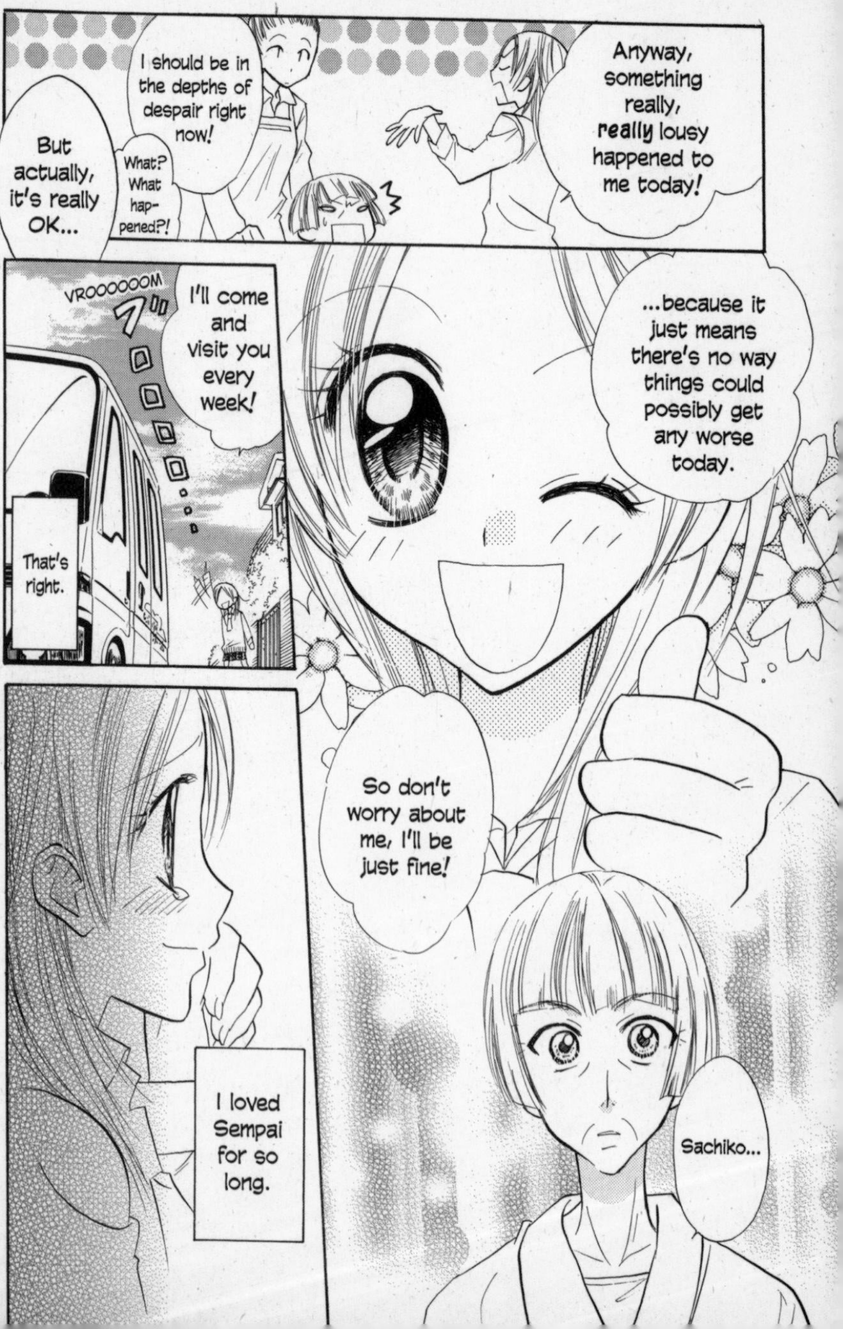
Anyway, something really, really lousy happened to me today!
I should be in the depths of despair right now!
What? What hap-pened?!
But actually, it's really OK...
...because it just means there's no way things could possibly get any worse today.
So don't worry about me, I'll be just fine!
Sachiko...
VROOOOOOM
I'll come and visit you every week!
That's right.
I loved Sempai for so long.

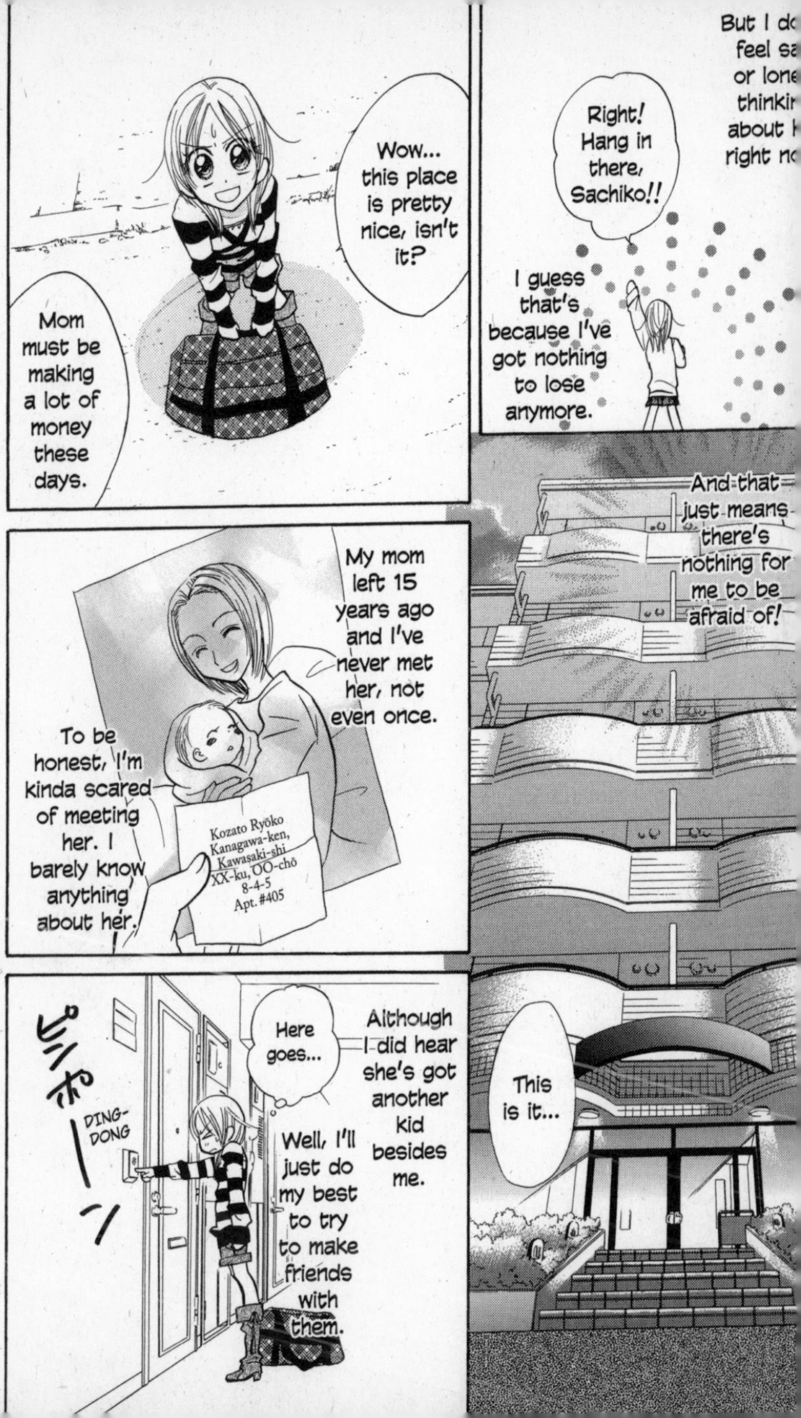

But I do feel sa or lone thinkin about h right no
Right! Hang in there, Sachiko!!
I guess that's because I've got nothing to lose anymore.
And that just means there's nothing for me to be afraid of!
This is it...
Wow... this place is pretty nice, isn't it?
Mom must be making a lot of money these days.
My mom left 15 years ago and I've never met her, not even once.
To be honest, I'm kinda scared of meeting her. I barely know anything about her.
Kozato Ryōko Kanagawa-ken, Kawasaki-shi XX-ku, OO-chō 8-4-5 Apt. #405
Here goes...
Although I did hear she's got another kid besides me.
Well, I'll just do my best to try to make friends with them.
ピンポーン
DING-DONG

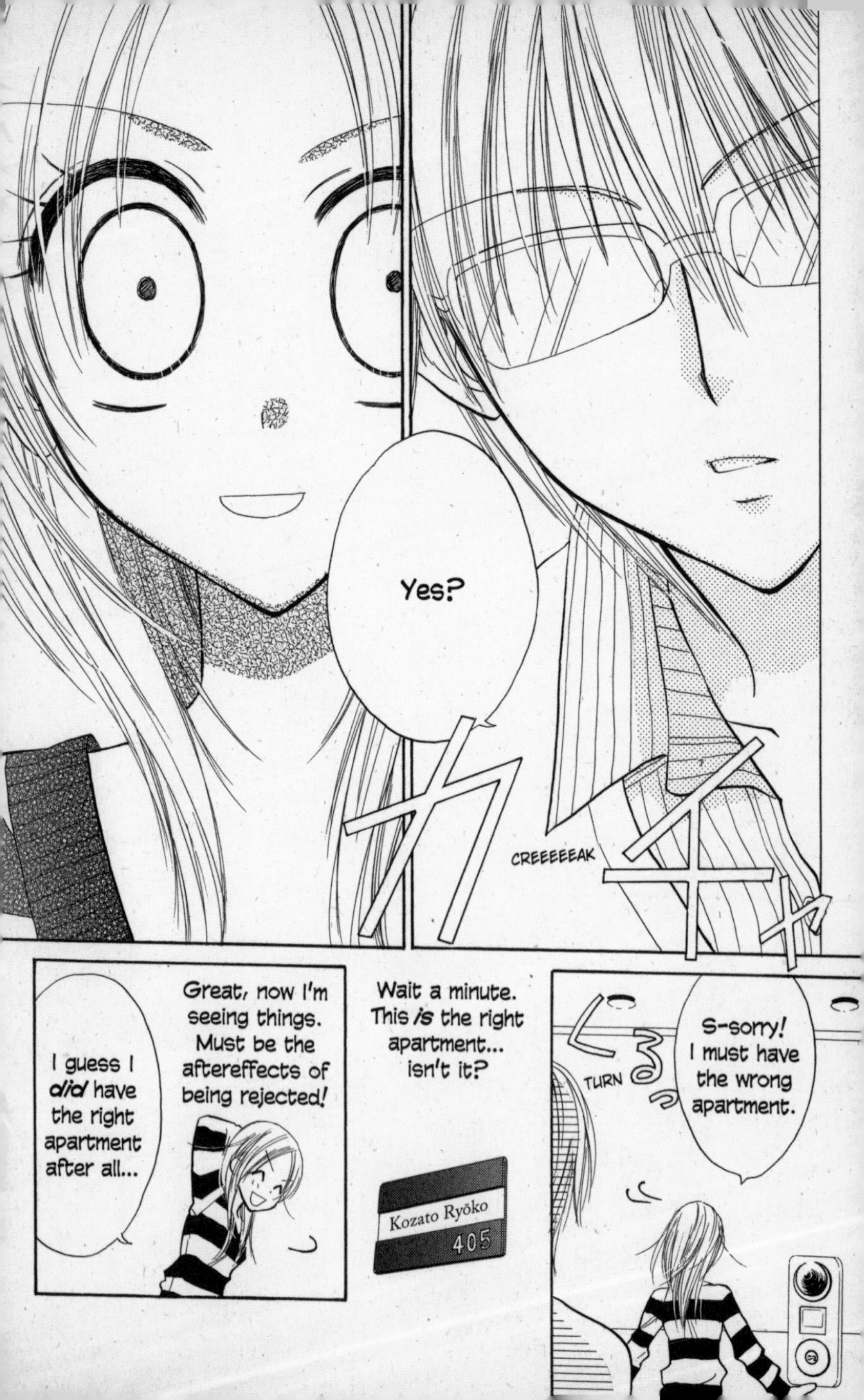
Yes?
CREEEEEAK
TURN
S-sorry! I must have the wrong apartment.
Wait a minute. This *is* the right apartment... isn't it?
Kozato Ryōko
405
Great, now I'm seeing things. Must be the aftereffects of being rejected!
I guess I *did* have the right apartment after all...

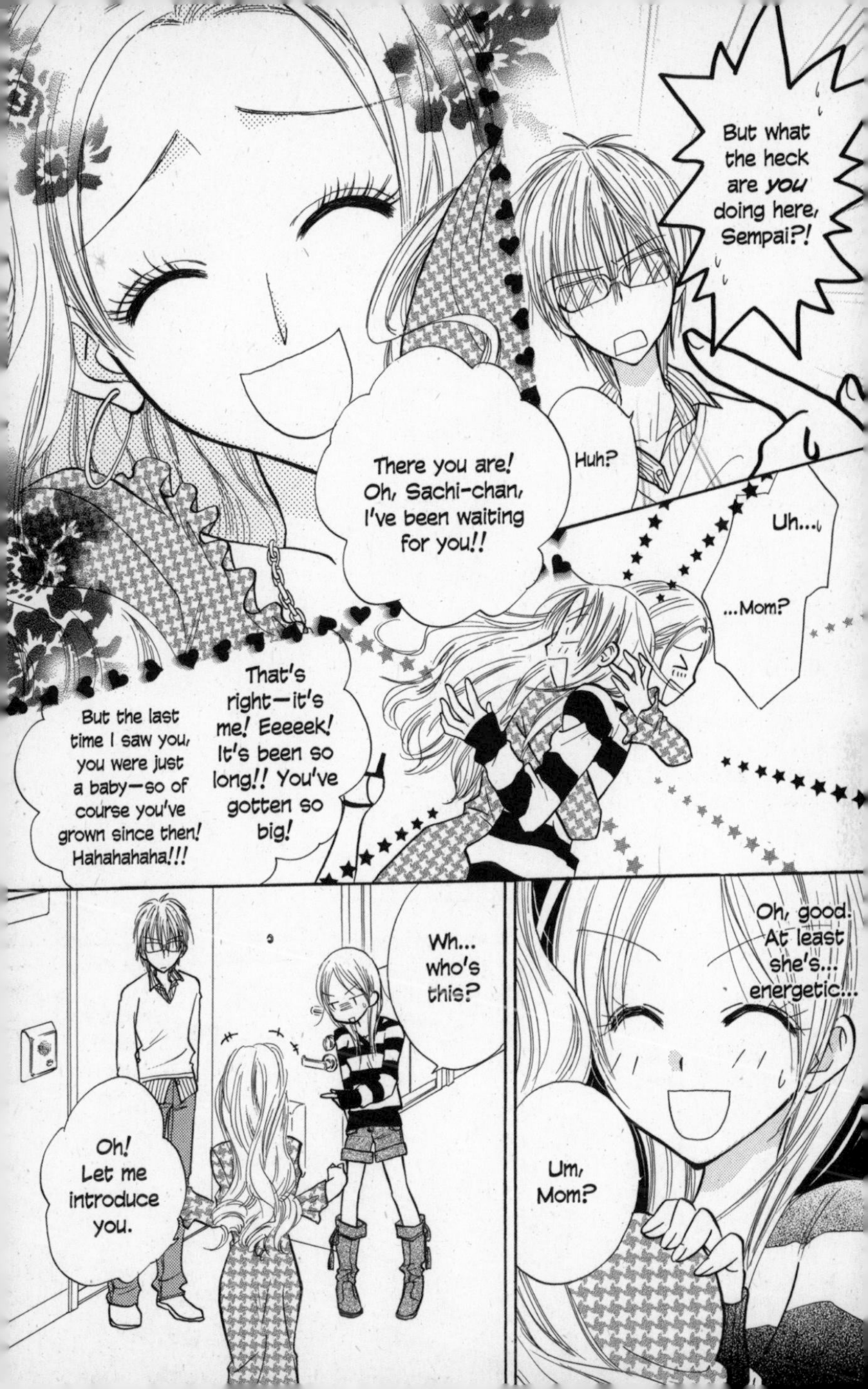

But what the heck are *you* doing here, Sempai?!
Huh?
Uh...
...Mom?
There you are! Oh, Sachi-chan, I've been waiting for you!!
That's right—it's me! Eeeeek! It's been so long!! You've gotten so big!
But the last time I saw you, you were just a baby—so of course you've grown since then! Hahahahaha!!!
Oh, good. At least she's... energetic...
Um, Mom?
Wh... who's this?
Oh! Let me introduce you.

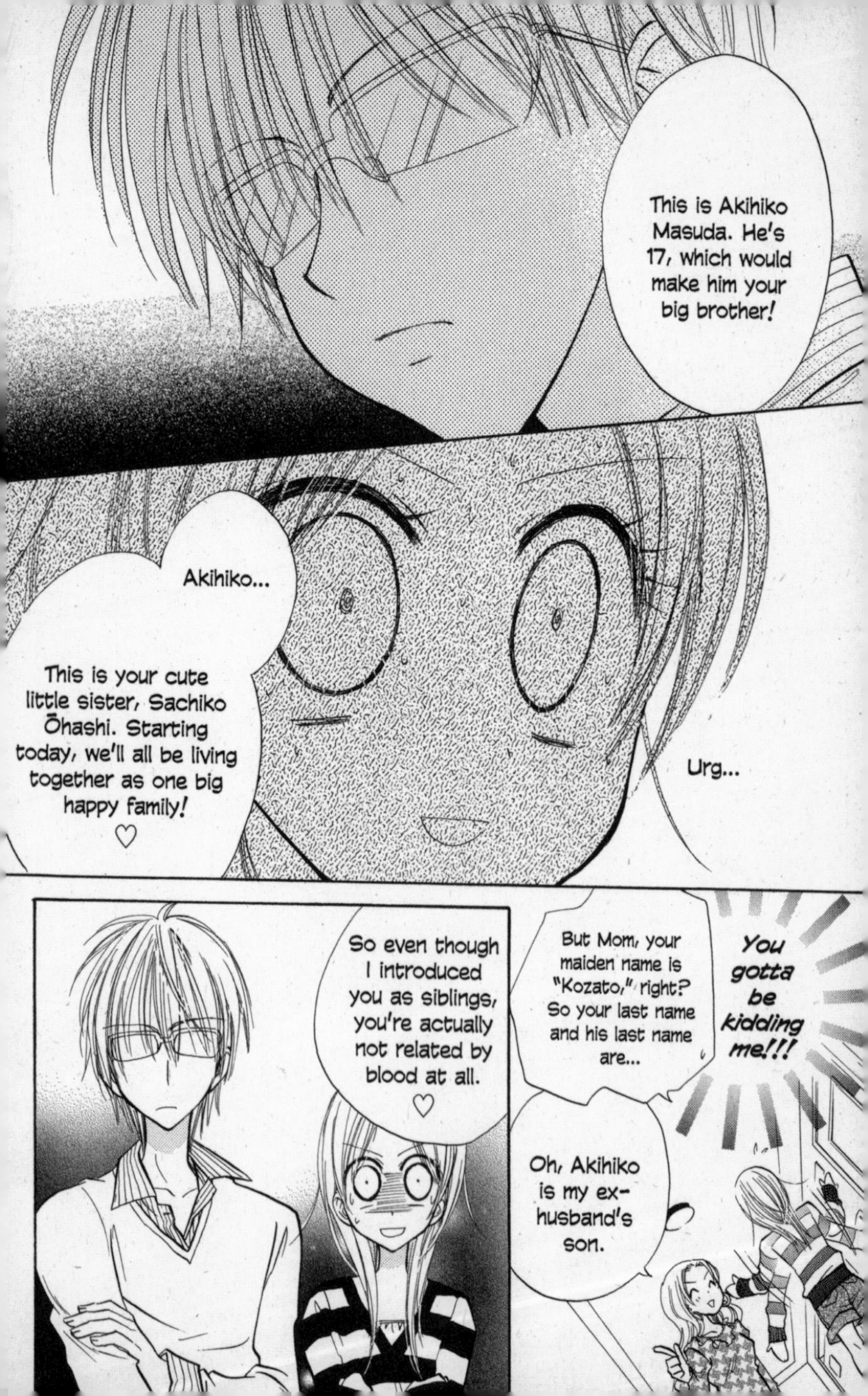

This is Akihiko Masuda. He's 17, which would make him your big brother!
Akihiko...
This is your cute little sister, Sachiko Ōhashi. Starting today, we'll all be living together as one big happy family! ♡
Urg...
You gotta be kidding me!!!
But Mom, your maiden name is "Kozato," right? So your last name and his last name are...
Oh, Akihiko is my ex-husband's son.
So even though I introduced you as siblings, you're actually not related by blood at all. ♡

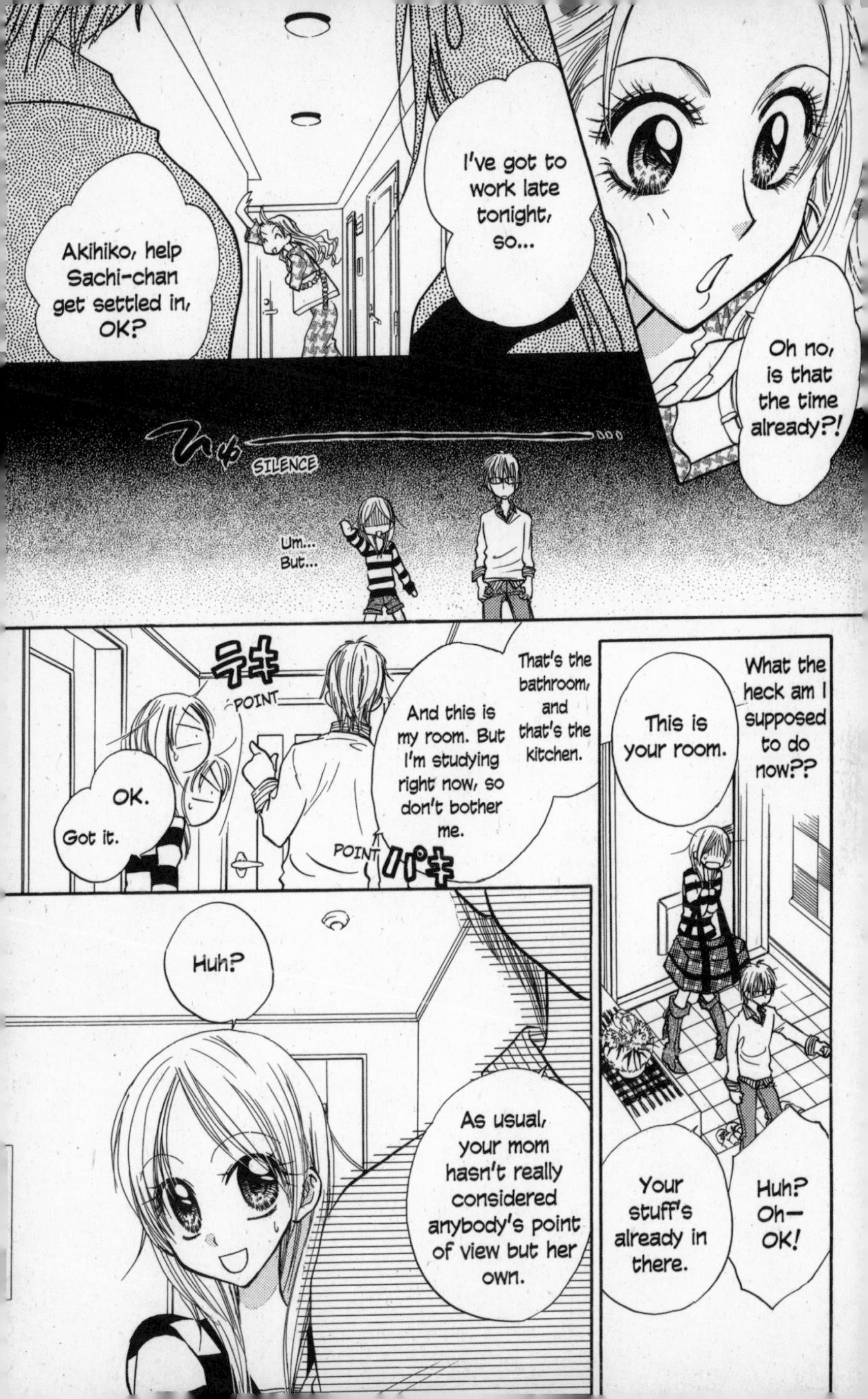
Oh no, is that the time already?!
I've got to work late tonight, so...
Akihiko, help Sachi-chan get settled in, OK?
SILENCE
Um... But...
What the heck am I supposed to do now??
This is your room.
Huh? Oh—OK!
Your stuff's already in there.
That's the bathroom, and that's the kitchen.
And this is my room. But I'm studying right now, so don't bother me.
POINT
POINT
OK.
Got it.
As usual, your mom hasn't really considered anybody's point of view but her own.
Huh?

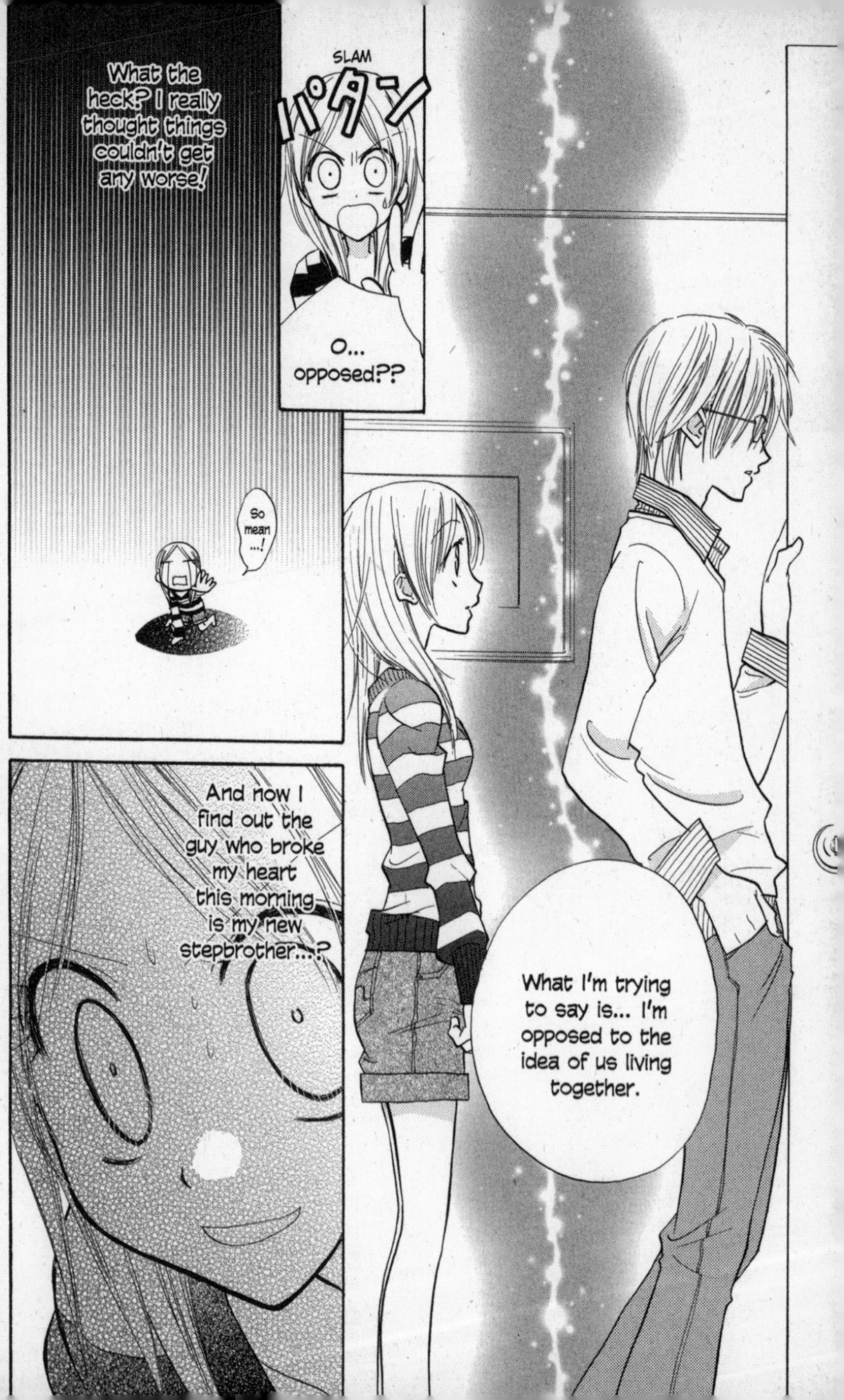
What I'm trying to say is... I'm opposed to the idea of us living together.
SLAM
パターン
O... opposed??
What the heck? I really thought things couldn't get any worse!
So mean ...!
And now I find out the guy who broke my heart this morning is my new stepbrother...?

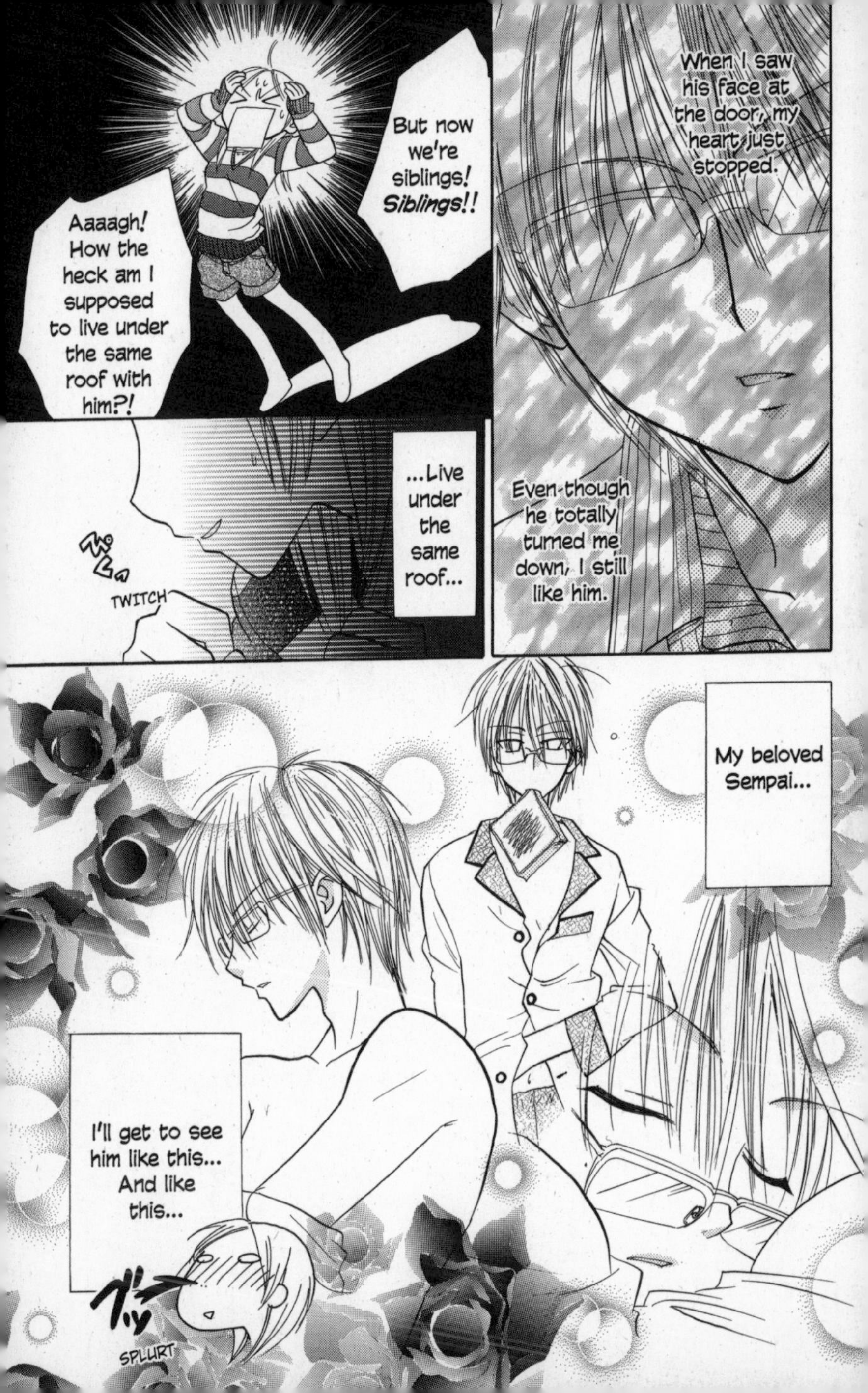
When I saw his face at the door, my heart just stopped.
Even though he totally turned me down, I still like him.
But now we're siblings! *Siblings!!*
Aaaagh! How the heck am I supposed to live under the same roof with him?!
...Live under the same roof...
TWITCH
My beloved Sempai...
I'll get to see him like this... And like this...
SPLURT

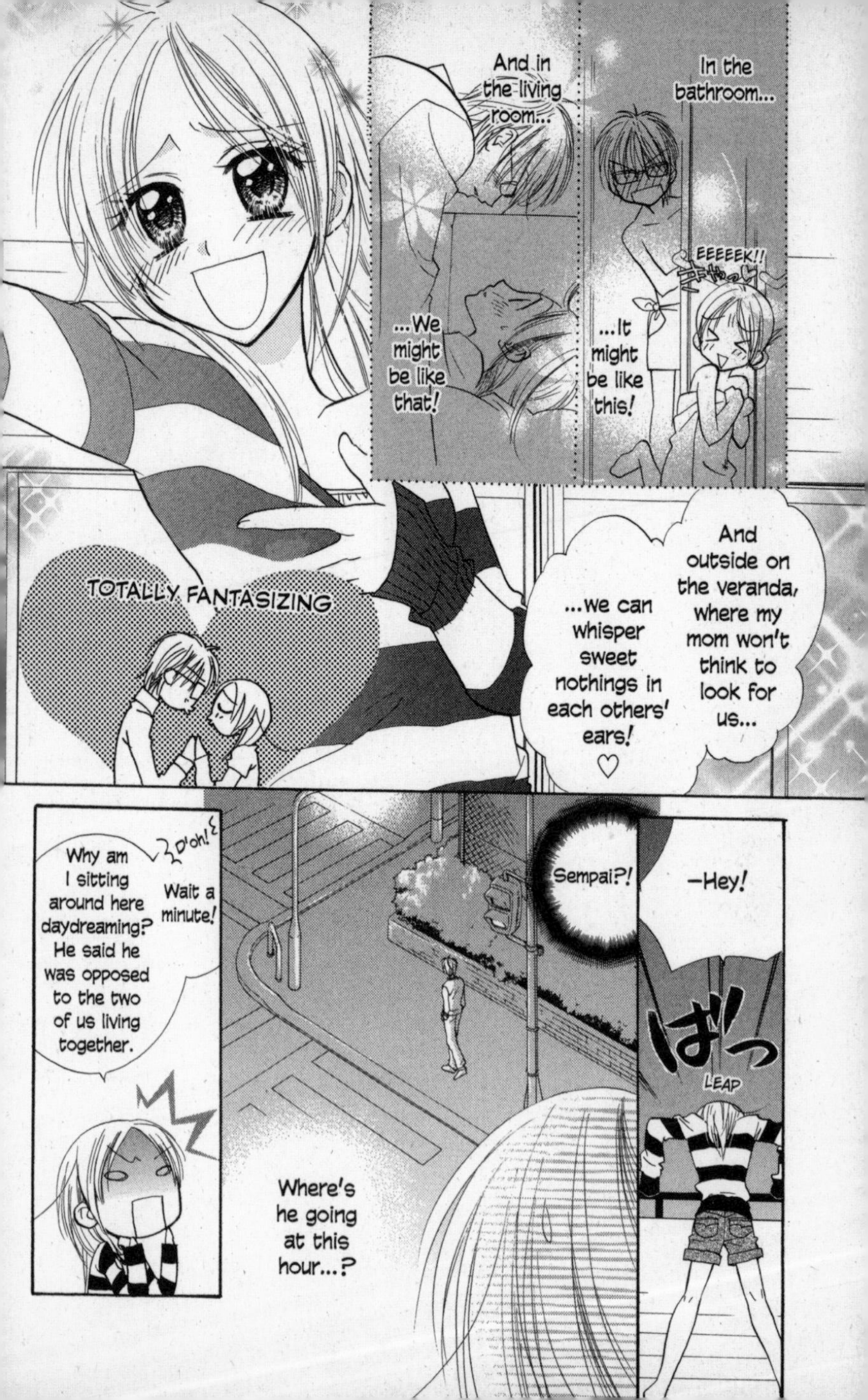
In the bathroom...
EEEEEK!!
...It might be like this!
And in the living room...
...We might be like that!
And outside on the veranda, where my mom won't think to look for us...
...we can whisper sweet nothings in each others' ears! ♡
TOTALLY FANTASIZING
—Hey!
LEAP
Sempai?!
Where's he going at this hour...?
D'oh!
Wait a minute!
Why am I sitting around here daydreaming? He said he was opposed to the two of us living together.

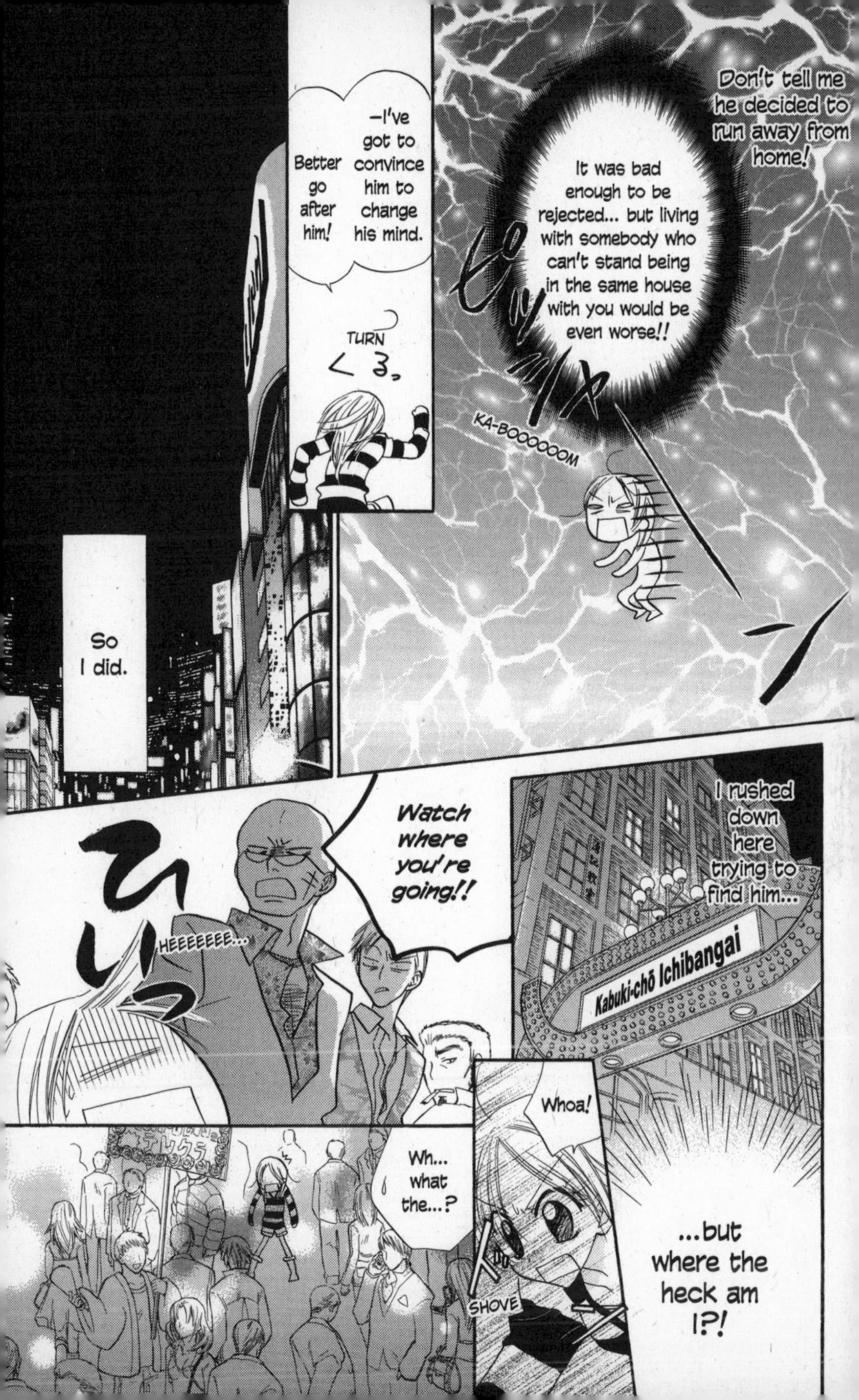
Don't tell me he decided to run away from home!
It was bad enough to be rejected... but living with somebody who can't stand being in the same house with you would be even worse!!
KA-BOOOOOOOM
—I've got to convince him to change his mind.
Better go after him!
TURN
So I did.
I rushed down here trying to find him...
Kabuki-chō Ichibangai
Whoa!
SHOVE
Watch where you're going!!
HEEEEEEEE...
Wh... what the...?
...but where the heck am I?!

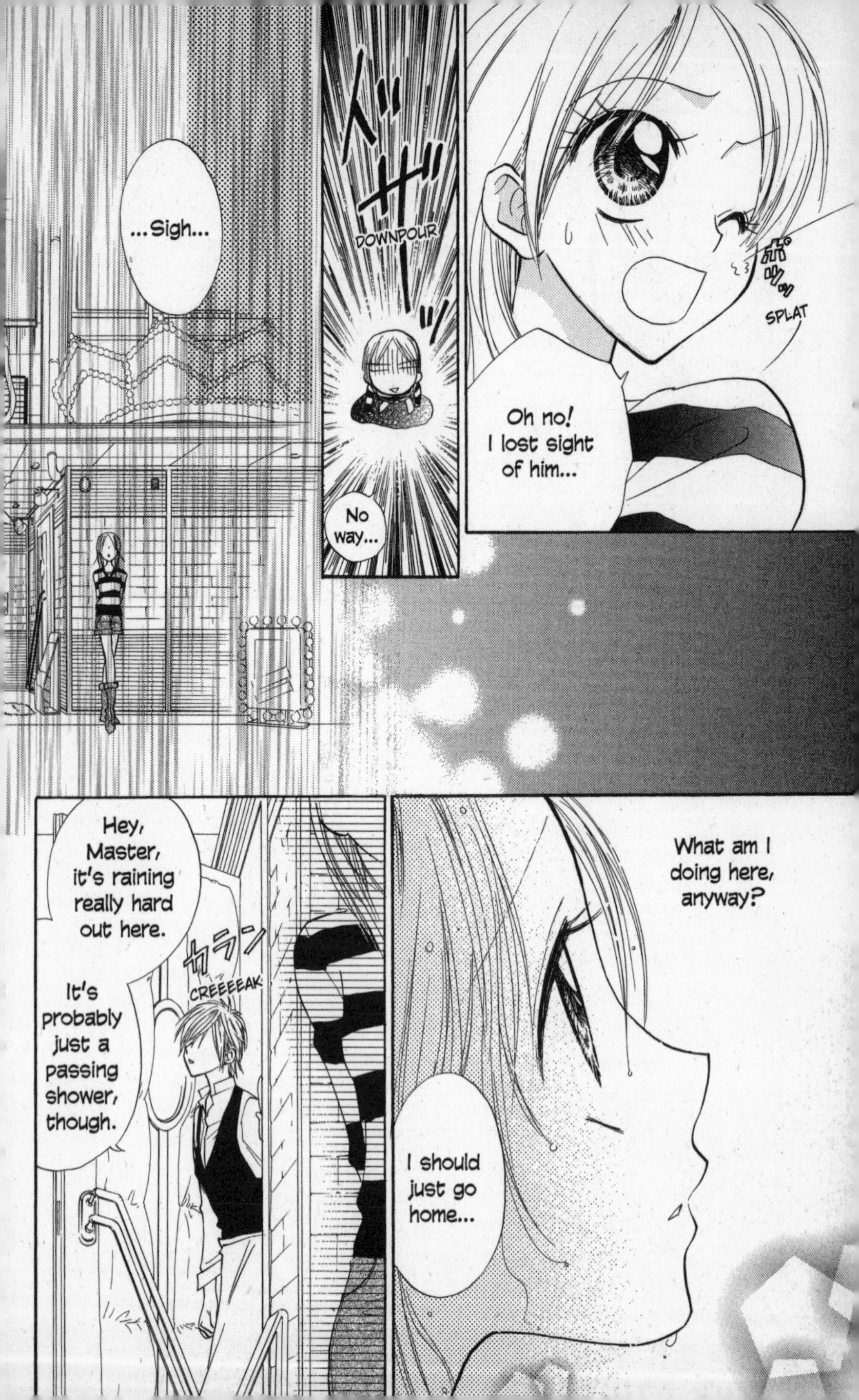
SPLAT
Oh no! I lost sight of him...
DOWNPOUR
No way...
...Sigh...
What am I doing here, anyway?
I should just go home...
Hey, Master, it's raining really hard out here.
CREEEEAK
It's probably just a passing shower, though.

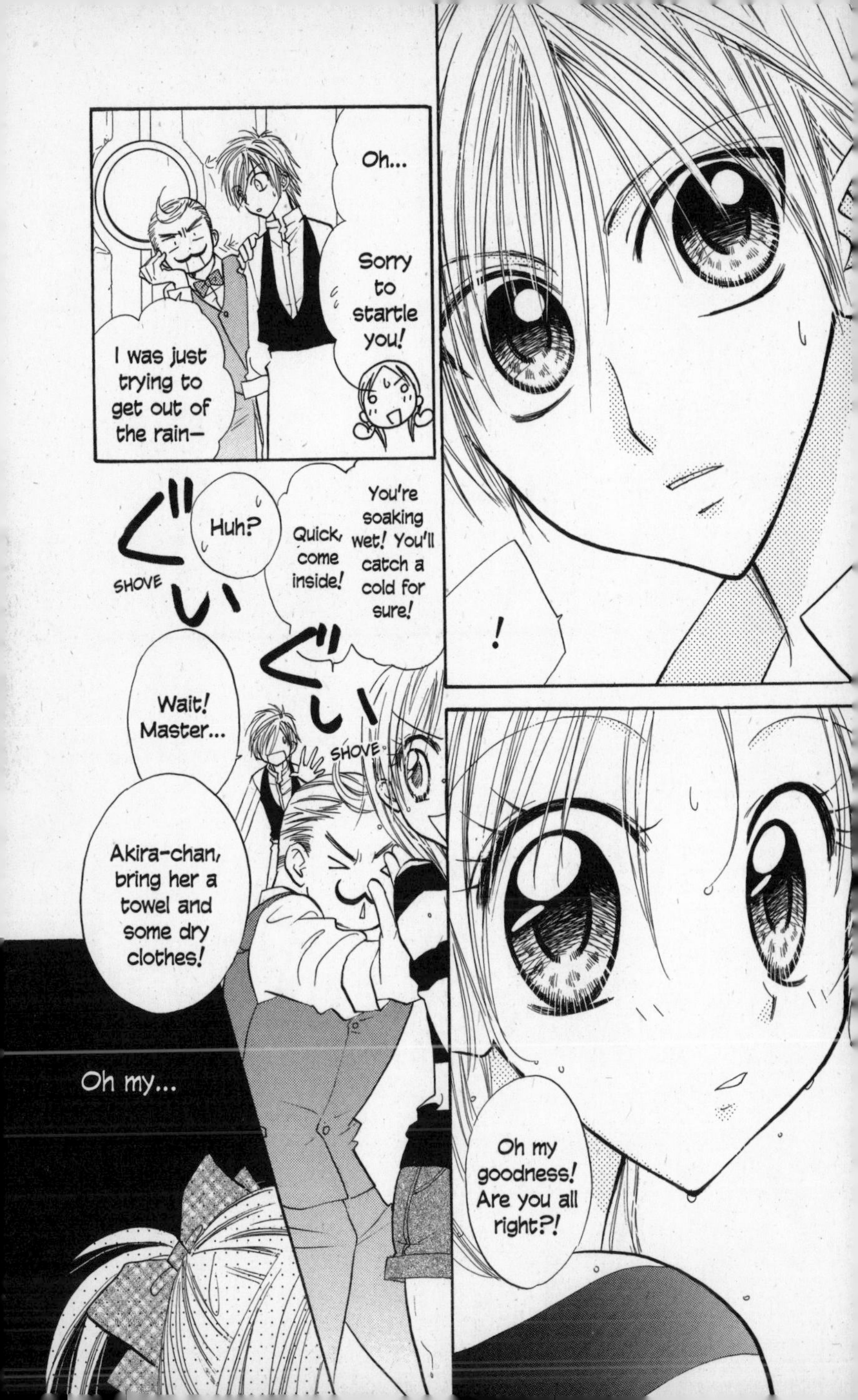
!
Oh my goodness! Are you all right?!
Oh...
Sorry to startle you!
I was just trying to get out of the rain—
You're soaking wet! You'll catch a cold for sure!
Quick, come inside!
Huh?
ぐい
SHOVE
ぐい
SHOVE
Wait! Master...
Akira-chan, bring her a towel and some dry clothes!
Oh my...

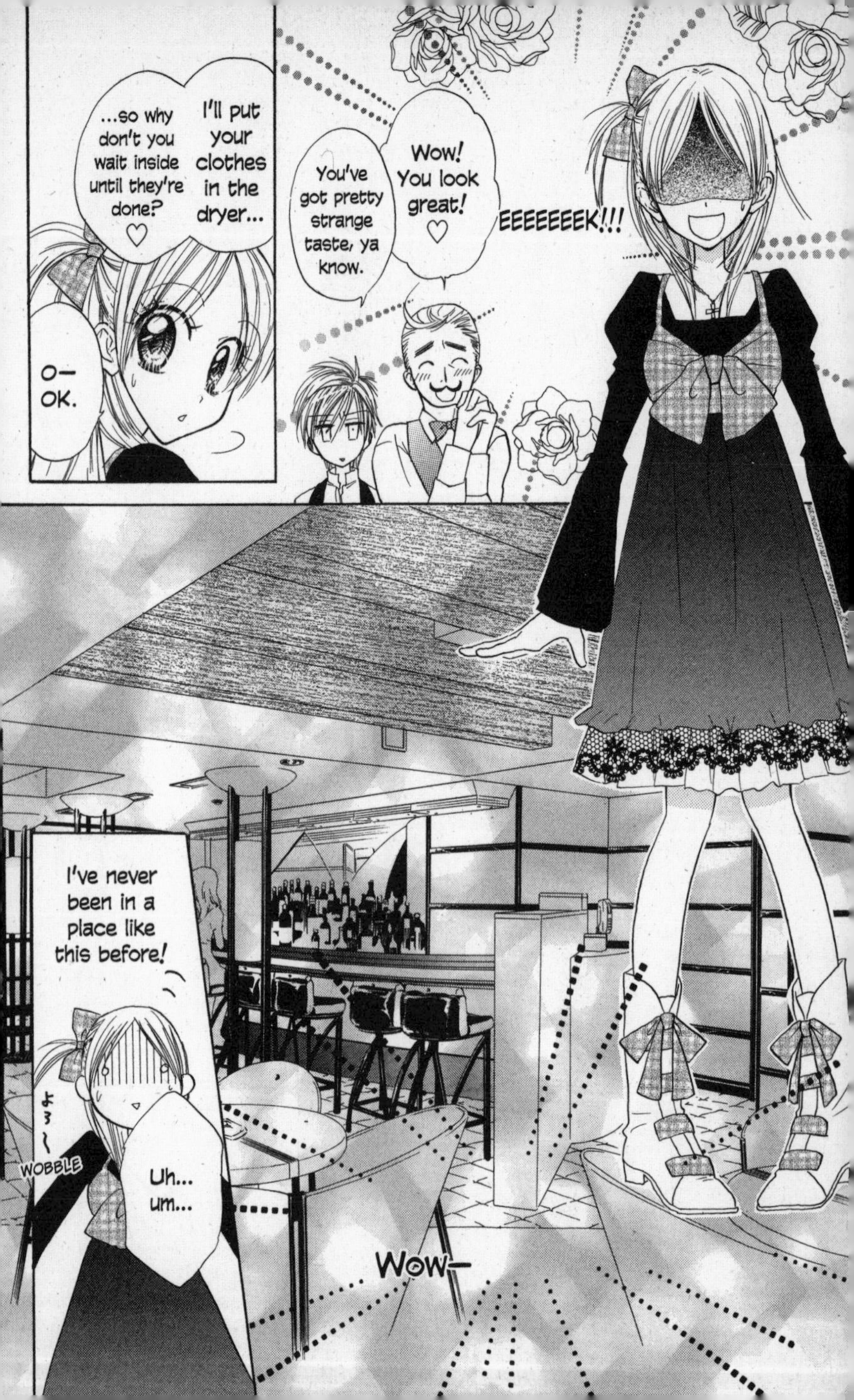
EEEEEEEK!!!
Wow! You look great! ♡
You've got pretty strange taste, ya know.
I'll put your clothes in the dryer...
...so why don't you wait inside until they're done? ♡
O—OK.
Wow—
I've never been in a place like this before!
Uh... um...
よろ~
WOBBLE

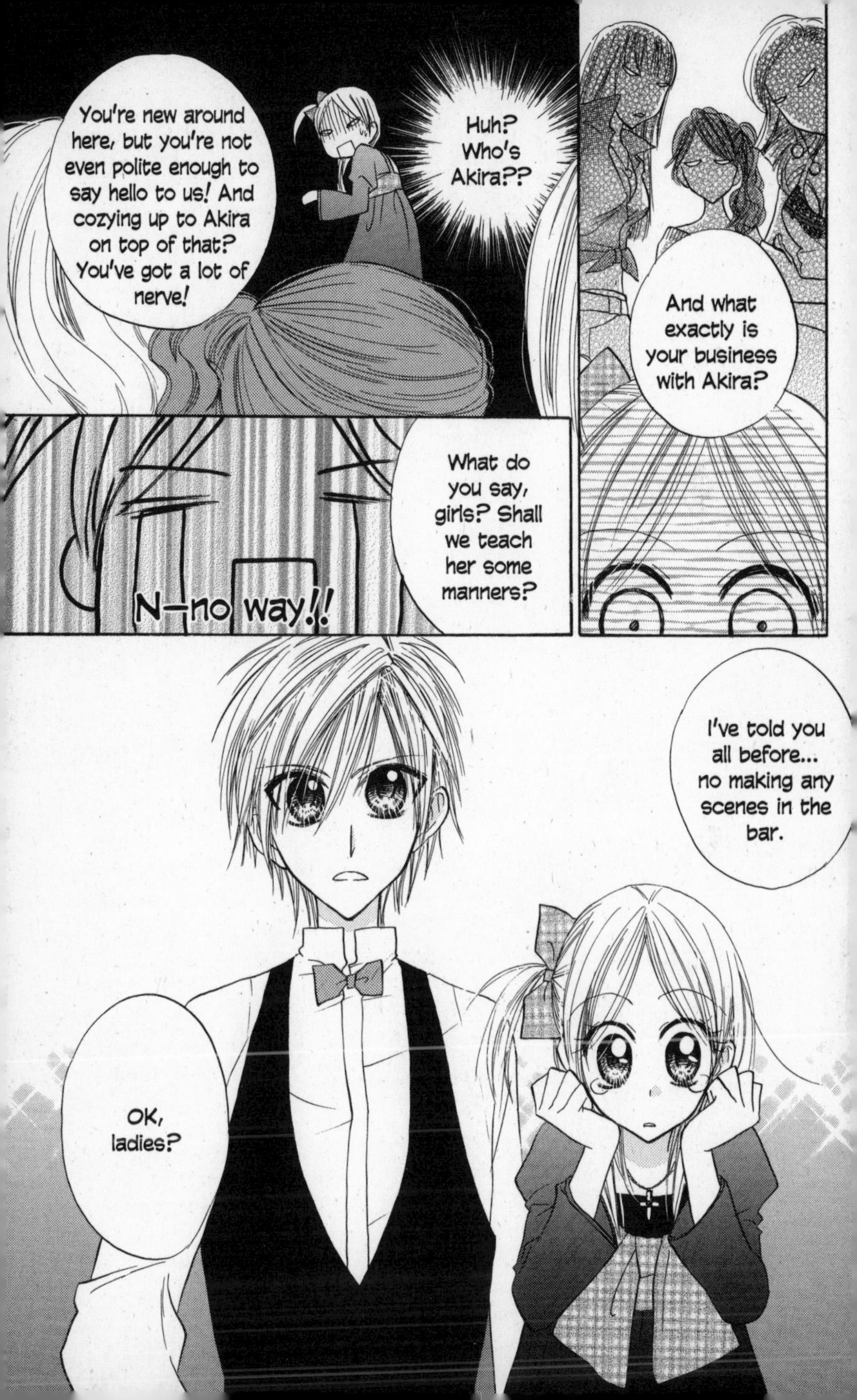

And what exactly is your business with Akira?
You're new around here, but you're not even polite enough to say hello to us! And cozying up to Akira on top of that? You've got a lot of nerve!
Huh? Who's Akira??
What do you say, girls? Shall we teach her some manners?
N-no way!!
I've told you all before... no making any scenes in the bar.
OK, ladies?

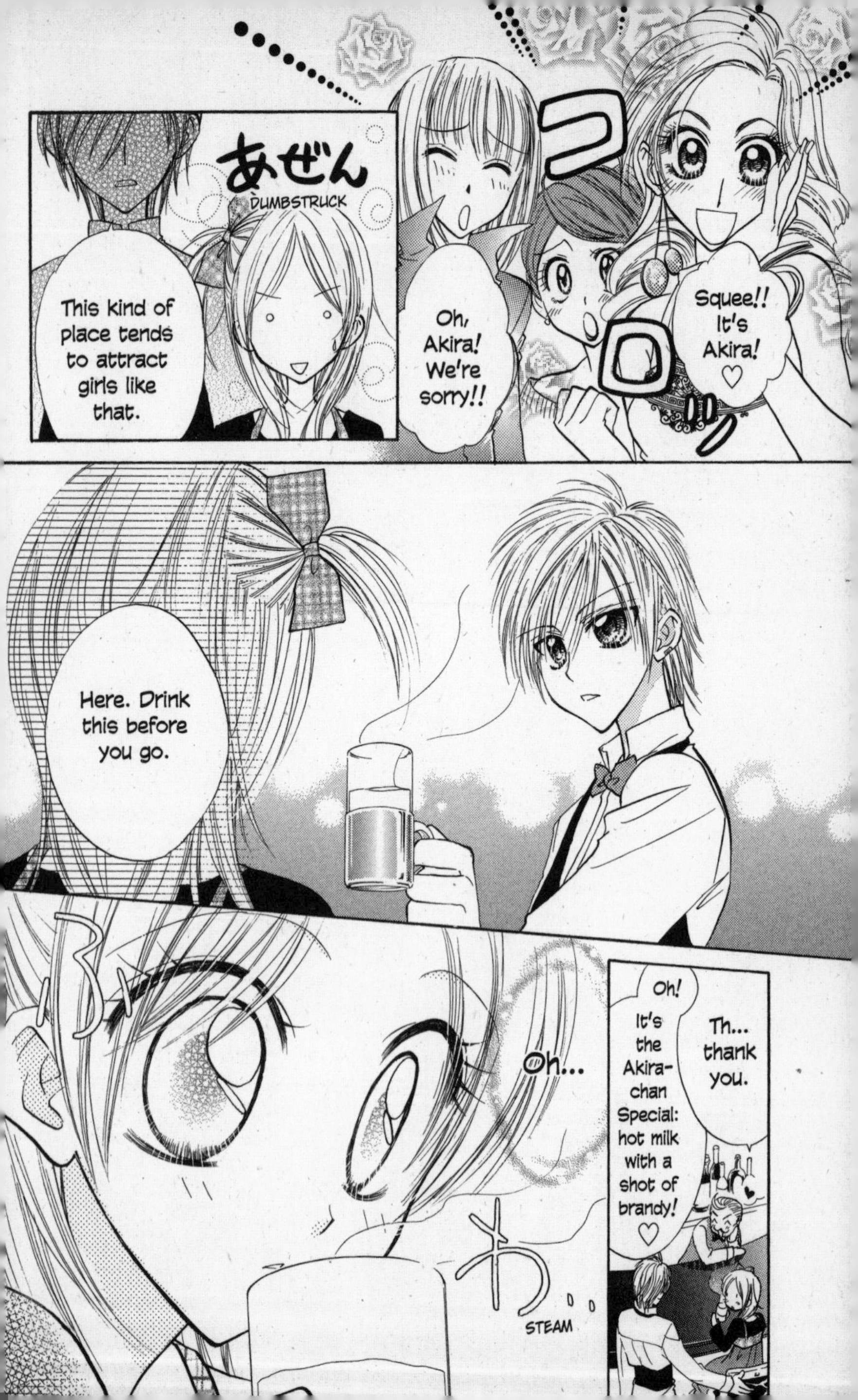

Squee!! It's Akira! ♡
Oh, Akira! We're sorry!!
あぜん
DUMBSTRUCK
This kind of place tends to attract girls like that.
Here. Drink this before you go.
Th... thank you.
Oh!
It's the Akira-chan Special: hot milk with a shot of brandy! ♡
Oh...
STEAM

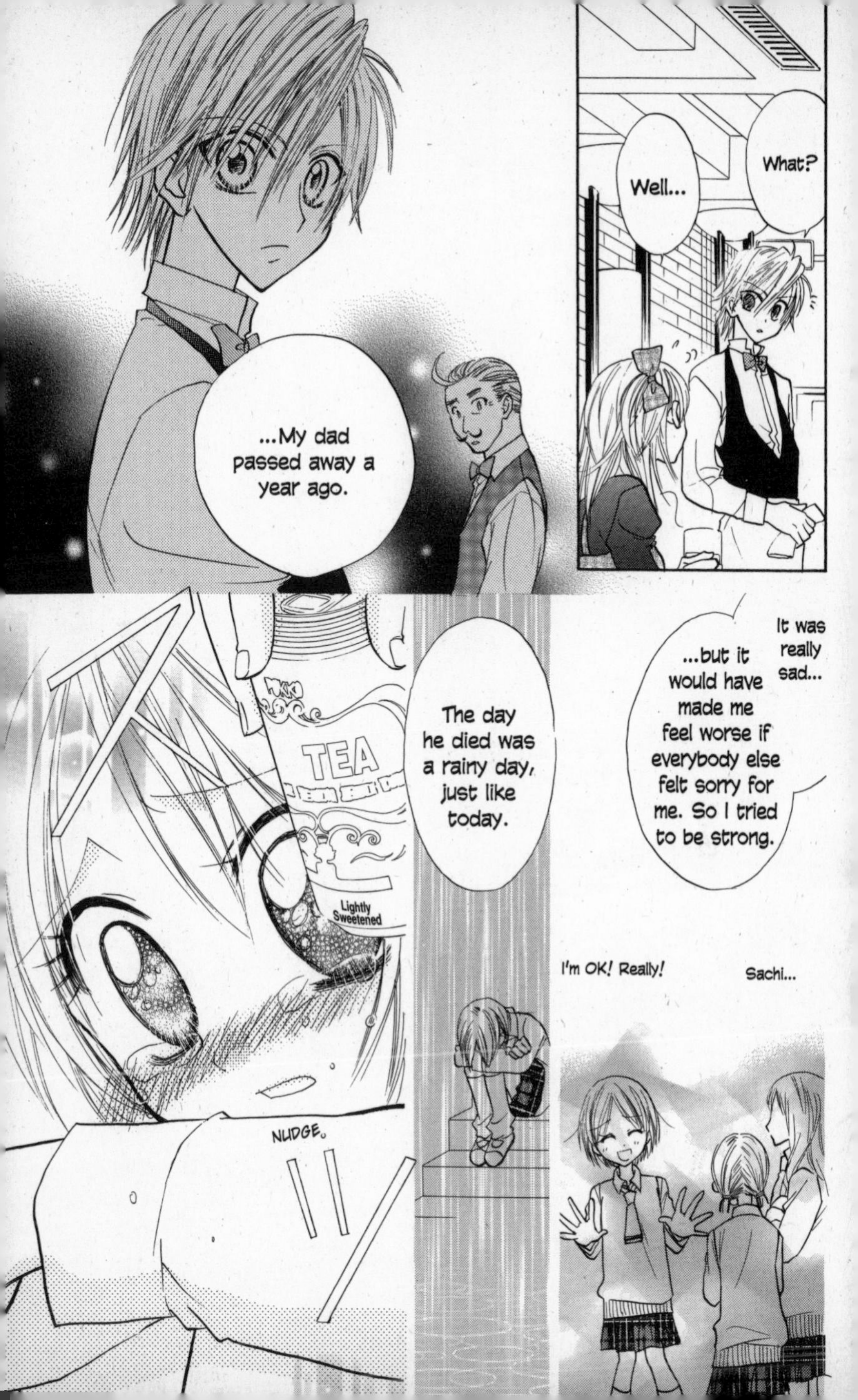
What?
Well...
...My dad passed away a year ago.
It was really sad...
...but it would have made me feel worse if everybody else felt sorry for me. So I tried to be strong.
Sachi...
I'm OK! Really!
The day he died was a rainy day, just like today.
TEA
Lightly Sweetened
NUDGE.

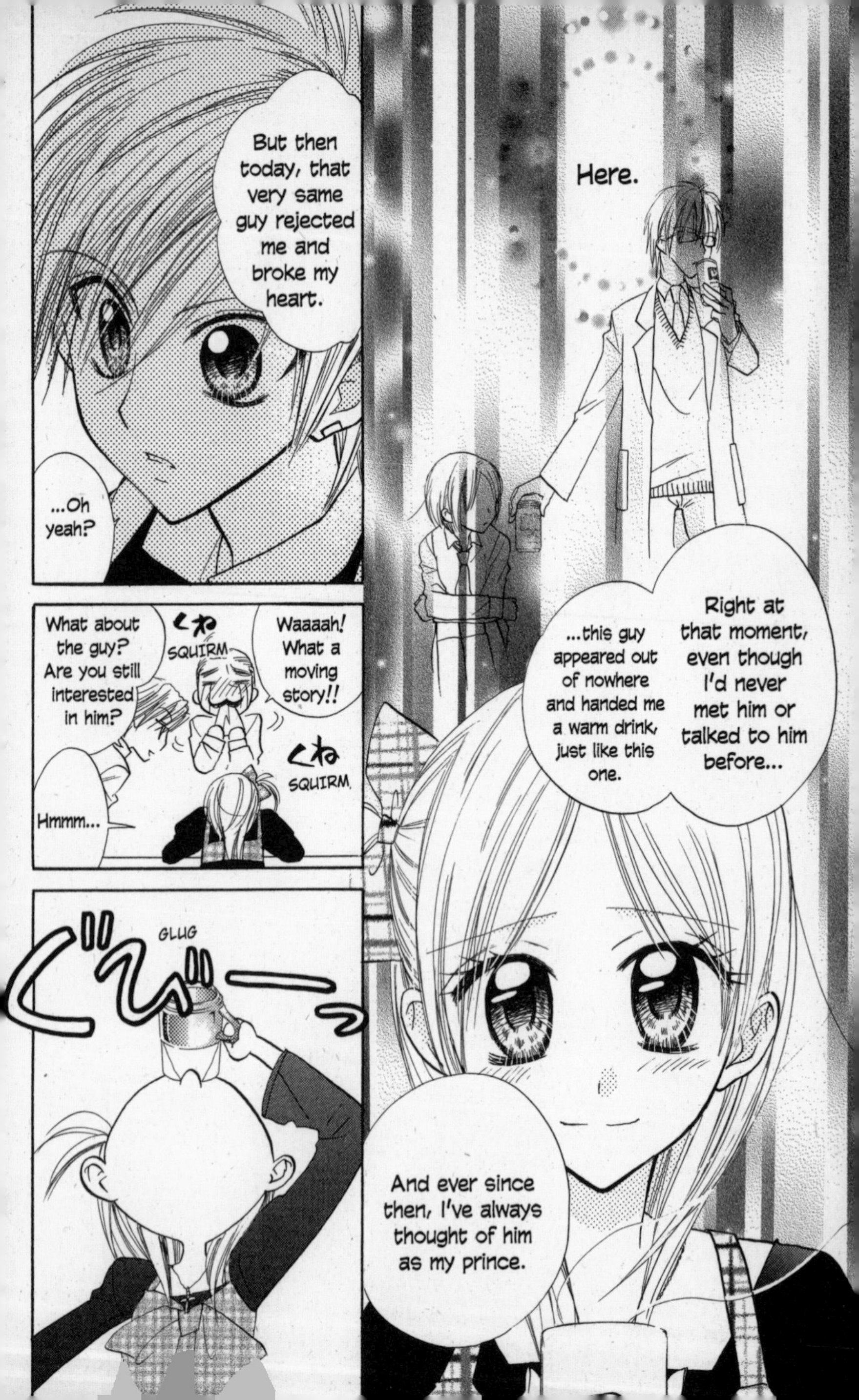
Here.
Right at that moment, even though I'd never met him or talked to him before...
...this guy appeared out of nowhere and handed me a warm drink, just like this one.
And ever since then, I've always thought of him as my prince.
But then today, that very same guy rejected me and broke my heart.
...Oh yeah?
Waaaah! What a moving story!!
くね SQUIRM
くね SQUIRM
What about the guy? Are you still interested in him?
Hmmm...
ぐびーっ
GLUG

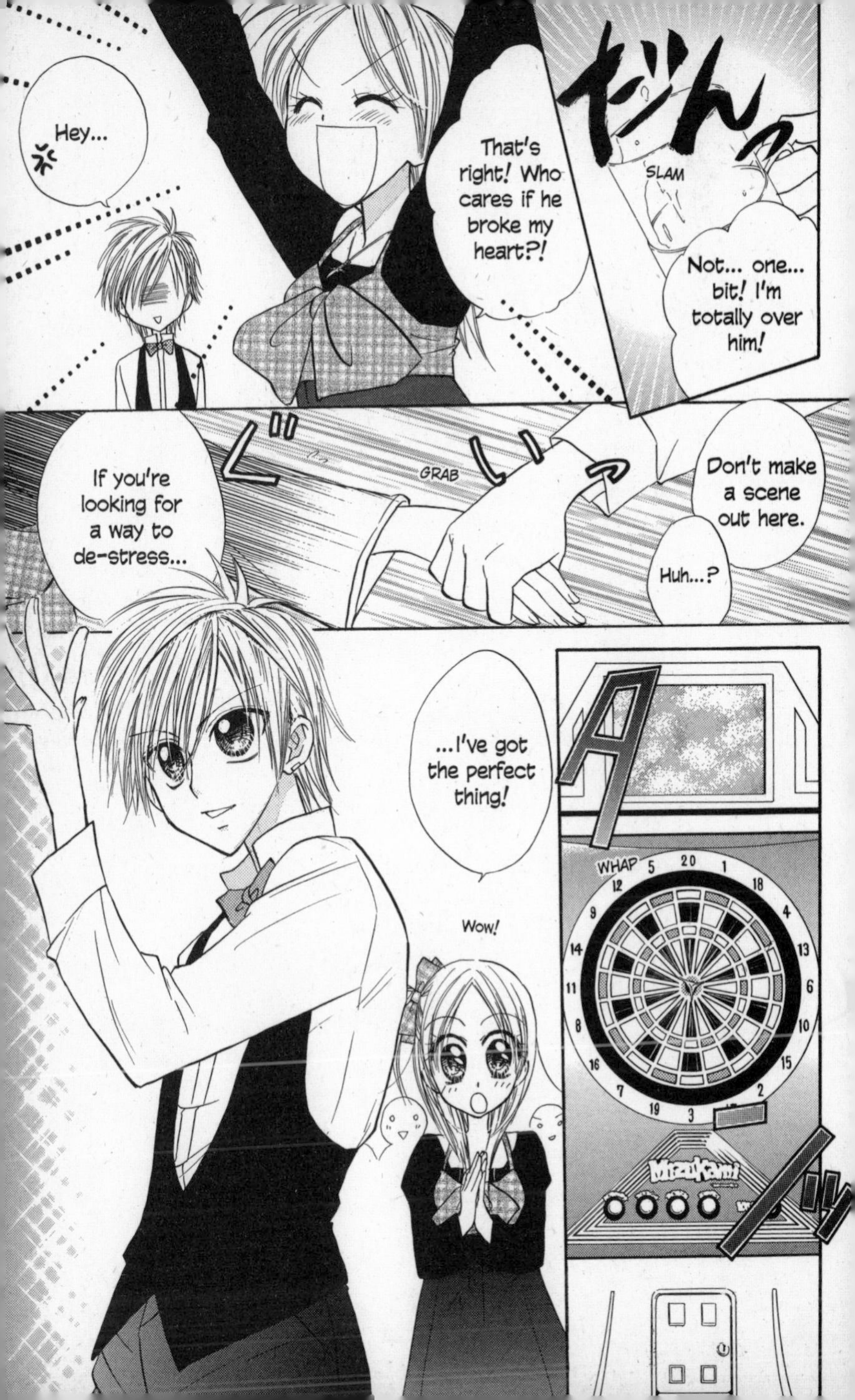
SLAM
Not... one... bit! I'm totally over him!
That's right! Who cares if he broke my heart?!
Hey...
Don't make a scene out here.
Huh...?
GRAB
If you're looking for a way to de-stress...
WHAP
...I've got the perfect thing!
Wow!

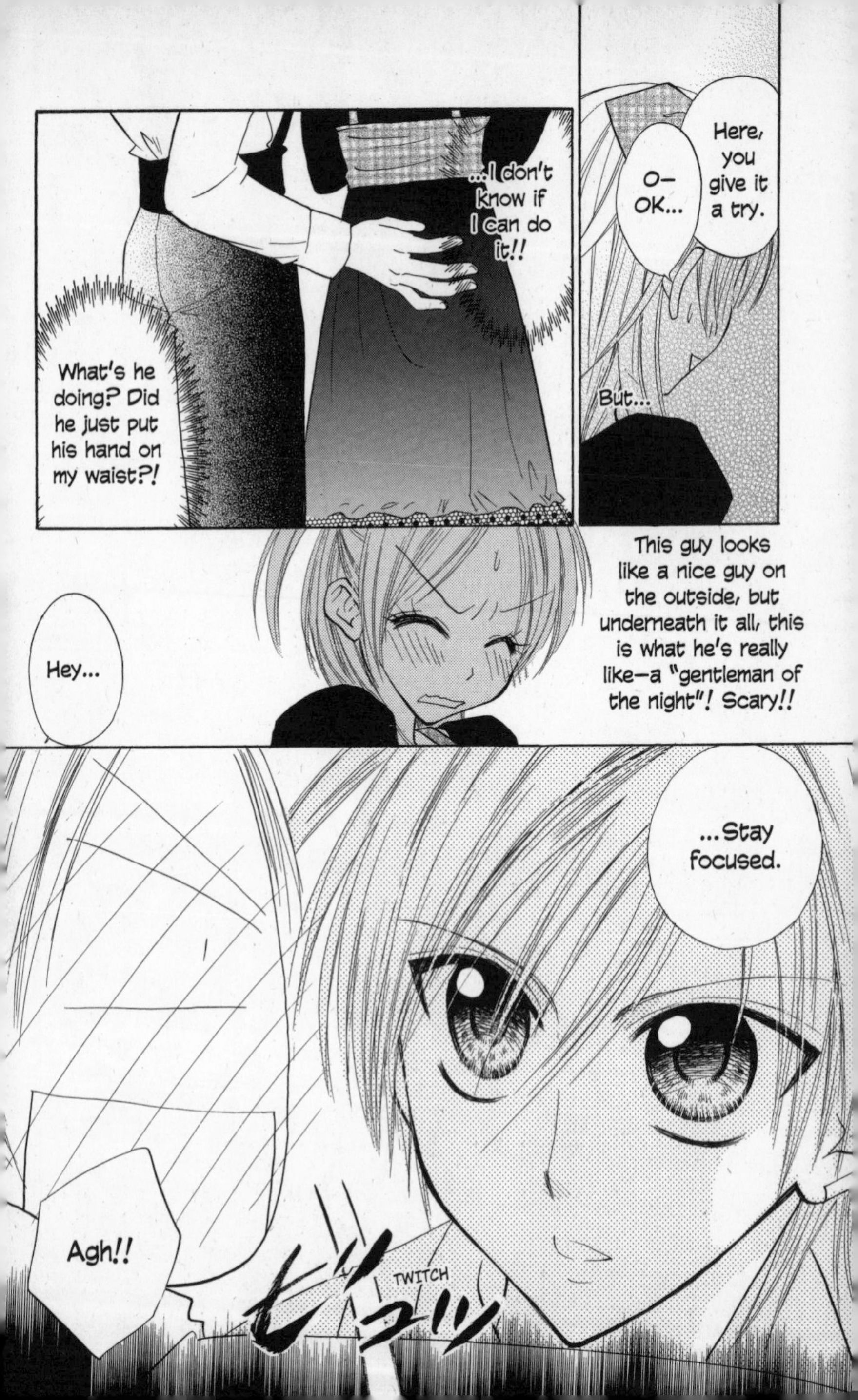
Here, you give it a try.
O-OK...
But...
...I don't know if I can do it!!
What's he doing? Did he just put his hand on my waist?!
This guy looks like a nice guy on the outside, but underneath it all, this is what he's really like—a "gentleman of the night"! Scary!!
Hey...
...Stay focused.
TWITCH
Agh!!

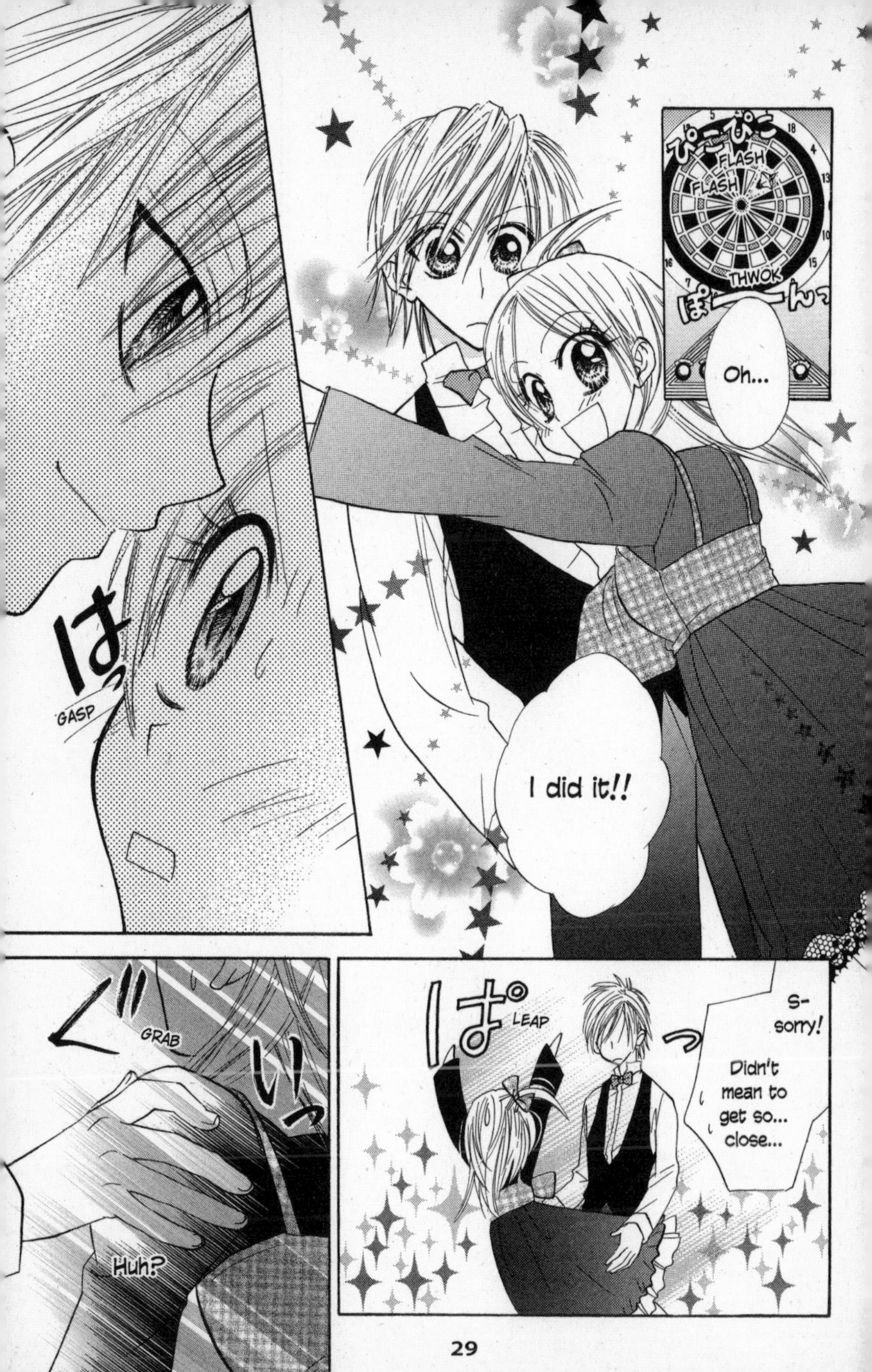
ぴこぴこ
FLASH
FLASH
THWOK
ぽーーんっ
Oh...
I did it!!
はっ
GASP
ぱっ
LEAP
S-sorry!
Didn't mean to get so... close...
ぐいっ
GRAB
Huh?

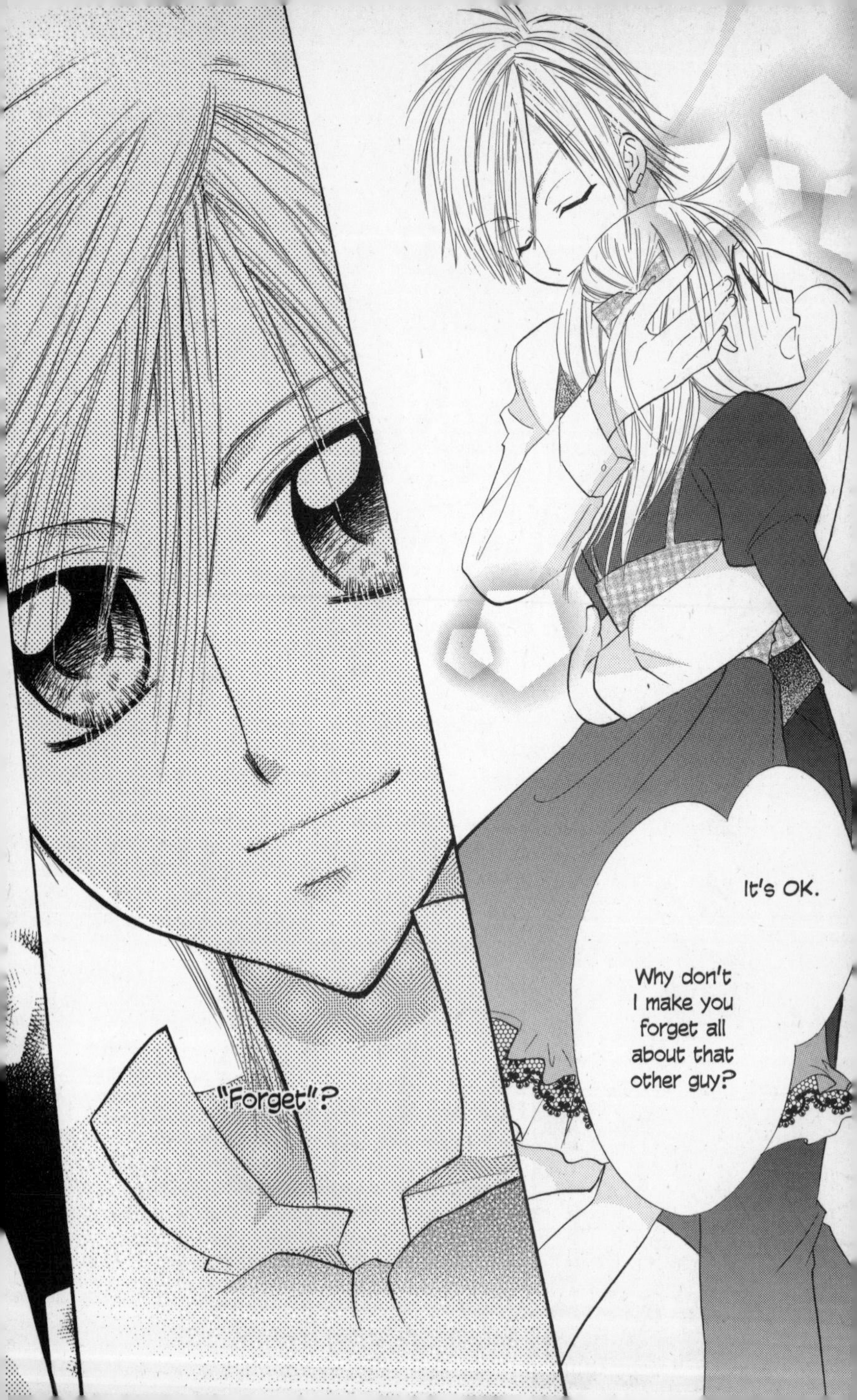
It's OK.
Why don't I make you forget all about that other guy?
"Forget"?

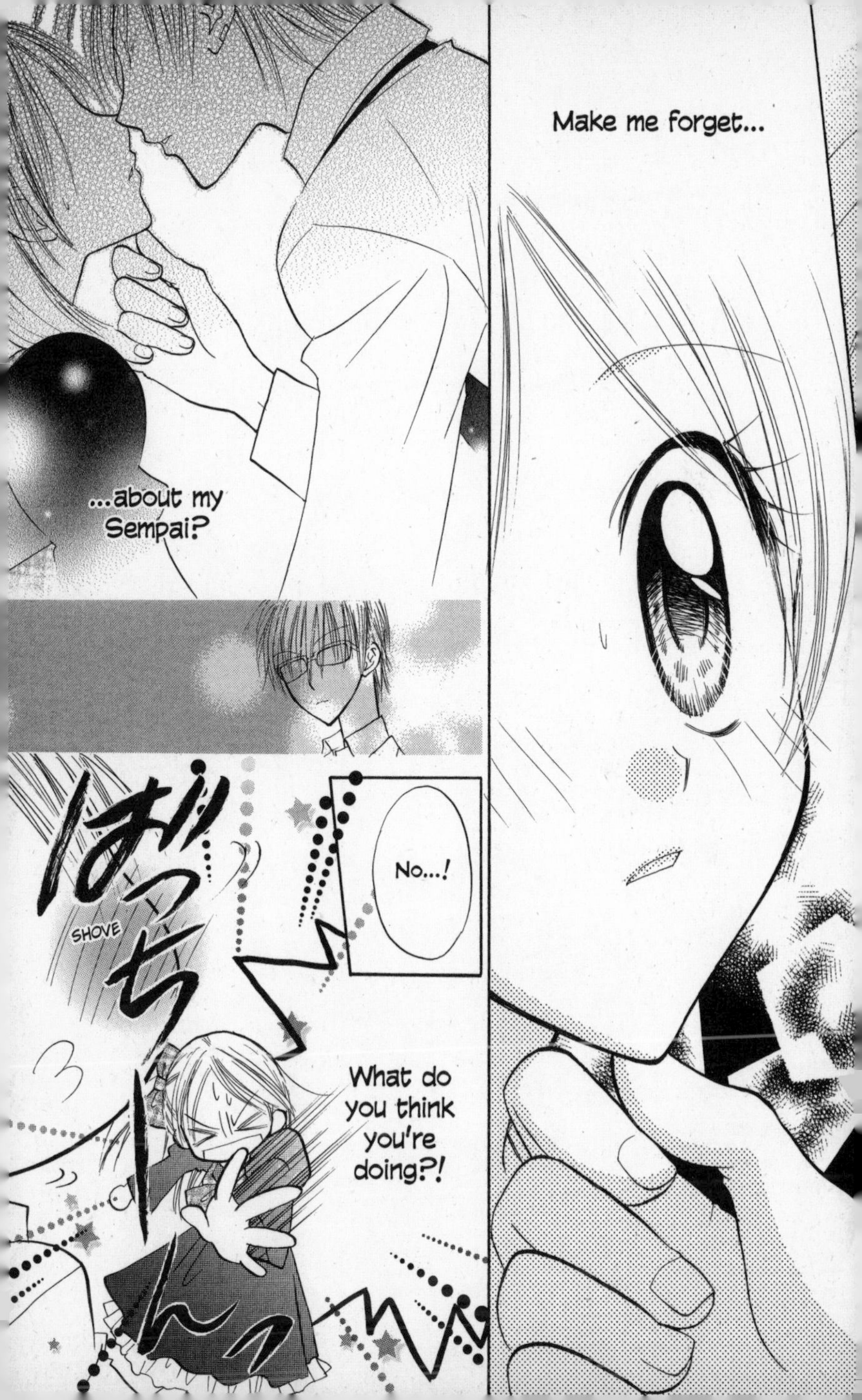

Make me forget...
...about my Sempai?
No...!
What do you think you're doing?!
SHOVE

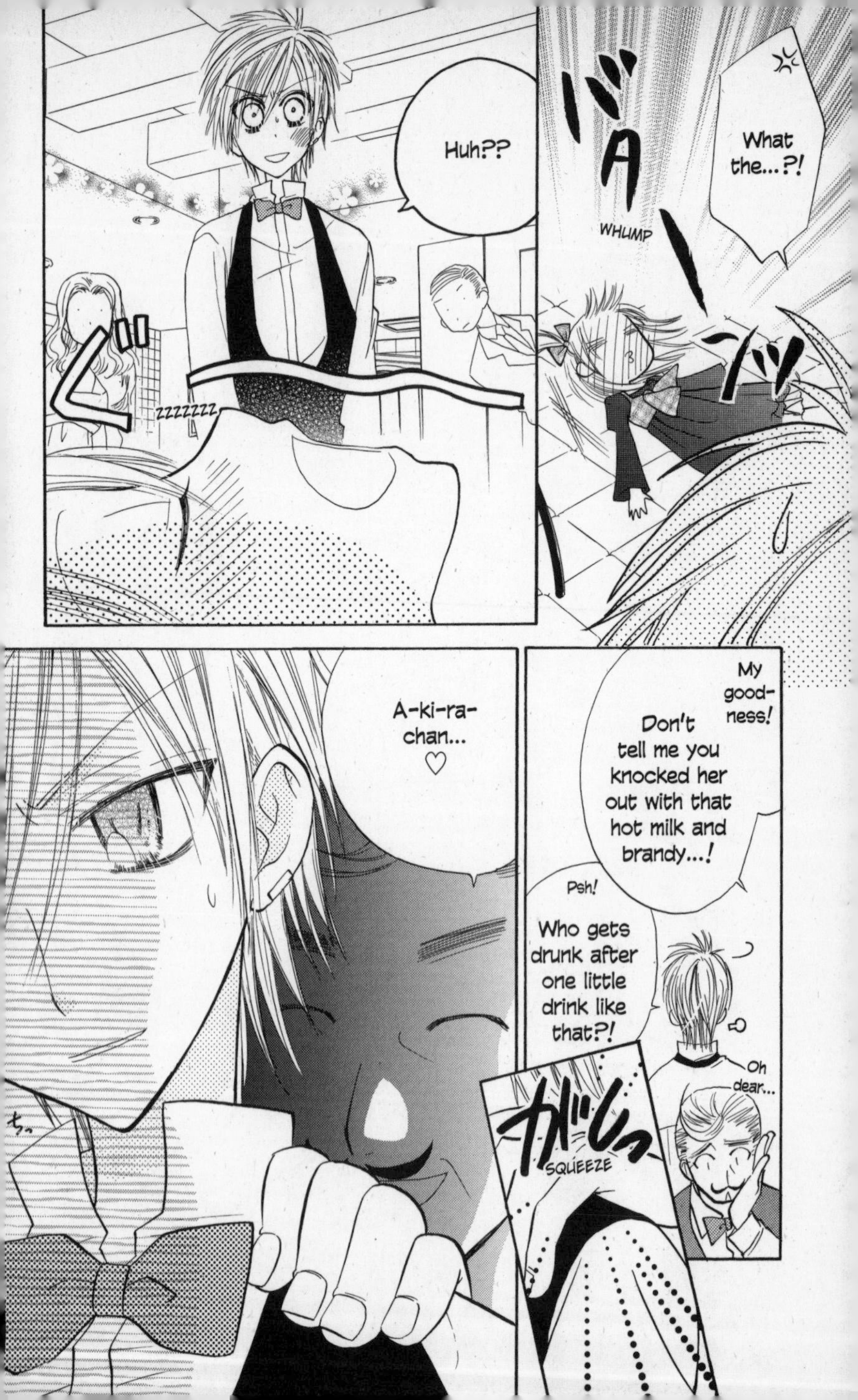
What the...?!
WHUMP
Huh??
ZZZZZZZ
My goodness!
Don't tell me you knocked her out with that hot milk and brandy...!
Psh!
Who gets drunk after one little drink like that?!
Oh dear...
SQUEEZE
A-ki-ra-chan... ♡

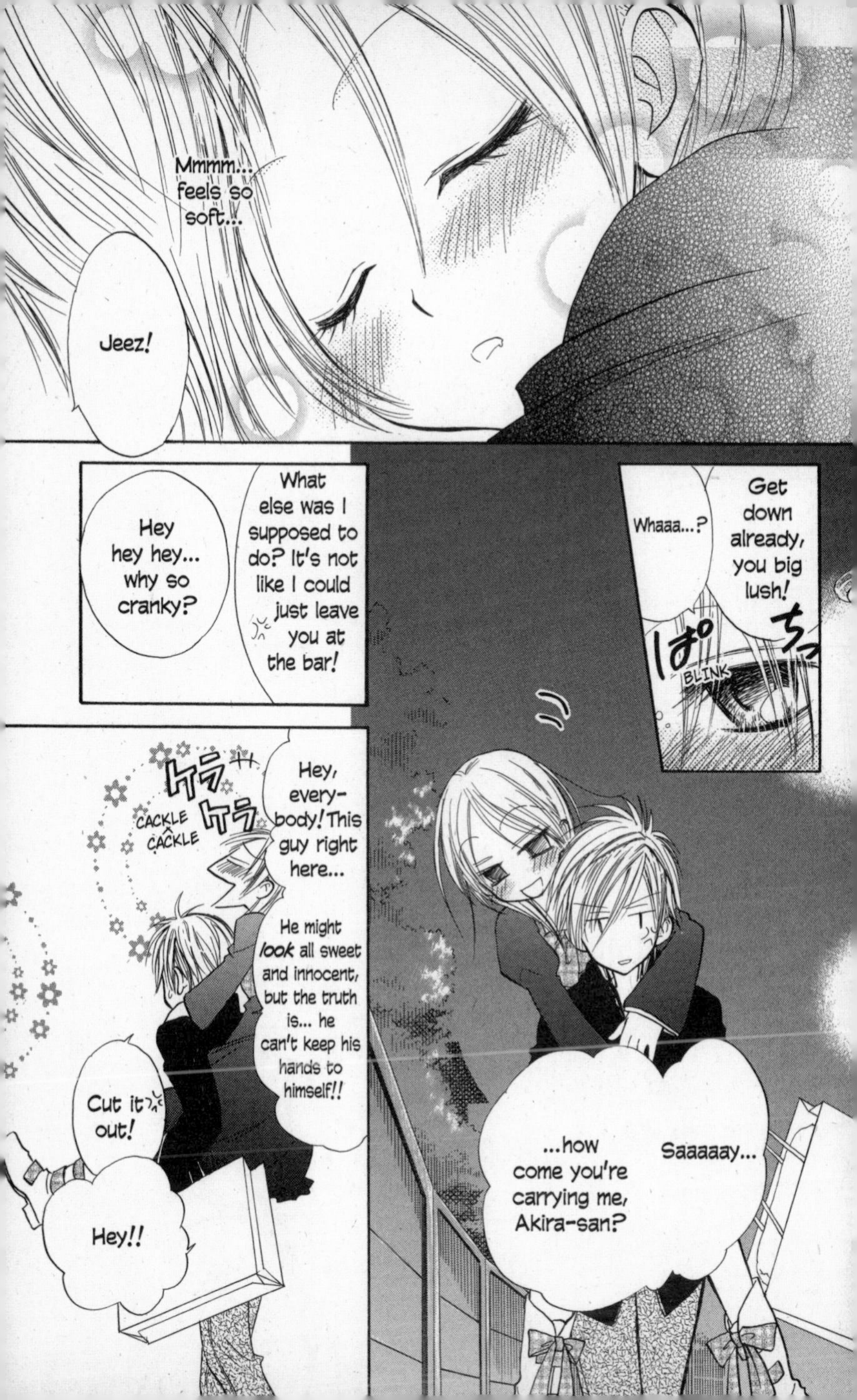
Mmmm... feels so soft...
Jeez!
Saaaaay...
...how come you're carrying me, Akira-san?
ぱち
BLINK
Whaaa...?
Get down already, you big lush!
What else was I supposed to do? It's not like I could just leave you at the bar!
Hey hey hey... why so cranky?
ケラケラ
CACKLE CACKLE
Hey, everybody! This guy right here...
He might *look* all sweet and innocent, but the truth is... he can't keep his hands to himself!!
Cut it out!
Hey!!

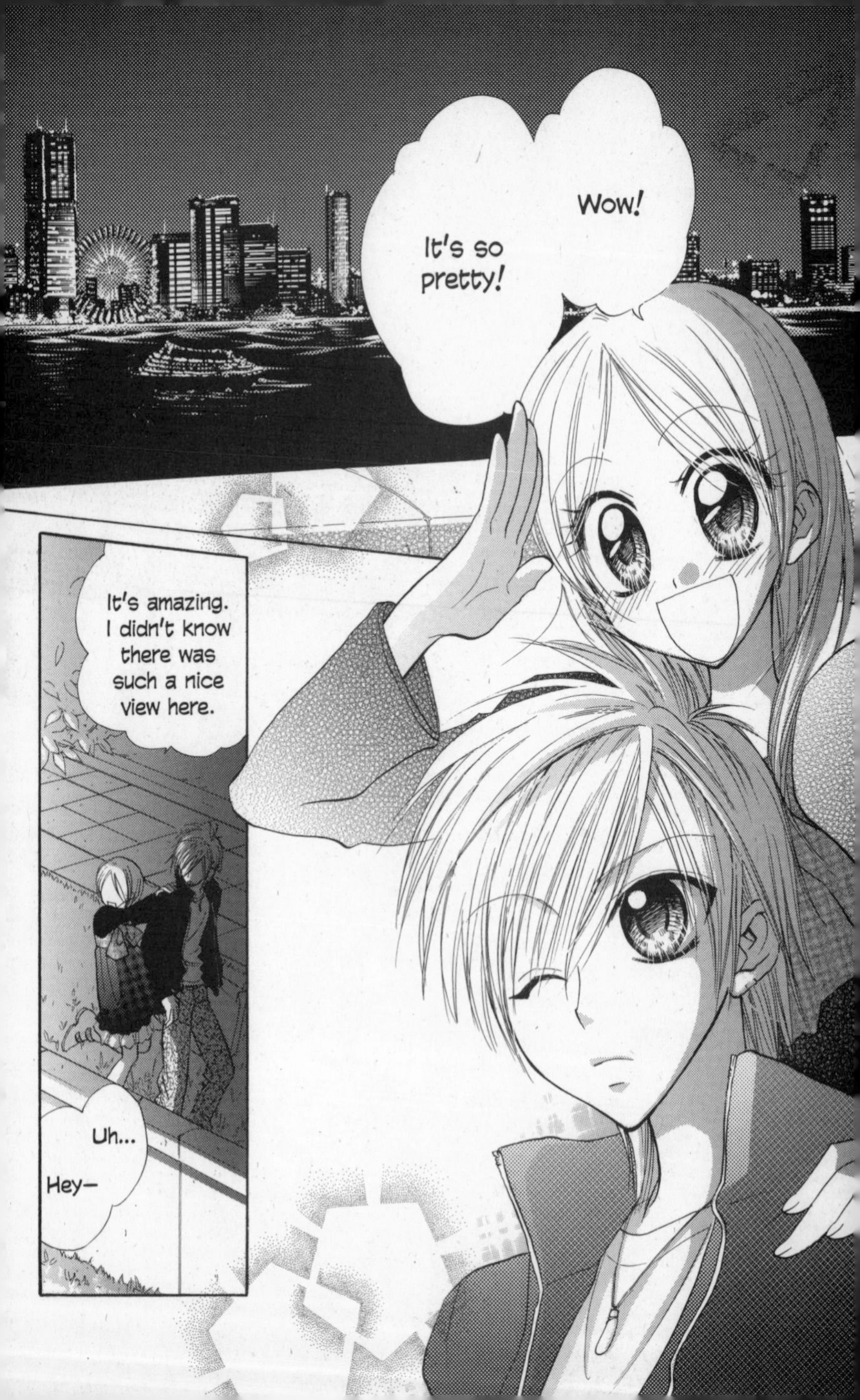
Wow!
It's so pretty!
It's amazing. I didn't know there was such a nice view here.
Uh...
Hey—

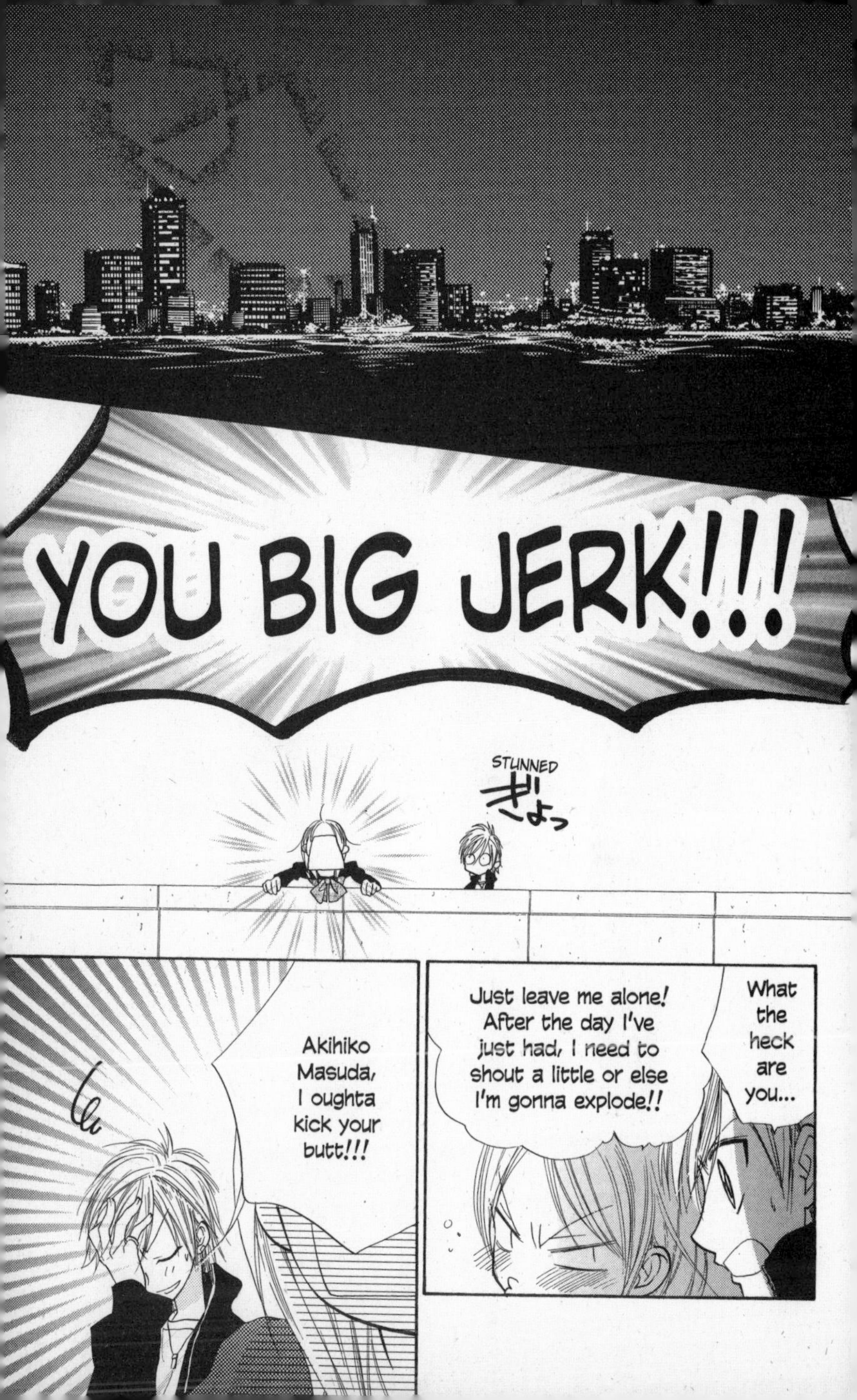
YOU BIG JERK!!!
STUNNED
ぎょっ
What the heck are you...
Just leave me alone! After the day I've just had, I need to shout a little or else I'm gonna explode!!
Akihiko Masuda, I oughta kick your butt!!!

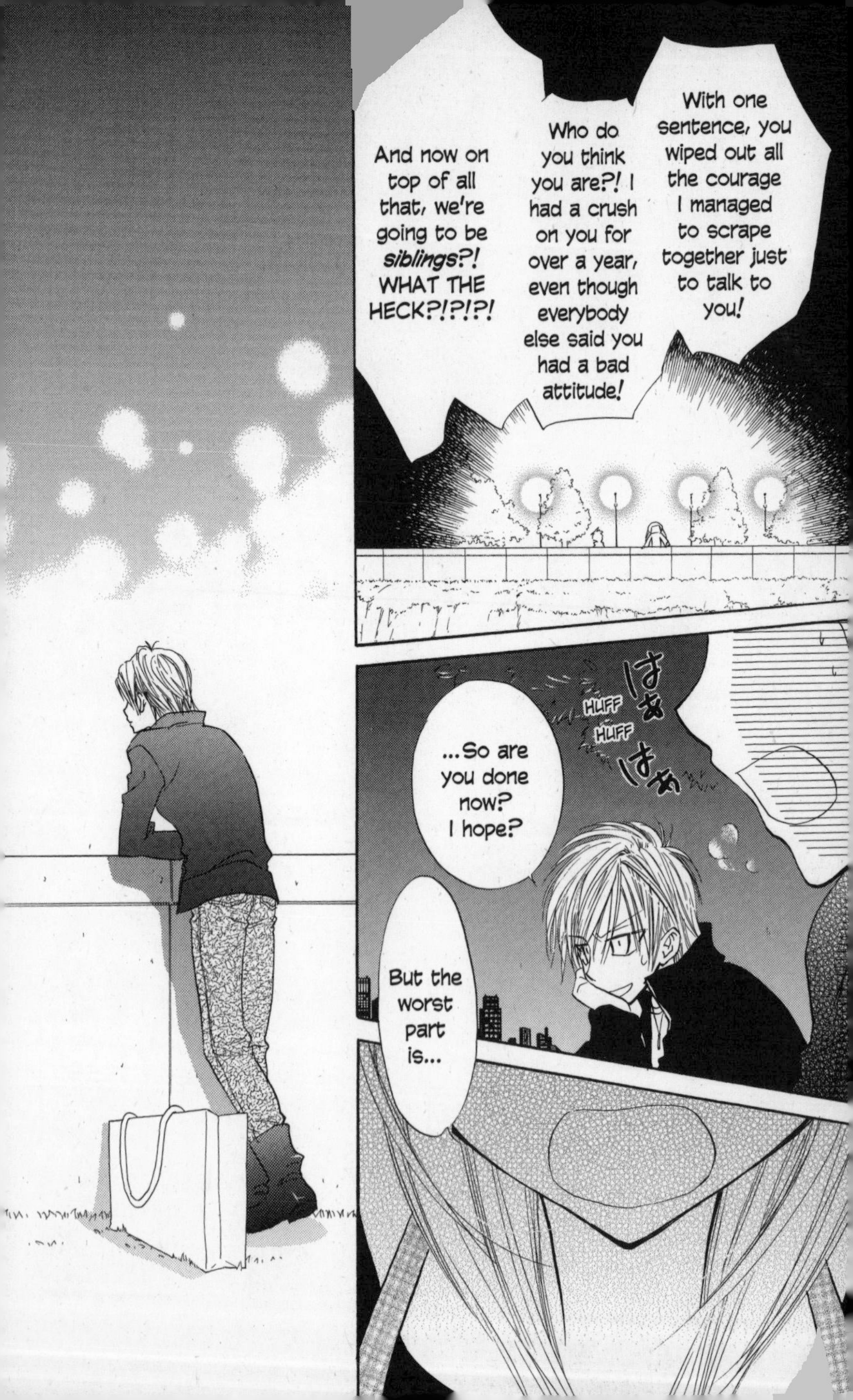
With one sentence, you wiped out all the courage I managed to scrape together just to talk to you!
Who do you think you are?! I had a crush on you for over a year, even though everybody else said you had a bad attitude!
And now on top of all that, we're going to be *siblings*?! WHAT THE HECK?!?!?!
はぁ はぁ
HUFF HUFF
...So are you done now? I hope?
But the worst part is...

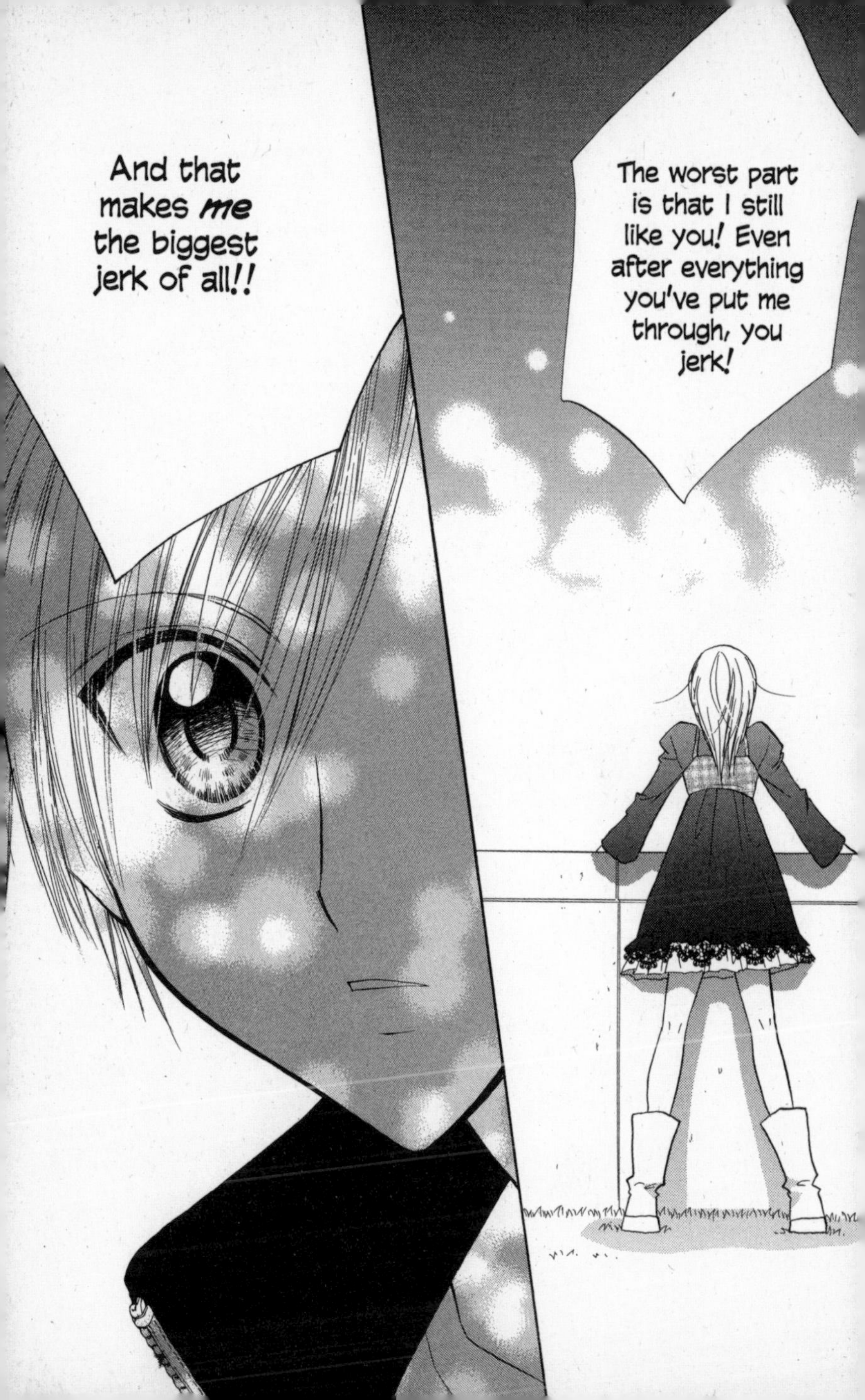
The worst part is that I still like you! Even after everything you've put me through, you jerk!
And that makes *me* the biggest jerk of all!!

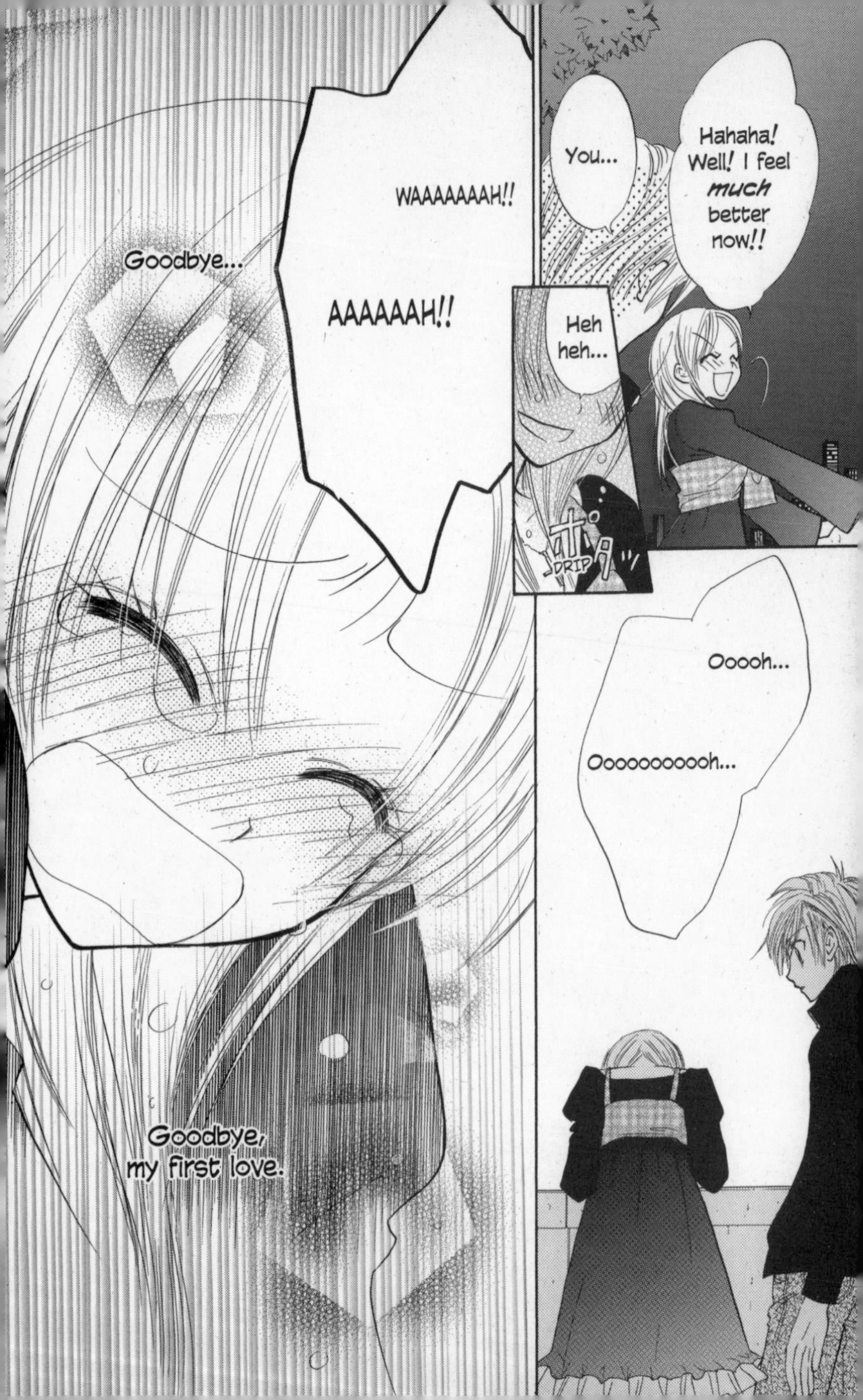

Hahaha! Well! I feel *much* better now!!
You...
Heh heh...
DRIP
Ooooh...
Oooooooooh...
WAAAAAAAH!!
AAAAAAH!!
Goodbye...
Goodbye, my first love.

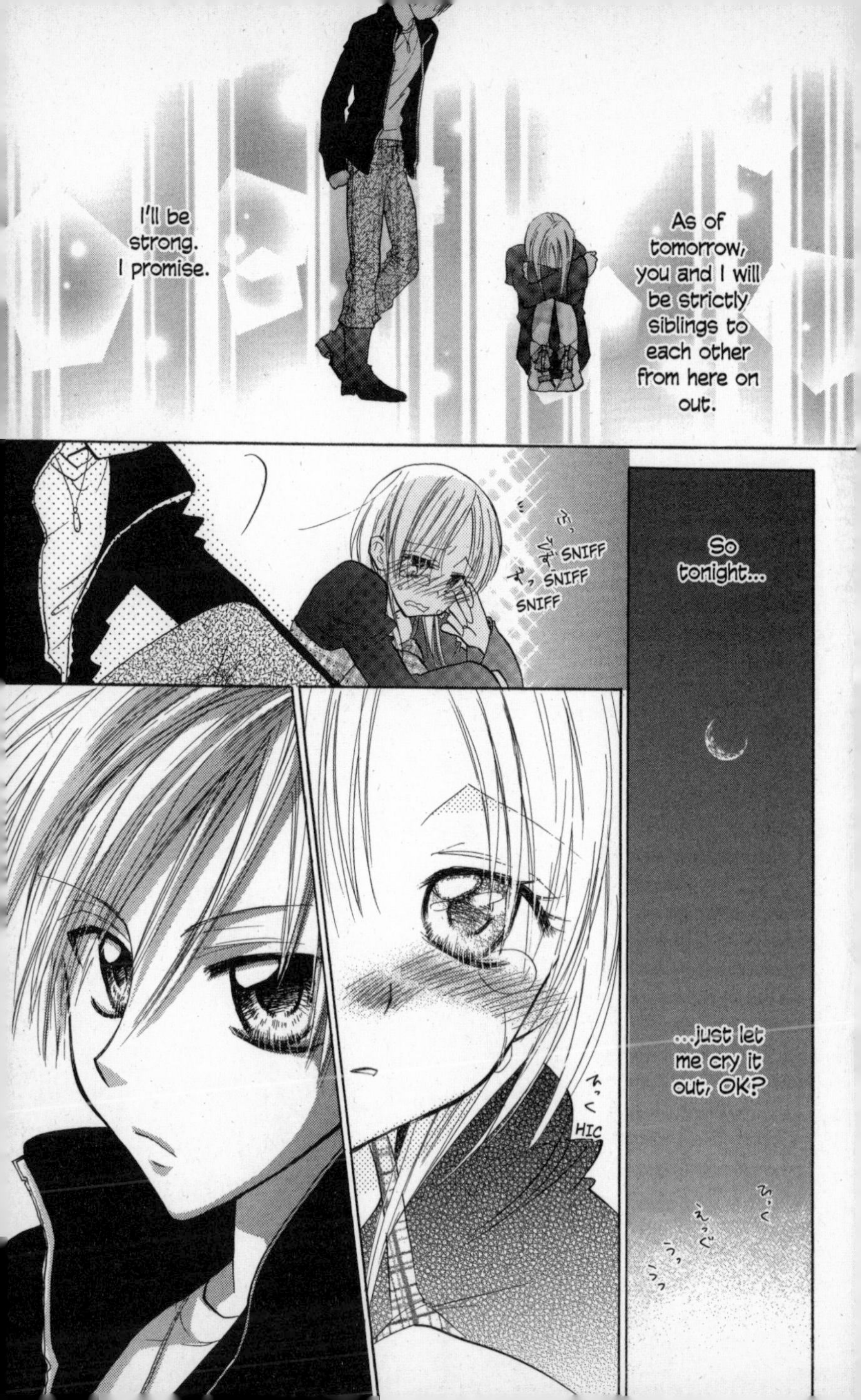
As of tomorrow, you and I will be strictly siblings to each other from here on out.
I'll be strong. I promise.
So tonight...
...just let me cry it out, OK?
SNIFF
SNIFF
SNIFF
HIC

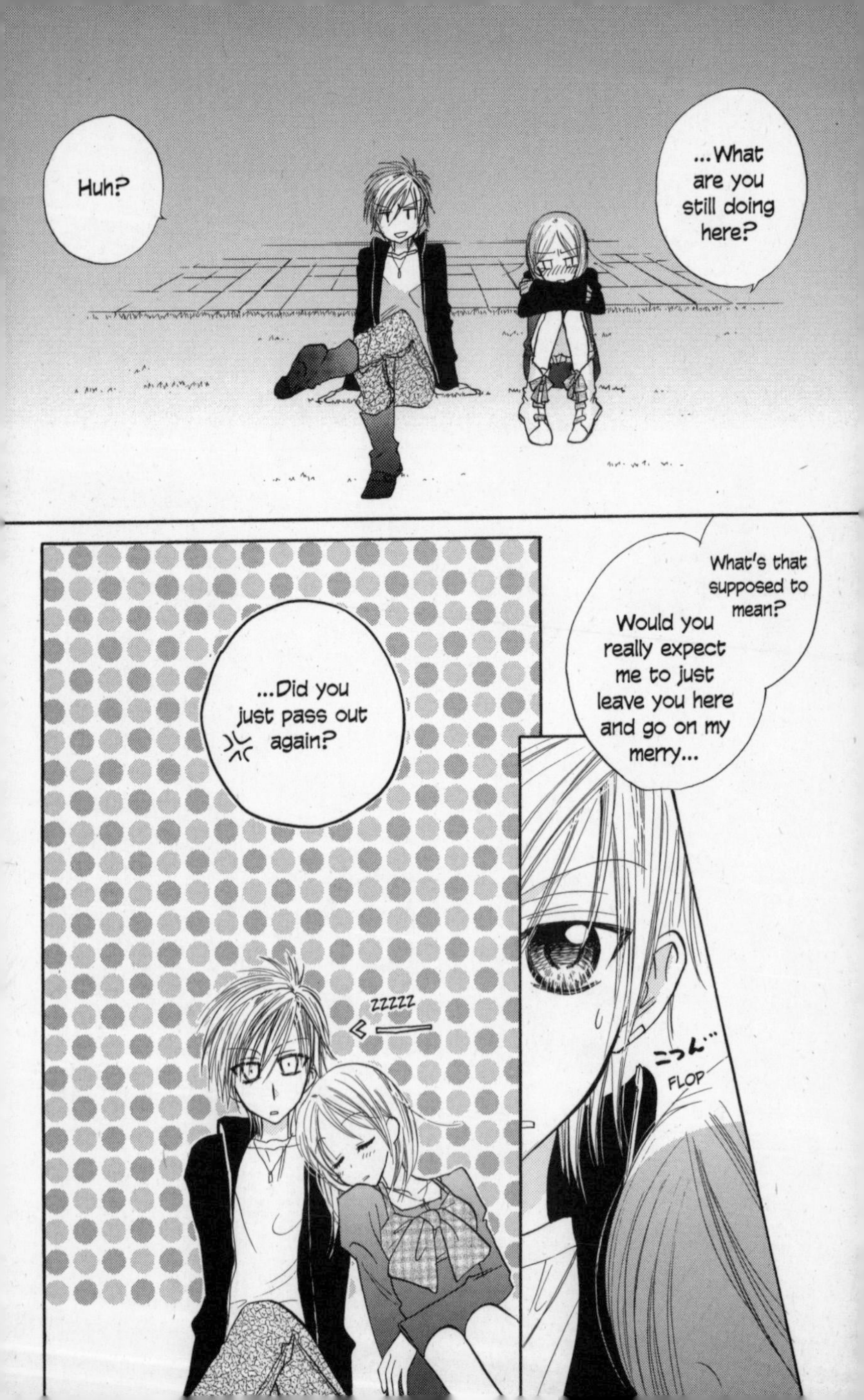
...What are you still doing here?
Huh?
What's that supposed to mean?
Would you really expect me to just leave you here and go on my merry...
FLOP
...Did you just pass out again?
ZZZZZ

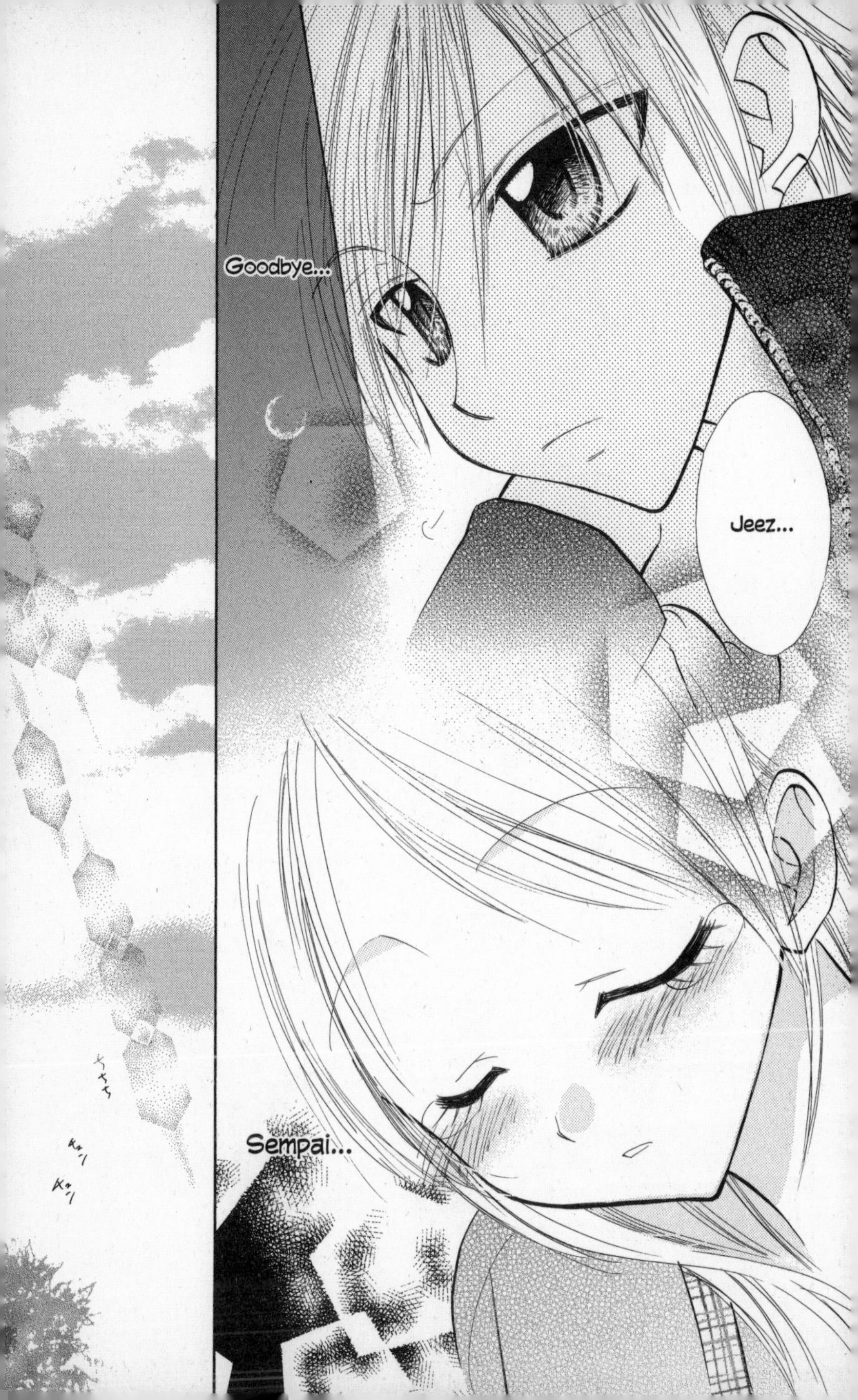
Jeez...
Goodbye...
Sempai...

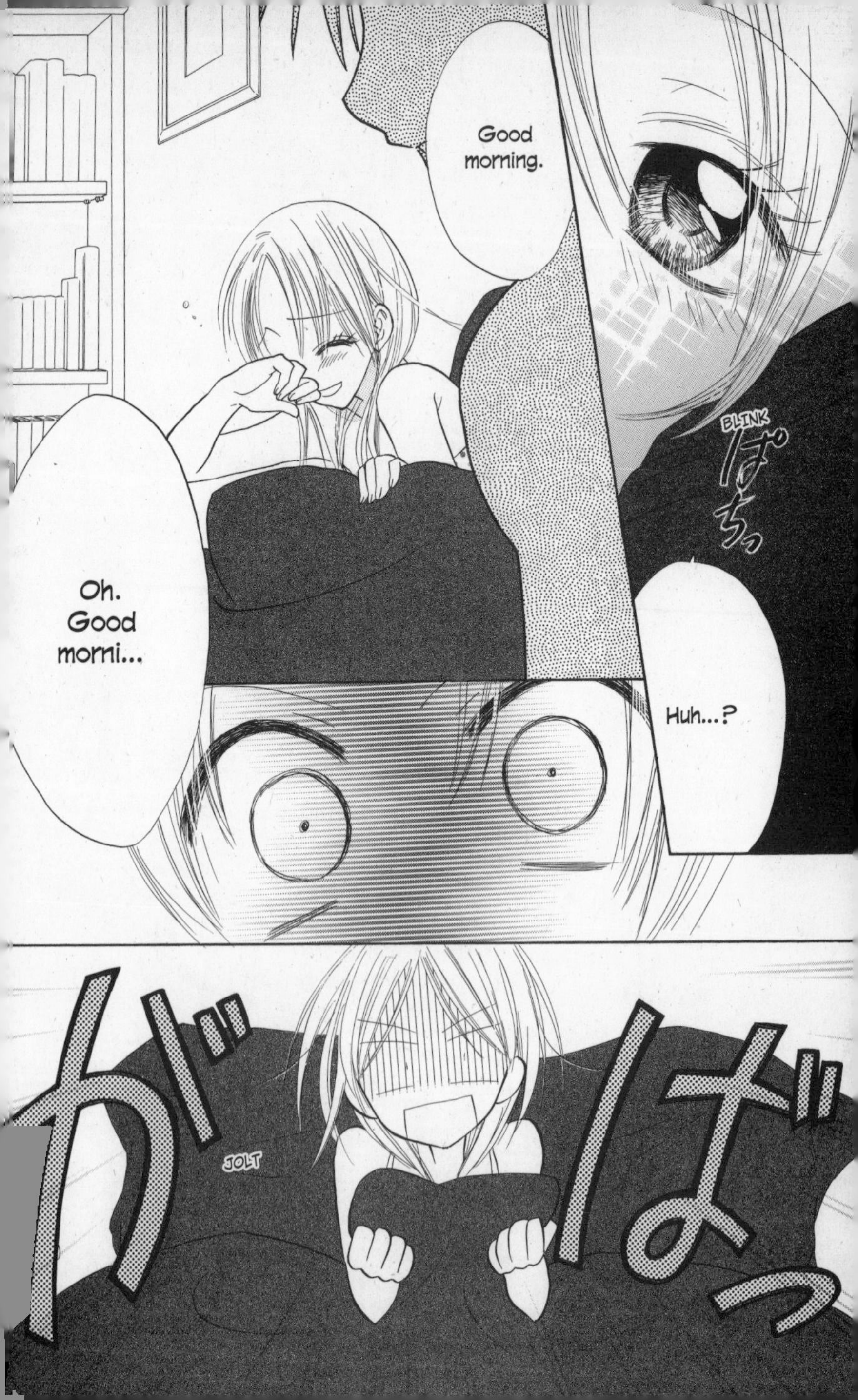
Good morning.
BLINK
ぱちっ
Oh. Good morni...
Huh...?
がばっ
JOLT

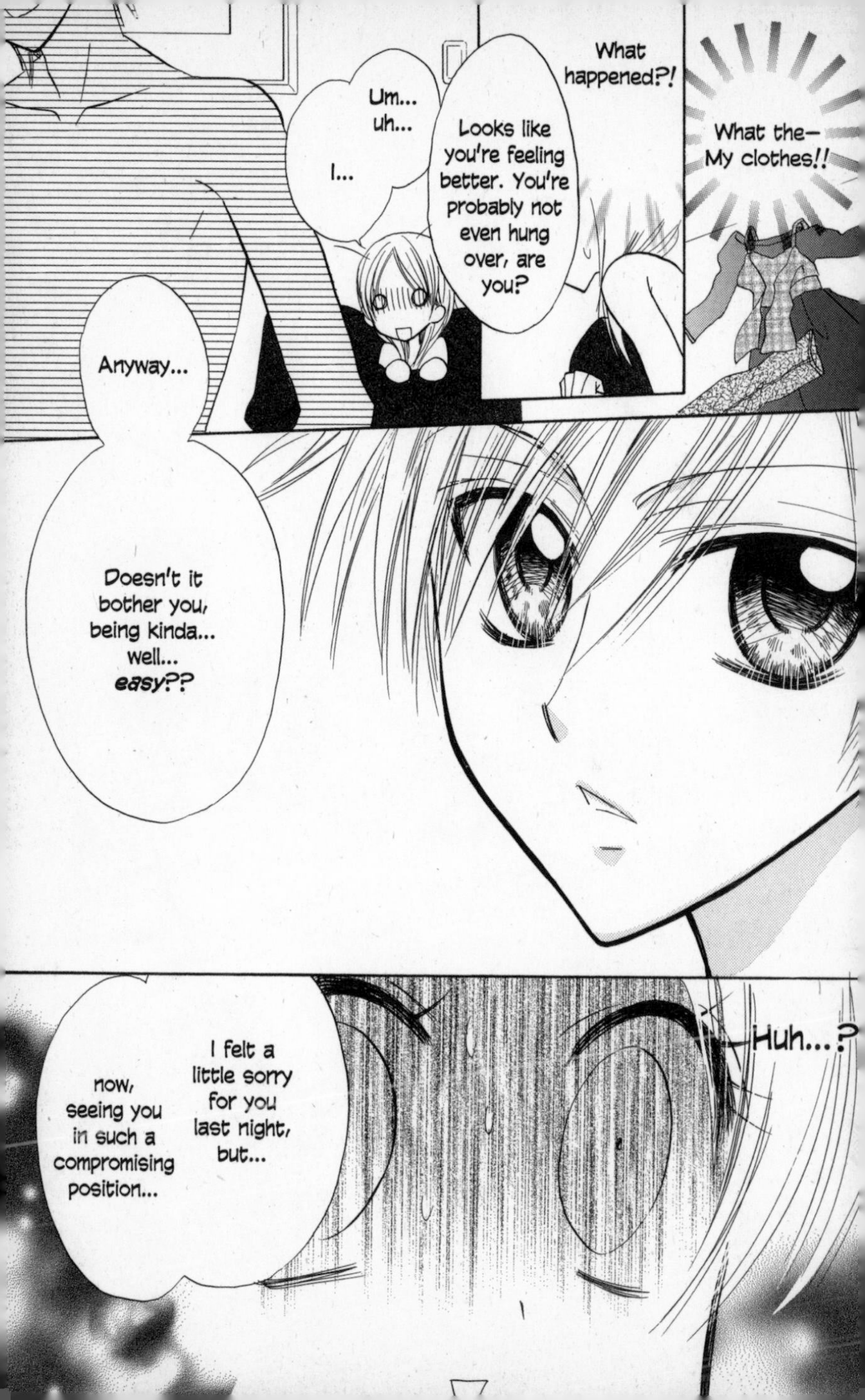

What the— My clothes!!
What happened?!
Looks like you're feeling better. You're probably not even hung over, are you?
Um... uh... I...
Anyway...
Doesn't it bother you, being kinda... well... *easy*??
Huh...?
I felt a little sorry for you last night, but...
now, seeing you in such a compromising position...

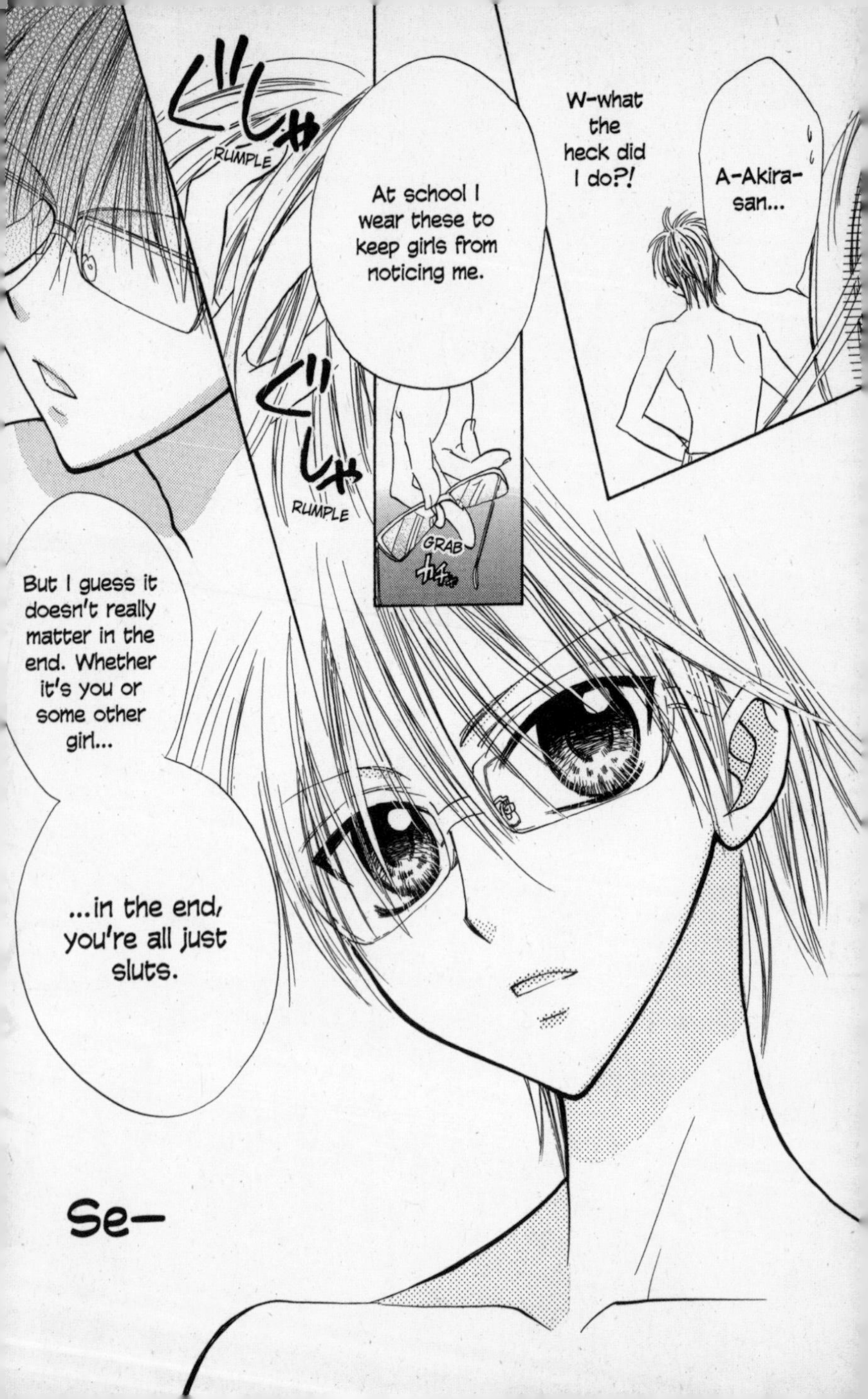
A-Akira-san...
W-what the heck did I do?!
At school I wear these to keep girls from noticing me.
GRAB
RUMPLE
RUMPLE
But I guess it doesn't really matter in the end. Whether it's you or some other girl...
...in the end, you're all just sluts.
Se-

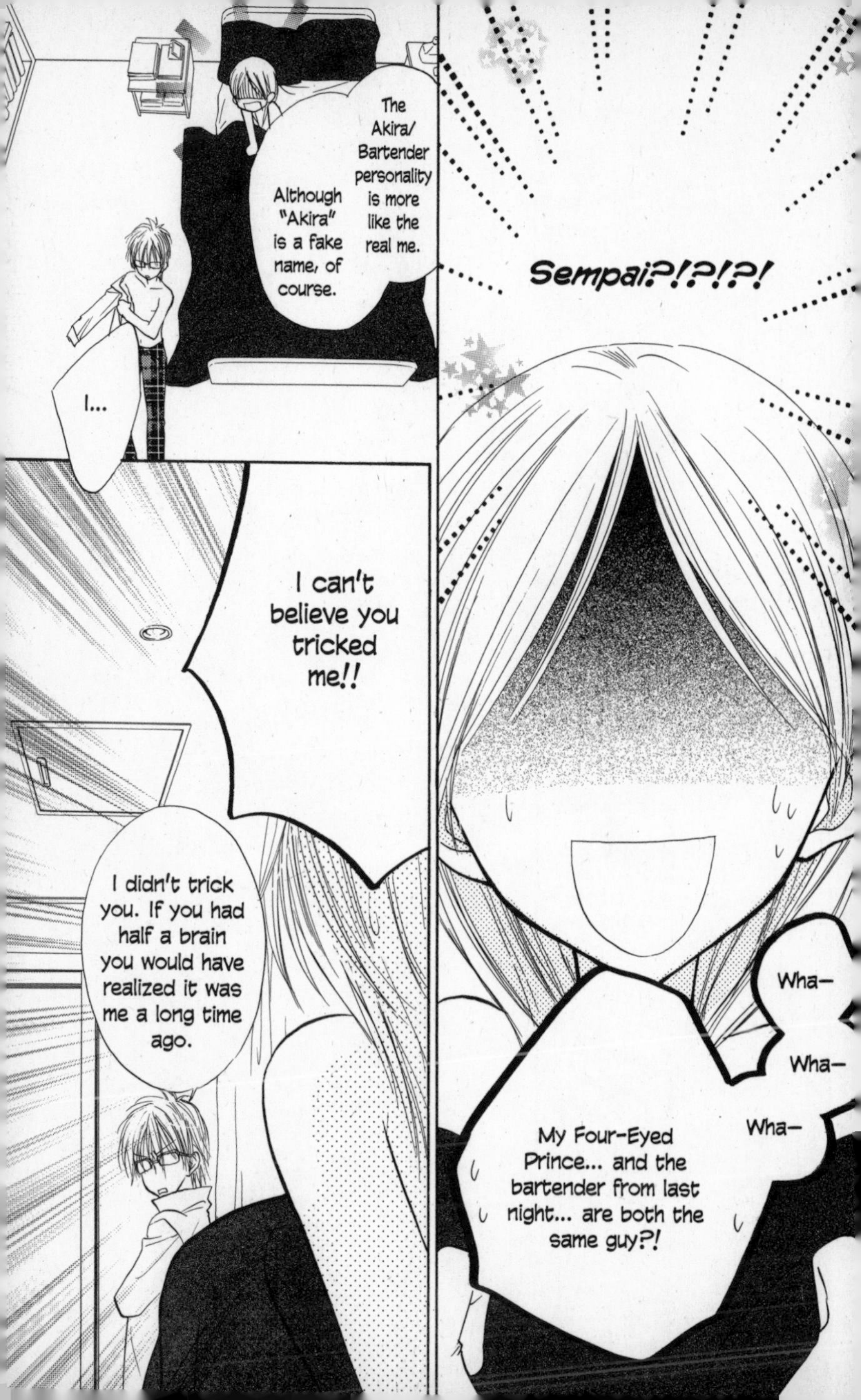
Sempai?!?!?!
Wha— Wha— Wha—
My Four-Eyed Prince... and the bartender from last night... are both the same guy?!
The Akira/ Bartender personality is more like the real me.
Although "Akira" is a fake name, of course.
I...
I can't believe you tricked me!!
I didn't trick you. If you had half a brain you would have realized it was me a long time ago.

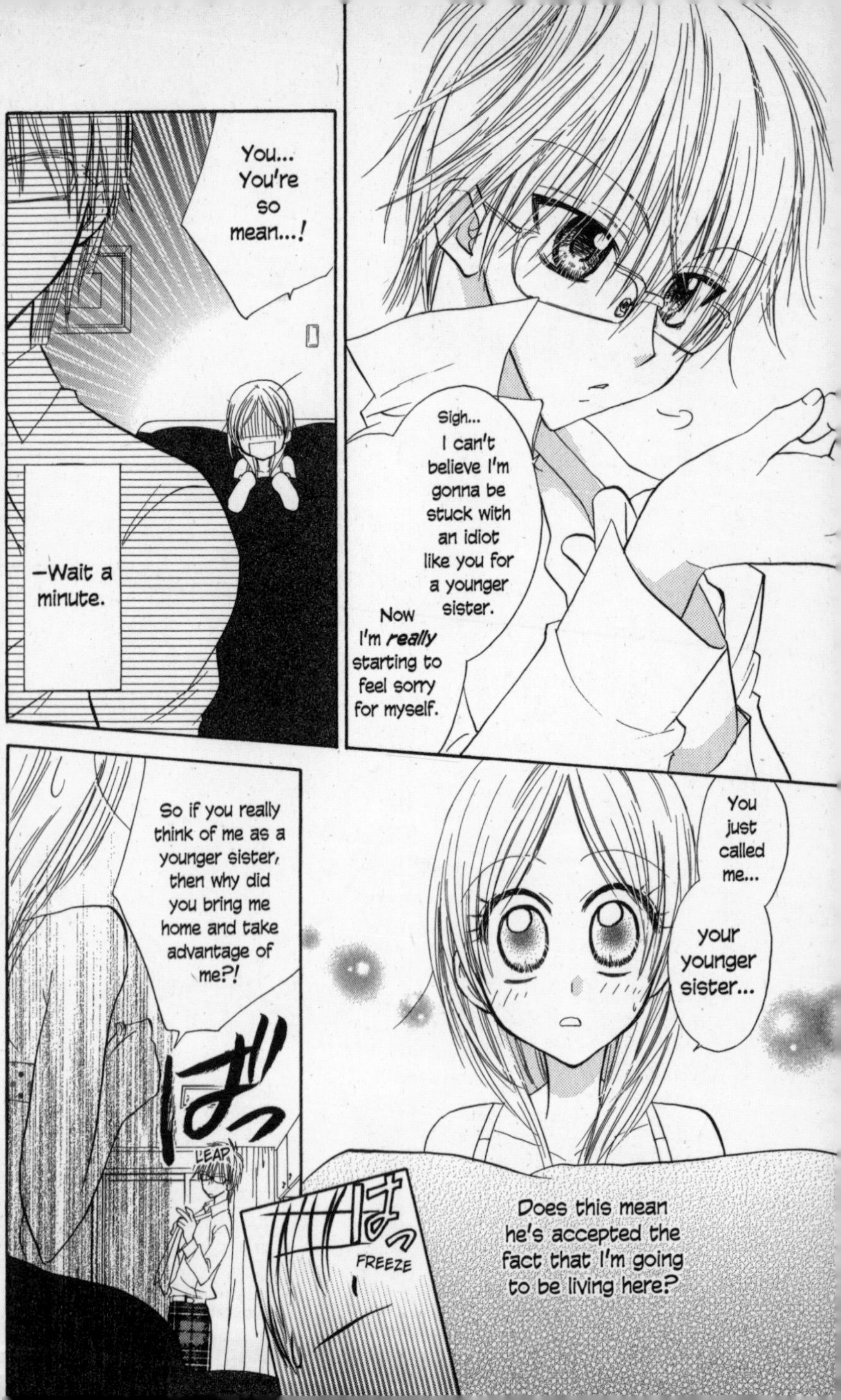
Sigh... I can't believe I'm gonna be stuck with an idiot like you for a younger sister.
Now I'm *really* starting to feel sorry for myself.
You... You're so mean...!
—Wait a minute.
You just called me...
your younger sister...
Does this mean he's accepted the fact that I'm going to be living here?
FREEZE
So if you really think of me as a younger sister, then why did you bring me home and take advantage of me?!
LEAP

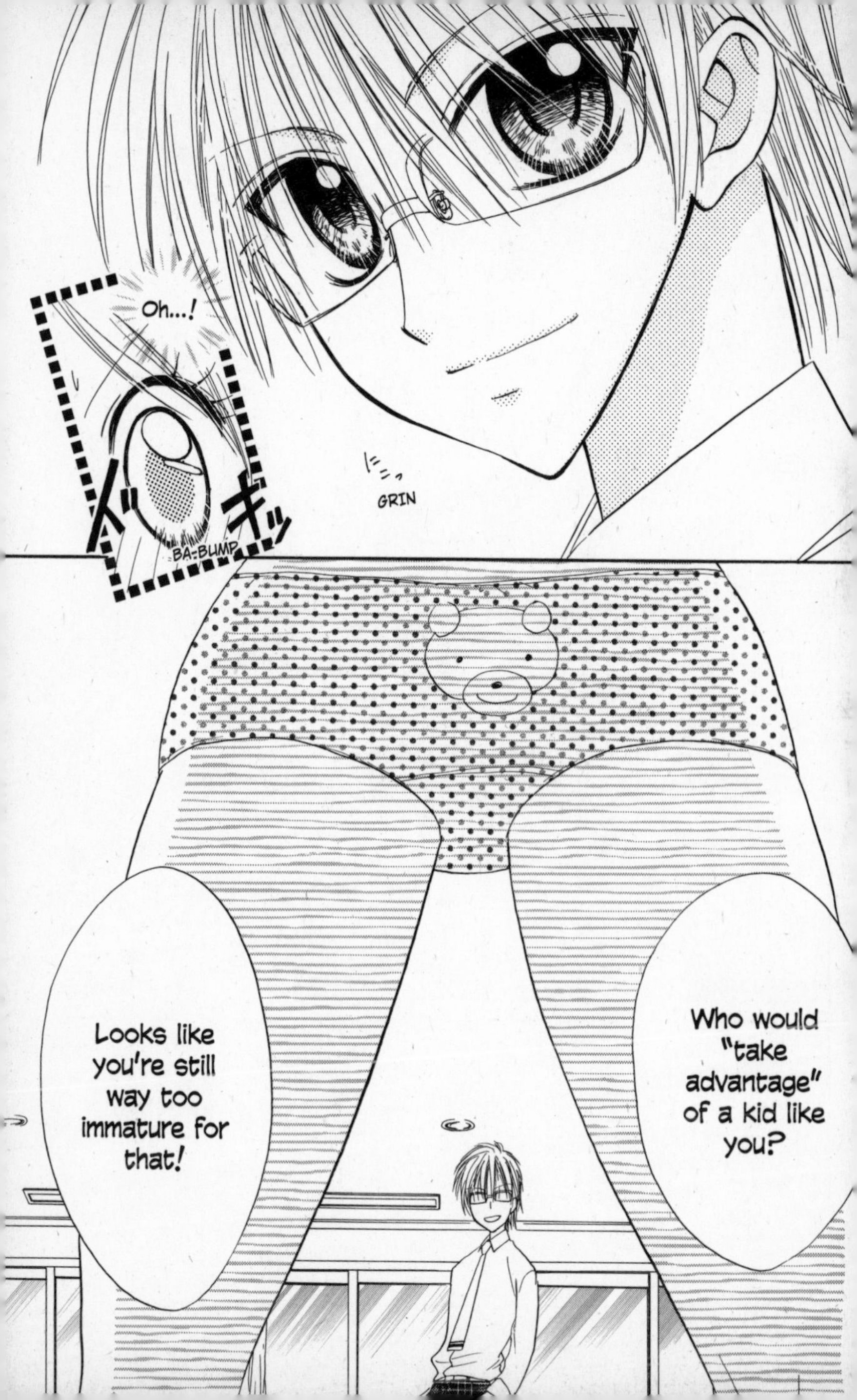
GRIN
Oh...!
BA-BUMP
Who would "take advantage" of a kid like you?
Looks like you're still way too immature for that!

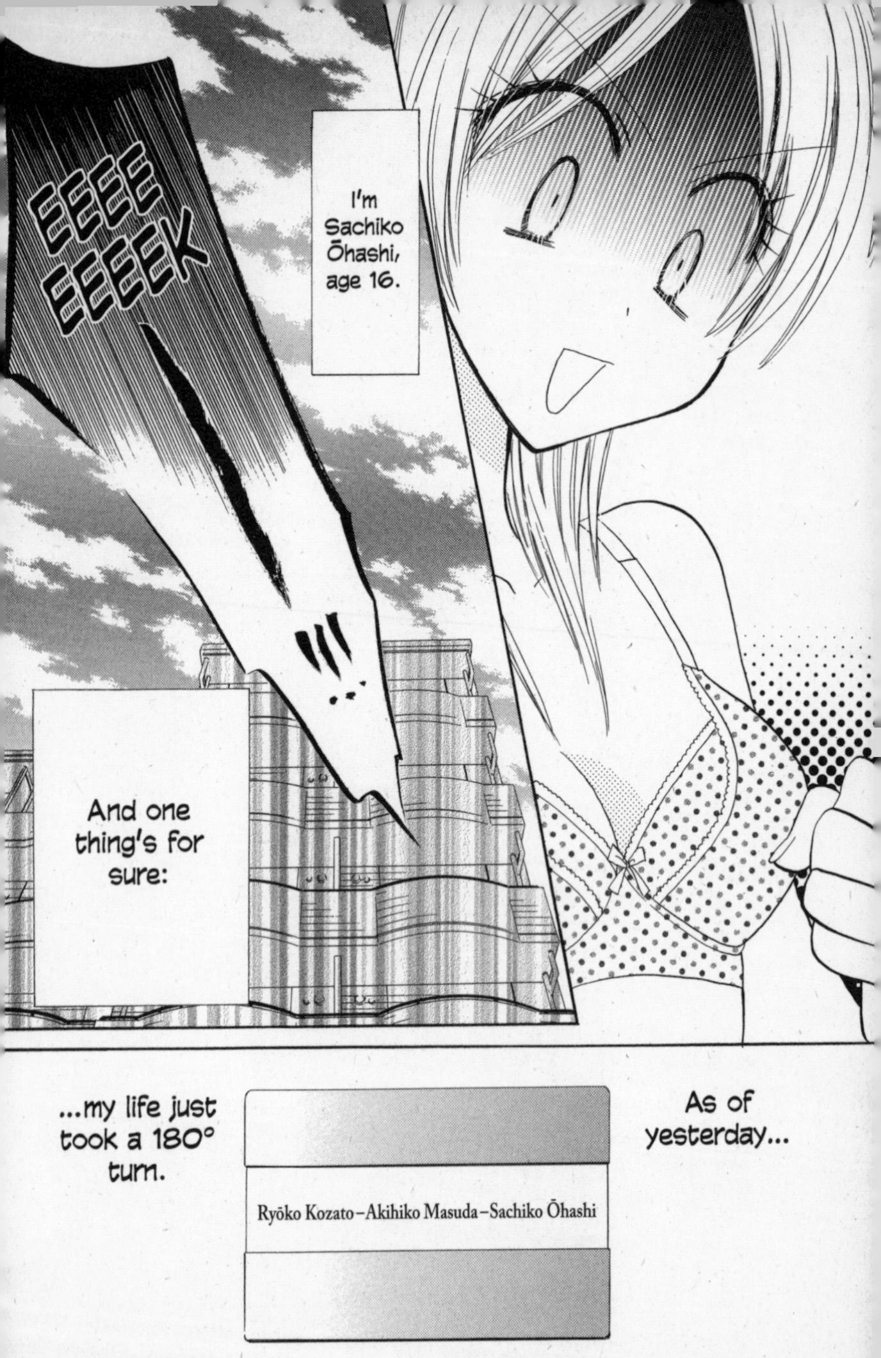
I'm Sachiko Ōhashi, age 16.
EEEE EEEEK
And one thing's for sure:
As of yesterday...
Ryōko Kozato–Akihiko Masuda–Sachiko Ōhashi
...my life just took a 180° turn.

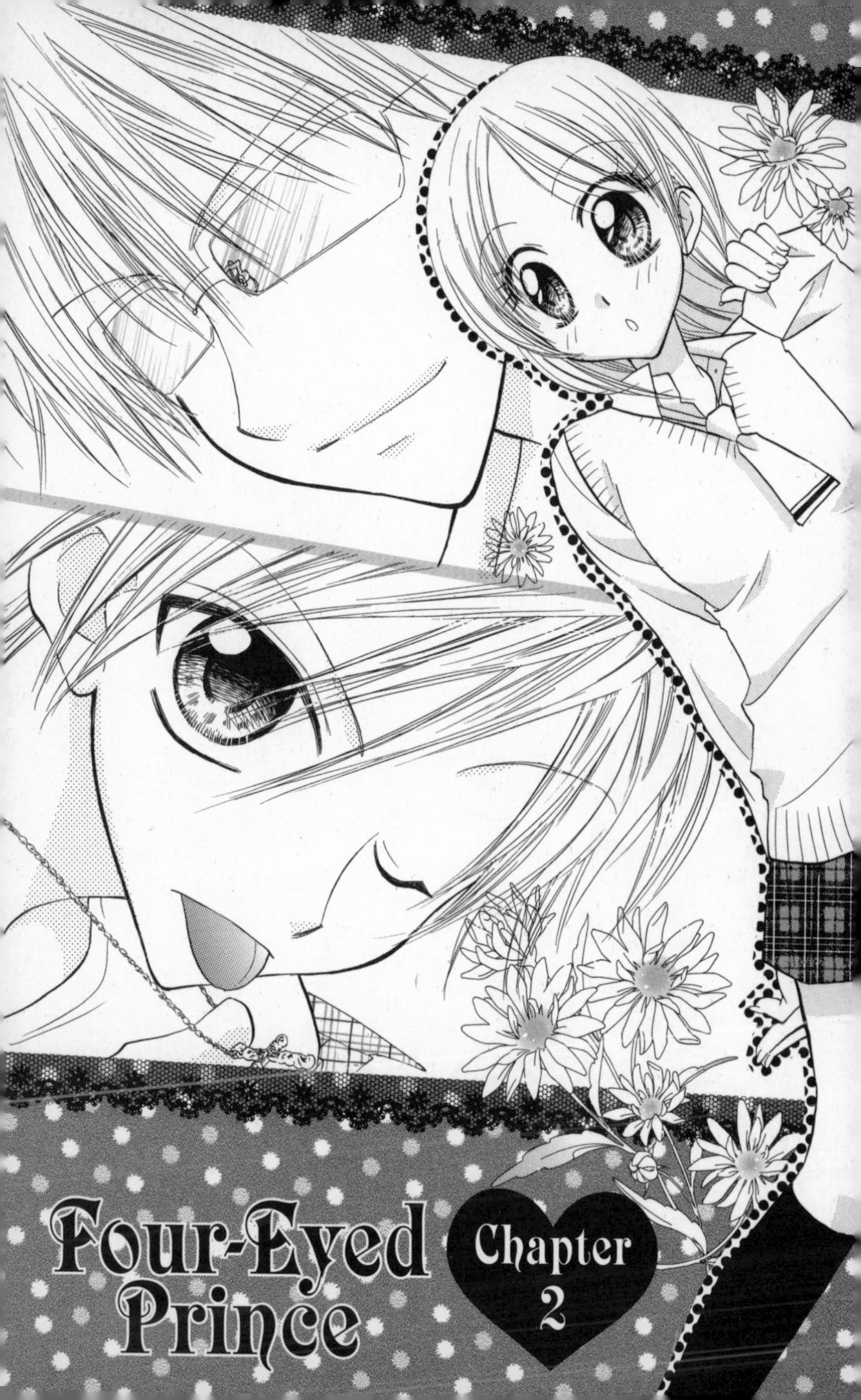
Four-Eyed Prince
Chapter 2

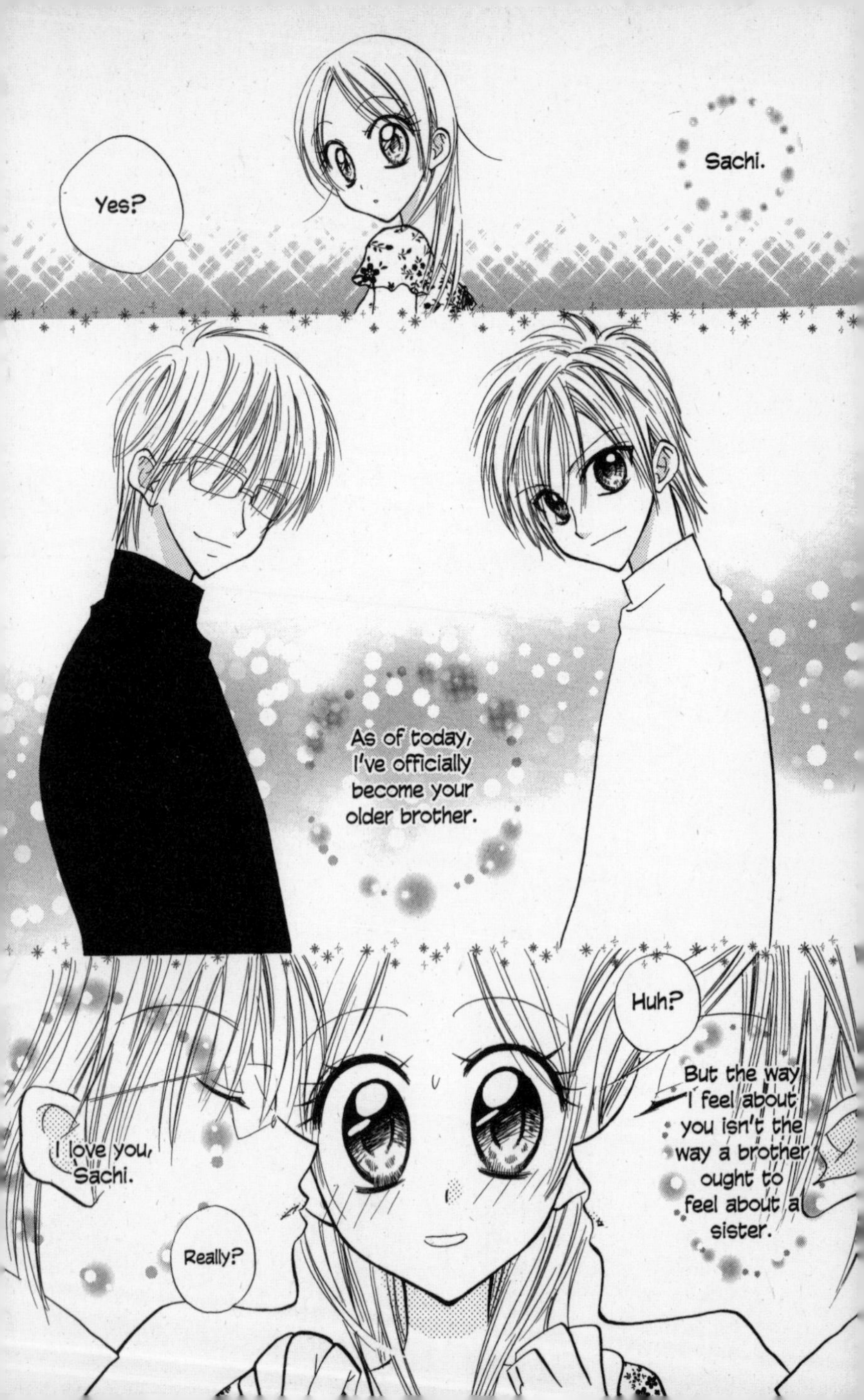
Sachi.
Yes?
As of today, I've officially become your older brother.
Huh?
But the way I feel about you isn't the way a brother ought to feel about a sister.
I love you, Sachi.
Really?

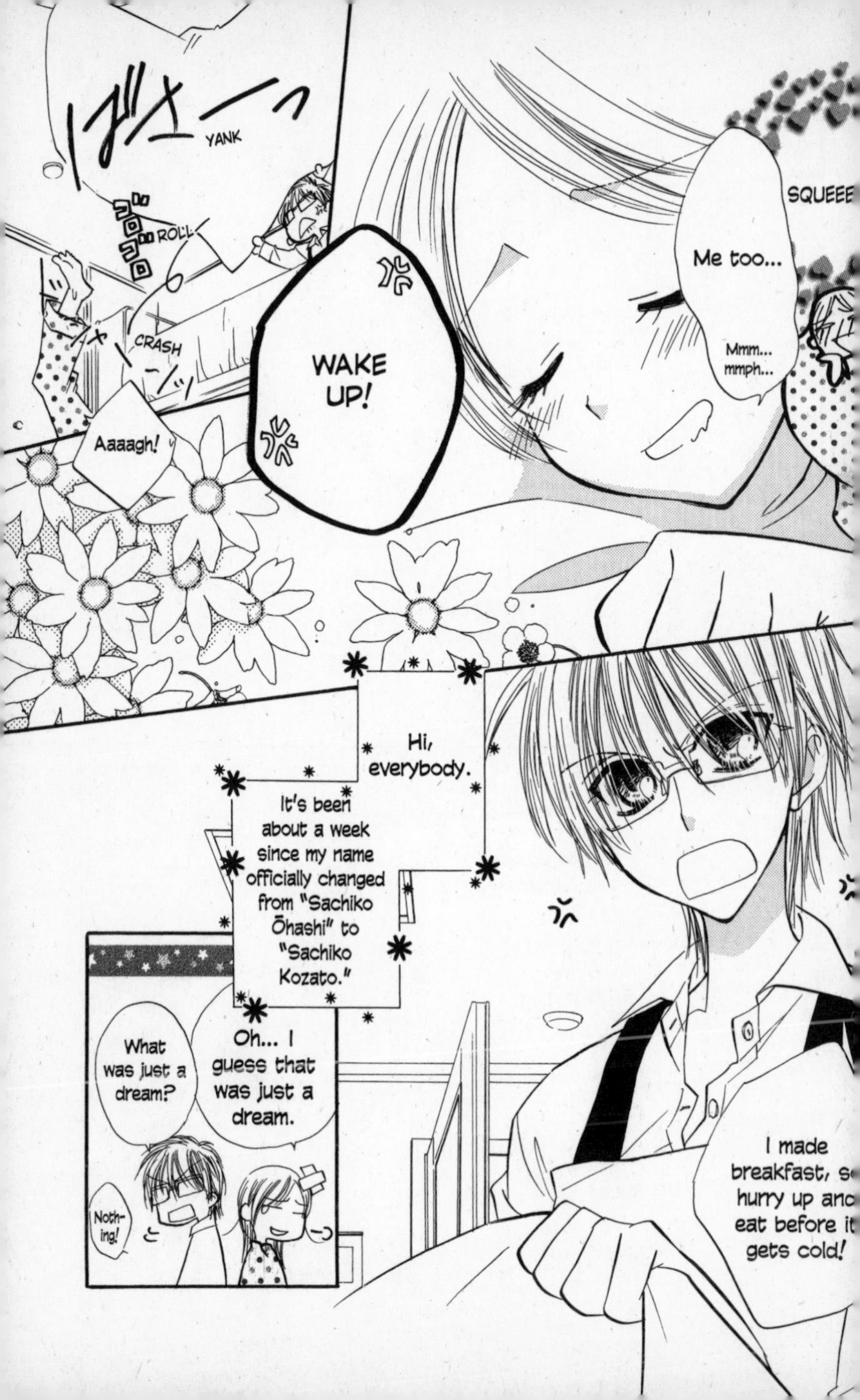
SQUEEE
Me too...
Mmm... mmph...
WAKE UP!
YANK
ROLL
CRASH
Aaaagh!
Hi, everybody.
It's been about a week since my name officially changed from "Sachiko Ōhashi" to "Sachiko Kozato."
I made breakfast, s hurry up anc eat before it gets cold!
Oh... I guess that was just a dream.
What was just a dream?
Nothing!

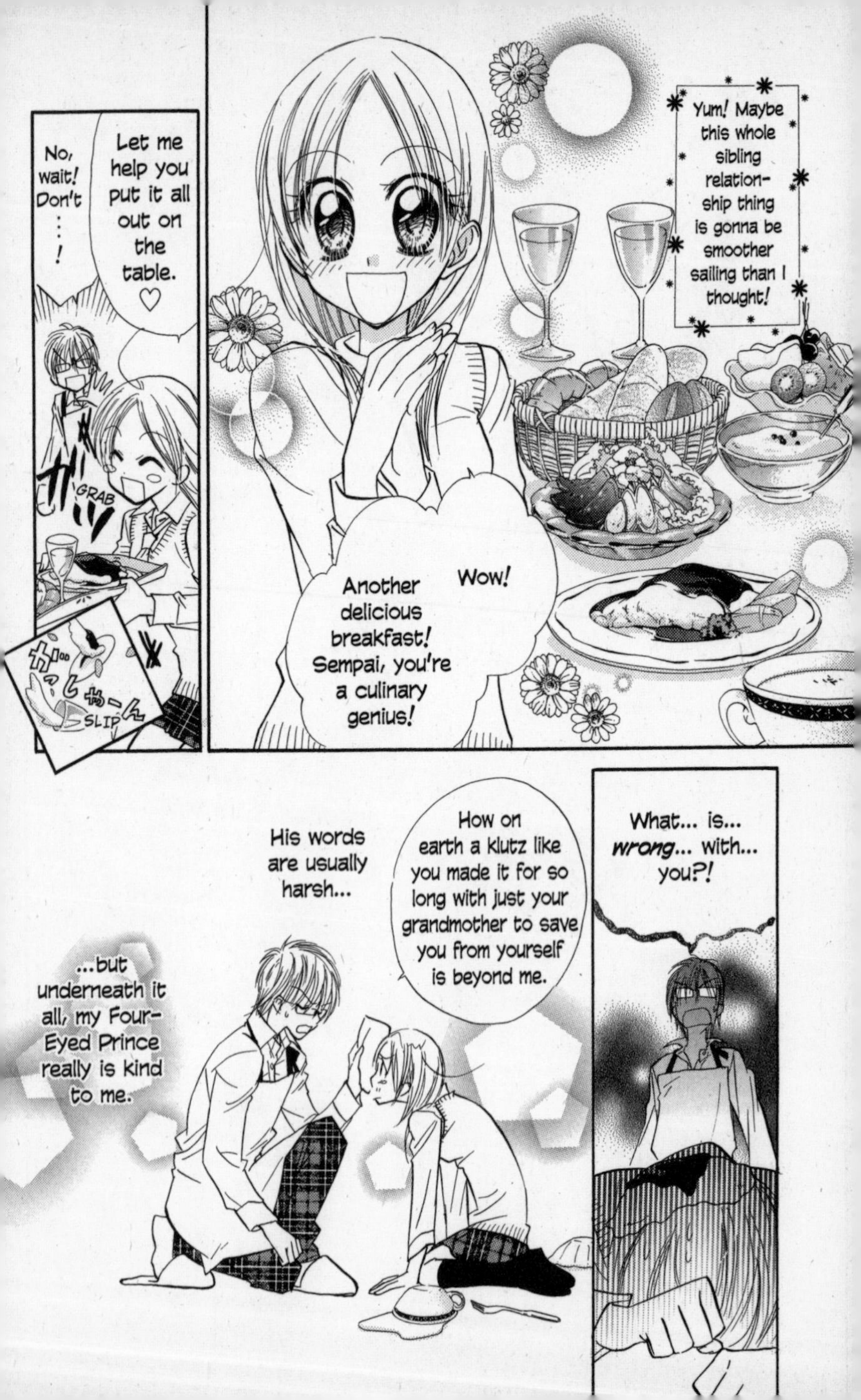
Yum! Maybe this whole sibling relation-ship thing is gonna be smoother sailing than I thought!
Wow!
Another delicious breakfast! Sempai, you're a culinary genius!
Let me help you put it all out on the table. ♡
No, wait! Don't . . . !
GRAB
がっしゃーん
SLIP
What... is... *wrong*... with... you?!
How on earth a klutz like you made it for so long with just your grandmother to save you from yourself is beyond me.
His words are usually harsh...
...but underneath it all, my Four-Eyed Prince really is kind to me.

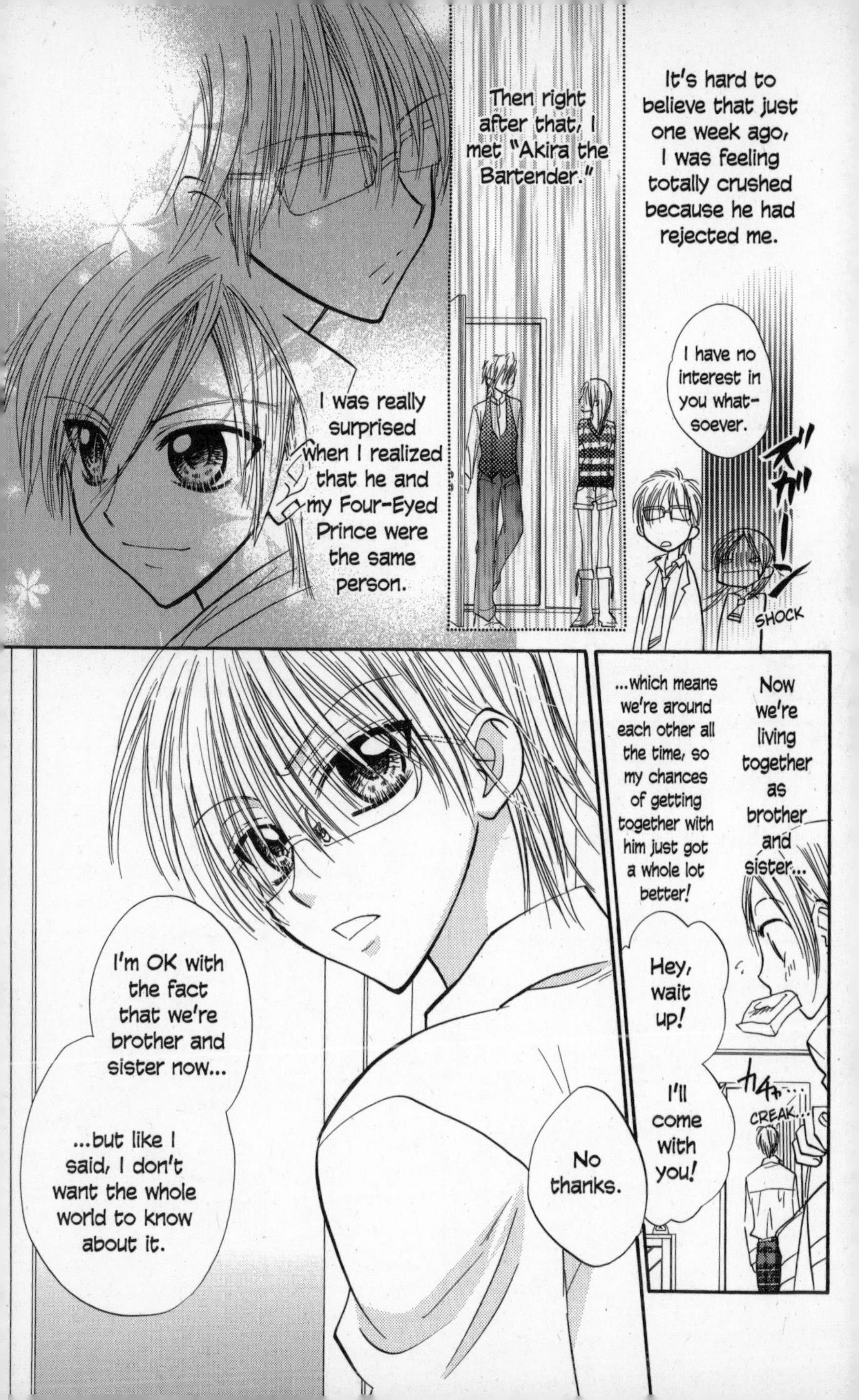
It's hard to believe that just one week ago, I was feeling totally crushed because he had rejected me.
I have no interest in you whatsoever.
SHOCK
Then right after that, I met "Akira the Bartender."
I was really surprised when I realized that he and my Four-Eyed Prince were the same person.
Now we're living together as brother and sister...
...which means we're around each other all the time, so my chances of getting together with him just got a whole lot better!
Hey, wait up!
I'll come with you!
CREAK...
No thanks.
I'm OK with the fact that we're brother and sister now...
...but like I said, I don't want the whole world to know about it.

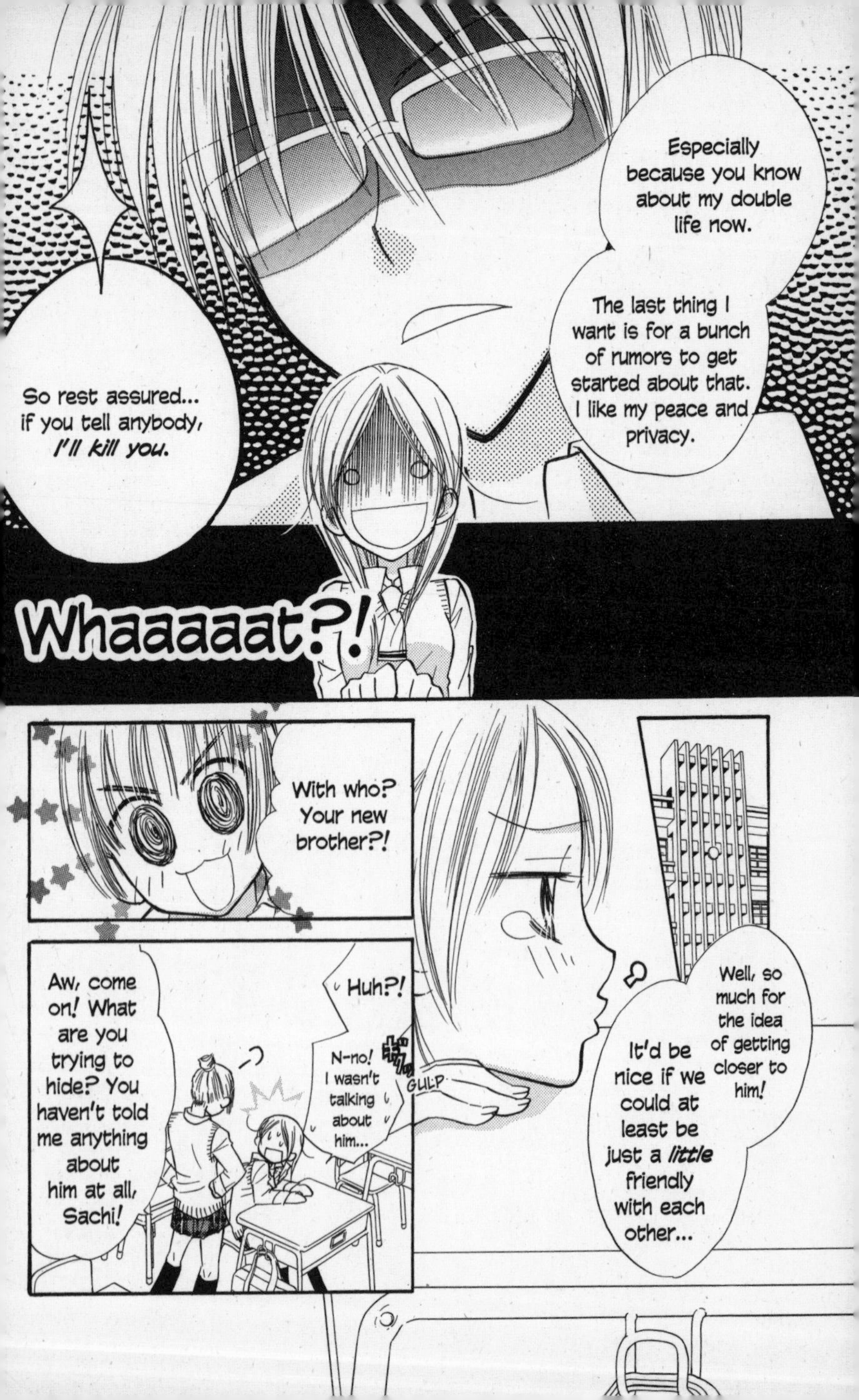
Especially because you know about my double life now.
The last thing I want is for a bunch of rumors to get started about that. I like my peace and privacy.
So rest assured... if you tell anybody, *I'll kill you.*
Whaaaaaat?!
Well, so much for the idea of getting closer to him!
It'd be nice if we could at least be just a *little* friendly with each other...
With who? Your new brother?!
Huh?!
N-no! I wasn't talking about him...
GULP
Aw, come on! What are you trying to hide? You haven't told me anything about him at all, Sachi!

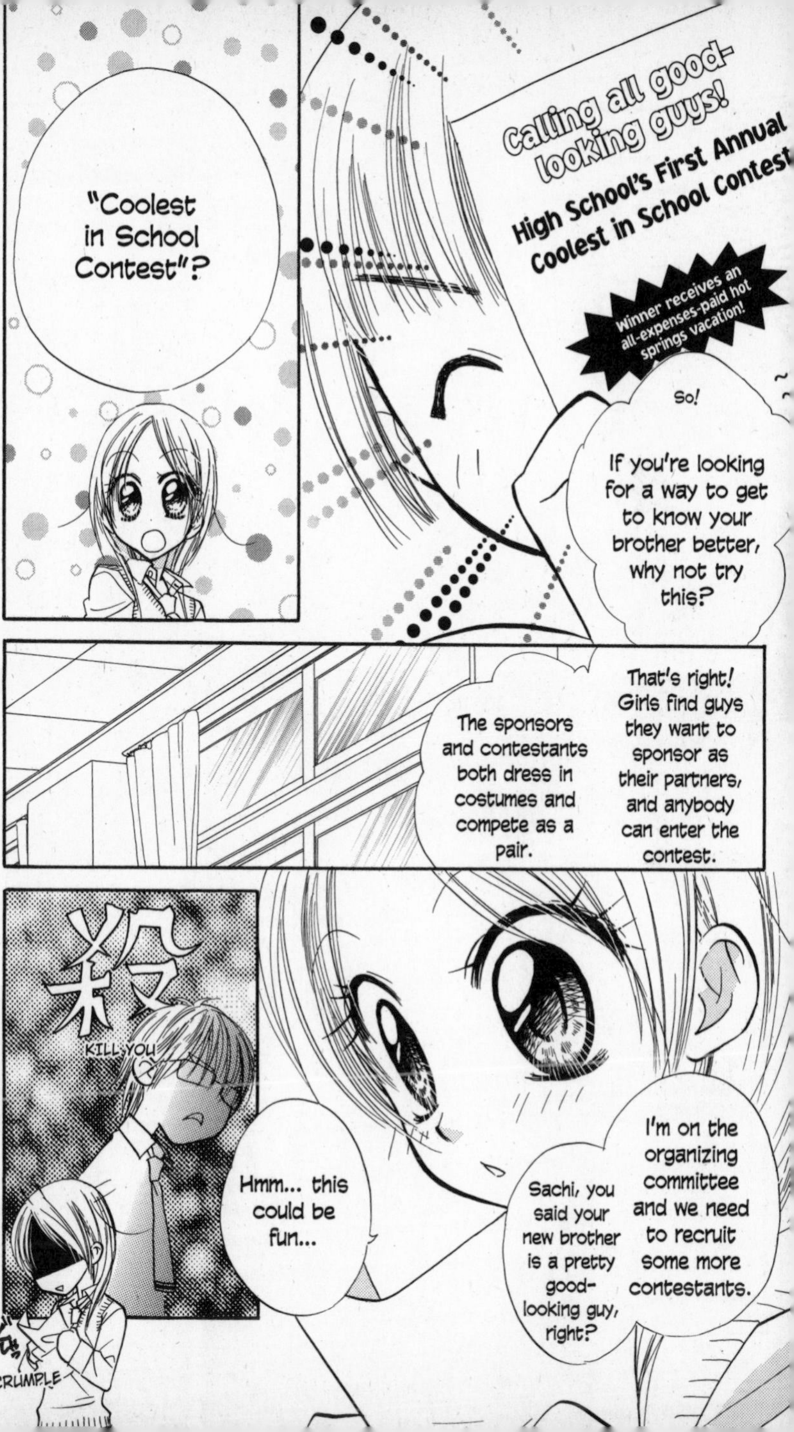
Calling all good-looking guys!
High School's First Annual Coolest in School Contest
Winner receives an all-expenses-paid hot springs vacation!
So!
If you're looking for a way to get to know your brother better, why not try this?
"Coolest in School Contest"?
That's right! Girls find guys they want to sponsor as their partners, and anybody can enter the contest.
The sponsors and contestants both dress in costumes and compete as a pair.
I'm on the organizing committee and we need to recruit some more contestants.
Sachi, you said your new brother is a pretty good-looking guy, right?
Hmm... this could be fun...
殺
KILL YOU
CRUMPLE

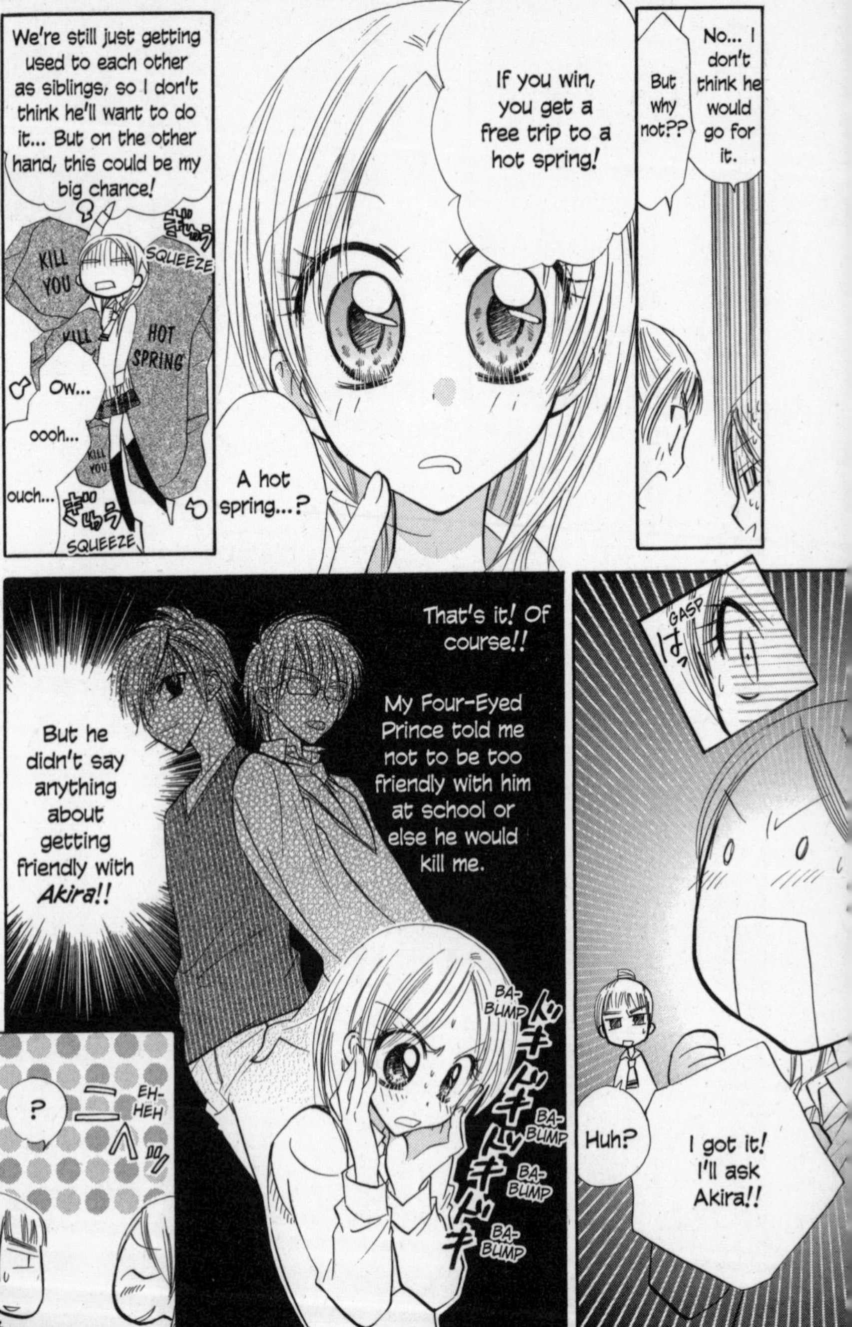
No... I don't think he would go for it.
But why not??
If you win, you get a free trip to a hot spring!
A hot spring...?
We're still just getting used to each other as siblings, so I don't think he'll want to do it... But on the other hand, this could be my big chance!
SQUEEZE
KILL YOU
KILL
HOT SPRING
KILL YOU
Ow...
oooh...
ouch...
SQUEEZE
GASP
I got it! I'll ask Akira!!
Huh?
That's it! Of course!!
My Four-Eyed Prince told me not to be too friendly with him at school or else he would kill me.
But he didn't say anything about getting friendly with *Akira*!!
BA-BUMP
BA-BUMP
BA-BUMP
BA-BUMP
EH-HEH
?

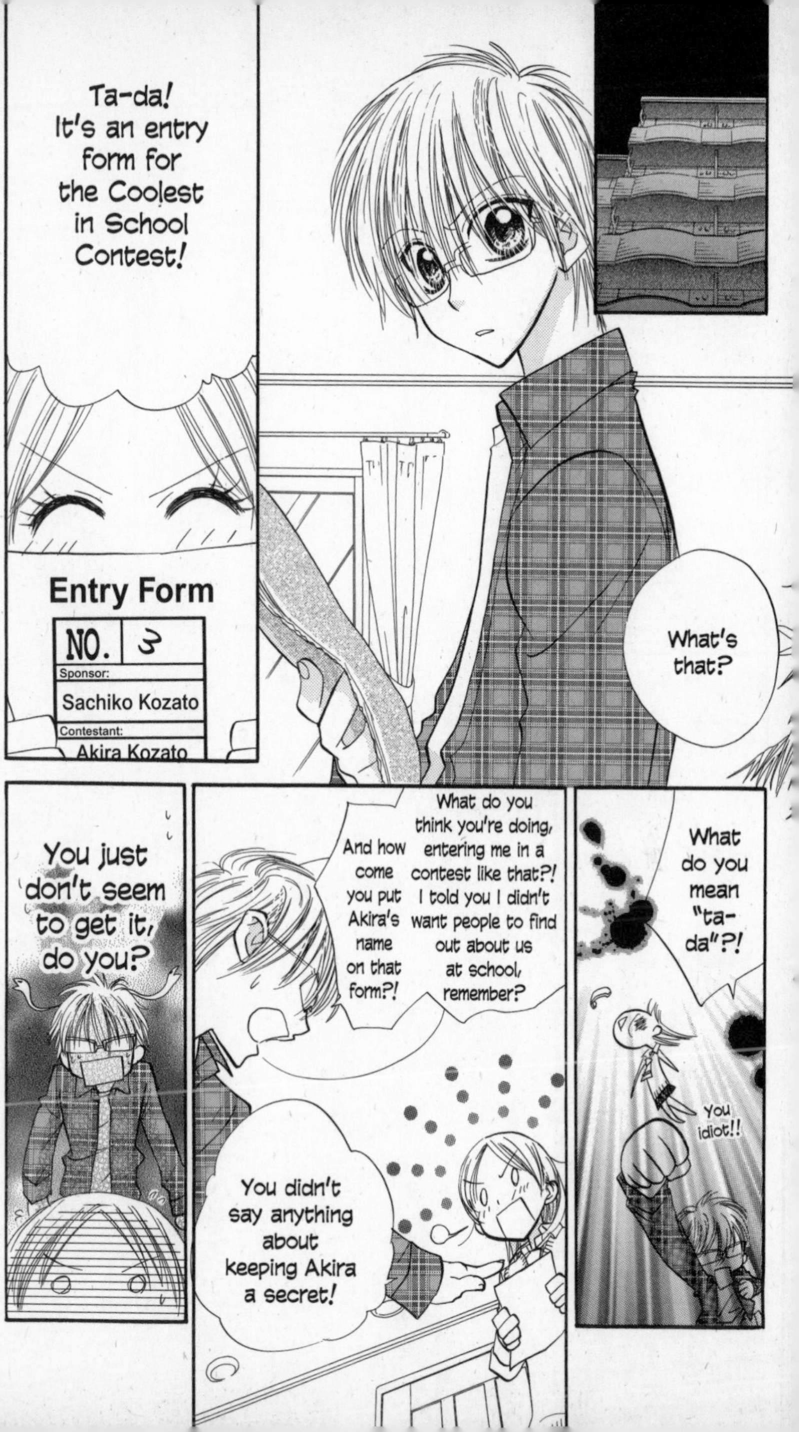
What's that?
Ta-da! It's an entry form for the Coolest in School Contest!
Entry Form
NO. 3
Sponsor:
Sachiko Kozato
Contestant:
Akira Kozato
What do you mean "ta-da"?!
You idiot!!
What do you think you're doing, entering me in a contest like that?! I told you I didn't want people to find out about us at school, remember?
And how come you put Akira's name on that form?!
You didn't say anything about keeping Akira a secret!
You just don't seem to get it, do you?

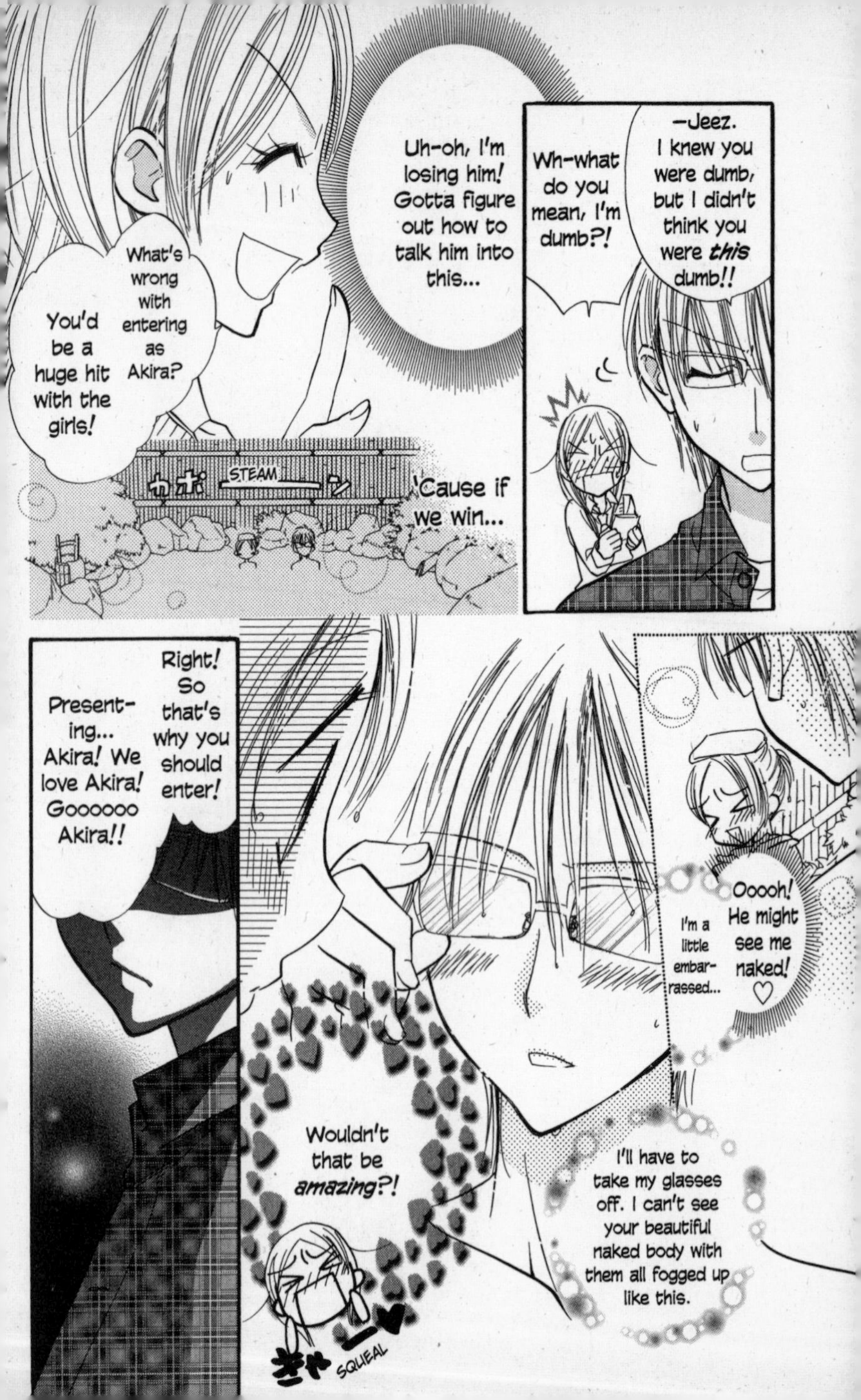
—Jeez. I knew you were dumb, but I didn't think you were *this* dumb!!
Wh-what do you mean, I'm dumb?!
Uh-oh, I'm losing him! Gotta figure out how to talk him into this...
What's wrong with entering as Akira?
You'd be a huge hit with the girls!
STEAM
'Cause if we win...
Ooooh! He might see me naked! ♡
I'm a little embar-rassed...
I'll have to take my glasses off. I can't see your beautiful naked body with them all fogged up like this.
Wouldn't that be *amazing*?!
SQUEAL
Right! So that's why you should enter!
Present-ing... Akira! We love Akira! Goooooo Akira!!

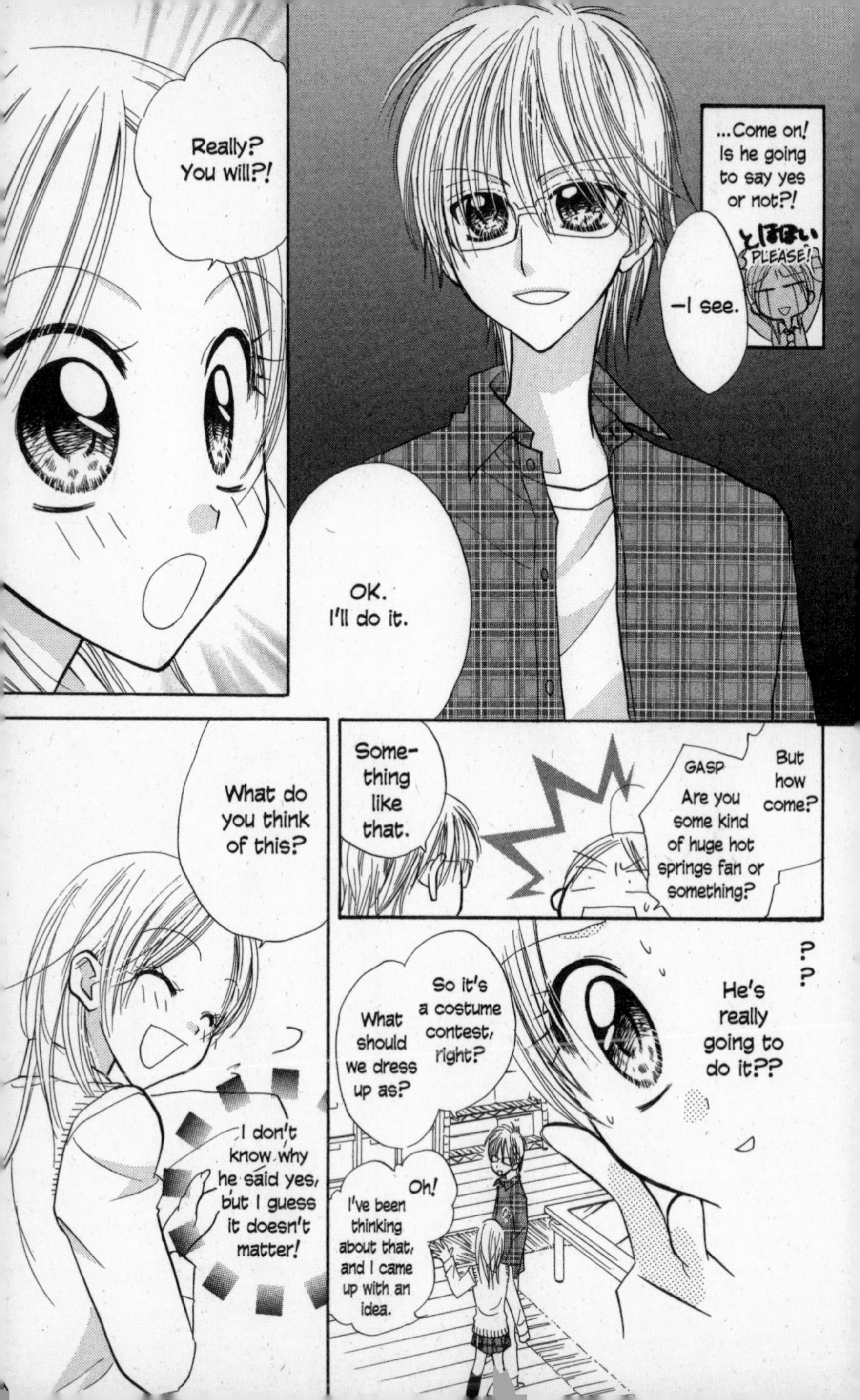
...Come on! Is he going to say yes or not?!
とほほい
PLEASE!
—I see.
OK. I'll do it.
Really? You will?!
But how come?
GASP
Are you some kind of huge hot springs fan or something?
Something like that.
??
He's really going to do it??
So it's a costume contest, right?
What should we dress up as?
Oh!
I've been thinking about that, and I came up with an idea.
What do you think of this?
I don't know why he said yes, but I guess it doesn't matter!

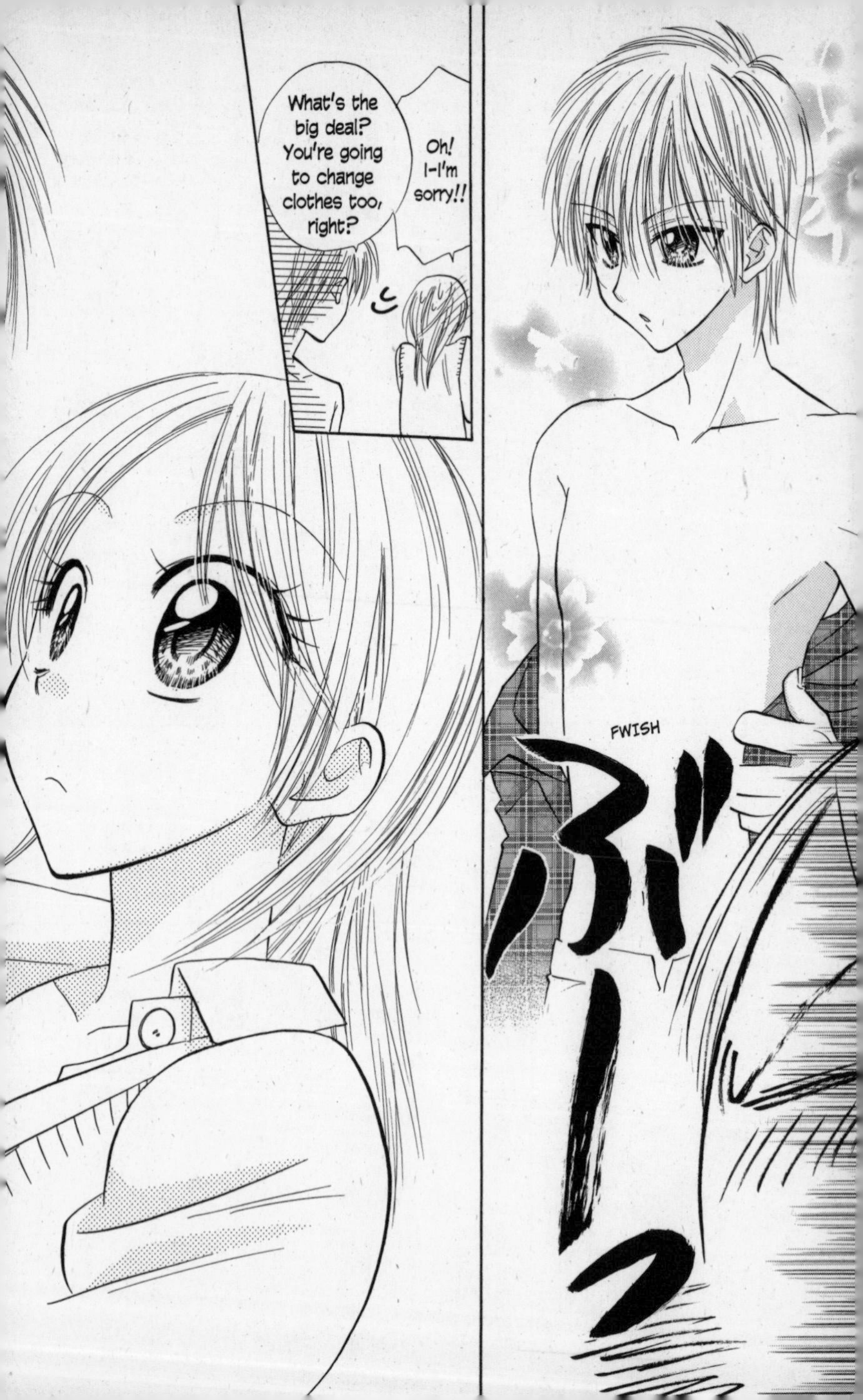
FWISH
Oh! I-I'm sorry!!
What's the big deal? You're going to change clothes too, right?

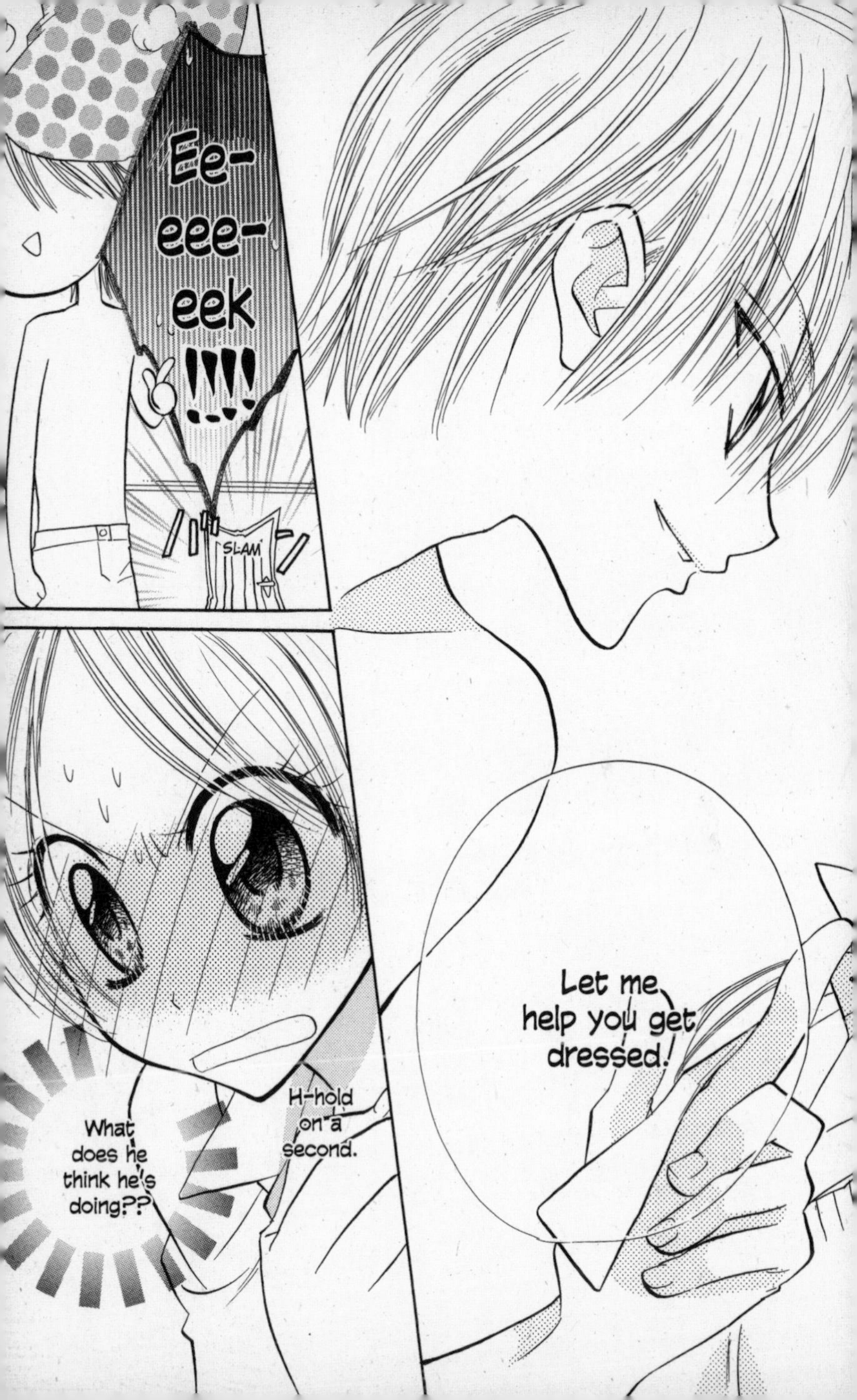
Let me help you get dressed!
Ee-eee-eek!!!!
SLAM
H-hold on a second.
What does he think he's doing??

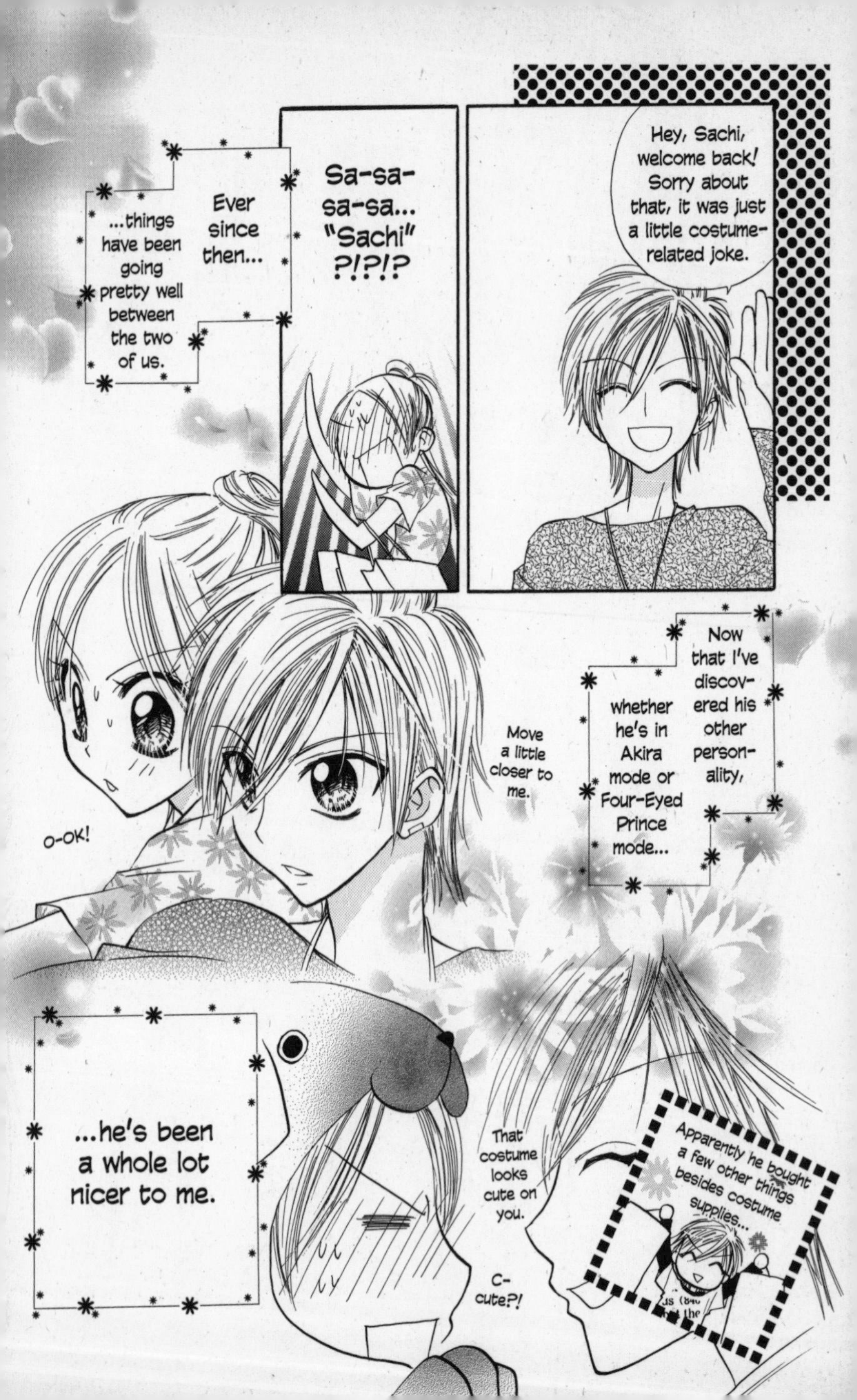

Hey, Sachi, welcome back! Sorry about that, it was just a little costume-related joke.
Sa-sa-sa-sa... "Sachi" ?!?!?
Ever since then...
...things have been going pretty well between the two of us.
Now that I've discovered his other personality,
whether he's in Akira mode or Four-Eyed Prince mode...
Move a little closer to me.
O-OK!
Apparently he bought a few other things besides costume supplies...
That costume looks cute on you.
C-cute?!
...he's been a whole lot nicer to me.

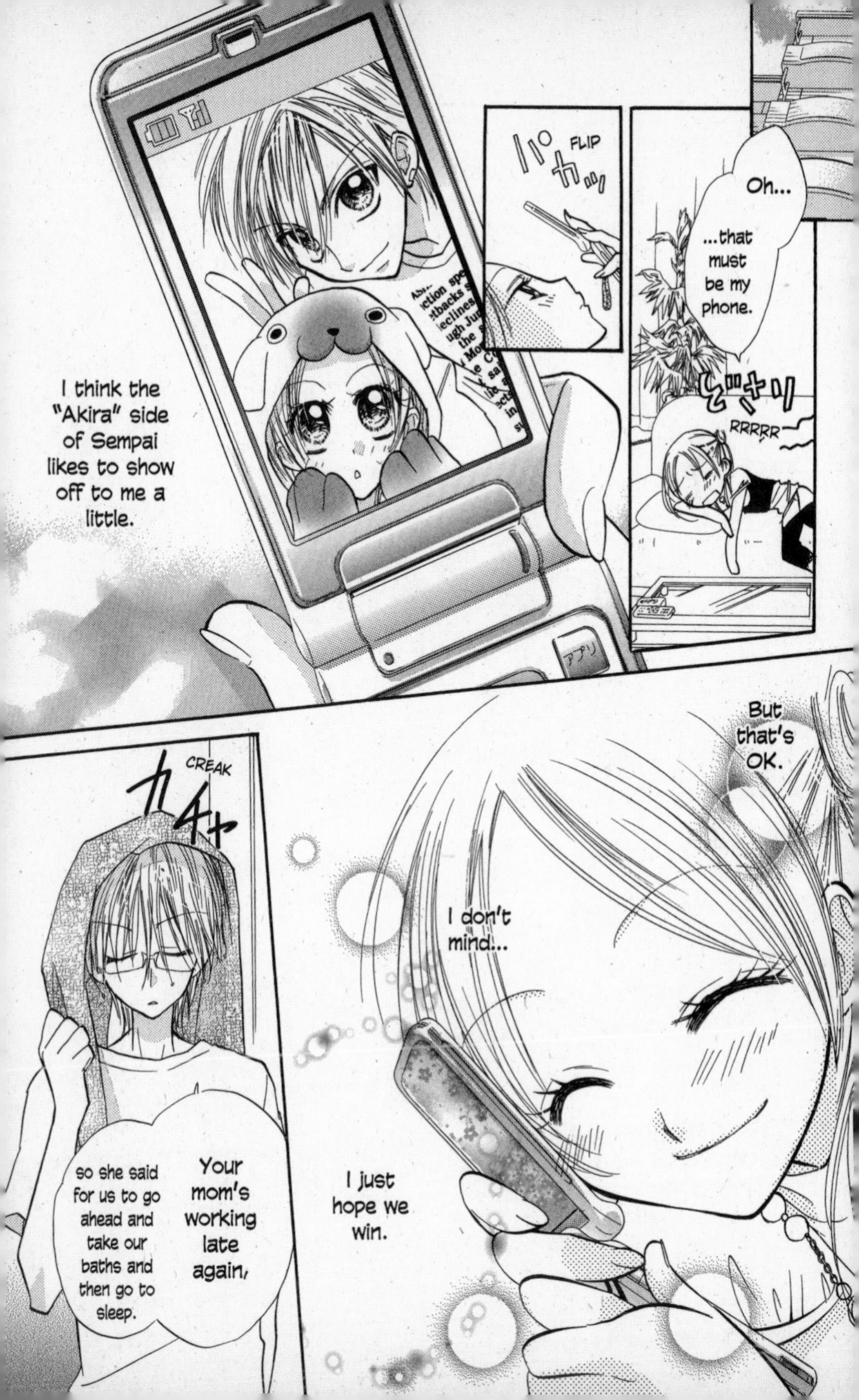
Oh...
...that must be my phone.
RRRRR
FLIP
I think the "Akira" side of Sempai likes to show off to me a little.
But that's OK.
I don't mind...
I just hope we win.
CREAK
Your mom's working late again,
so she said for us to go ahead and take our baths and then go to sleep.

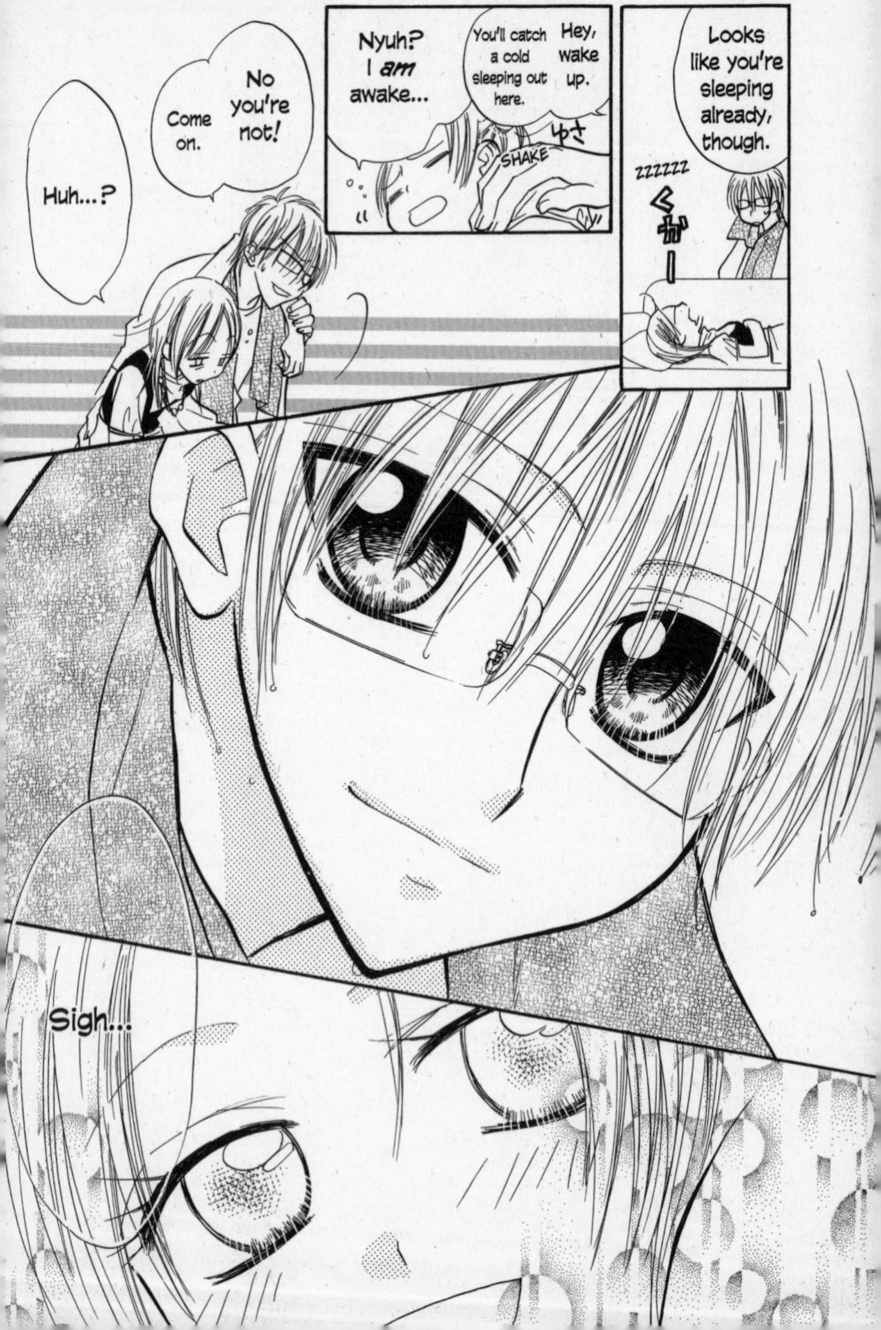
Looks like you're sleeping already, though.
zzzzzz
ぐかー
Hey, wake up.
You'll catch a cold sleeping out here.
ゆさ
SHAKE
Nyuh? I *am* awake...
No you're not!
Come on.
Huh...?
Sigh...

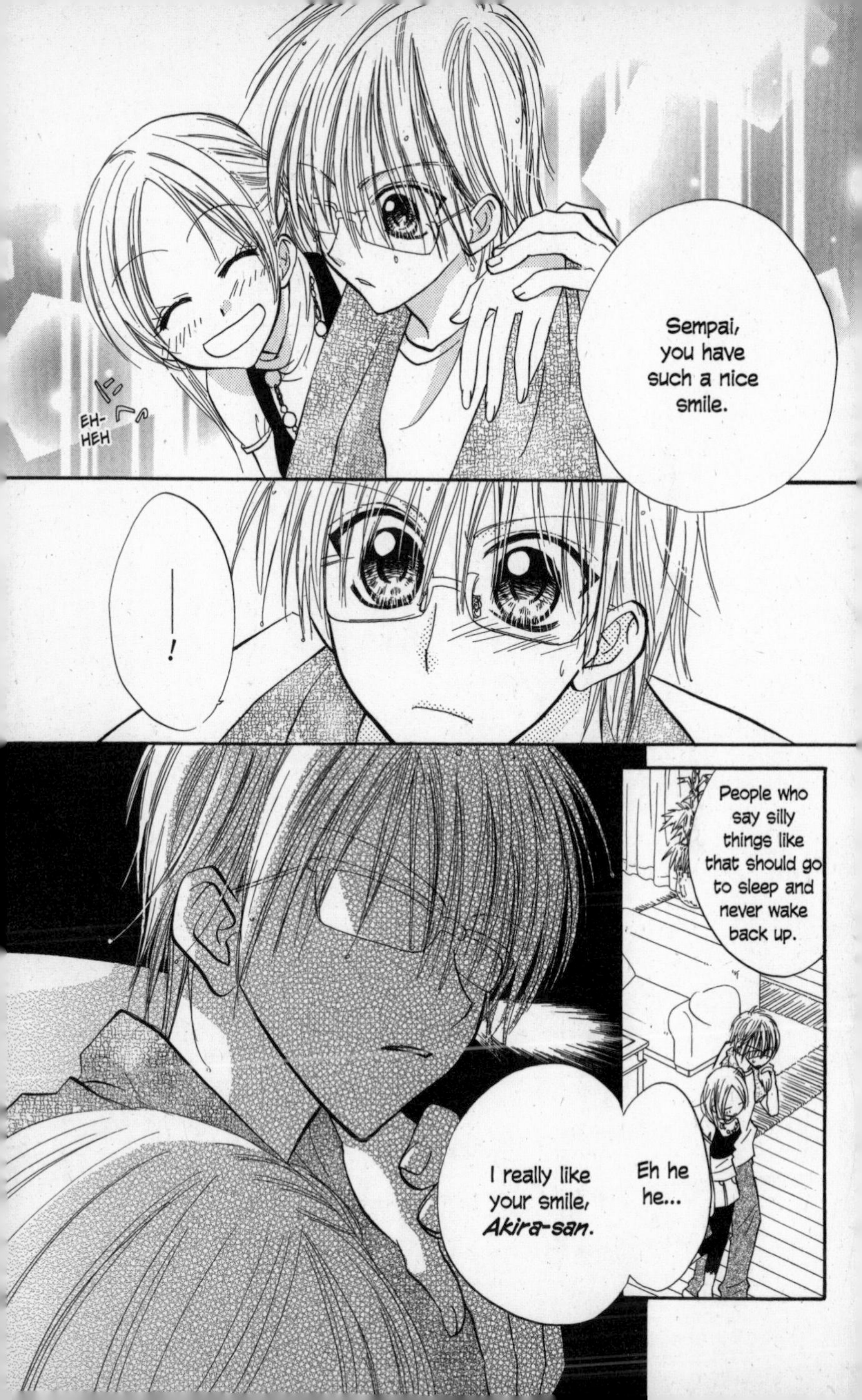

Sempai, you have such a nice smile.
EH-HEH
—!
People who say silly things like that should go to sleep and never wake back up.
Eh he he...
I really like your smile, *Akira-san*.

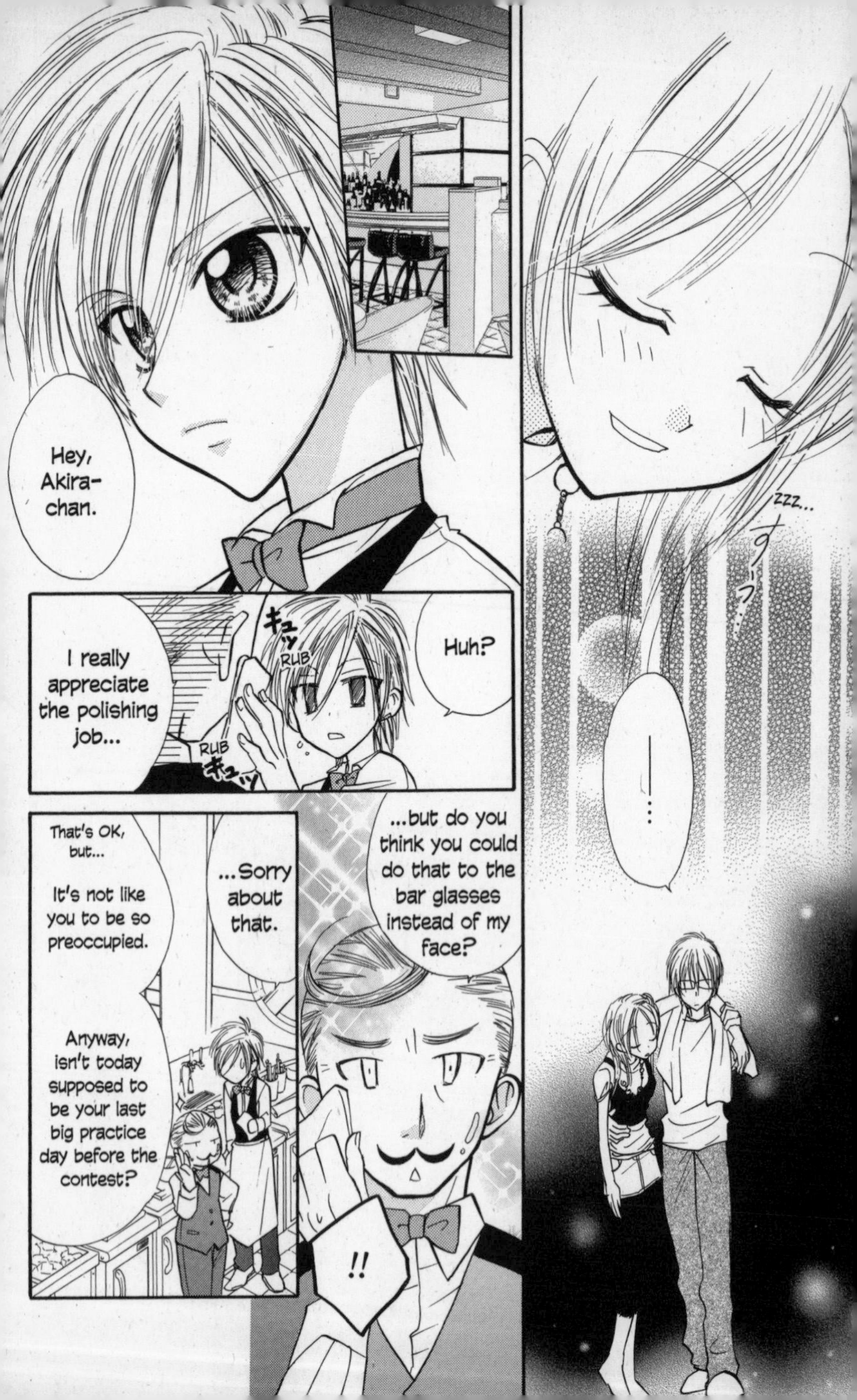
zzz...
すーっ…
—...
Hey, Akira-chan.
Huh?
キュッ RUB
キュッ RUB
I really appreciate the polishing job...
...but do you think you could do that to the bar glasses instead of my face?
!!
...Sorry about that.
That's OK, but...
It's not like you to be so preoccupied.
Anyway, isn't today supposed to be your last big practice day before the contest?

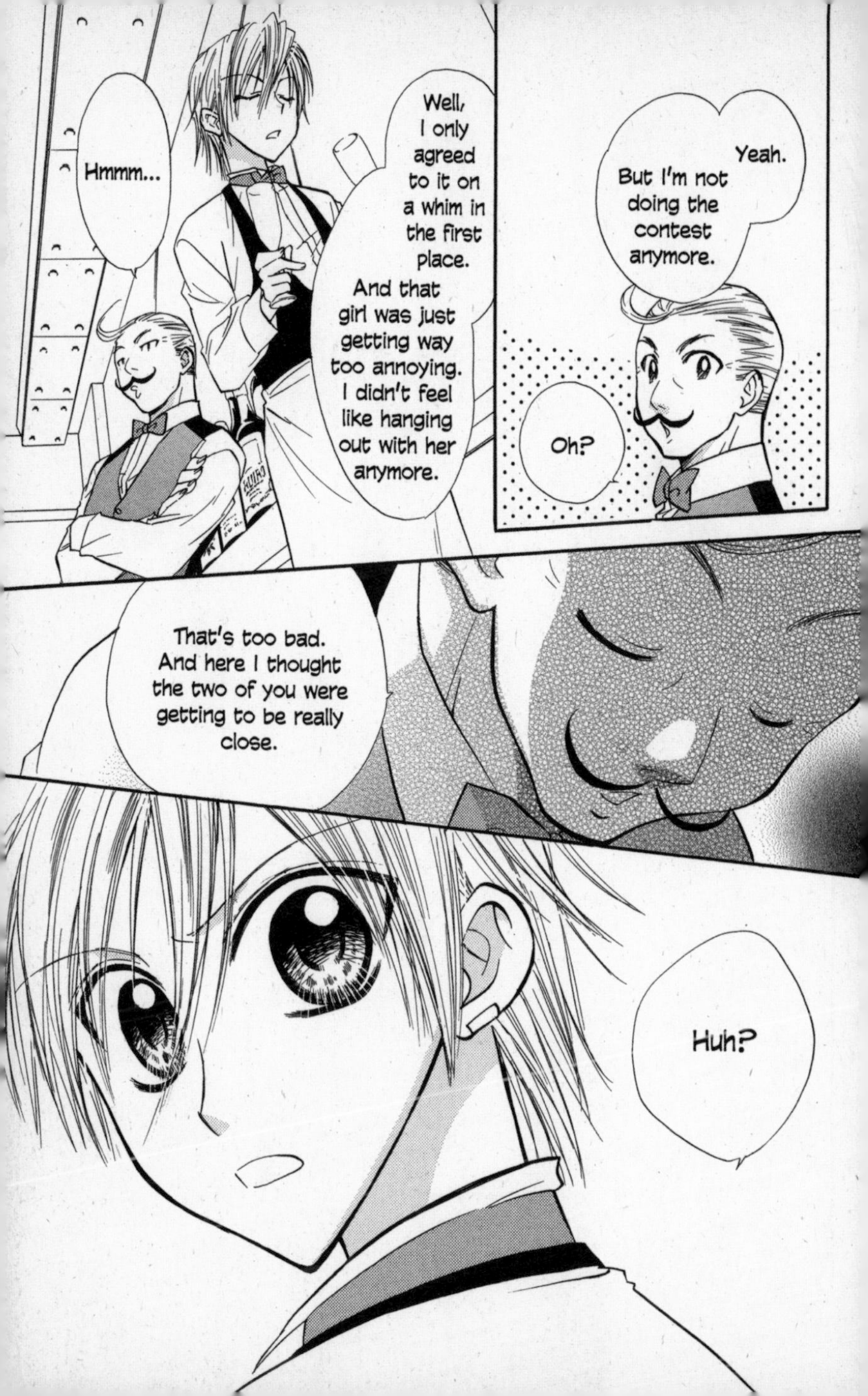
Yeah. But I'm not doing the contest anymore.
Oh?
Well, I only agreed to it on a whim in the first place. And that girl was just getting way too annoying. I didn't feel like hanging out with her anymore.
Hmmm...
That's too bad. And here I thought the two of you were getting to be really close.
Huh?

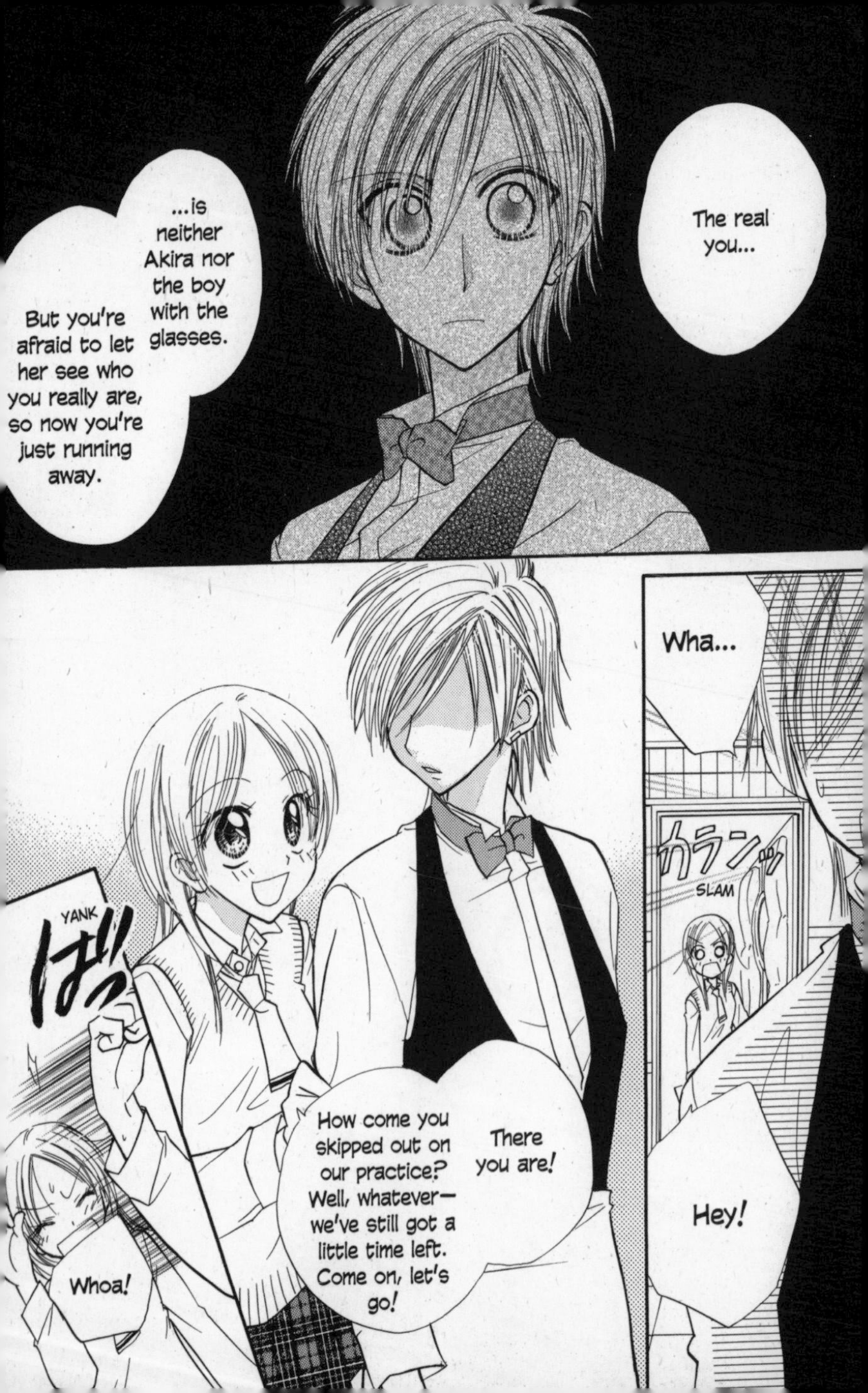
The real you...
...is neither Akira nor the boy with the glasses.
But you're afraid to let her see who you really are, so now you're just running away.
Wha...
カランッ
SLAM
Hey!
There you are!
How come you skipped out on our practice? Well, whatever—we've still got a little time left. Come on, let's go!
ぱっ
YANK
Whoa!

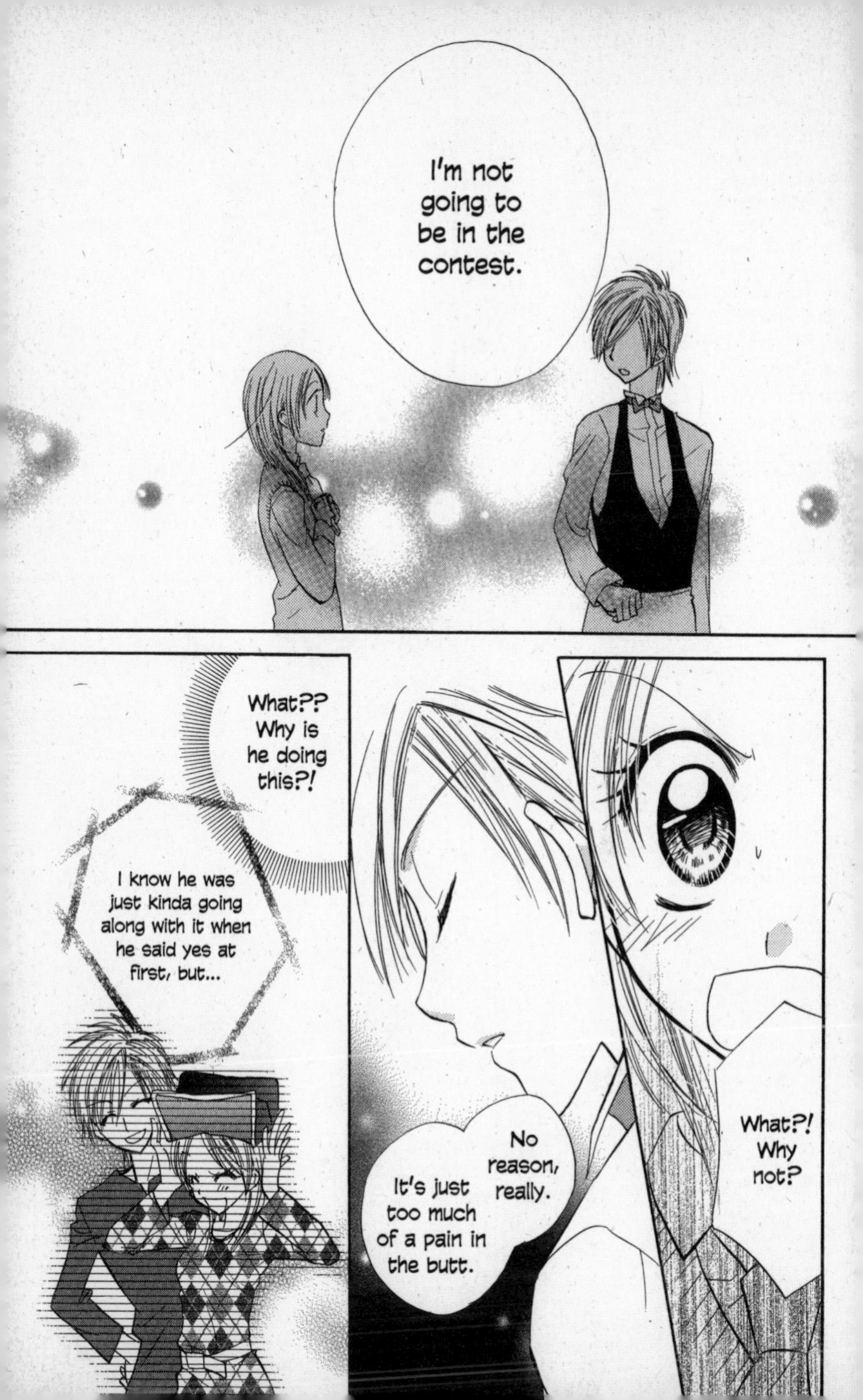
I'm not going to be in the contest.
What?! Why not?
No reason, really.
It's just too much of a pain in the butt.
What?? Why is he doing this?!
I know he was just kinda going along with it when he said yes at first, but...

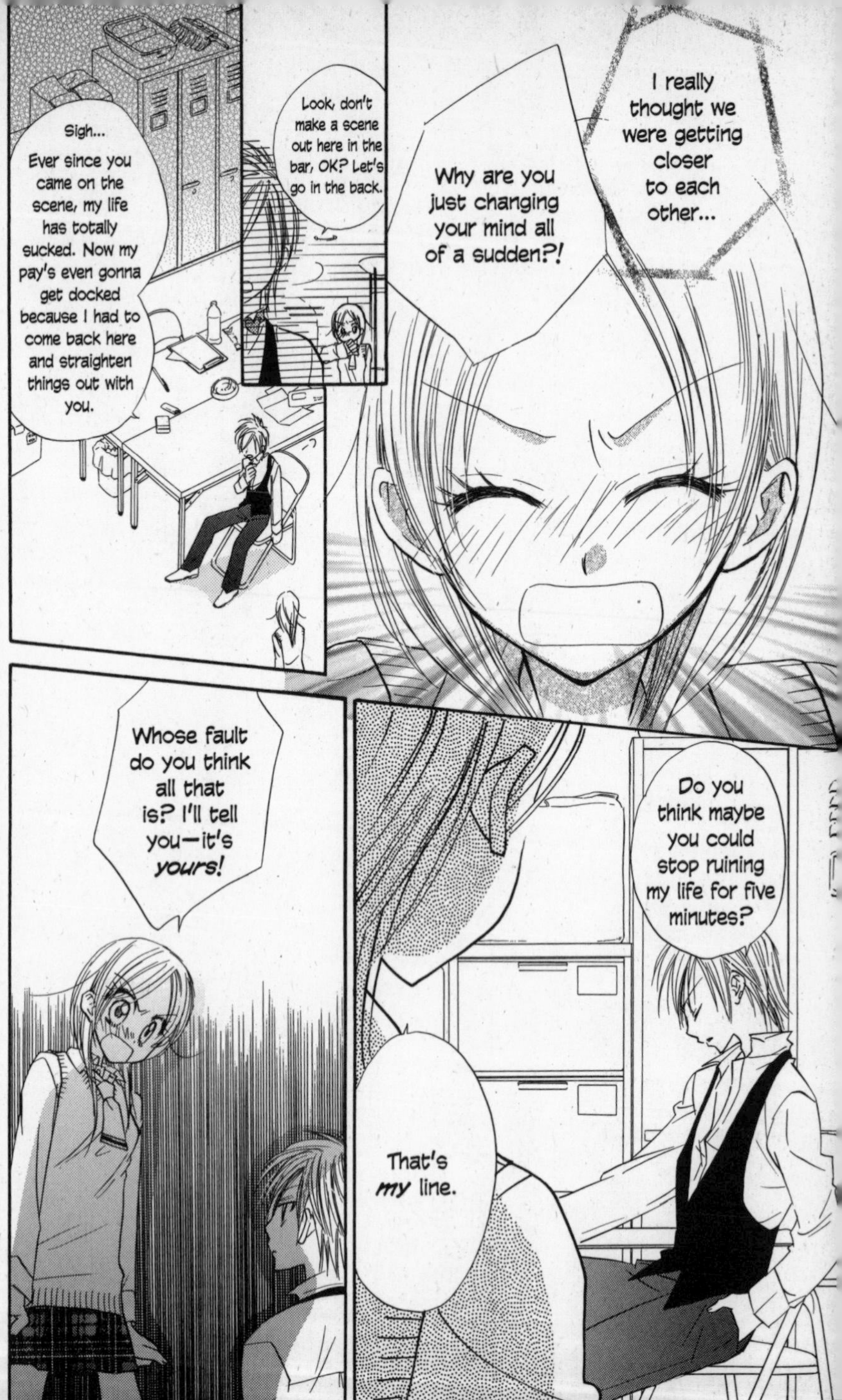
I really thought we were getting closer to each other...
Why are you just changing your mind all of a sudden?!
Look, don't make a scene out here in the bar, OK? Let's go in the back.
Sigh... Ever since you came on the scene, my life has totally sucked. Now my pay's even gonna get docked because I had to come back here and straighten things out with you.
Do you think maybe you could stop ruining my life for five minutes?
That's *my* line.
Whose fault do you think all that is? I'll tell you—it's *yours!*

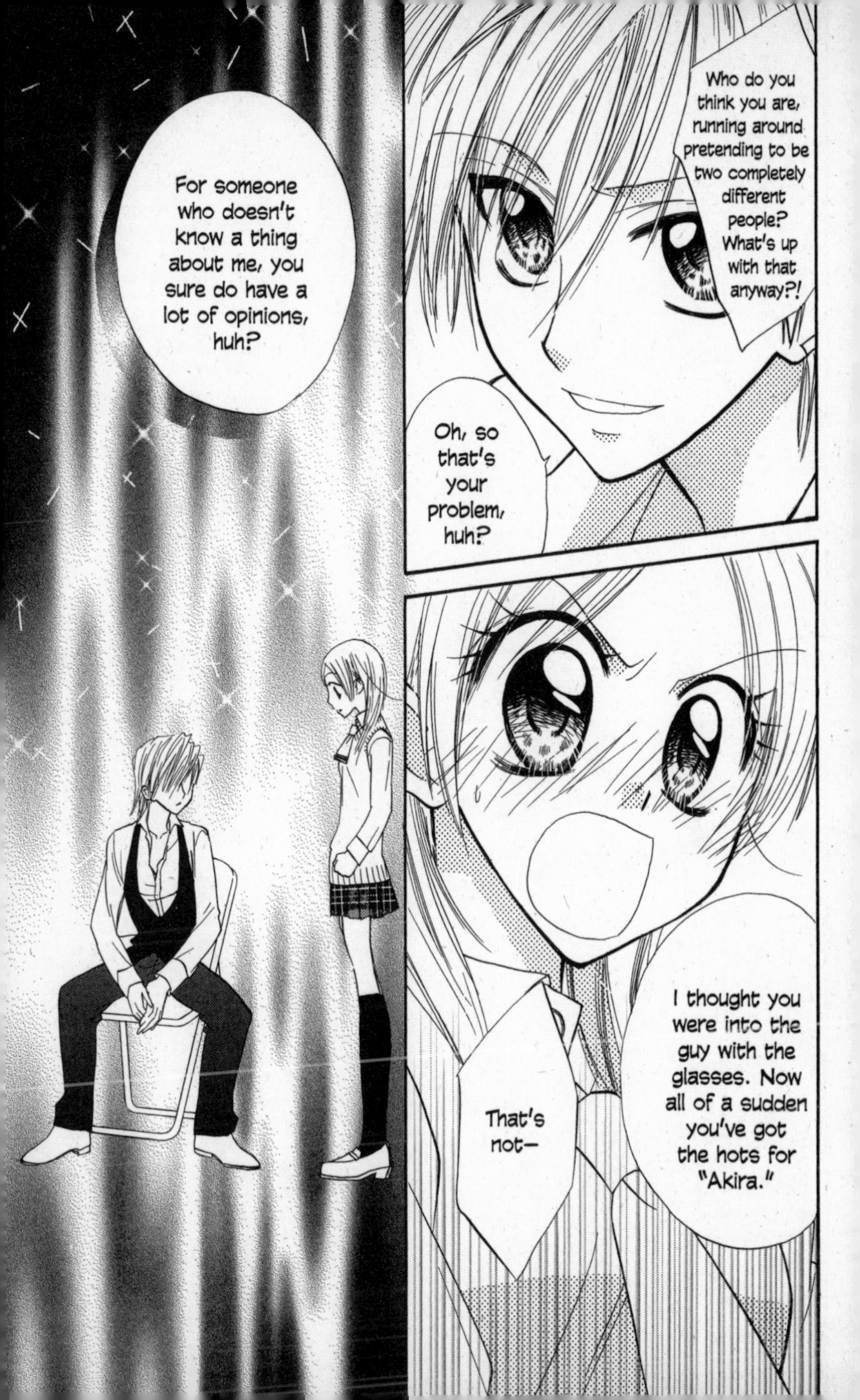
Who do you think you are, running around pretending to be two completely different people? What's up with that anyway?!
Oh, so that's your problem, huh?
I thought you were into the guy with the glasses. Now all of a sudden you've got the hots for "Akira."
That's not—
For someone who doesn't know a thing about me, you sure do have a lot of opinions, huh?

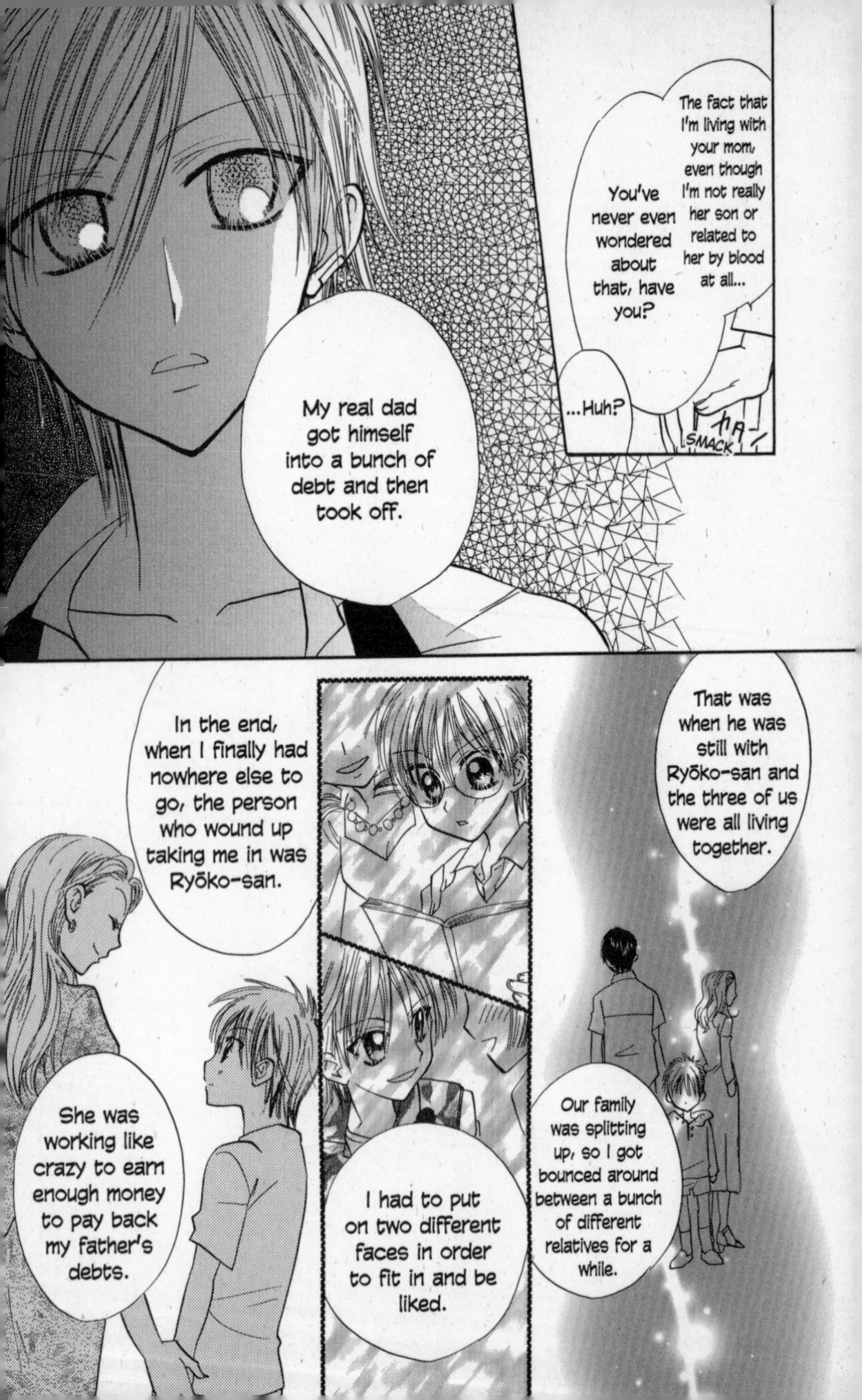
The fact that I'm living with your mom, even though I'm not really her son or related to her by blood at all...
You've never even wondered about that, have you?
...Huh?
SMACK
My real dad got himself into a bunch of debt and then took off.
That was when he was still with Ryōko-san and the three of us were all living together.
Our family was splitting up, so I got bounced around between a bunch of different relatives for a while.
I had to put on two different faces in order to fit in and be liked.
In the end, when I finally had nowhere else to go, the person who wound up taking me in was Ryōko-san.
She was working like crazy to earn enough money to pay back my father's debts.

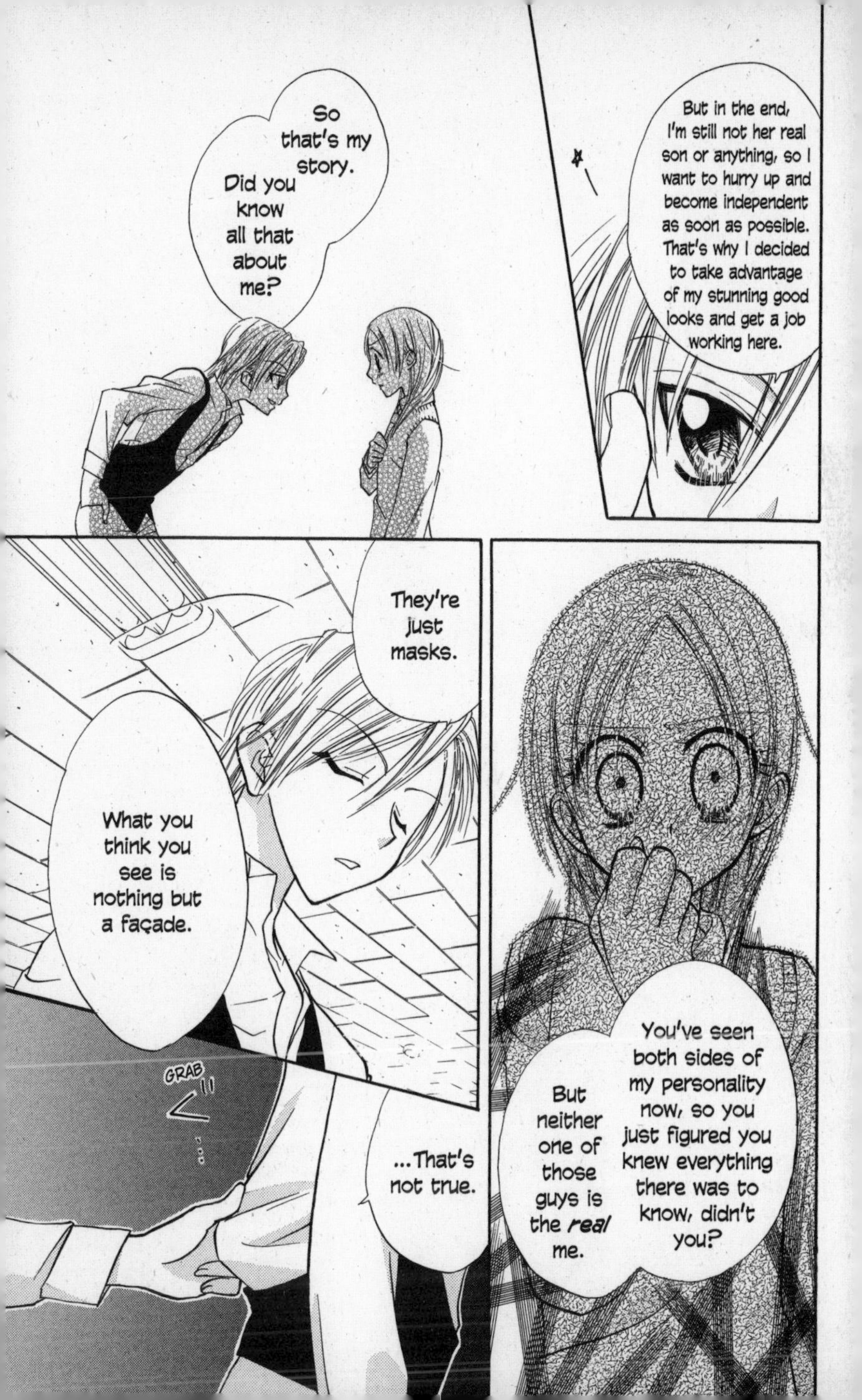
But in the end, I'm still not her real son or anything, so I want to hurry up and become independent as soon as possible. That's why I decided to take advantage of my stunning good looks and get a job working here.
So that's my story.
Did you know all that about me?
You've seen both sides of my personality now, so you just figured you knew everything there was to know, didn't you?
But neither one of those guys is the *real* me.
They're just masks.
What you think you see is nothing but a façade.
GRAB
...That's not true.

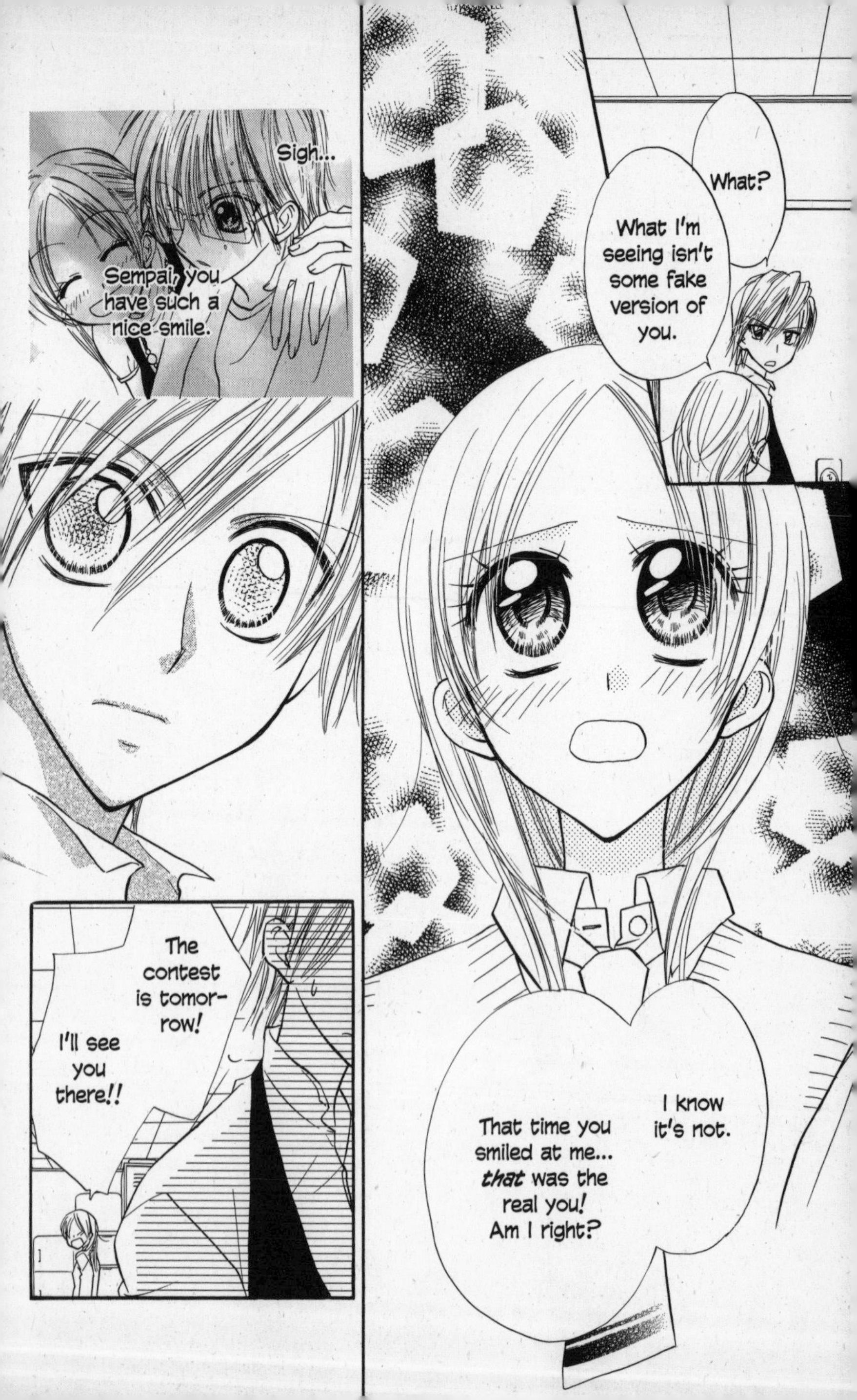
What?
What I'm seeing isn't some fake version of you.
I know it's not.
That time you smiled at me... *that* was the real you! Am I right?
Sigh...
Sempai, you have such a nice smile.
The contest is tomorrow!
I'll see you there!!

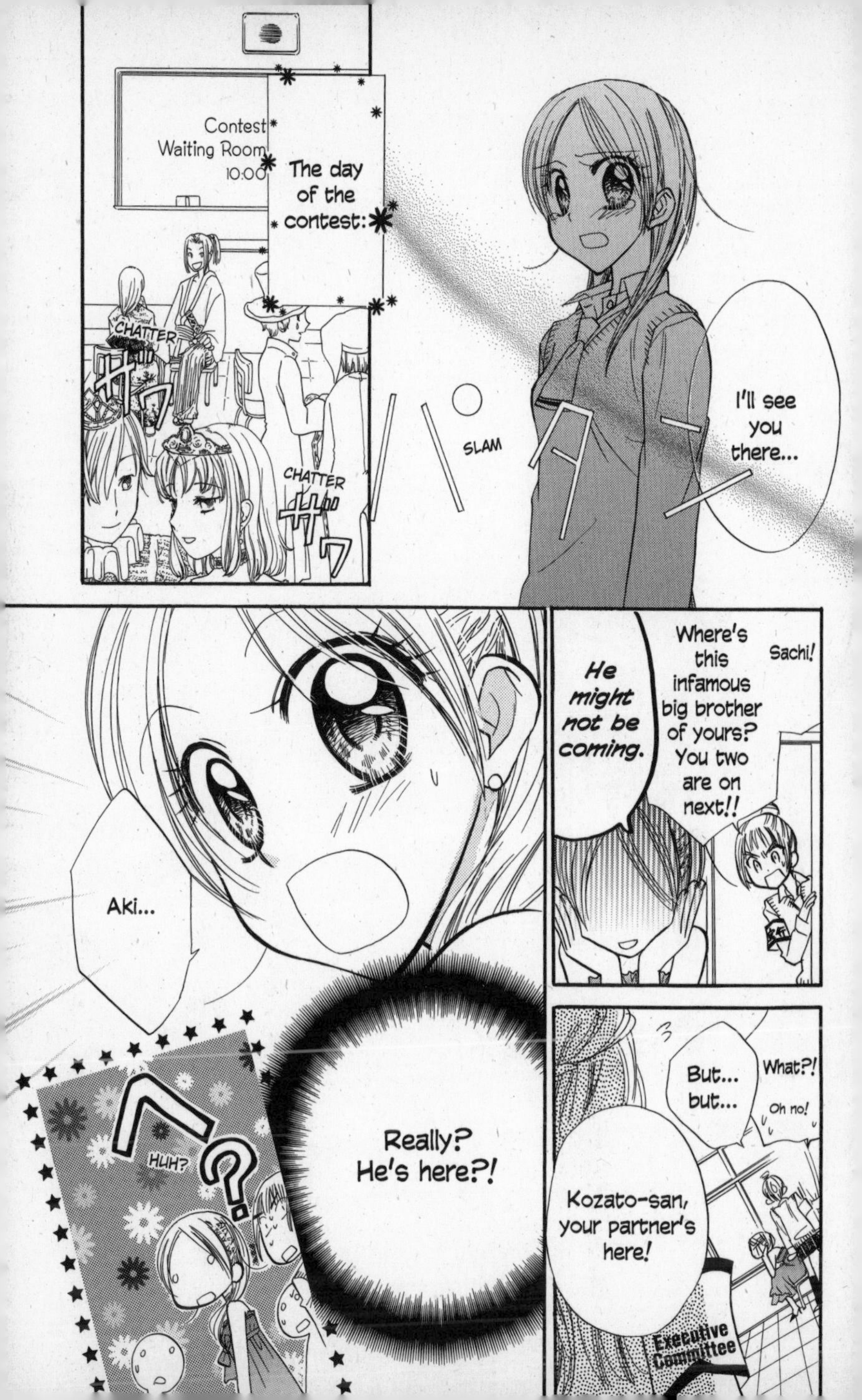
I'll see you there...
SLAM
Contest Waiting Room 10:00
The day of the contest:
CHATTER
CHATTER
Sachi!
Where's this infamous big brother of yours? You two are on next!!
He might not be coming.
What?!
Oh no!
But... but...
Kozato-san, your partner's here!
Executive Committee
Aki...
Really? He's here?!
HUH?

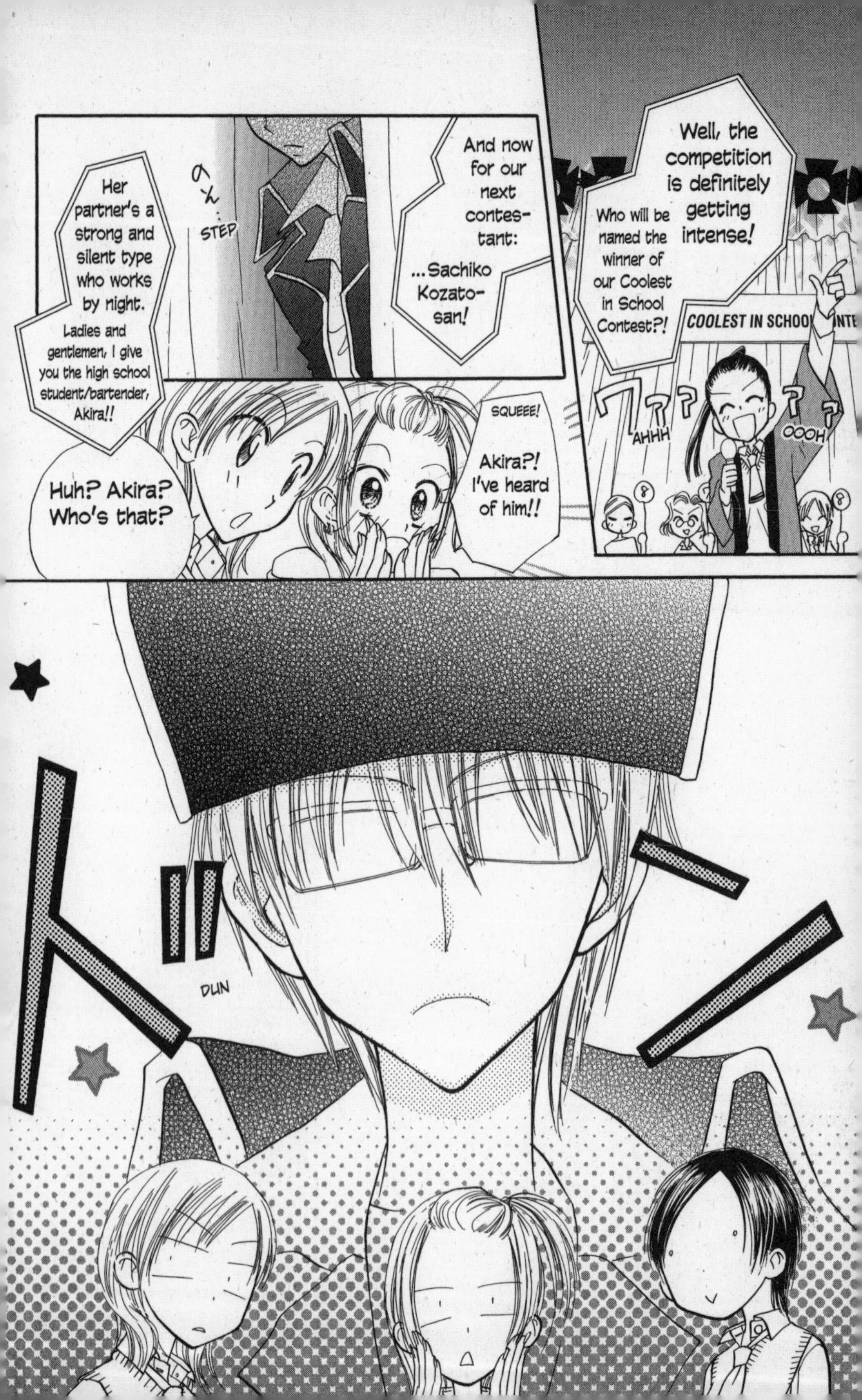
Well, the competition is definitely getting intense!
Who will be named the winner of our Coolest in School Contest?!
AHHH
OOOH
And now for our next contestant:
...Sachiko Kozato-san!
STEP
Her partner's a strong and silent type who works by night.
Ladies and gentlemen, I give you the high school student/bartender, Akira!!
SQUEEE!
Akira?! I've heard of him!!
Huh? Akira? Who's that?
DUN

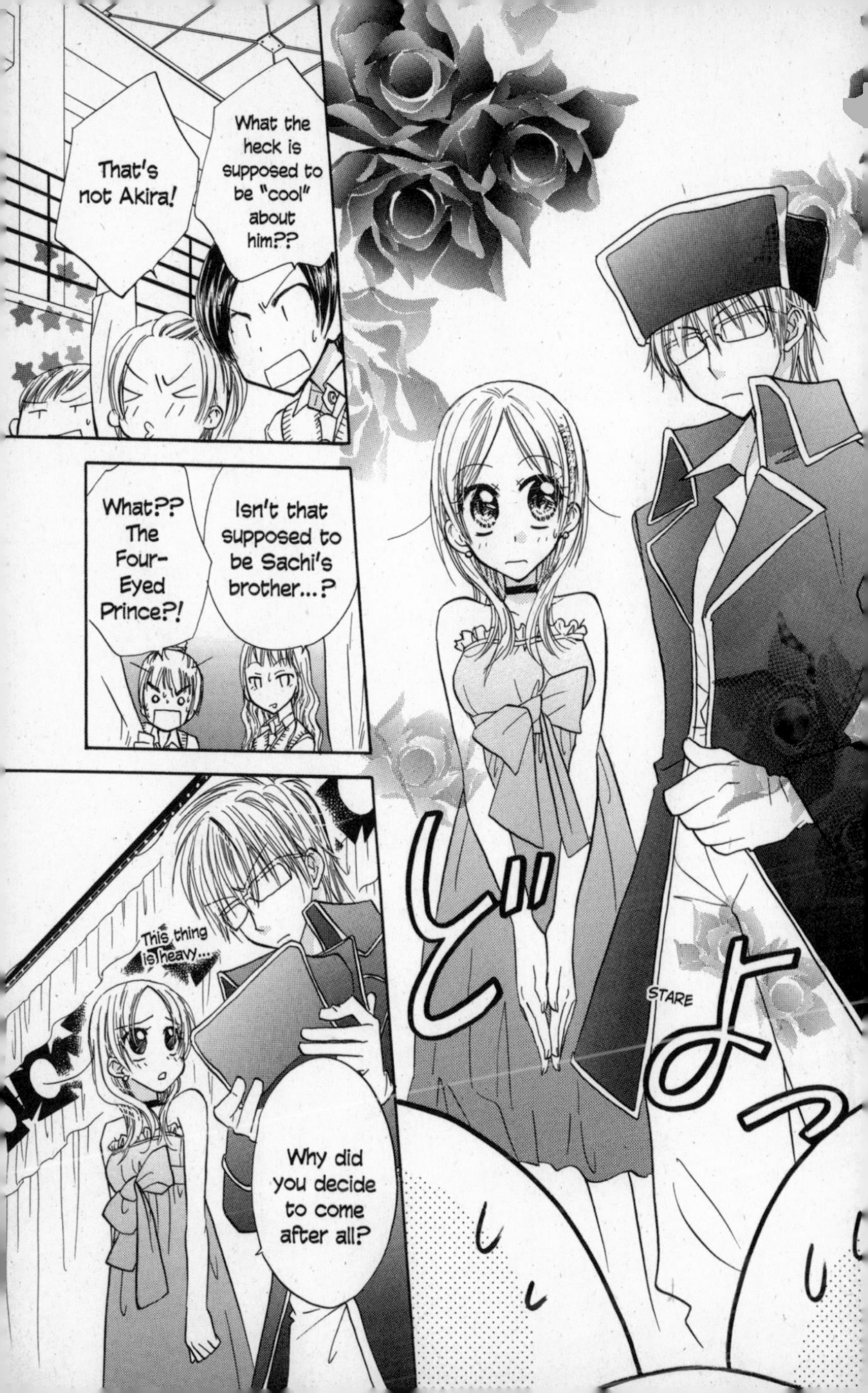
STARE
What the heck is supposed to be "cool" about him??
That's not Akira!
Isn't that supposed to be Sachi's brother...?
What?? The Four-Eyed Prince?!
This thing is heavy...
Why did you decide to come after all?

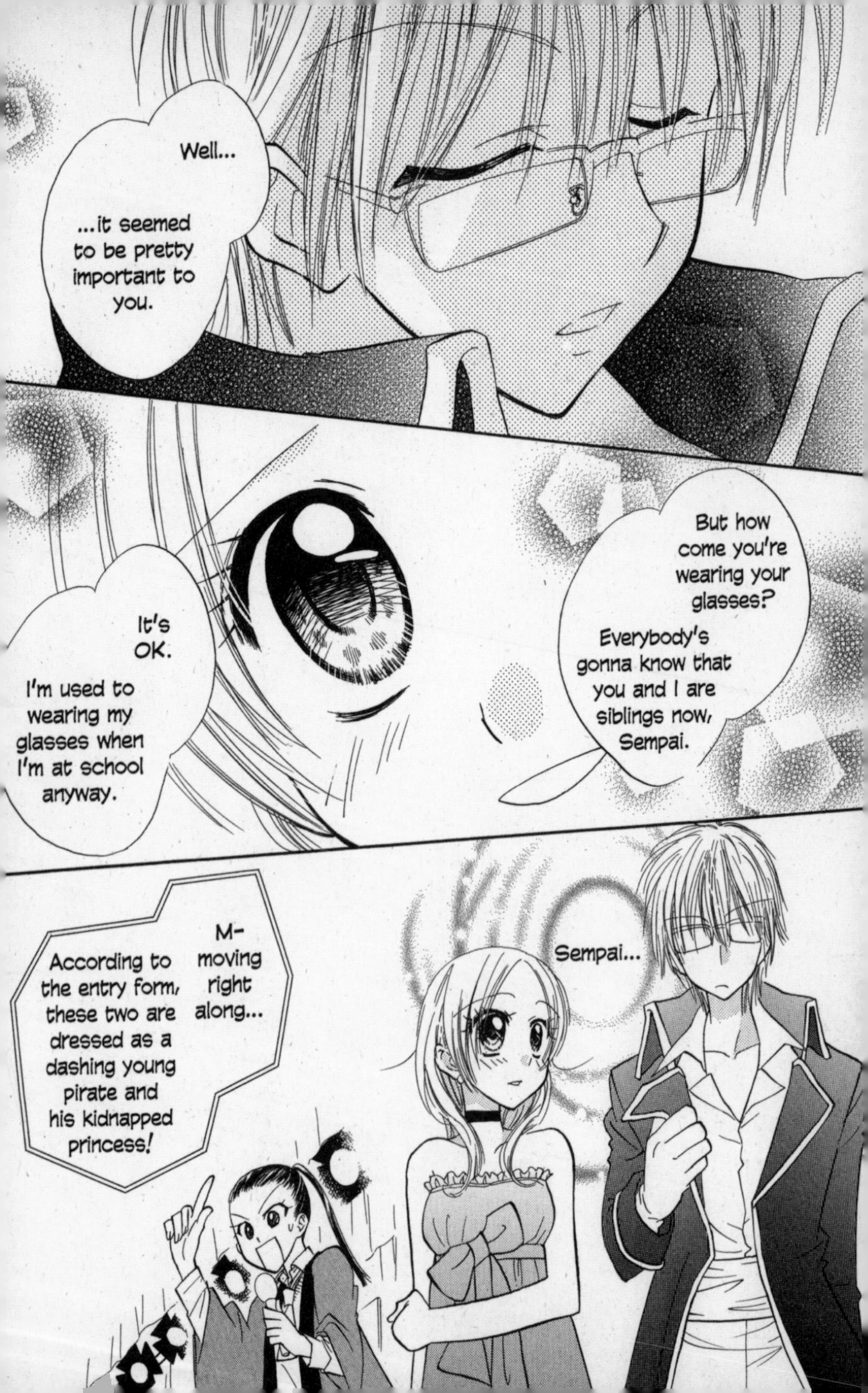
Well...
...it seemed to be pretty important to you.
But how come you're wearing your glasses?
Everybody's gonna know that you and I are siblings now, Sempai.
It's OK.
I'm used to wearing my glasses when I'm at school anyway.
Sempai...
M-moving right along...
According to the entry form, these two are dressed as a dashing young pirate and his kidnapped princess!

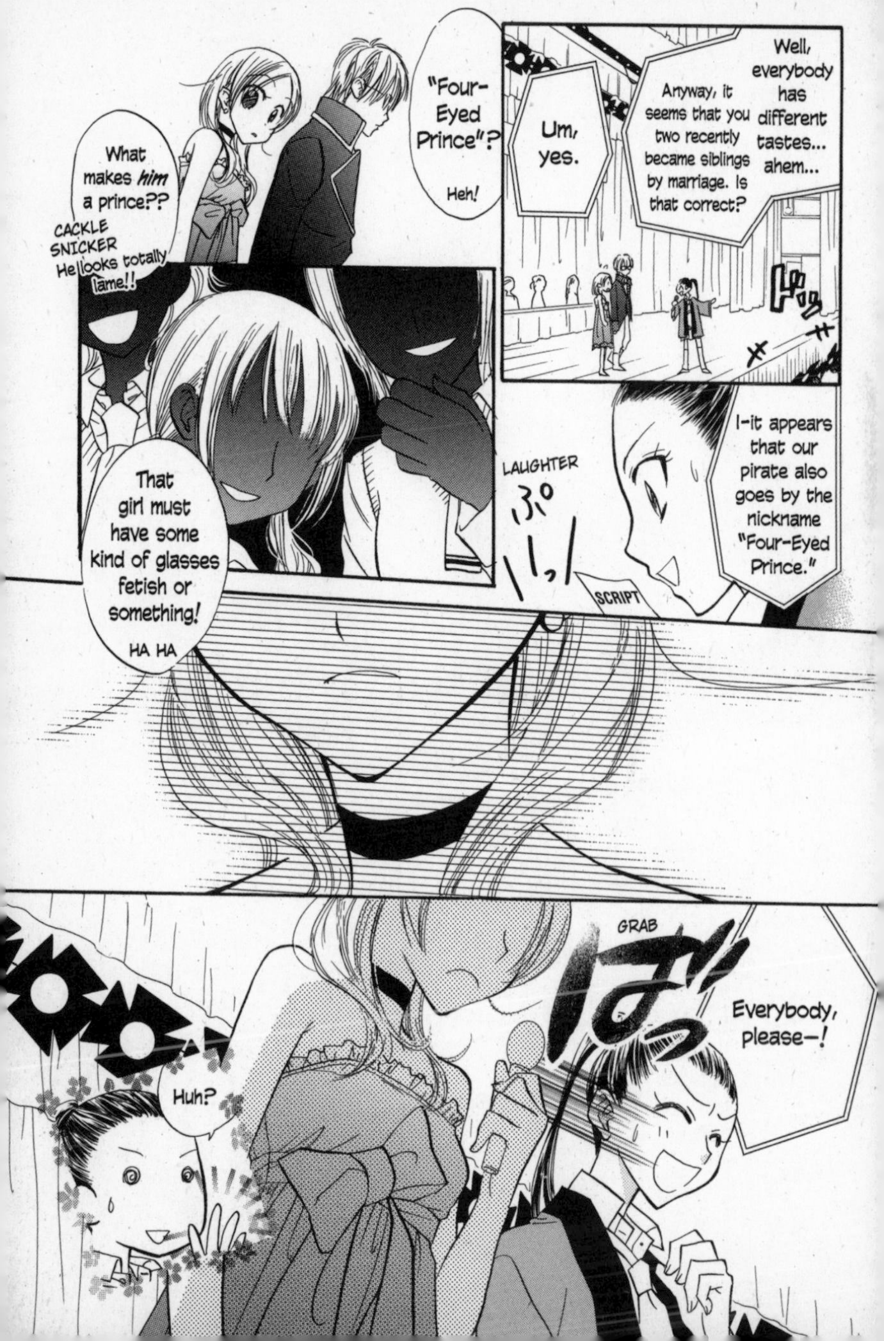
Well, everybody has different tastes... ahem...
Anyway, it seems that you two recently became siblings by marriage. Is that correct?
Um, yes.
I-it appears that our pirate also goes by the nickname "Four-Eyed Prince."
LAUGHTER
SCRIPT
"Four-Eyed Prince"?
Heh!
What makes *him* a prince??
CACKLE SNICKER
He looks totally lame!!
That girl must have some kind of glasses fetish or something!
HA HA
GRAB
Everybody, please—!
Huh?

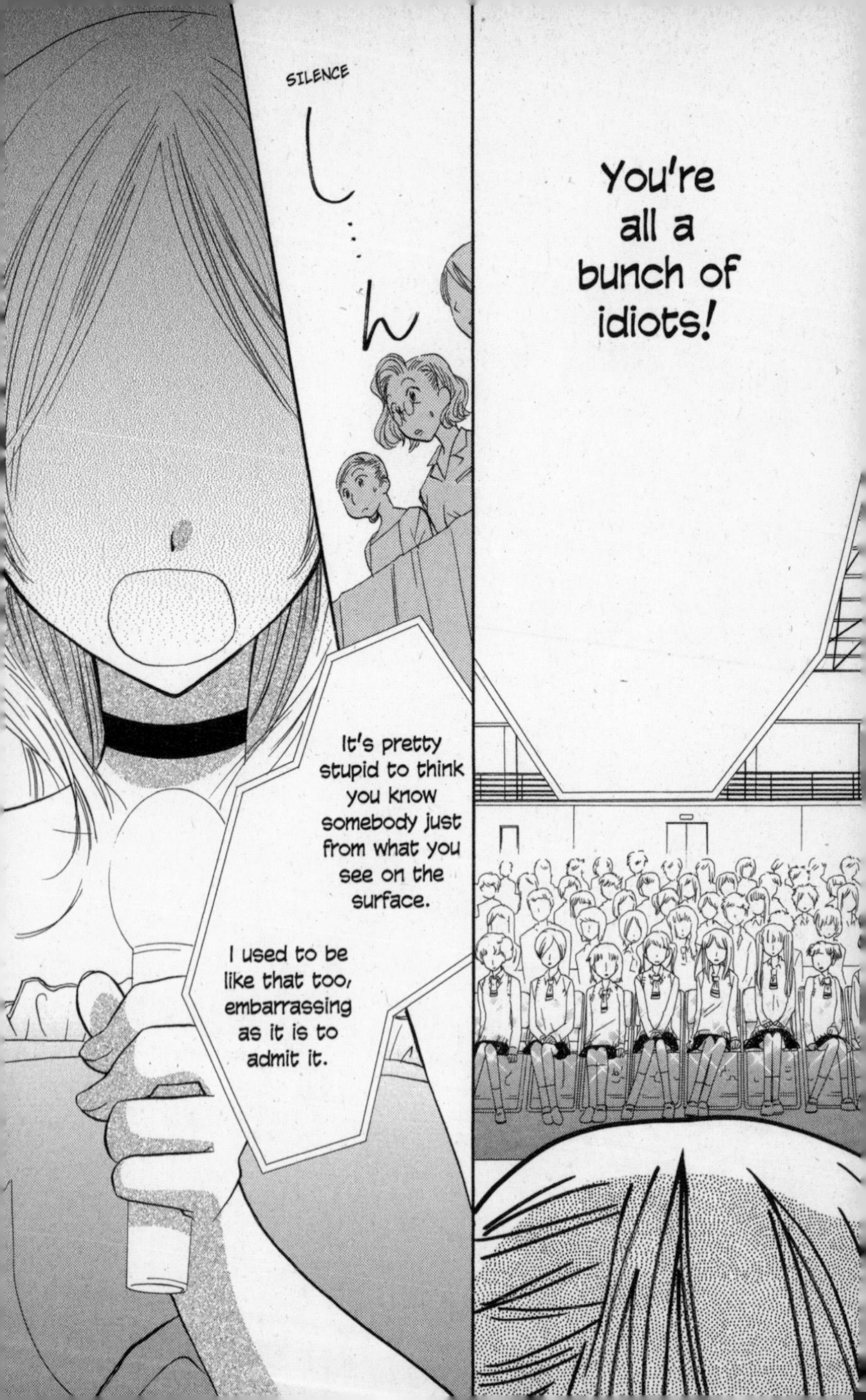
You're all a bunch of idiots!
SILENCE
It's pretty stupid to think you know somebody just from what you see on the surface.
I used to be like that too, embarrassing as it is to admit it.

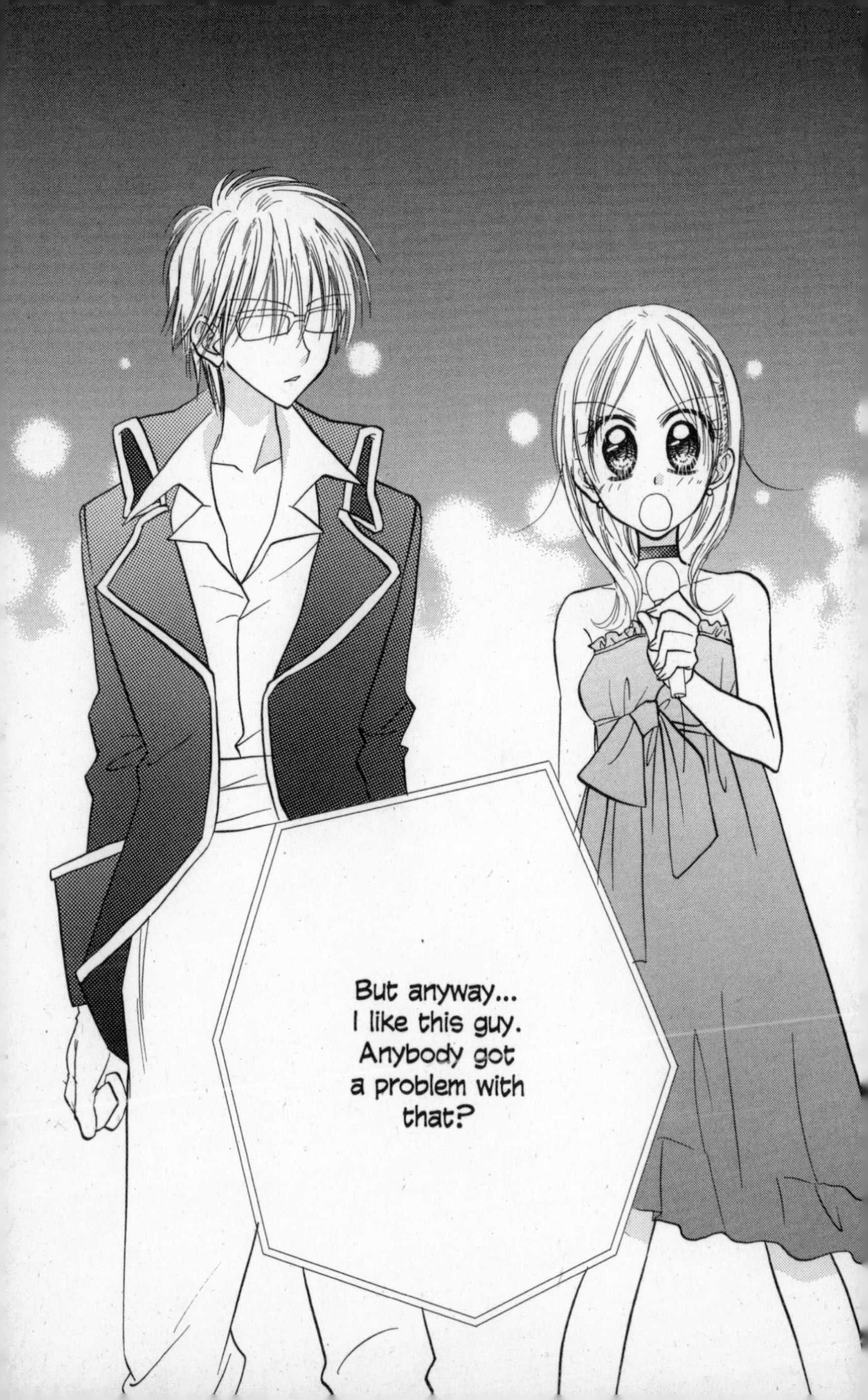
But anyway... I like this guy. Anybody got a problem with that?

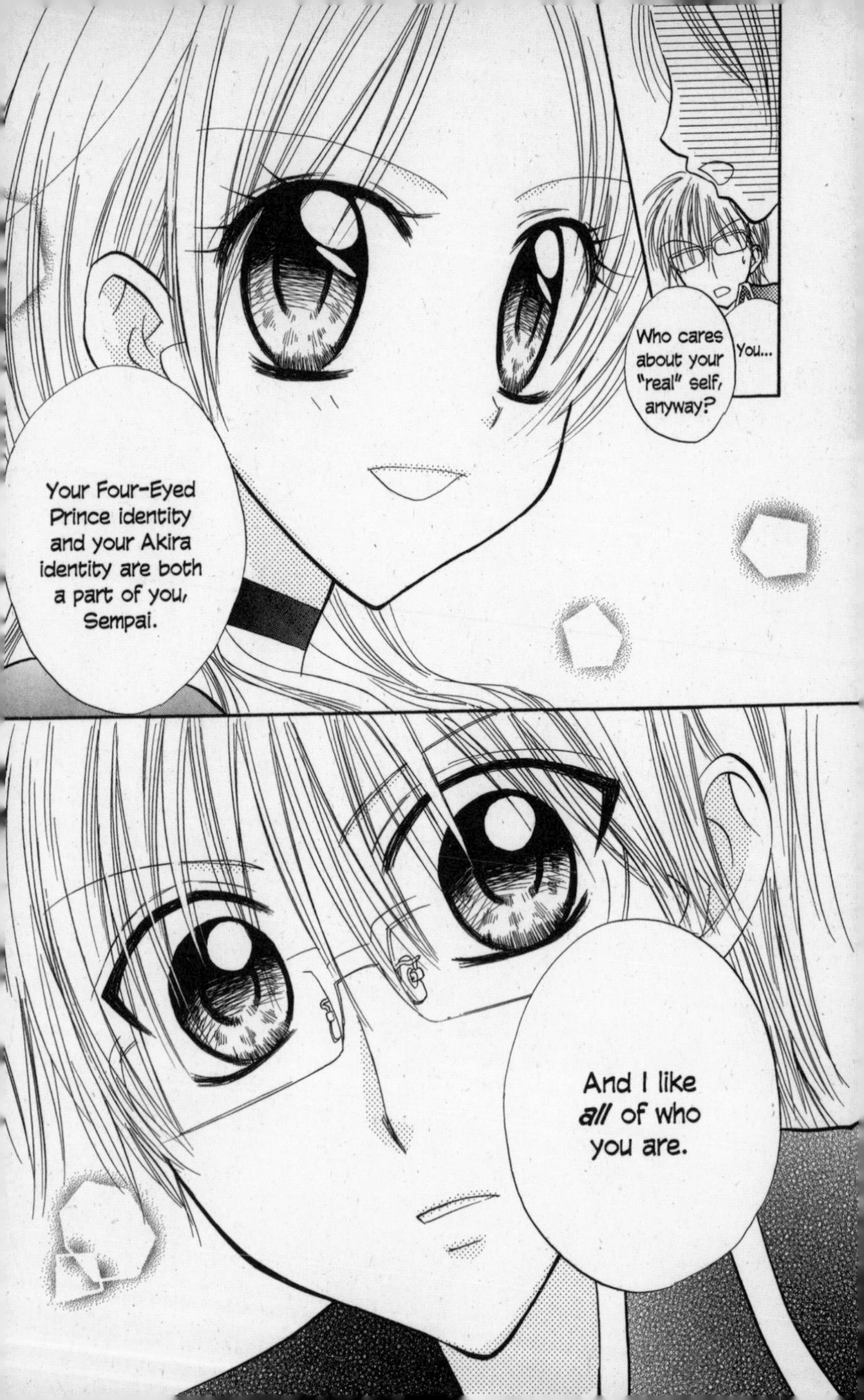
You...
Who cares about your "real" self, anyway?
Your Four-Eyed Prince identity and your Akira identity are both a part of you, Sempai.
And I like *all* of who you are.

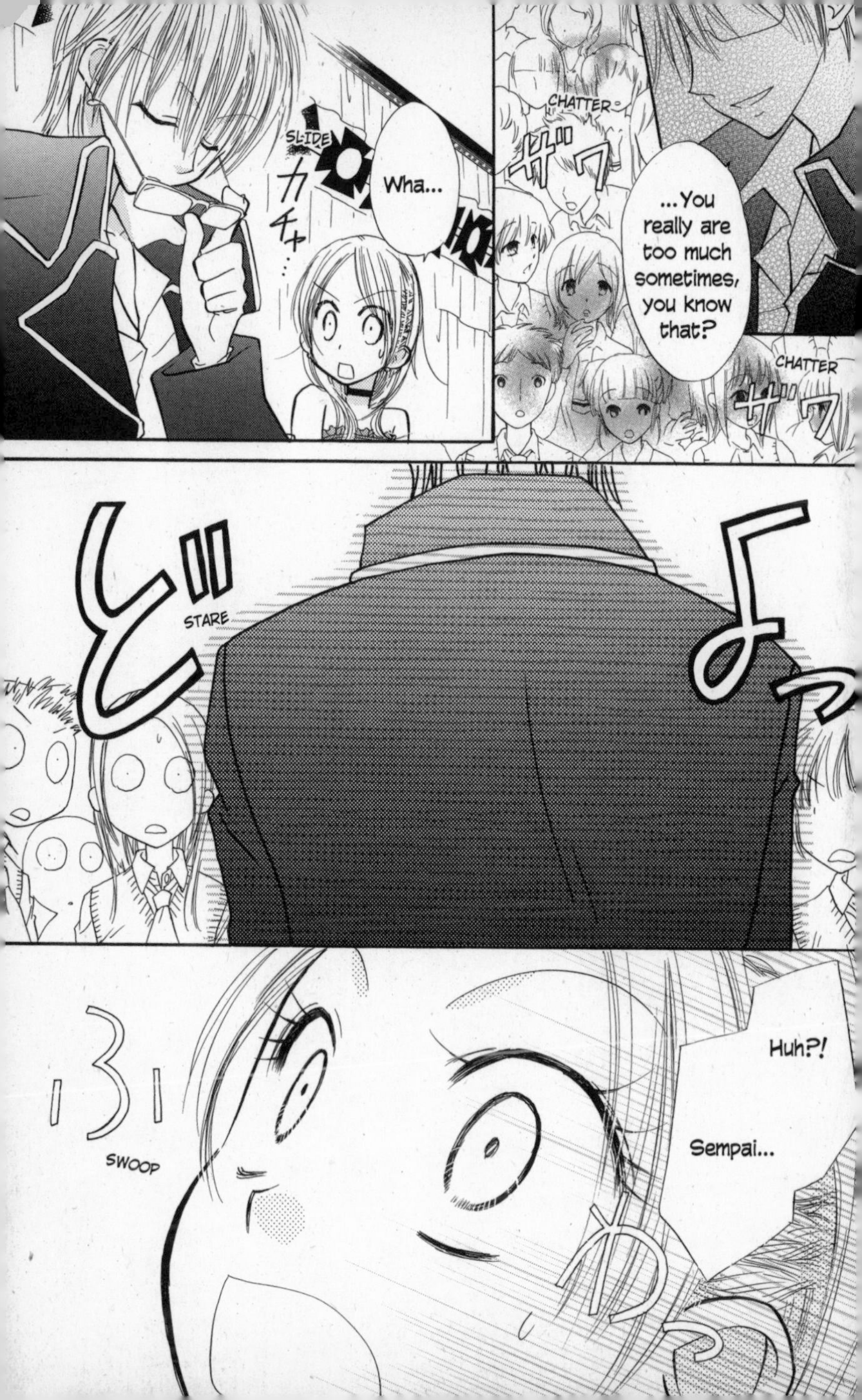
CHATTER
ザワ
...You really are too much sometimes, you know that?
CHATTER
ザワ
SLIDE
カチャ...
Wha...
STARE
Huh?!
Sempai...
SWOOP

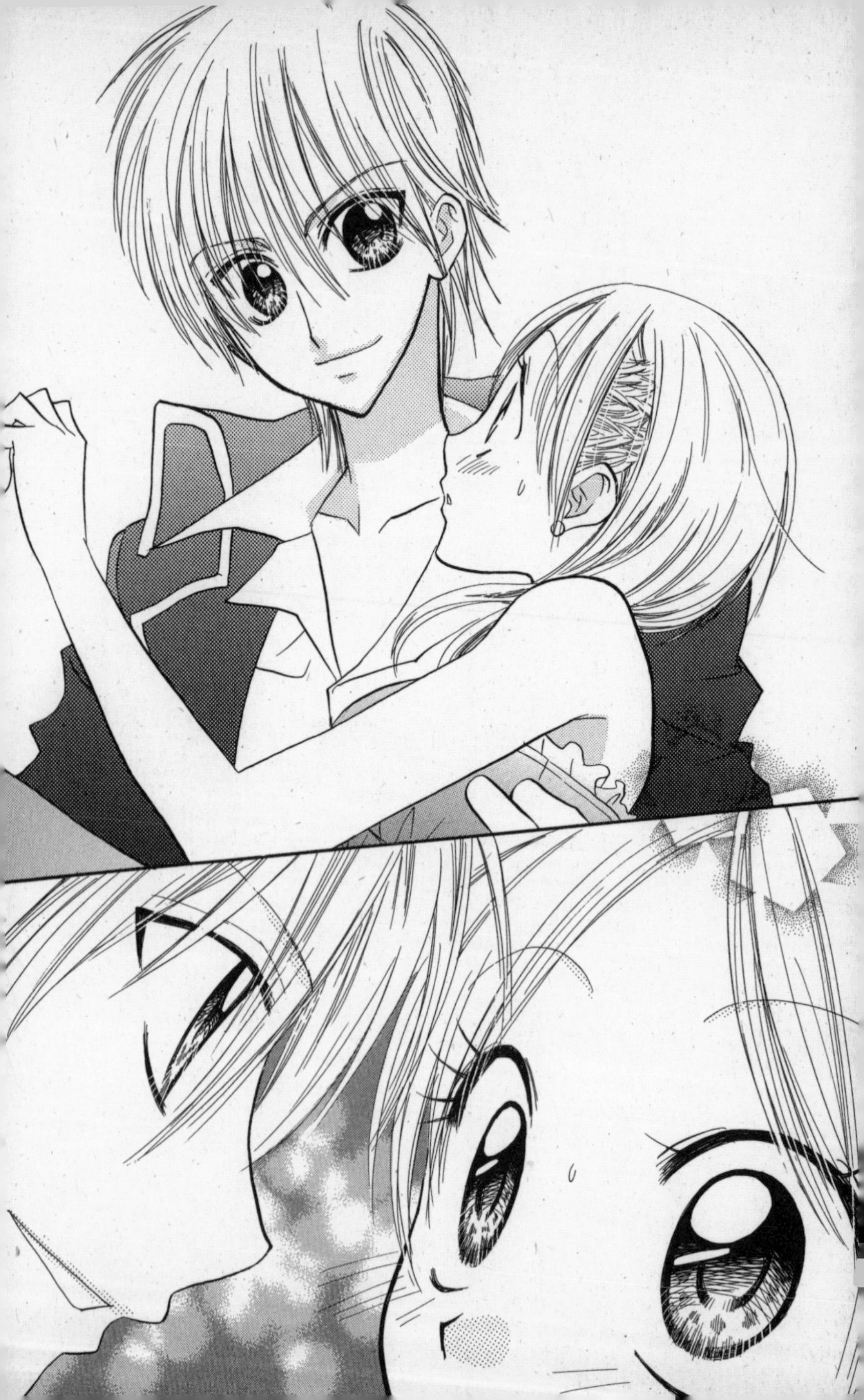

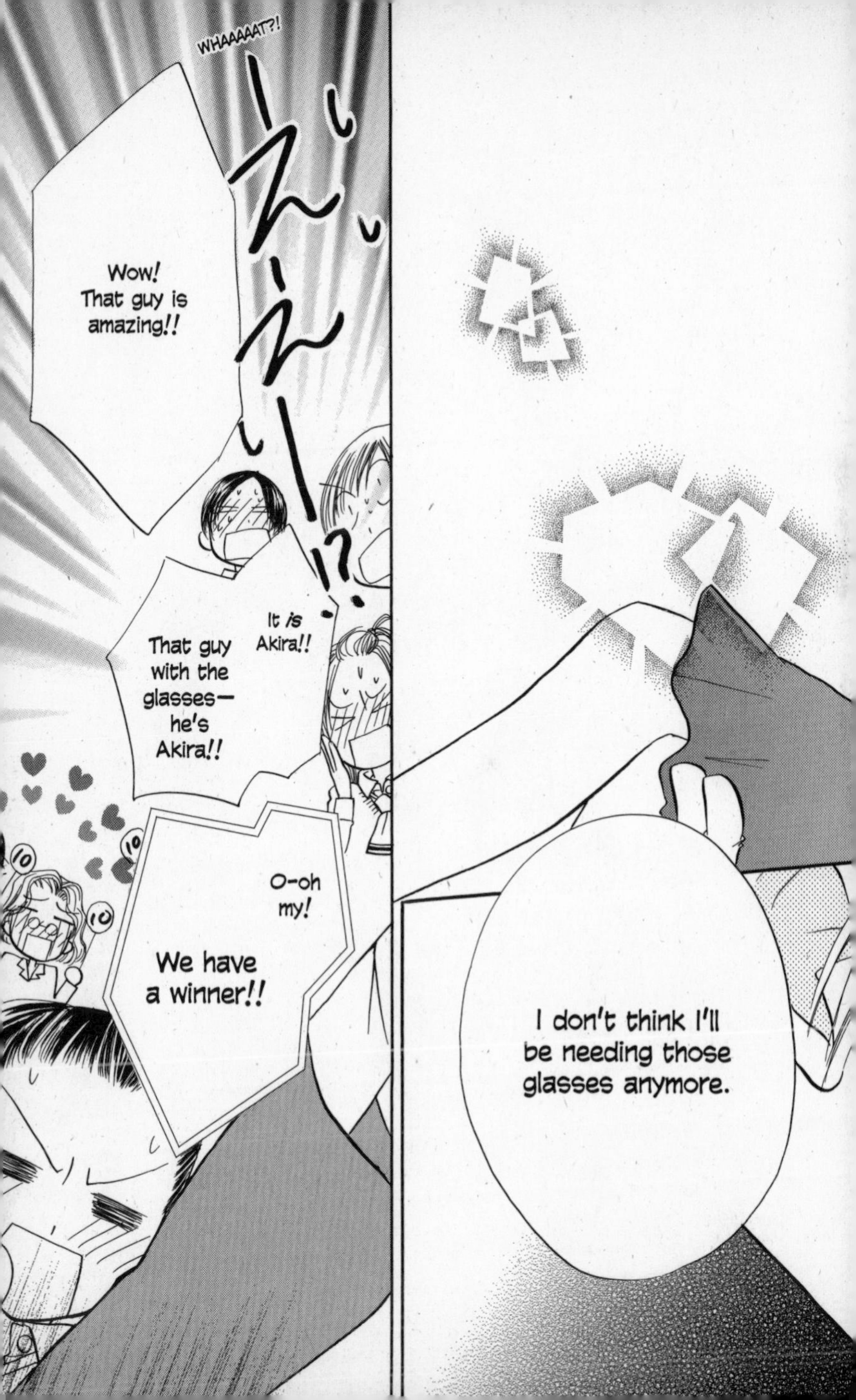
I don't think I'll be needing those glasses anymore.
WHAAAAAT?!
Wow! That guy is amazing!!
It is Akira!!
That guy with the glasses—he's Akira!!
O-oh my!
We have a winner!!

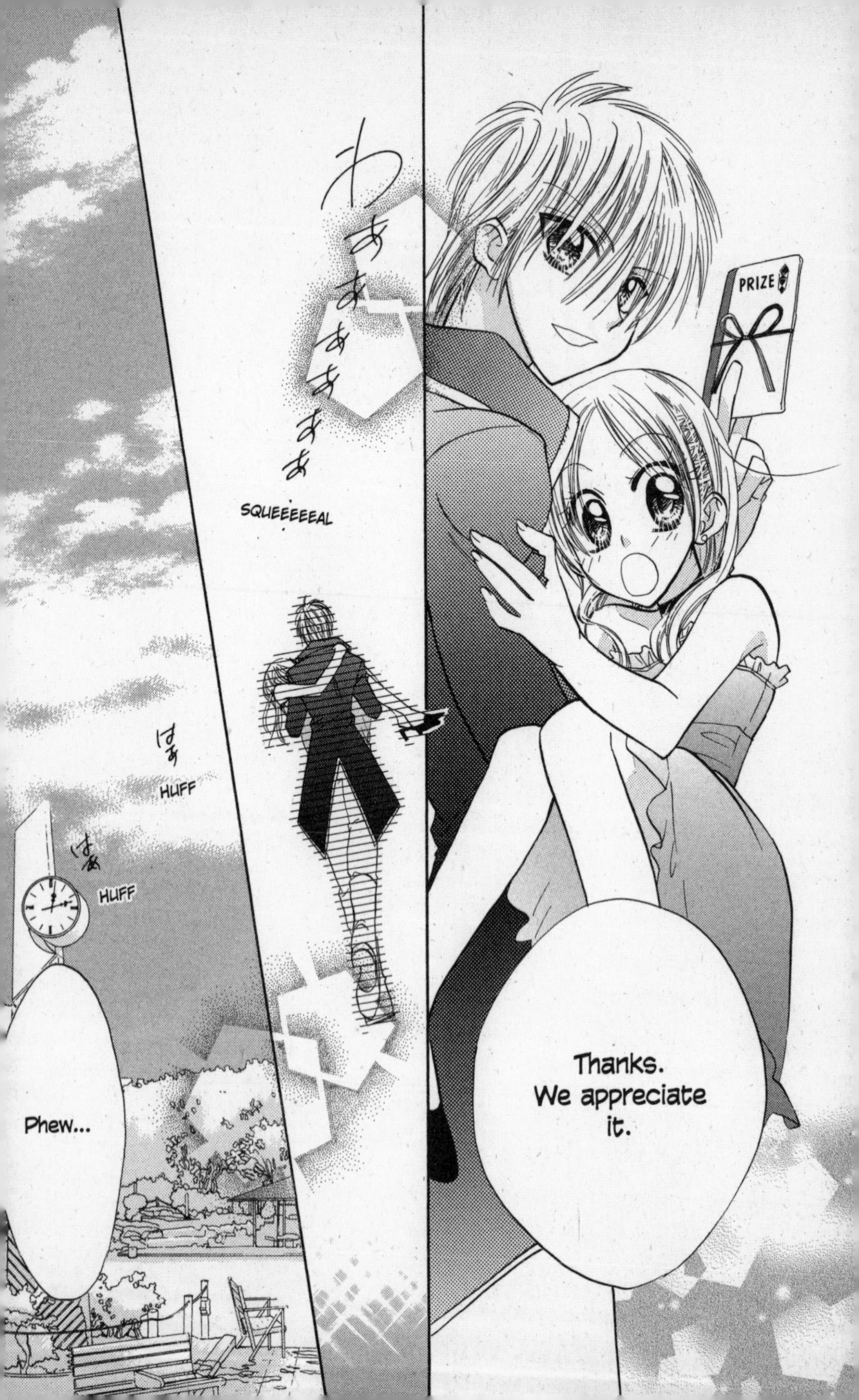
PRIZE
Thanks. We appreciate it.
わああああああ
SQUEEEEEEAL
はぁ
HUFF
はぁ
HUFF
Phew...

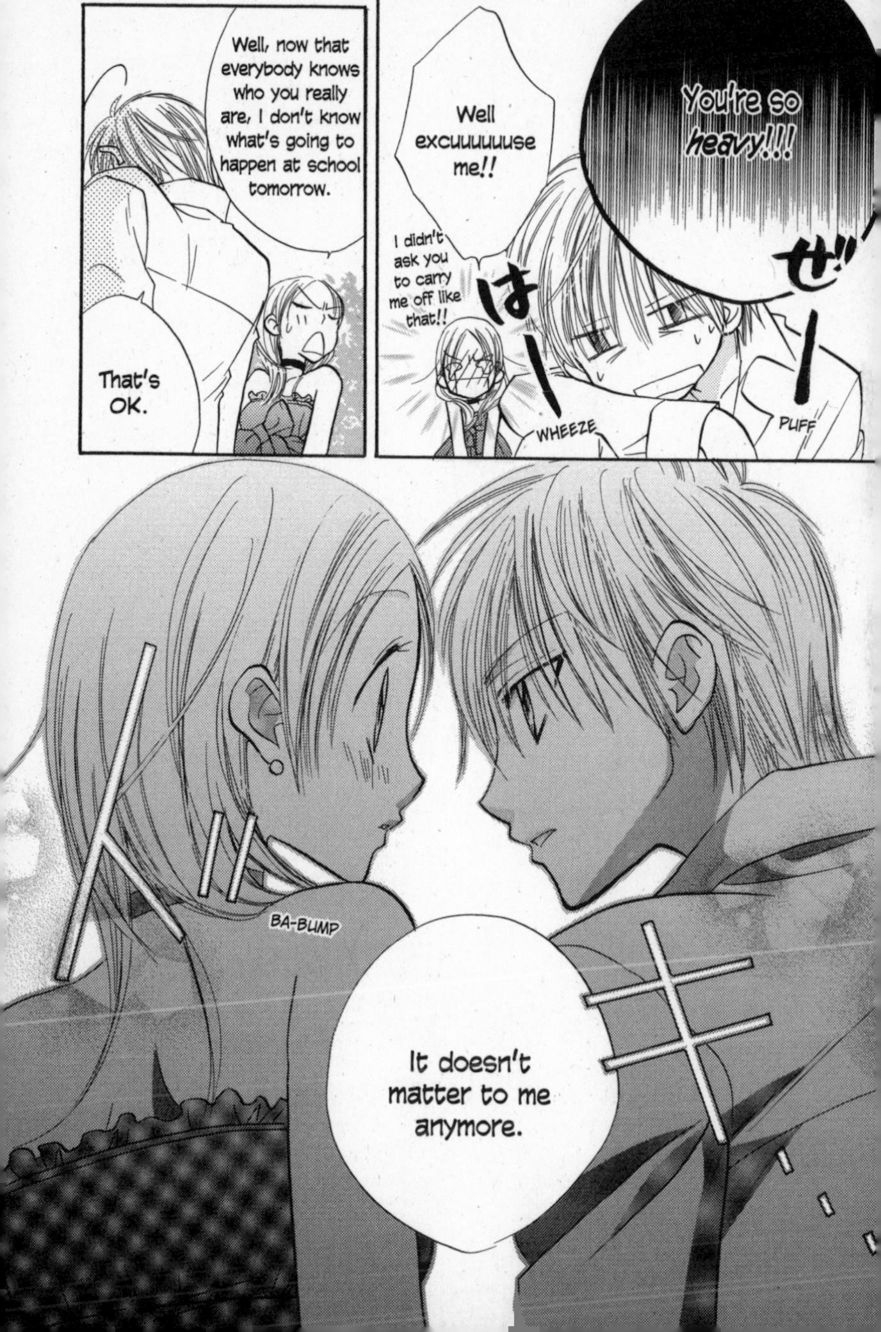
You're so heavy!!!
ぜーー
PUFF
Well excuuuuuuse me!!
はー
WHEEZE
I didn't ask you to carry me off like that!!
Well, now that everybody knows who you really are, I don't know what's going to happen at school tomorrow.
That's OK.
BA-BUMP
It doesn't matter to me anymore.

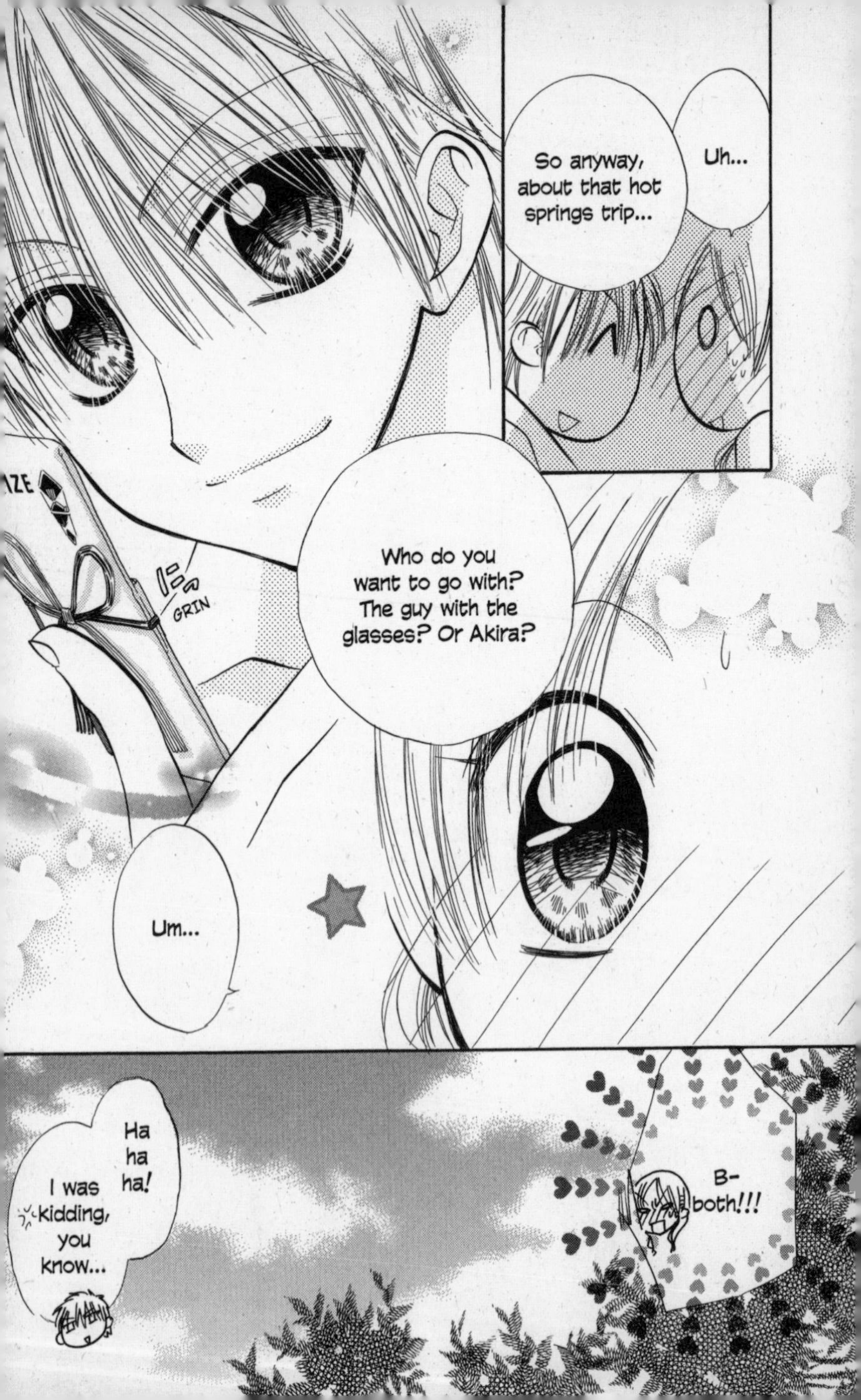
Uh...
So anyway, about that hot springs trip...
Who do you want to go with? The guy with the glasses? Or Akira?
GRIN
Um...
B-both!!!
Ha ha ha!
I was kidding, you know...

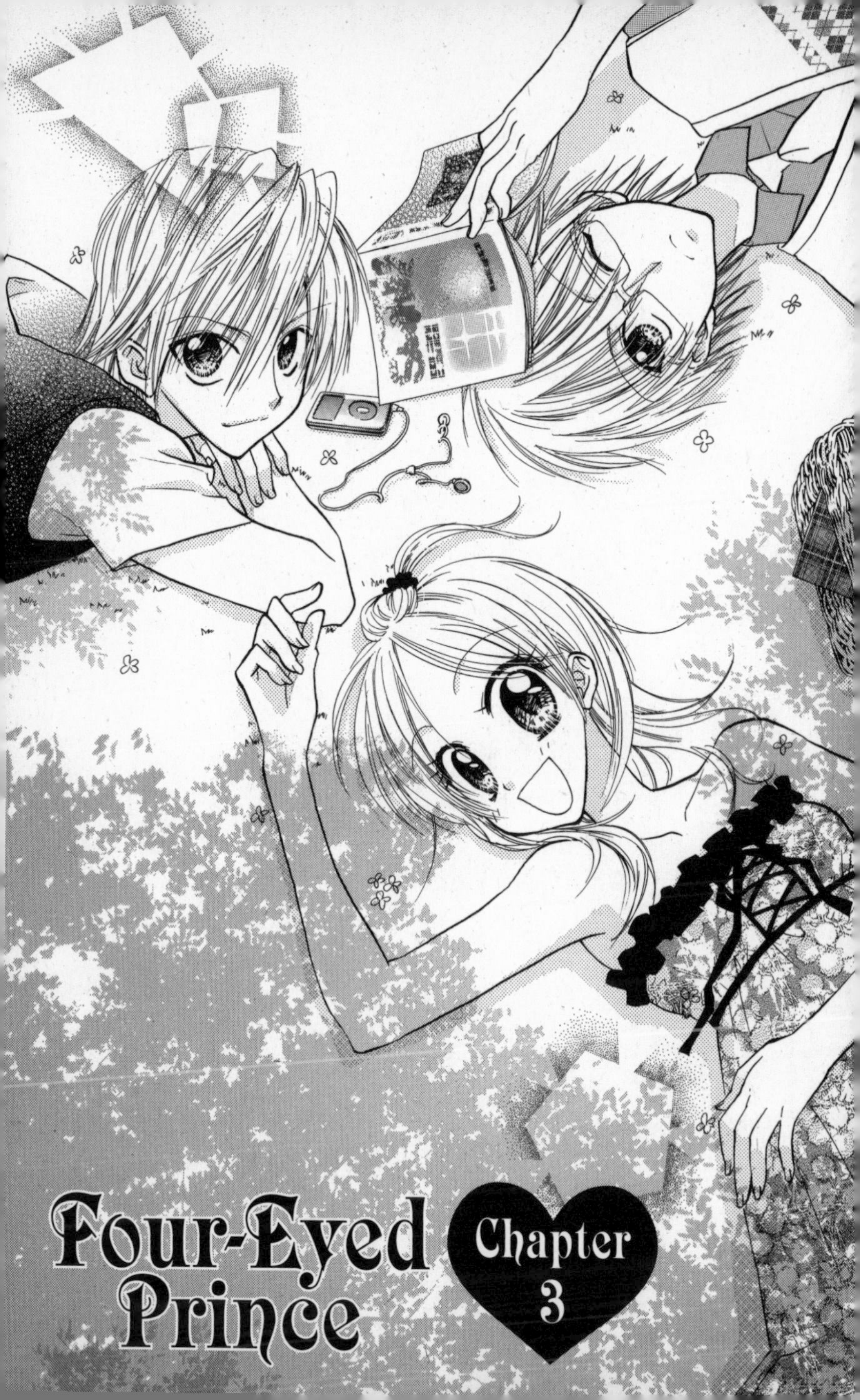
Four-Eyed Prince
Chapter 3

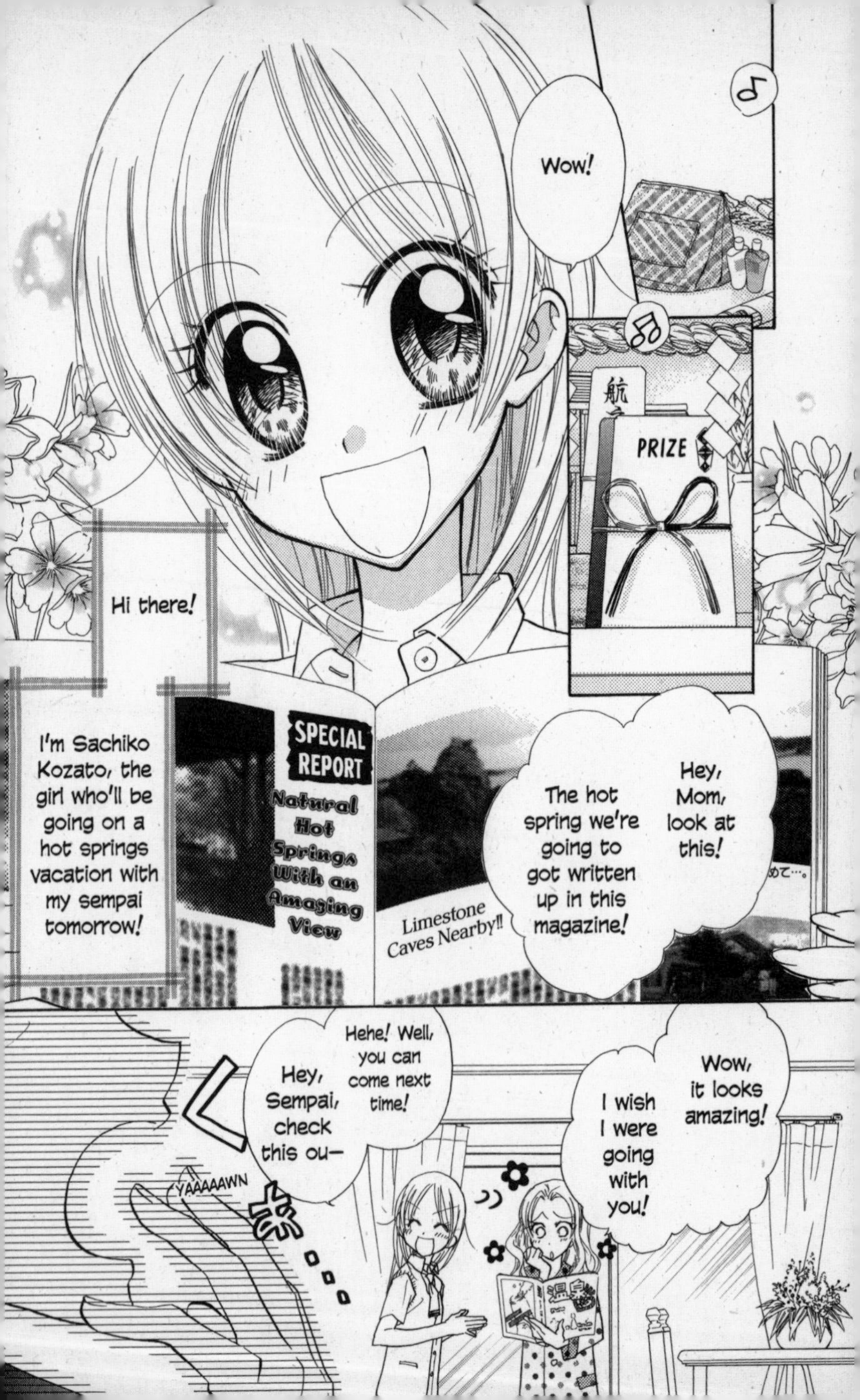
Wow!
PRIZE
Hi there!
I'm Sachiko Kozato, the girl who'll be going on a hot springs vacation with my sempai tomorrow!
SPECIAL REPORT
Natural Hot Springs With an Amazing View
Limestone Caves Nearby!!
Hey, Mom, look at this!
The hot spring we're going to got written up in this magazine!
Wow, it looks amazing!
I wish I were going with you!
Hehe! Well, you can come next time!
Hey, Sempai, check this ou—
YAAAAAWN

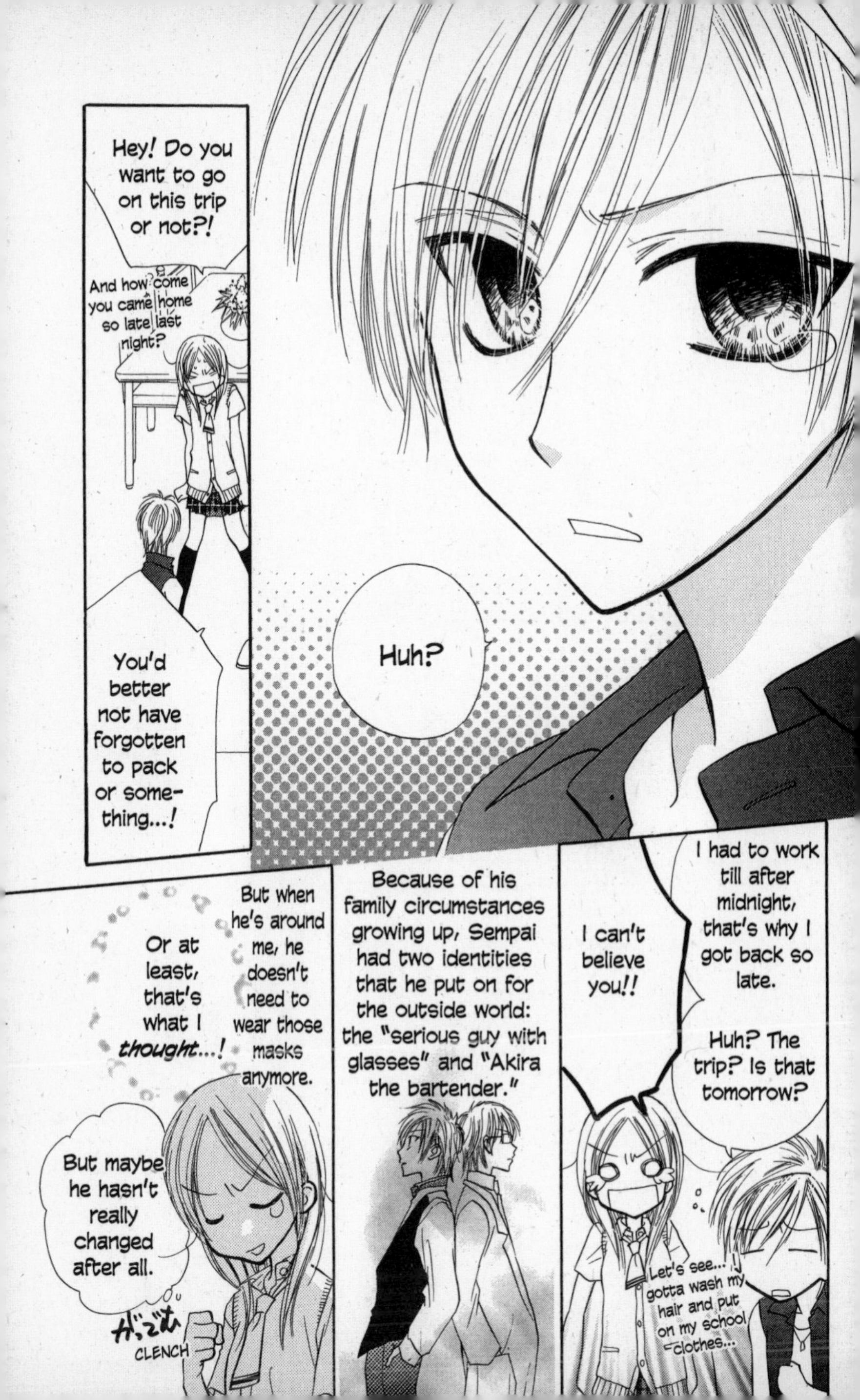
Huh?
Hey! Do you want to go on this trip or not?!
And how come you came home so late last night?
You'd better not have forgotten to pack or something...!
I had to work till after midnight, that's why I got back so late.
Huh? The trip? Is that tomorrow?
Let's see... gotta wash my hair and put on my school clothes...
I can't believe you!!
Because of his family circumstances growing up, Sempai had two identities that he put on for the outside world: the "serious guy with glasses" and "Akira the bartender."
But when he's around me, he doesn't need to wear those masks anymore.
Or at least, that's what I *thought*...!
But maybe he hasn't really changed after all.
がっ
CLENCH

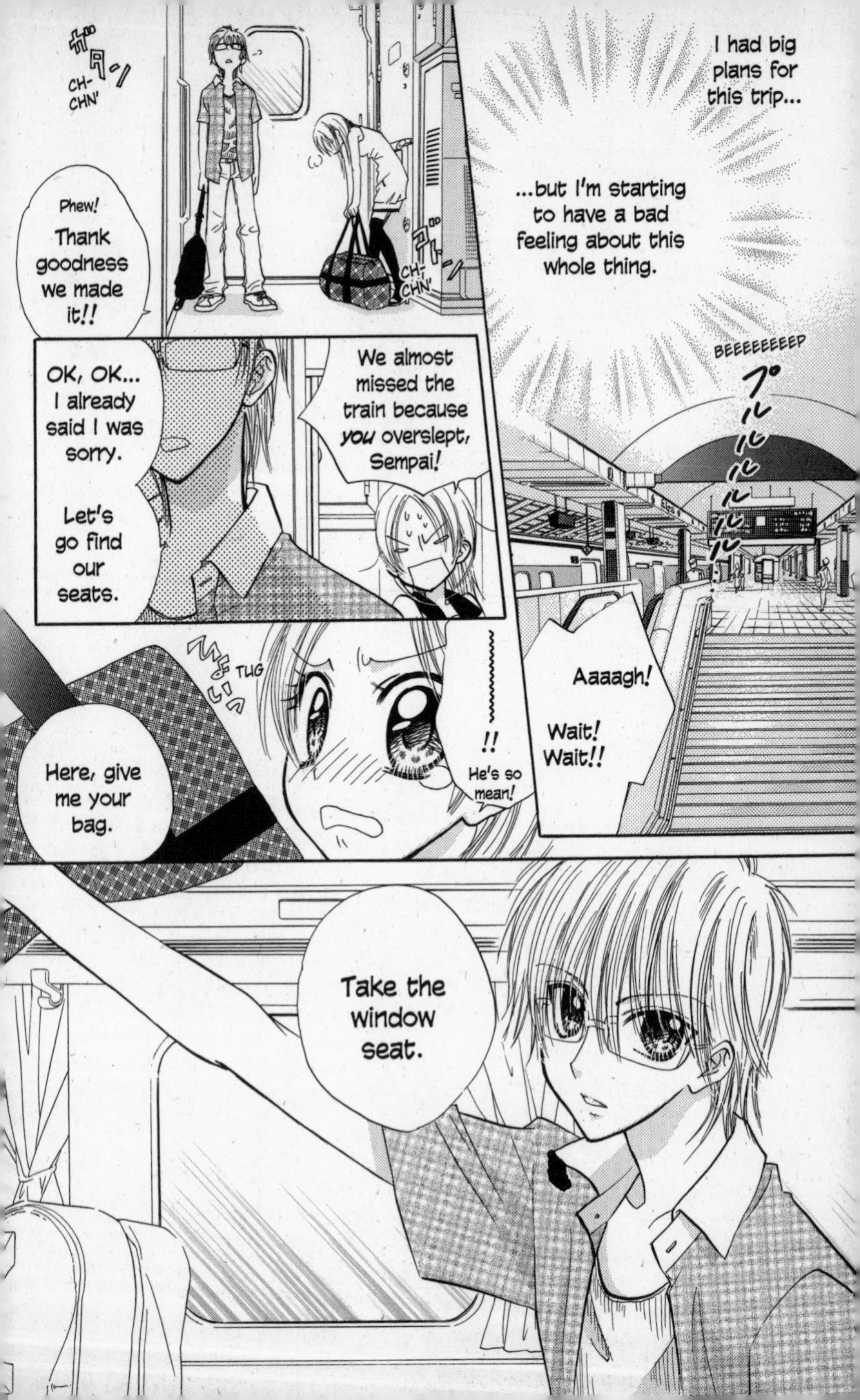
I had big plans for this trip...
...but I'm starting to have a bad feeling about this whole thing.
BEEEEEEEEP
Aaaagh!
Wait! Wait!!
CH-CHN'
CH-CHN'
Phew! Thank goodness we made it!!
We almost missed the train because *you* overslept, Sempai!
OK, OK... I already said I was sorry.
Let's go find our seats.
!!
He's so mean!
TUG
Here, give me your bag.
Take the window seat.

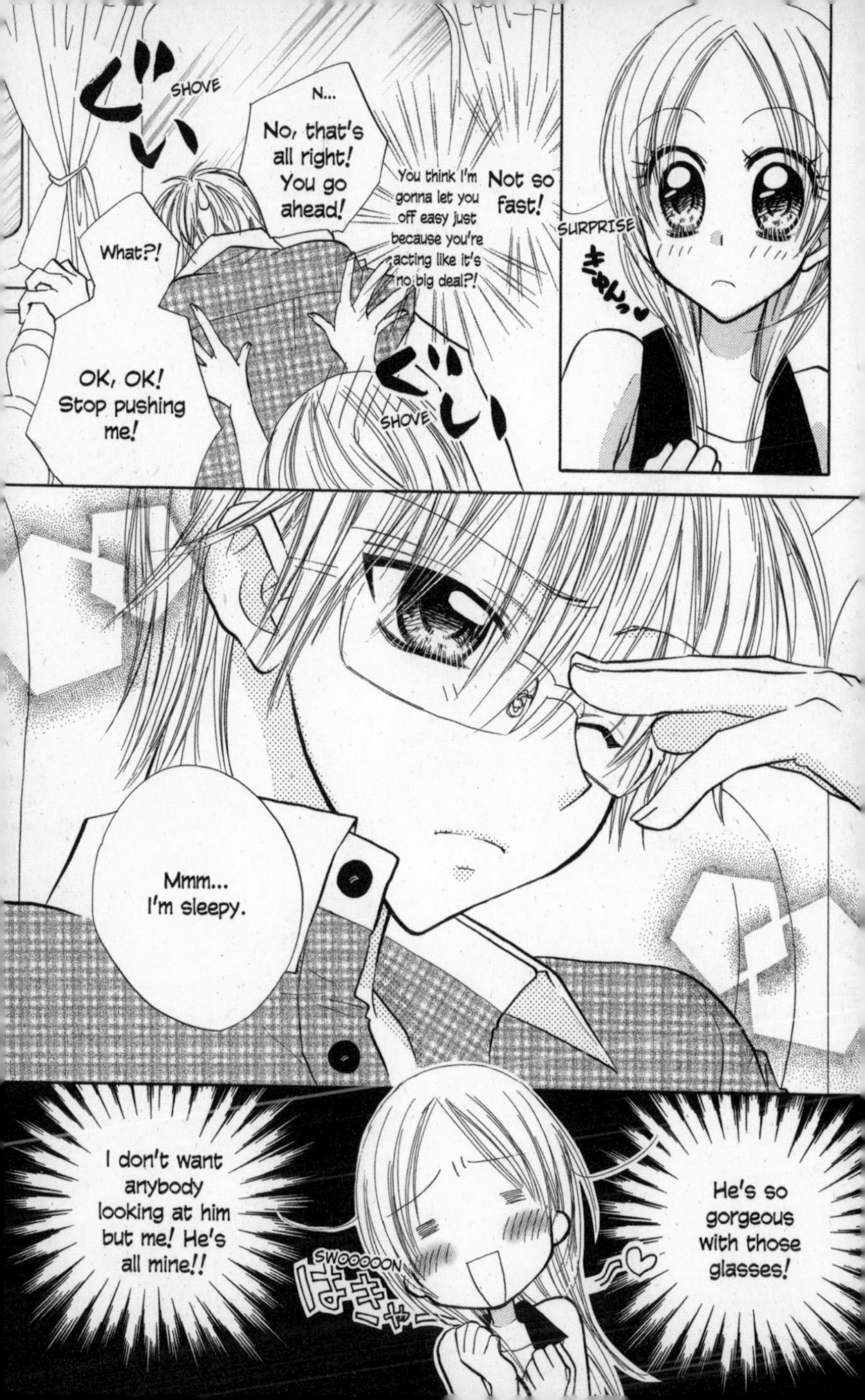
SURPRISE
きゅんっ
Not so fast!
You think I'm gonna let you off easy just because you're acting like it's no big deal?!
N...
No, that's all right! You go ahead!
ぐい
SHOVE
What?!
OK, OK! Stop pushing me!
ぐい
SHOVE
Mmm... I'm sleepy.
He's so gorgeous with those glasses!
SWOOOOON
I don't want anybody looking at him but me! He's all mine!!

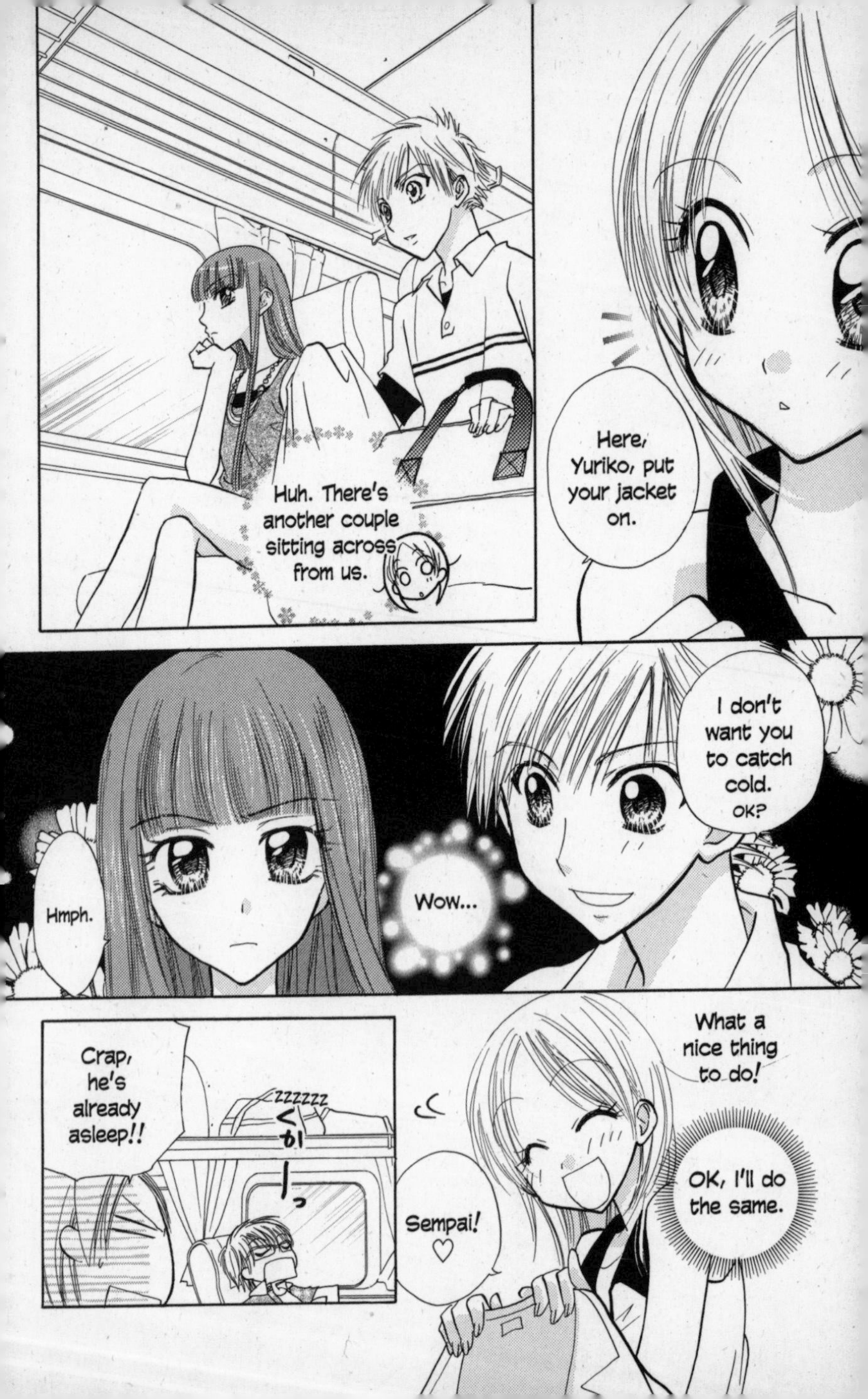
Here, Yuriko, put your jacket on.
Huh. There's another couple sitting across from us.
I don't want you to catch cold. OK?
Wow...
Hmph.
What a nice thing to do!
OK, I'll do the same.
Sempai! ♡
Crap, he's already asleep!!
zzzzzz

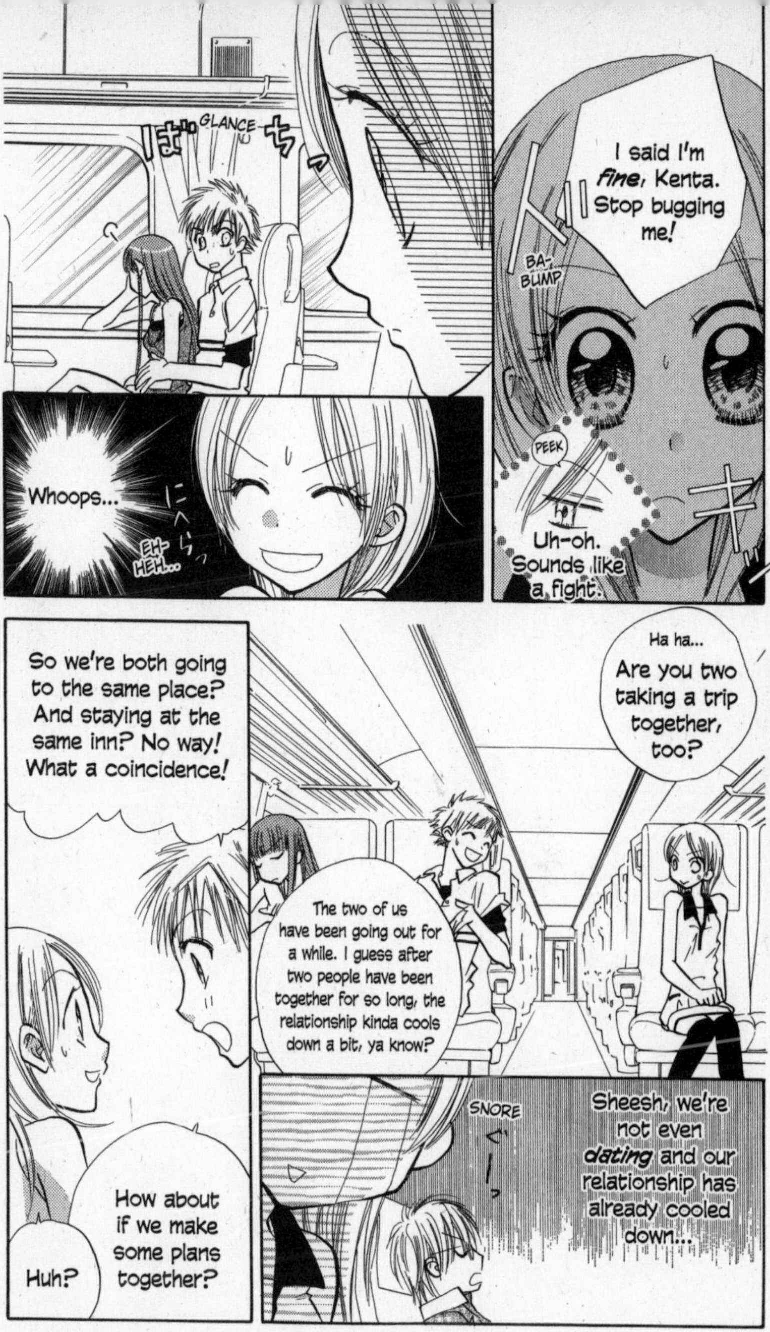
I said I'm *fine*, Kenta. Stop bugging me!
BA-BUMP
PEEK
Uh-oh. Sounds like a fight.
GLANCE
Whoops...
EH-HEH...
Ha ha...
Are you two taking a trip together, too?
The two of us have been going out for a while. I guess after two people have been together for so long, the relationship kinda cools down a bit, ya know?
SNORE
Sheesh, we're not even *dating* and our relationship has already cooled down...
So we're both going to the same place? And staying at the same inn? No way! What a coincidence!
How about if we make some plans together?
Huh?

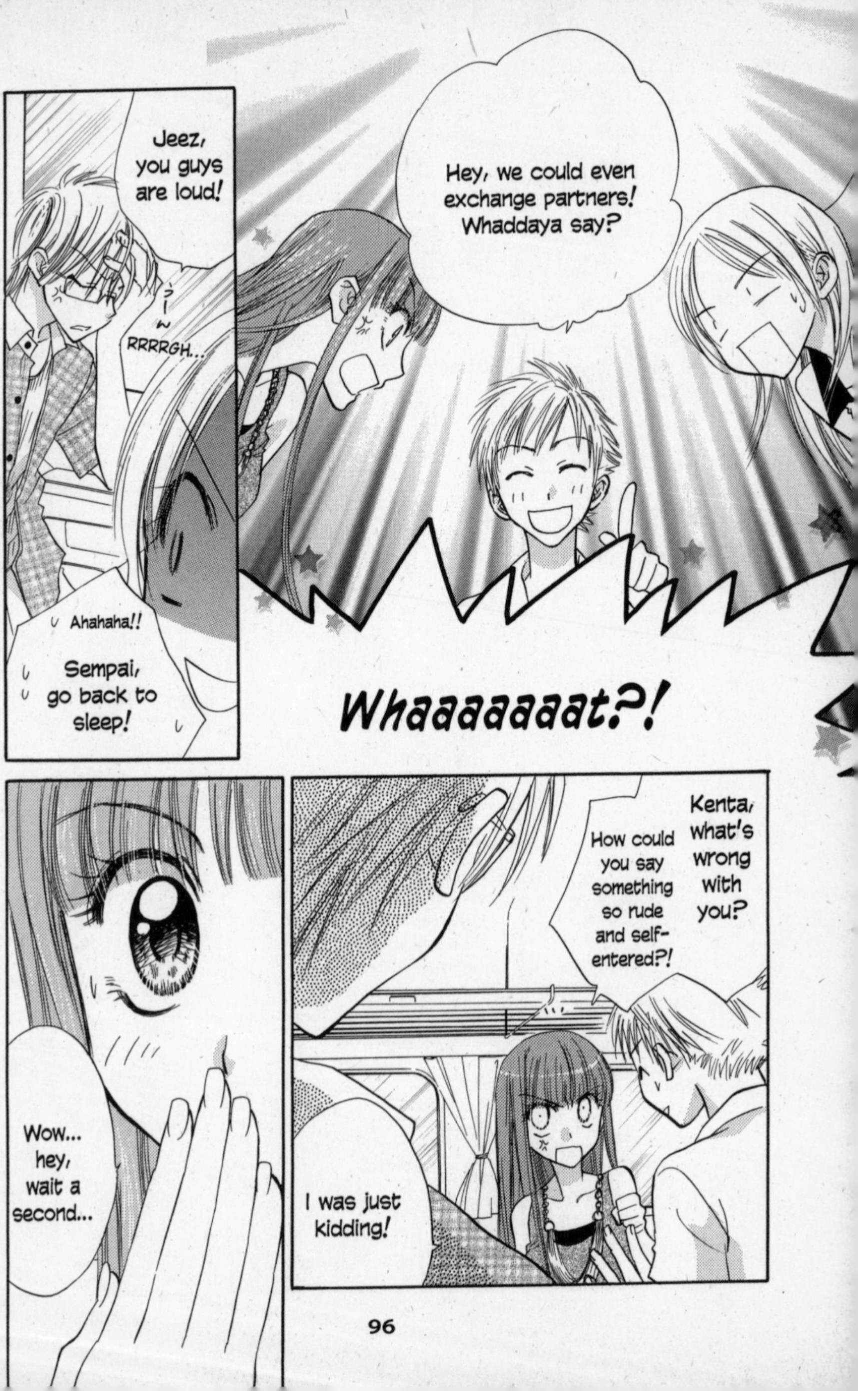
Hey, we could even exchange partners! Whaddaya say?
Whaaaaaaaat?!
Jeez, you guys are loud!
RRRRGH...
Ahahaha!!
Sempai, go back to sleep!
Kenta, what's wrong with you?
How could you say something so rude and self-entered?!
I was just kidding!
Wow... hey, wait a second...

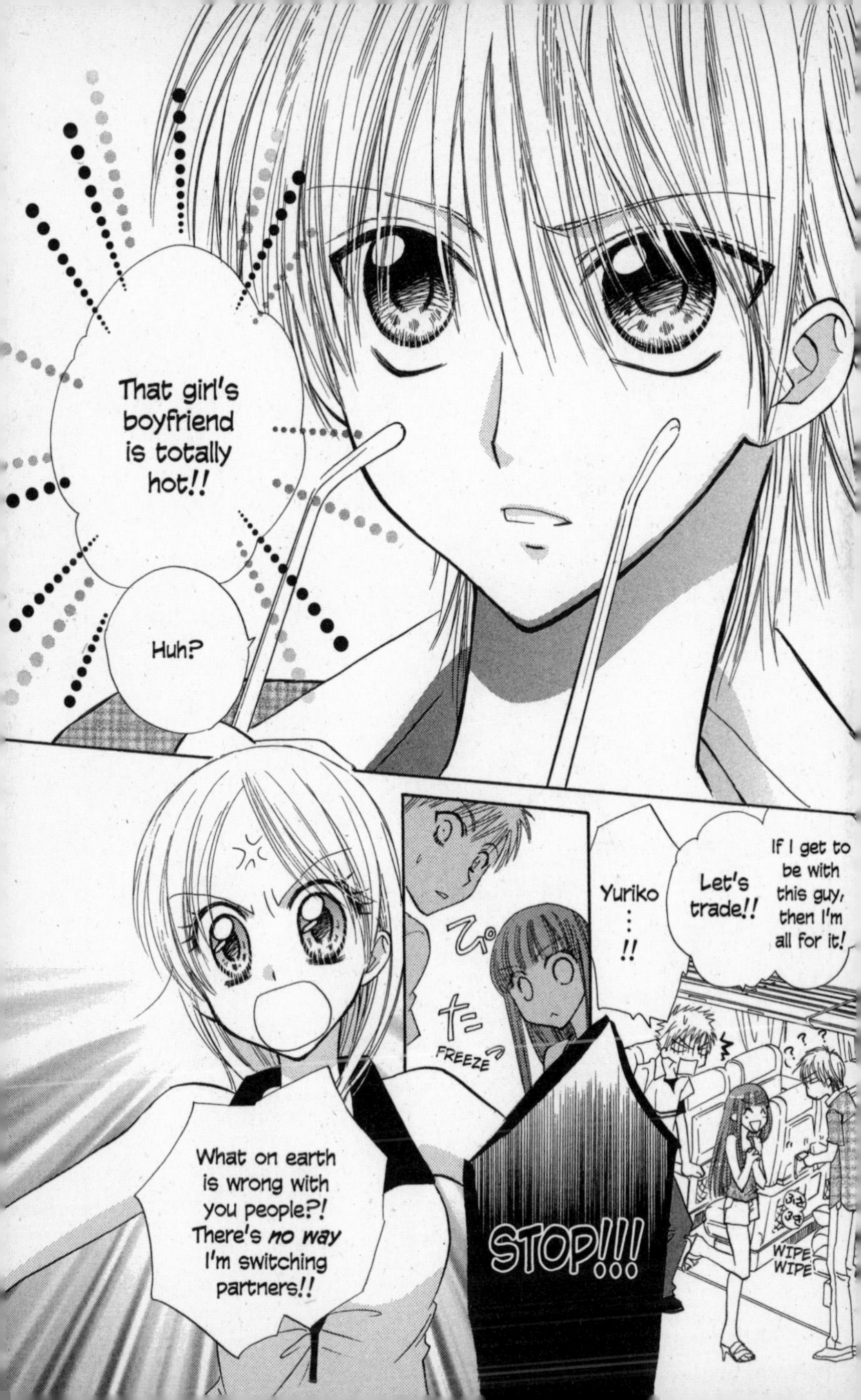
That girl's boyfriend is totally hot!!
Huh?
If I get to be with this guy, then I'm all for it!
Let's trade!!
Yuriko ... !!
WIPE WIPE
ぴた
FREEZE
What on earth is wrong with you people?! There's *no way* I'm switching partners!!
STOP!!!

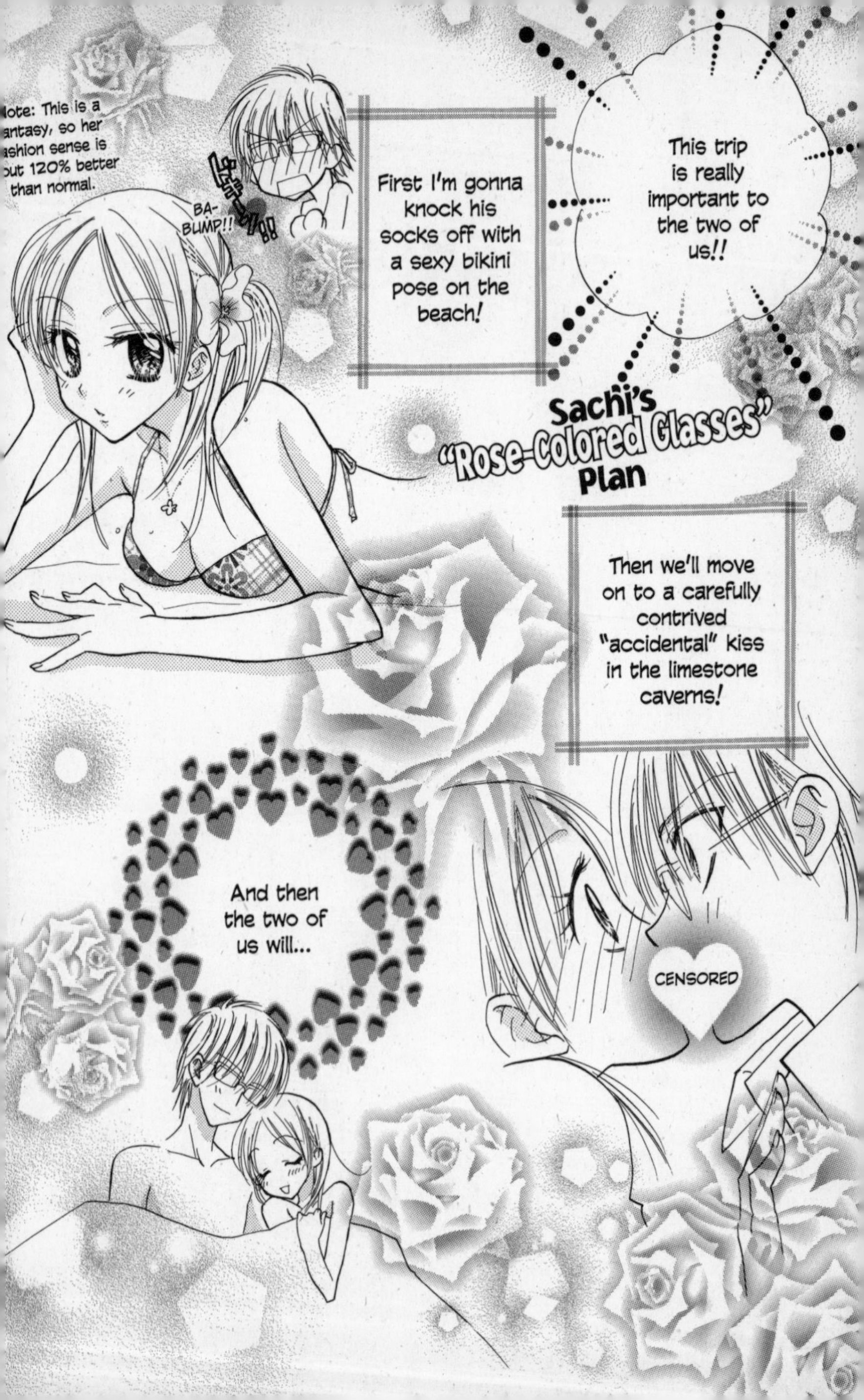

This trip is really important to the two of us!!
First I'm gonna knock his socks off with a sexy bikini pose on the beach!
lote: This is a antasy, so her ashion sense is out 120% better than normal.
BA-BUMP!!
Sachi's "Rose-Colored Glasses" Plan
Then we'll move on to a carefully contrived "accidental" kiss in the limestone caverns!
CENSORED
And then the two of us will...

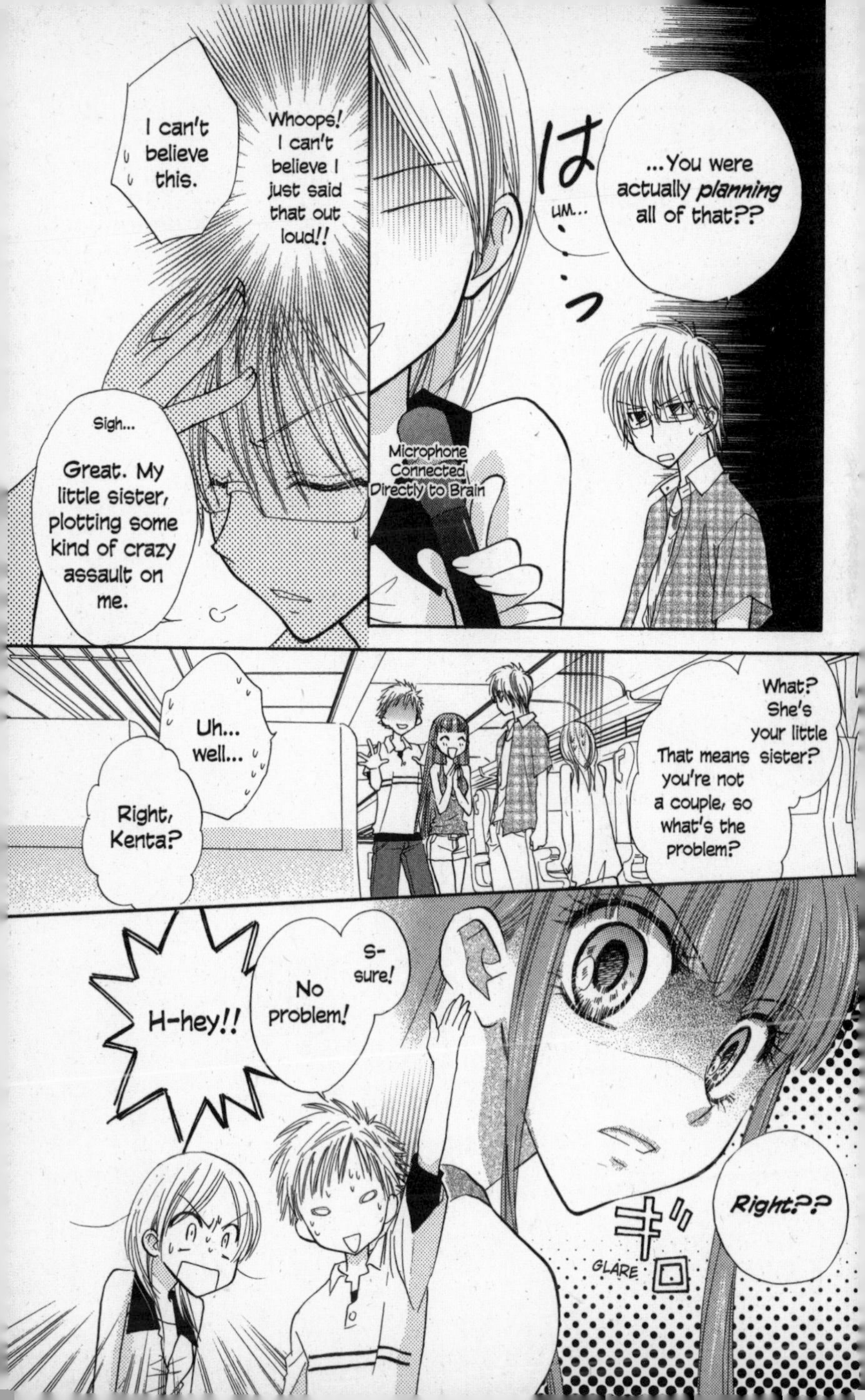
...You were actually *planning* all of that??
UM...
Microphone Connected Directly to Brain
Whoops! I can't believe I just said that out loud!!
I can't believe this.
Sigh...
Great. My little sister, plotting some kind of crazy assault on me.
What? She's your little sister? That means you're not a couple, so what's the problem?
Uh... well...
Right, Kenta?
Right??
GLARE
S-sure!
No problem!
H-hey!!

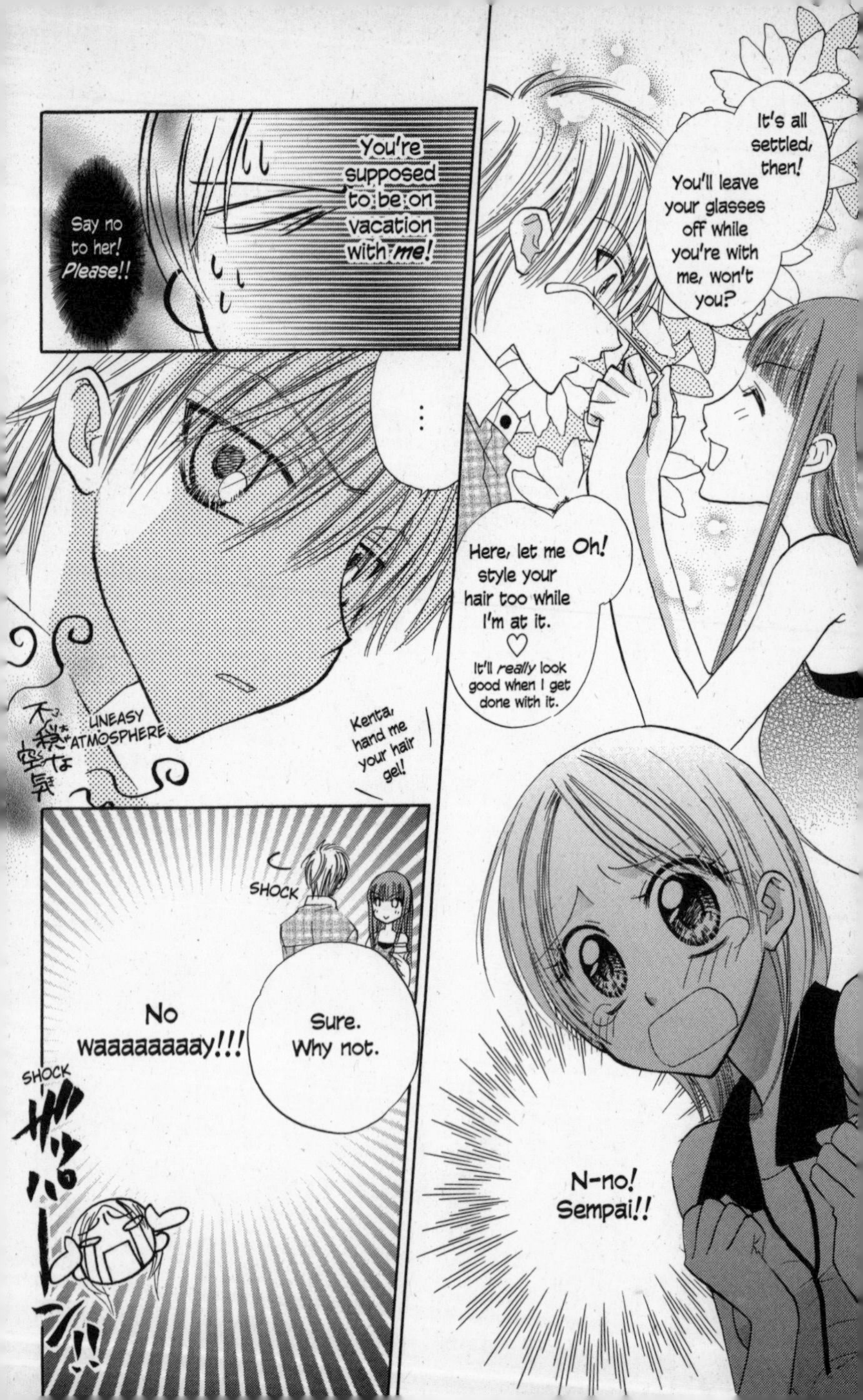

It's all settled, then! You'll leave your glasses off while you're with me, won't you?
Oh!
Here, let me style your hair too while I'm at it. ♡
It'll *really* look good when I get done with it.
N-no! Sempai!!
You're supposed to be on vacation with *me*!
Say no to her! *Please*!!
...
Kenta, hand me your hair gel!
UNEASY ATMOSPHERE
不穏な空気
SHOCK
Sure. Why not.
No waaaaaaaay!!!
SHOCK

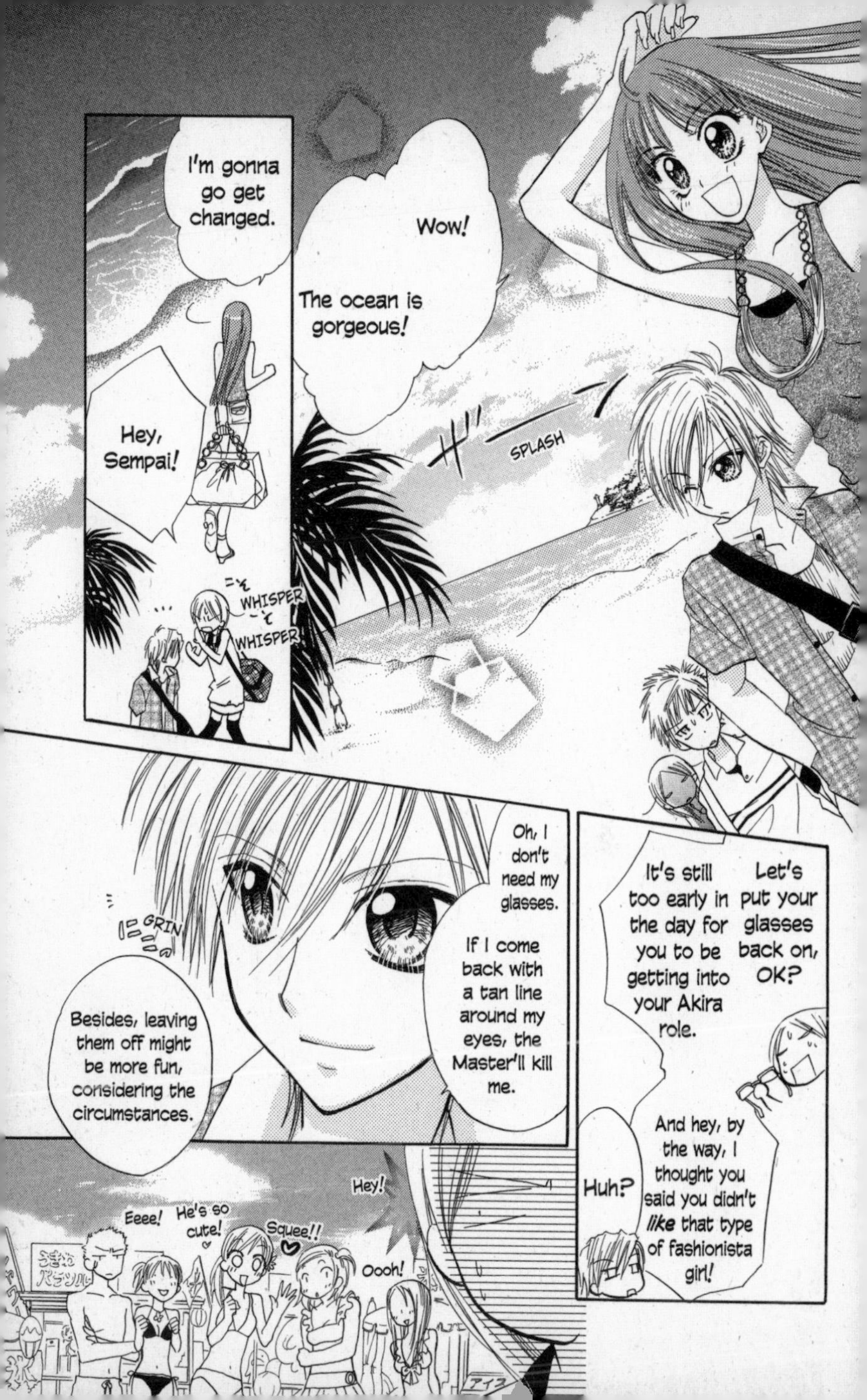
Wow!
The ocean is gorgeous!
SPLASH
I'm gonna go get changed.
Hey, Sempai!
WHISPER
WHISPER
Let's put your glasses back on, OK?
It's still too early in the day for you to be getting into your Akira role.
And hey, by the way, I thought you said you didn't *like* that type of fashionista girl!
Huh?
Oh, I don't need my glasses.
If I come back with a tan line around my eyes, the Master'll kill me.
GRIN
Besides, leaving them off might be more fun, considering the circumstances.
Hey!
He's so cute!
Eeee!
Squee!!
Oooh!

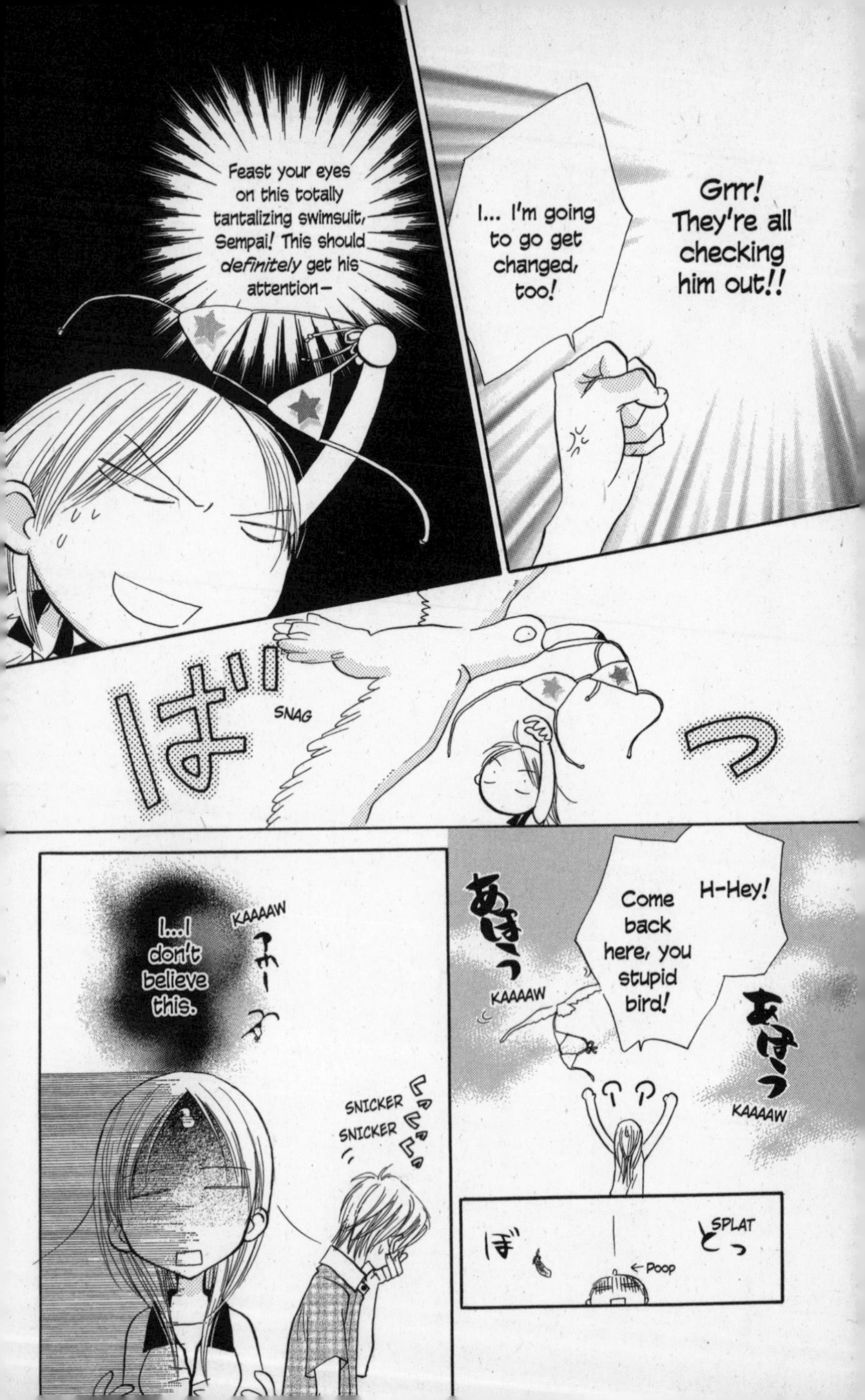
Grrr! They're all checking him out!!
I... I'm going to go get changed, too!
Feast your eyes on this totally tantalizing swimsuit, Sempai! This should *definitely* get his attention—
ばっ
SNAG
H-Hey!
あほう
KAAAAW
Come back here, you stupid bird!
あほう
KAAAAW
とっ
SPLAT
ぼ
← Poop
I...I don't believe this.
KAAAAW
あほー
SNICKER
SNICKER

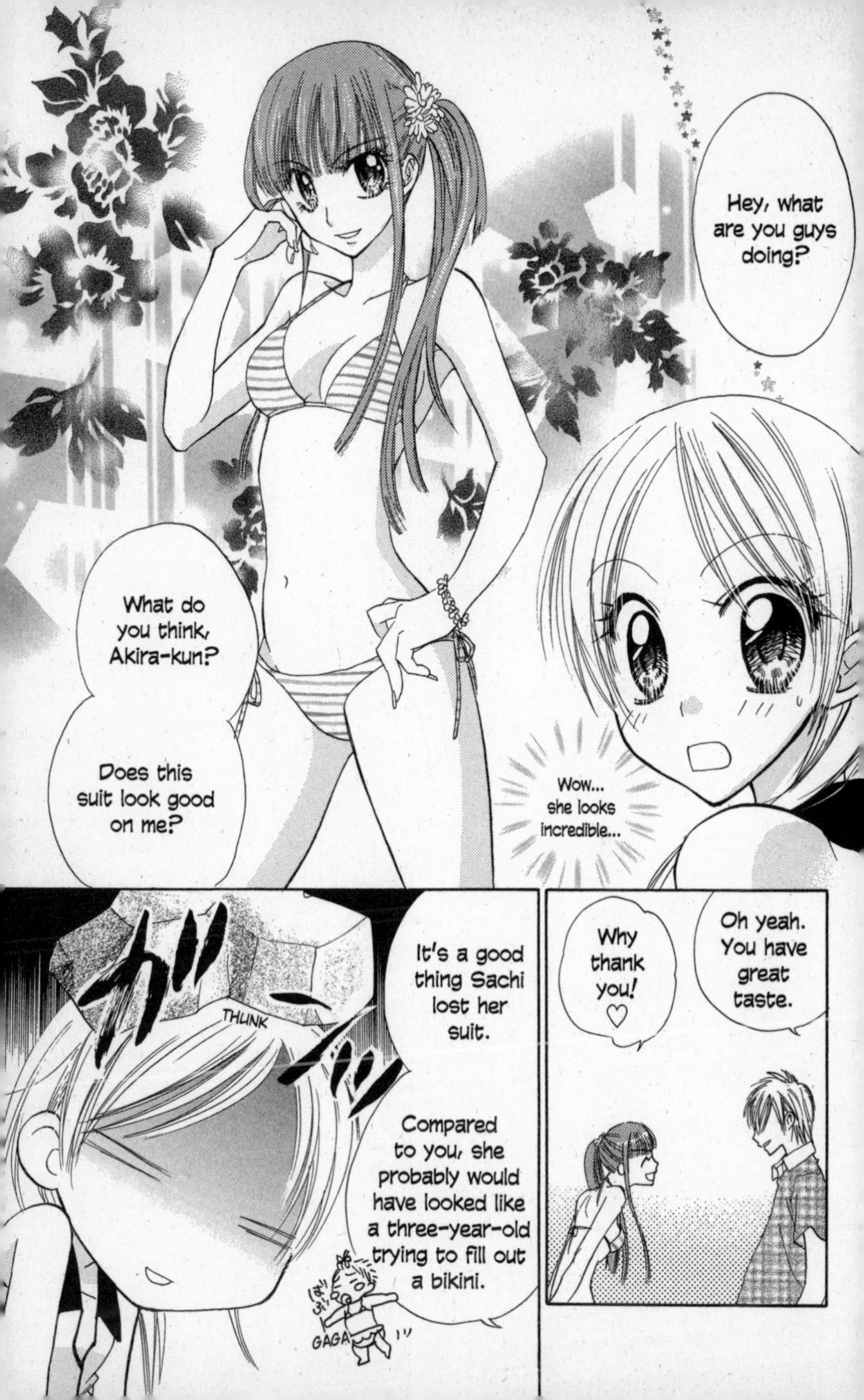

Hey, what are you guys doing?
What do you think, Akira-kun?
Does this suit look good on me?
Wow... she looks incredible...
Oh yeah. You have great taste.
Why thank you! ♡
THUNK
It's a good thing Sachi lost her suit.
Compared to you, she probably would have looked like a three-year-old trying to fill out a bikini.
GAGA

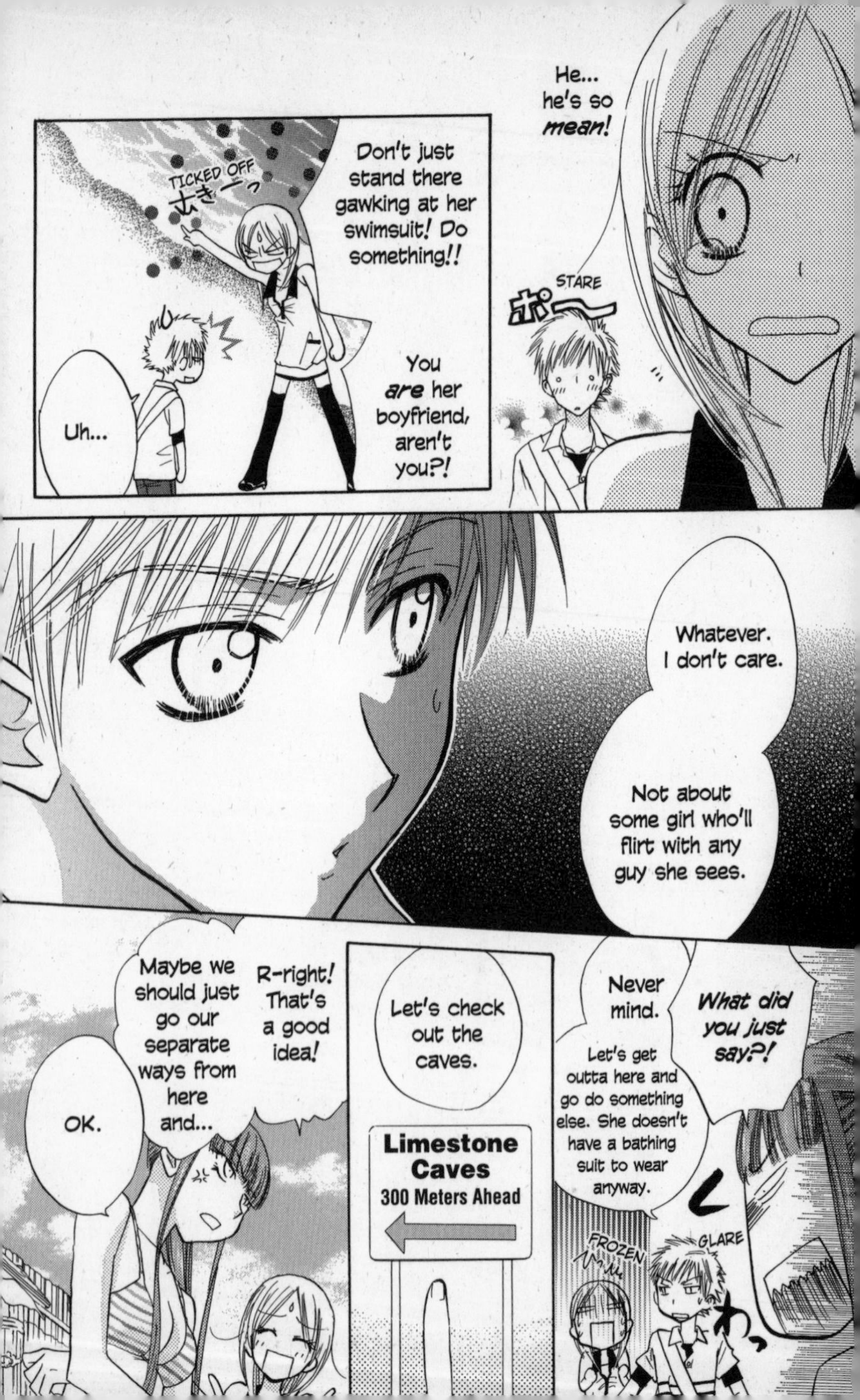
He... he's so *mean*!
STARE
Don't just stand there gawking at her swimsuit! Do something!!
TICKED OFF
You *are* her boyfriend, aren't you?!
Uh...
Whatever. I don't care.
Not about some girl who'll flirt with any guy she sees.
*What did you just say?!*
Never mind.
Let's get outta here and go do something else. She doesn't have a bathing suit to wear anyway.
GLARE
FROZEN
Let's check out the caves.
Limestone Caves
300 Meters Ahead
R-right! That's a good idea!
Maybe we should just go our separate ways from here and...
OK.

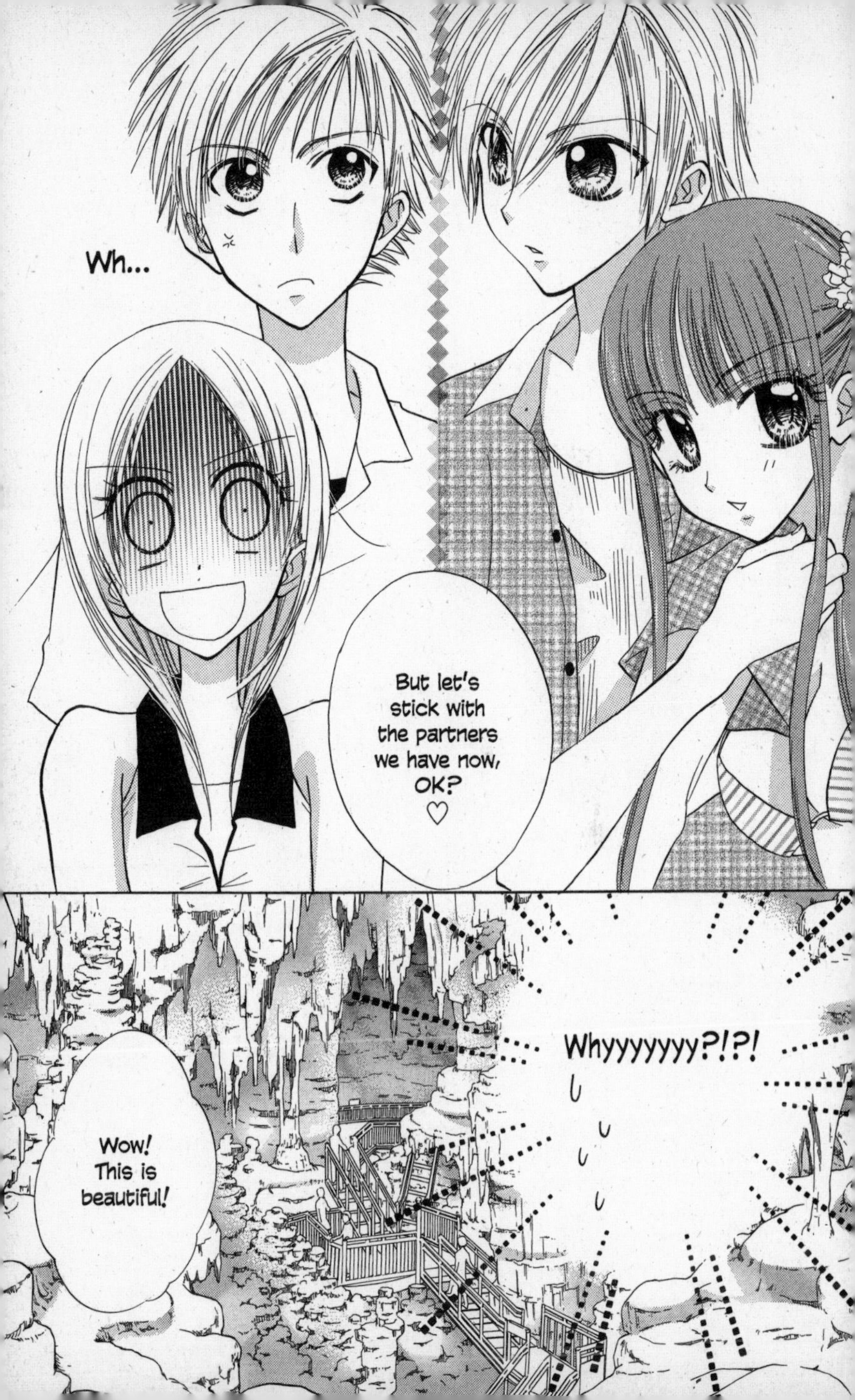
But let's stick with the partners we have now, OK? ♡
Wh...
Whyyyyyyy?!?!
Wow! This is beautiful!

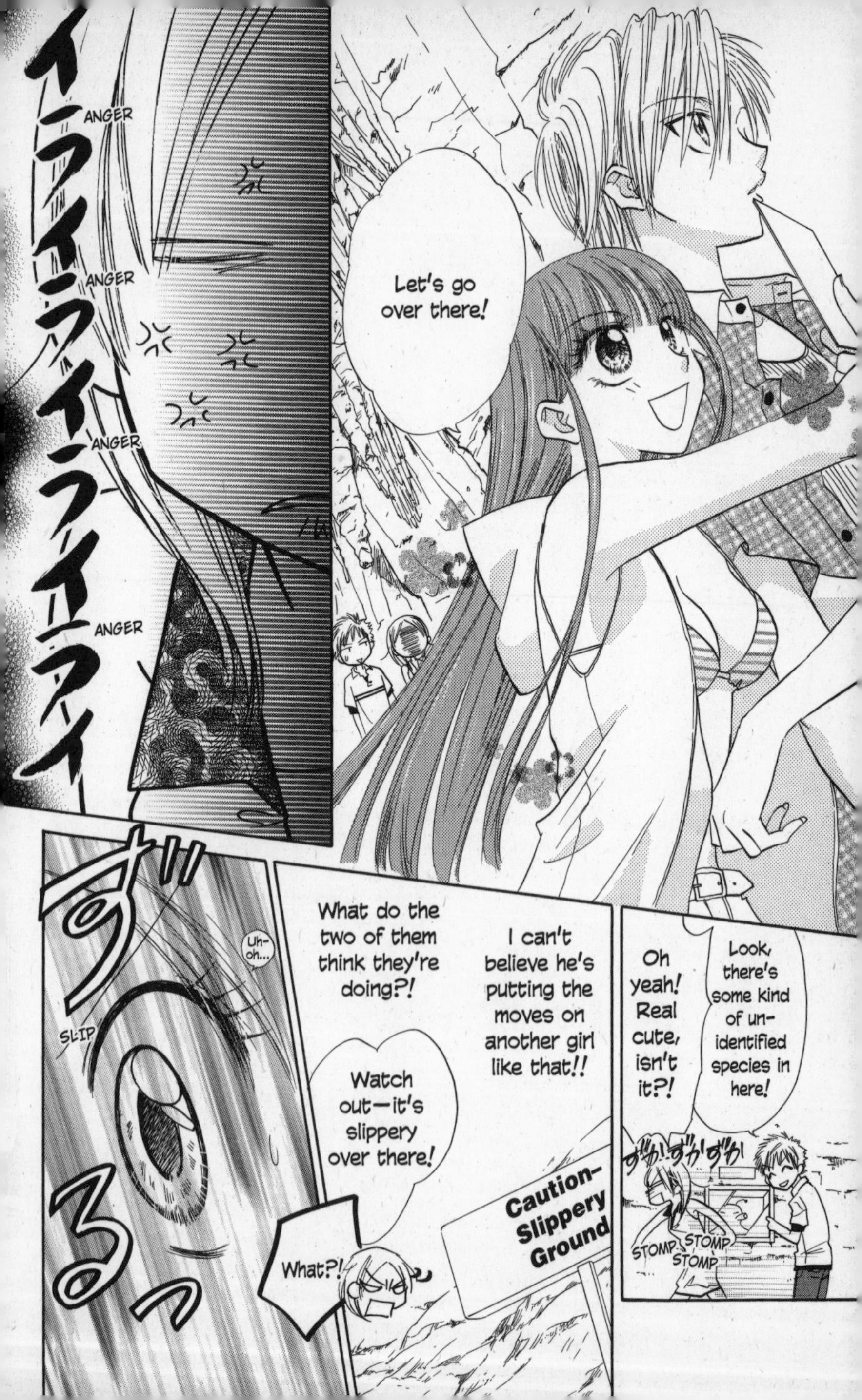
Let's go over there!
ANGER
ANGER
ANGER
ANGER
Look, there's some kind of un-identified species in here!
Oh yeah! Real cute, isn't it?!
STOMP STOMP STOMP
I can't believe he's putting the moves on another girl like that!!
What do the two of them think they're doing?!
Caution-Slippery Ground
Watch out—it's slippery over there!
What?!
Uh-oh...
SLIP

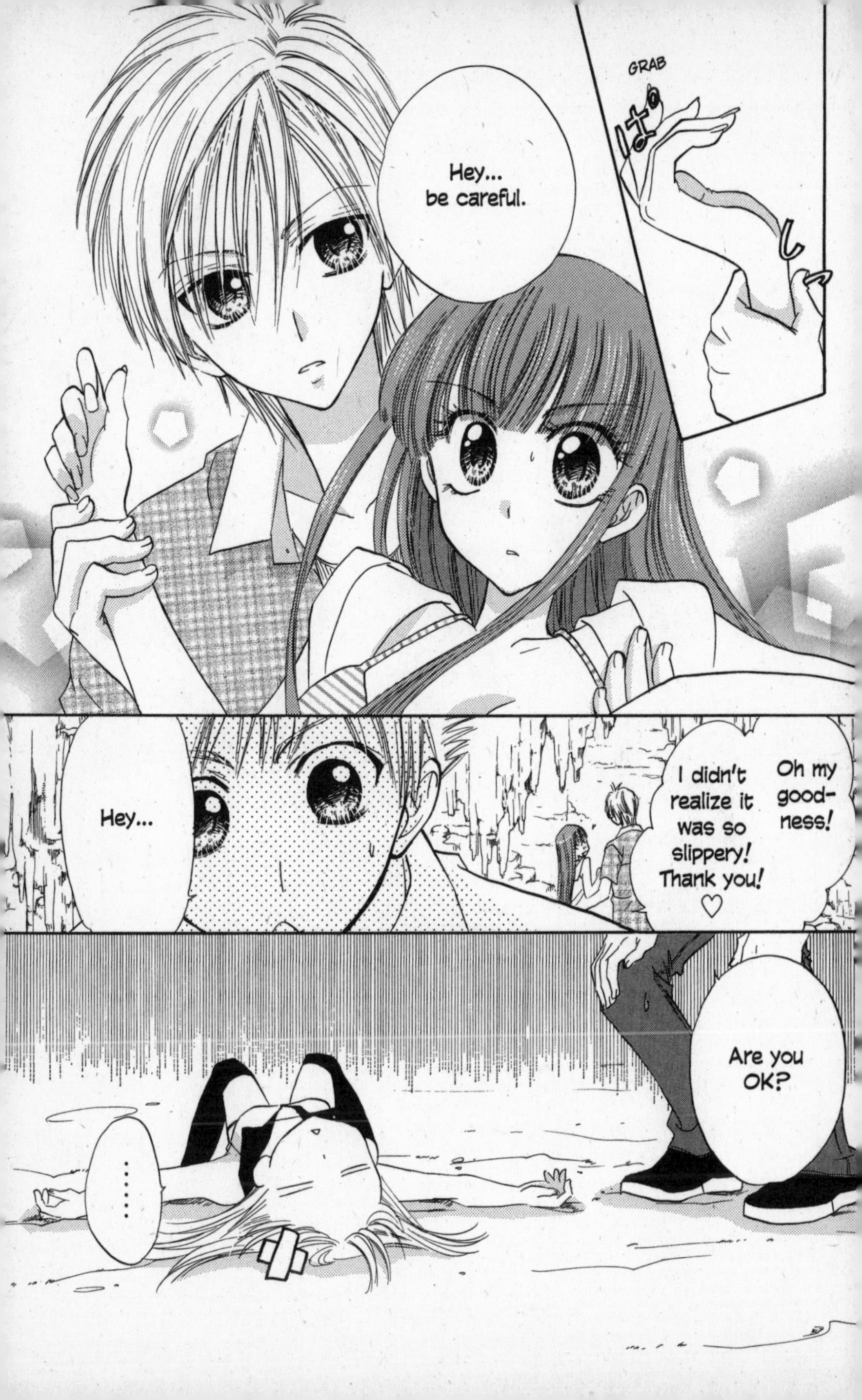
GRAB
Hey... be careful.
Oh my goodness!
I didn't realize it was so slippery! Thank you! ♡
Hey...
Are you OK?
......

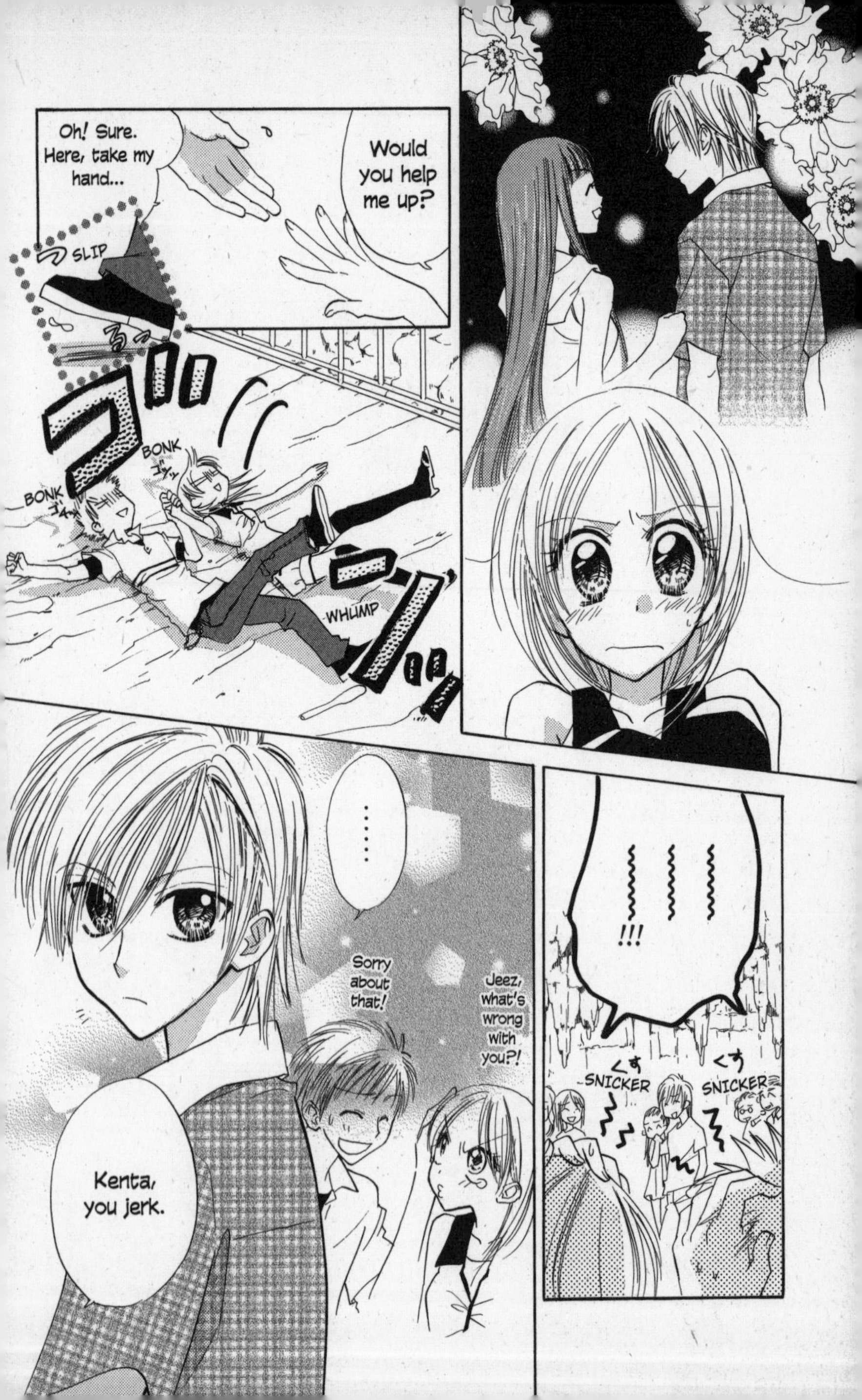
Would you help me up?
Oh! Sure. Here, take my hand...
SLIP
BONK
BONK
WHUMP
!!!
くす SNICKER
くす SNICKER
......
Jeez, what's wrong with you?!
Sorry about that!
Kenta, you jerk.

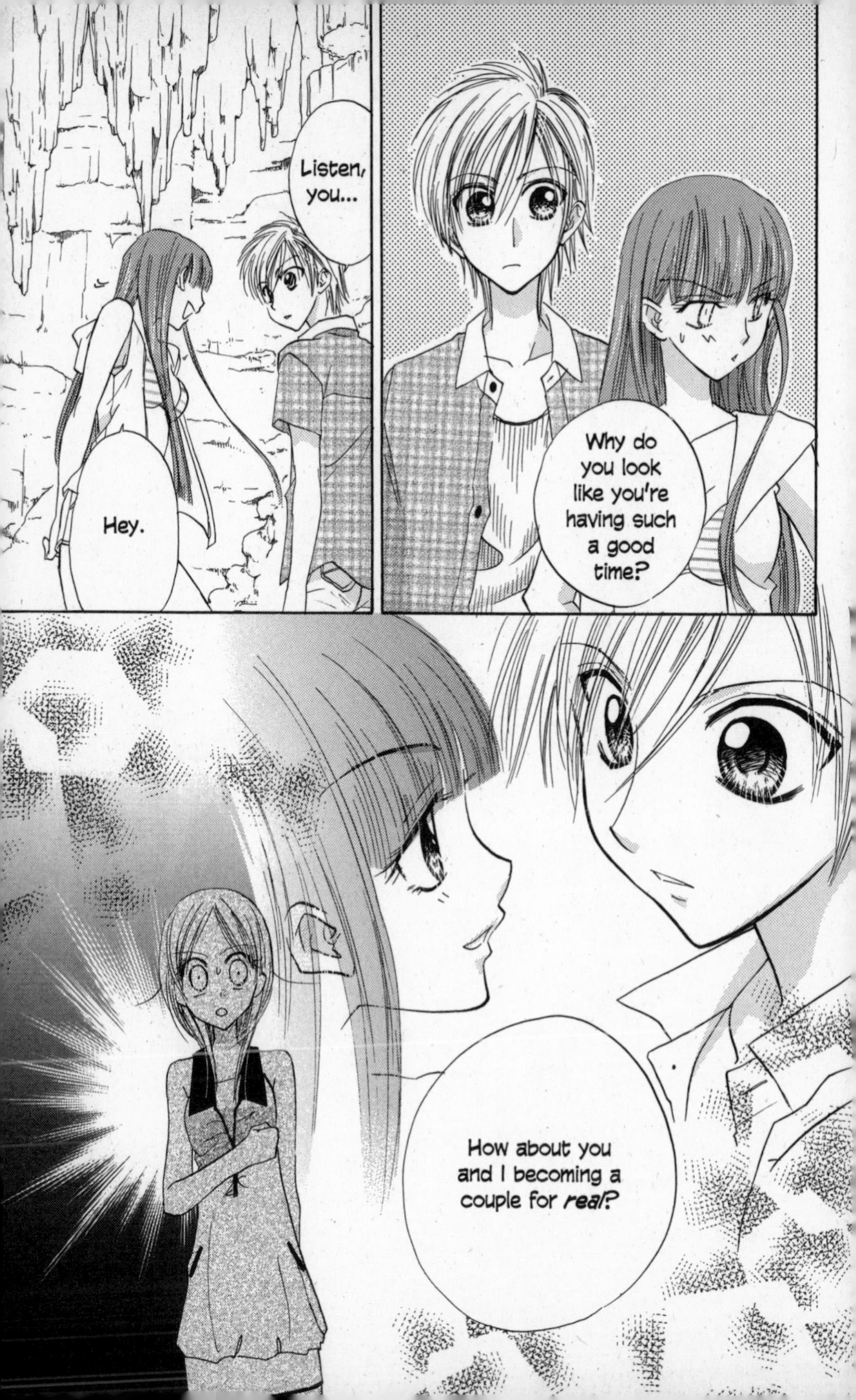
Why do you look like you're having such a good time?
Listen, you...
Hey.
How about you and I becoming a couple for *real*?

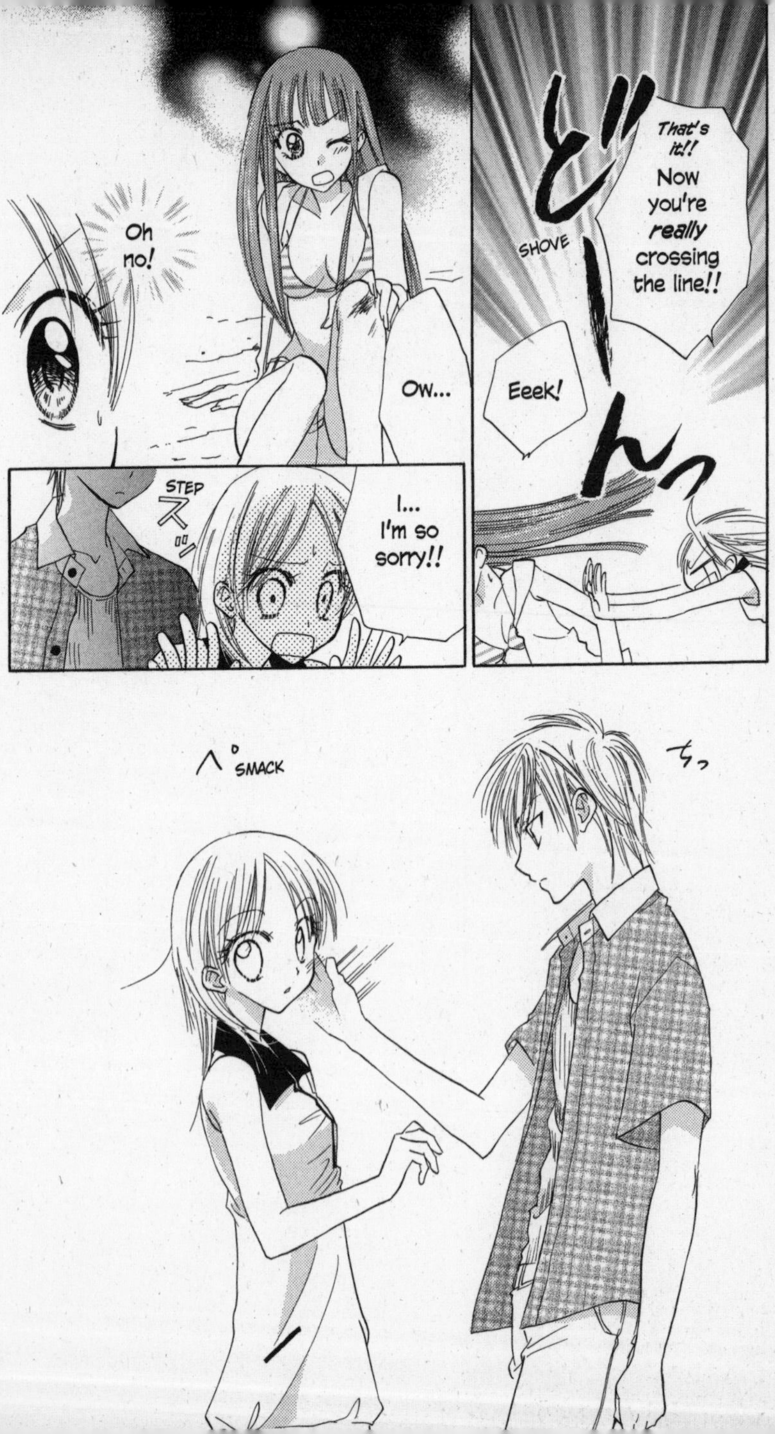
That's it!! Now you're really crossing the line!!
SHOVE
どーんっ
Eeek!
Oh no!
Ow...
STEP
スッ
I... I'm so sorry!!
ちっ
ペ
SMACK

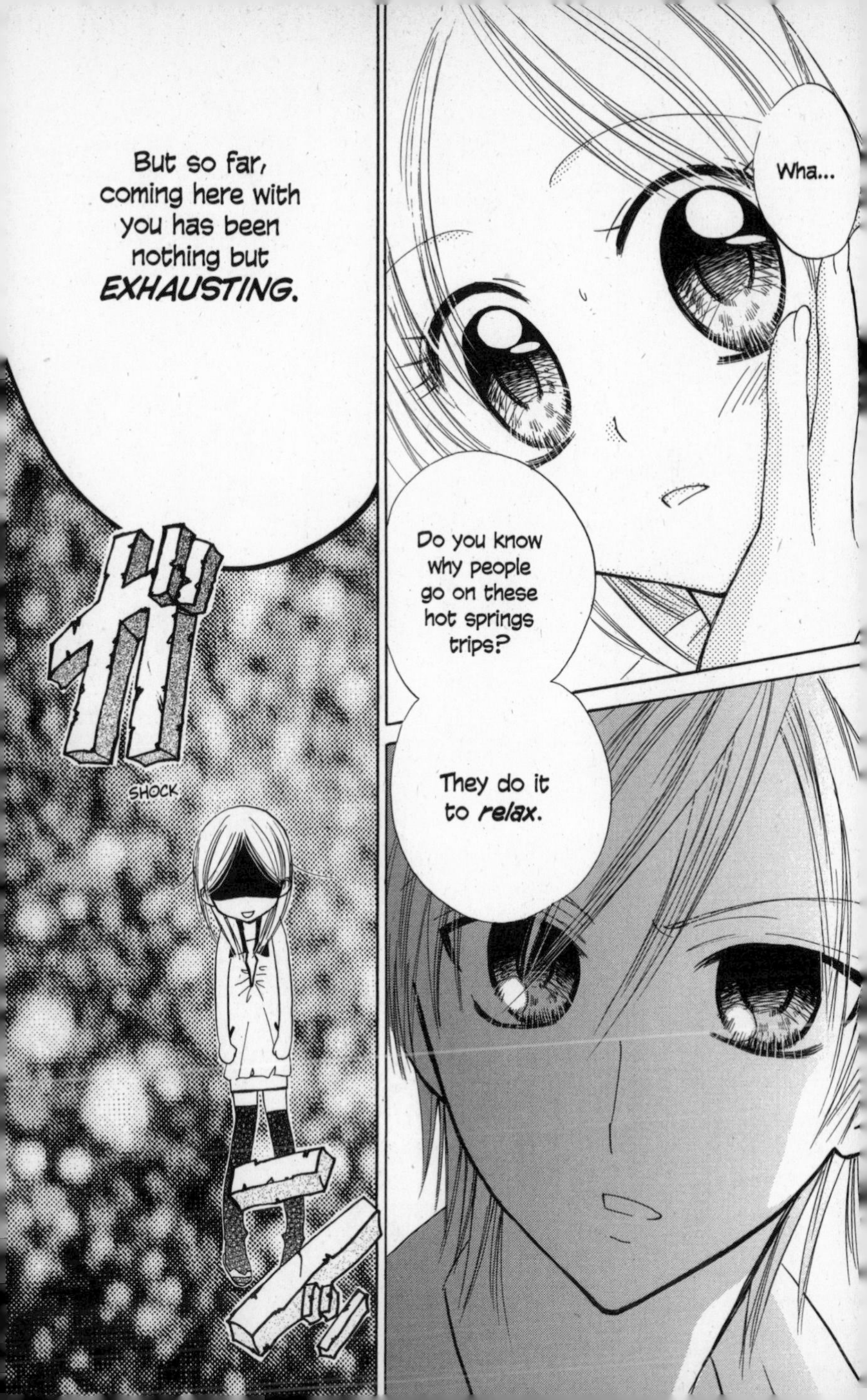
Wha...
Do you know why people go on these hot springs trips?
They do it to *relax*.
But so far, coming here with you has been nothing but ***EXHAUSTING.***
SHOCK

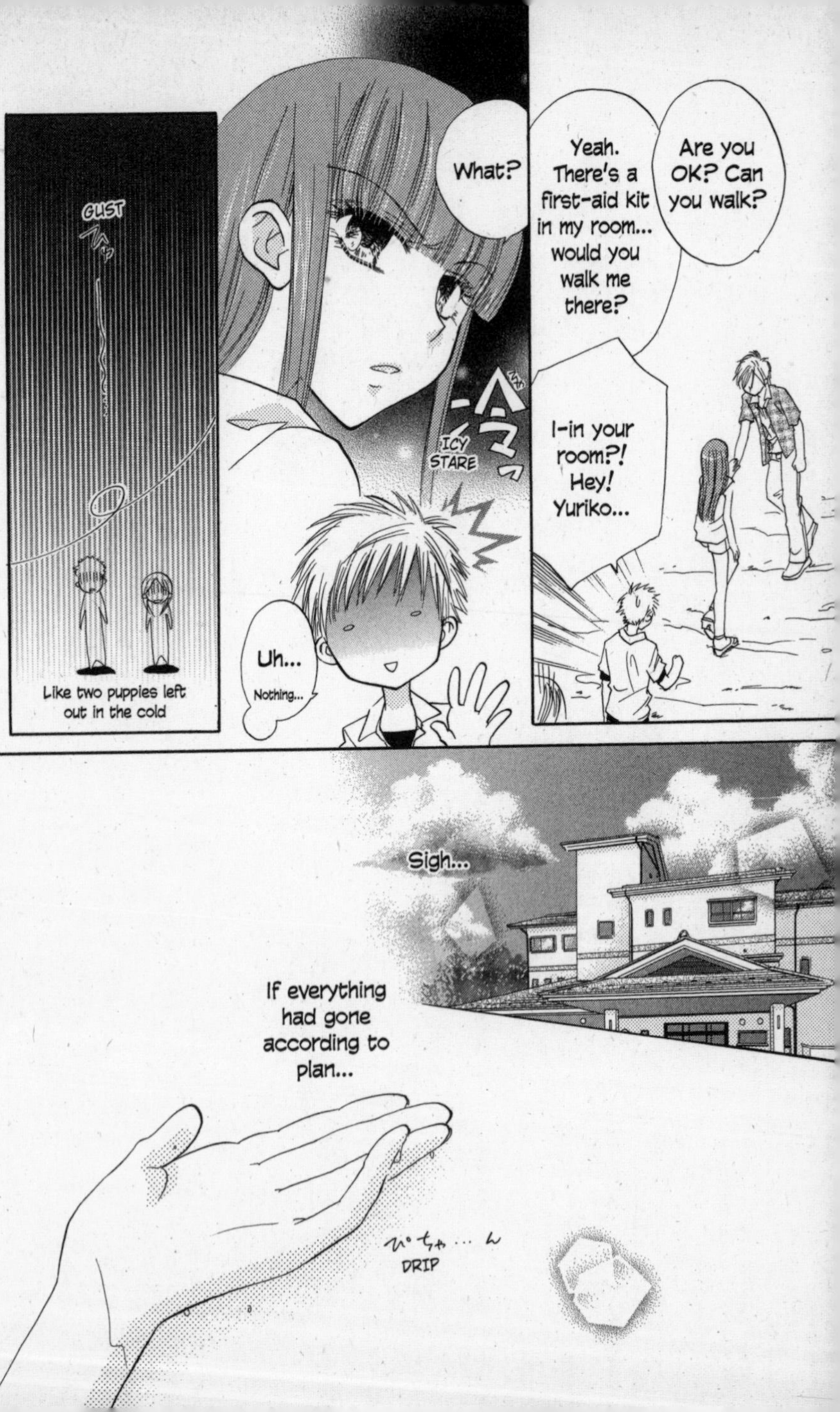
Are you OK? Can you walk?
Yeah. There's a first-aid kit in my room... would you walk me there?
I-in your room?! Hey! Yuriko...
What?
ICY STARE
Uh...
Nothing...
GUST
Like two puppies left out in the cold
Sigh...
If everything had gone according to plan...
DRIP

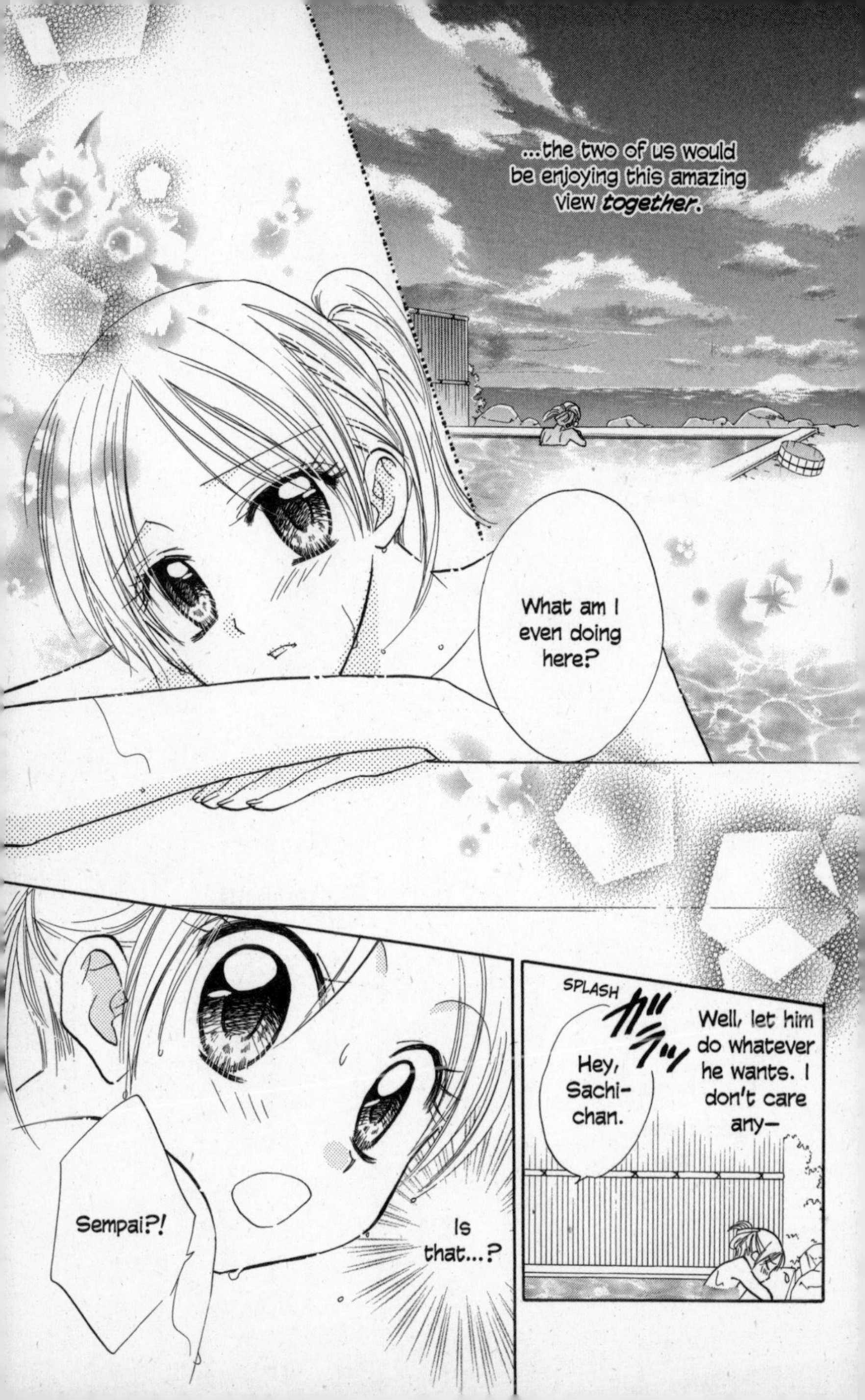
...the two of us would be enjoying this amazing view *together*.
What am I even doing here?
Well, let him do whatever he wants. I don't care any—
SPLASH
Hey, Sachi-chan.
Is that...?
Sempai?!

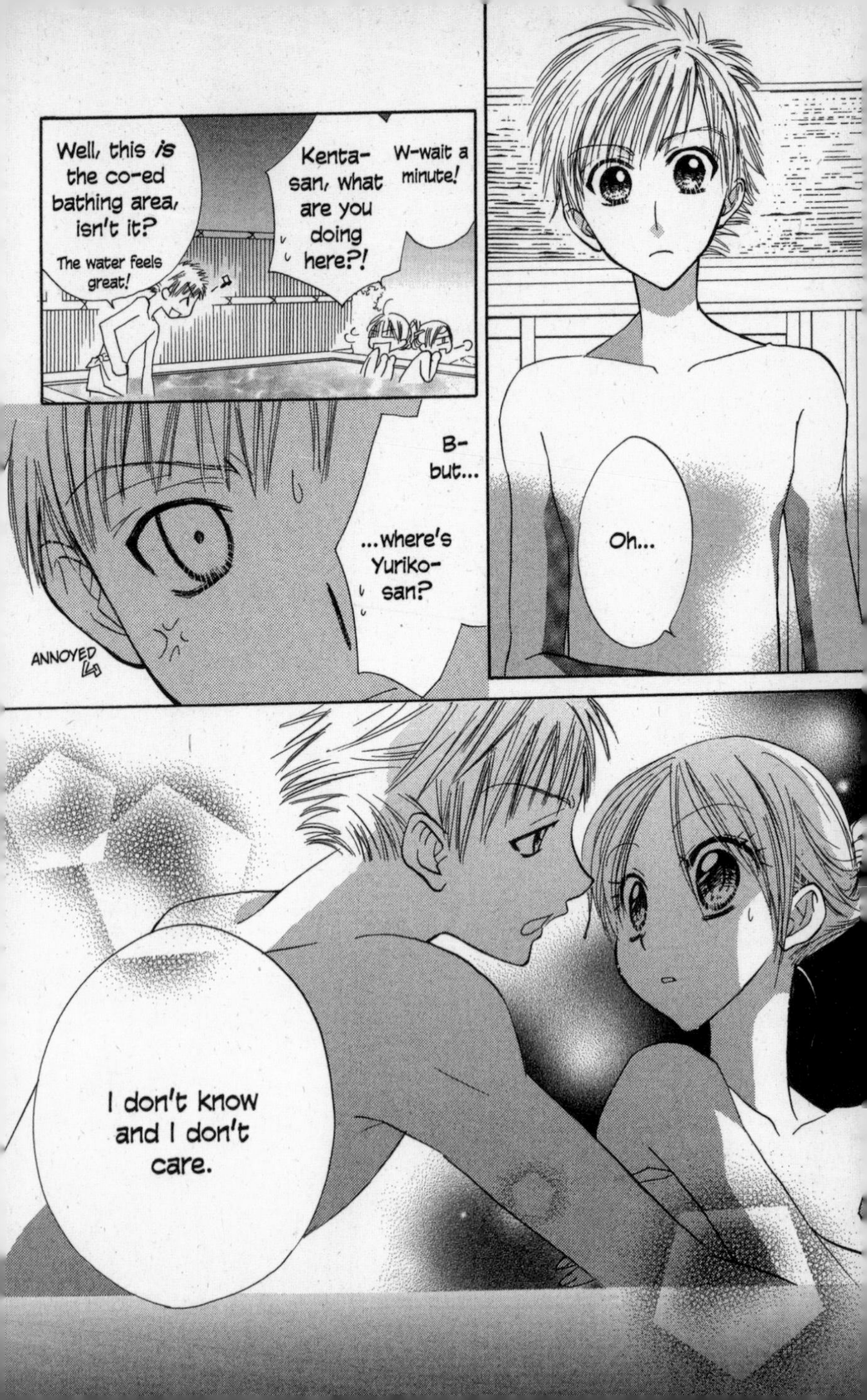
Oh...
W-wait a minute!
Kenta-san, what are you doing here?!
Well, this *is* the co-ed bathing area, isn't it?
The water feels great!
B-but...
...where's Yuriko-san?
ANNOYED
I don't know and I don't care.

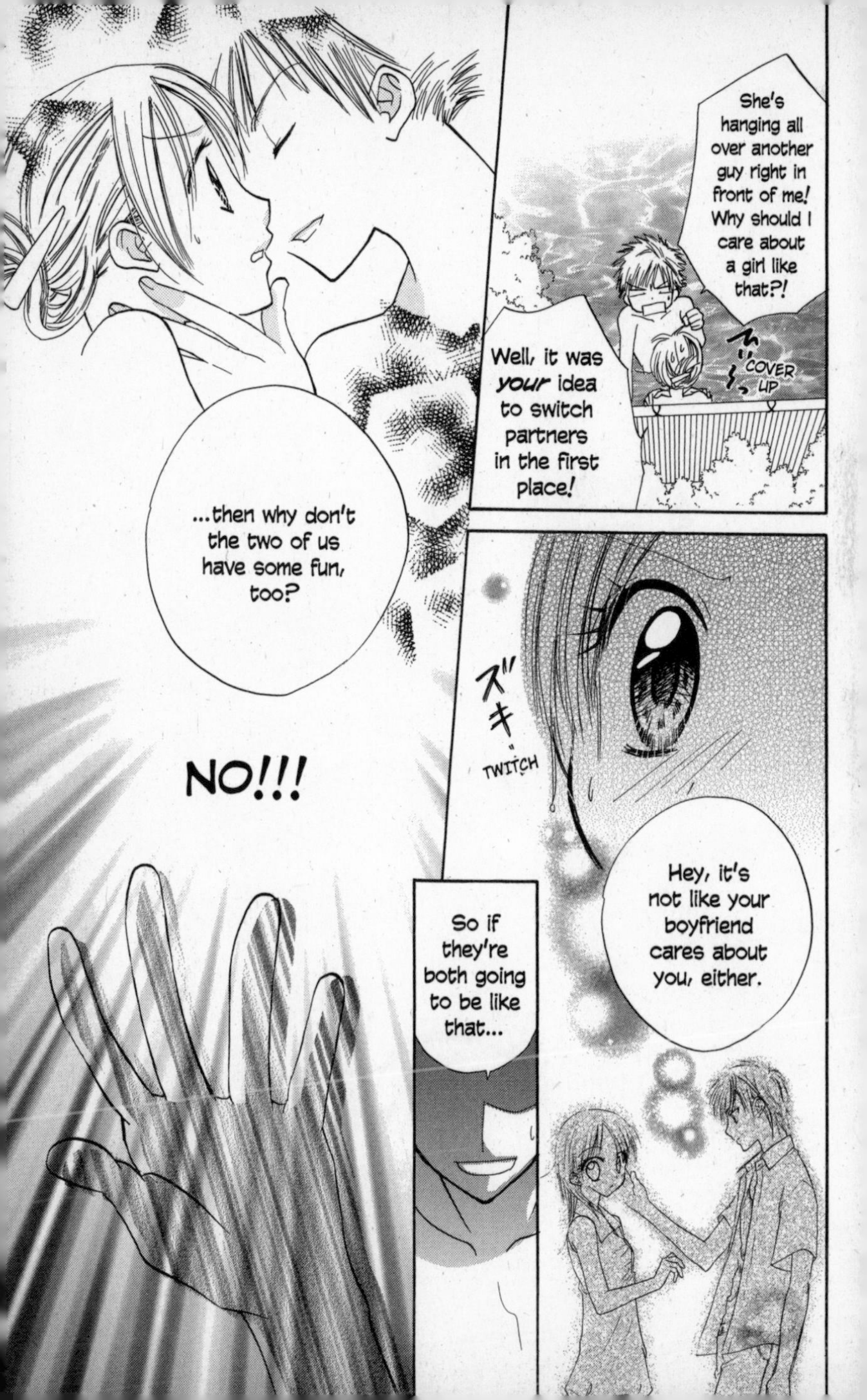

She's hanging all over another guy right in front of me! Why should I care about a girl like that?!
COVER UP
Well, it was *your* idea to switch partners in the first place!
TWITCH
Hey, it's not like your boyfriend cares about you, either.
So if they're both going to be like that...
...then why don't the two of us have some fun, too?
NO!!!

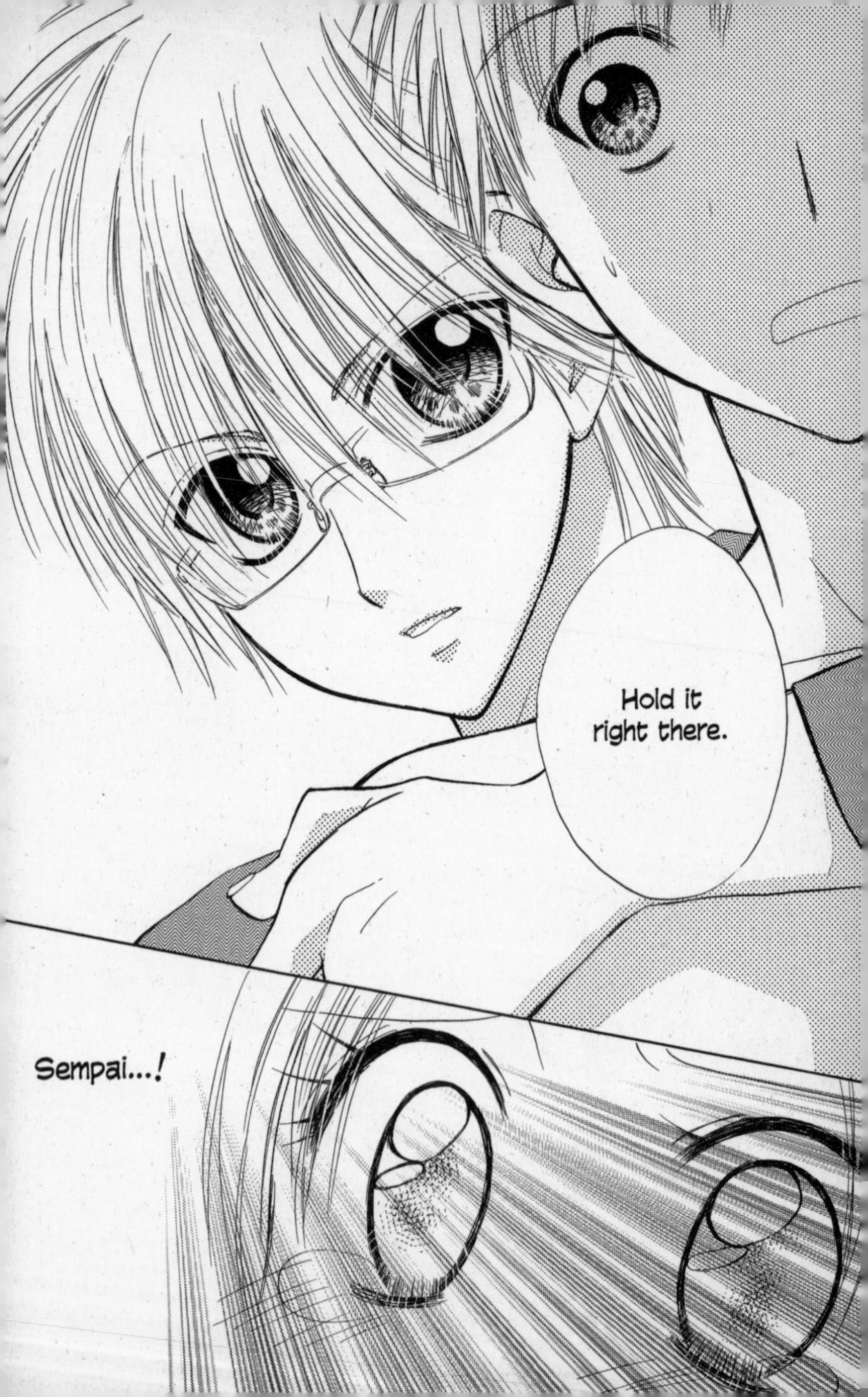
Hold it right there.
Sempai...!

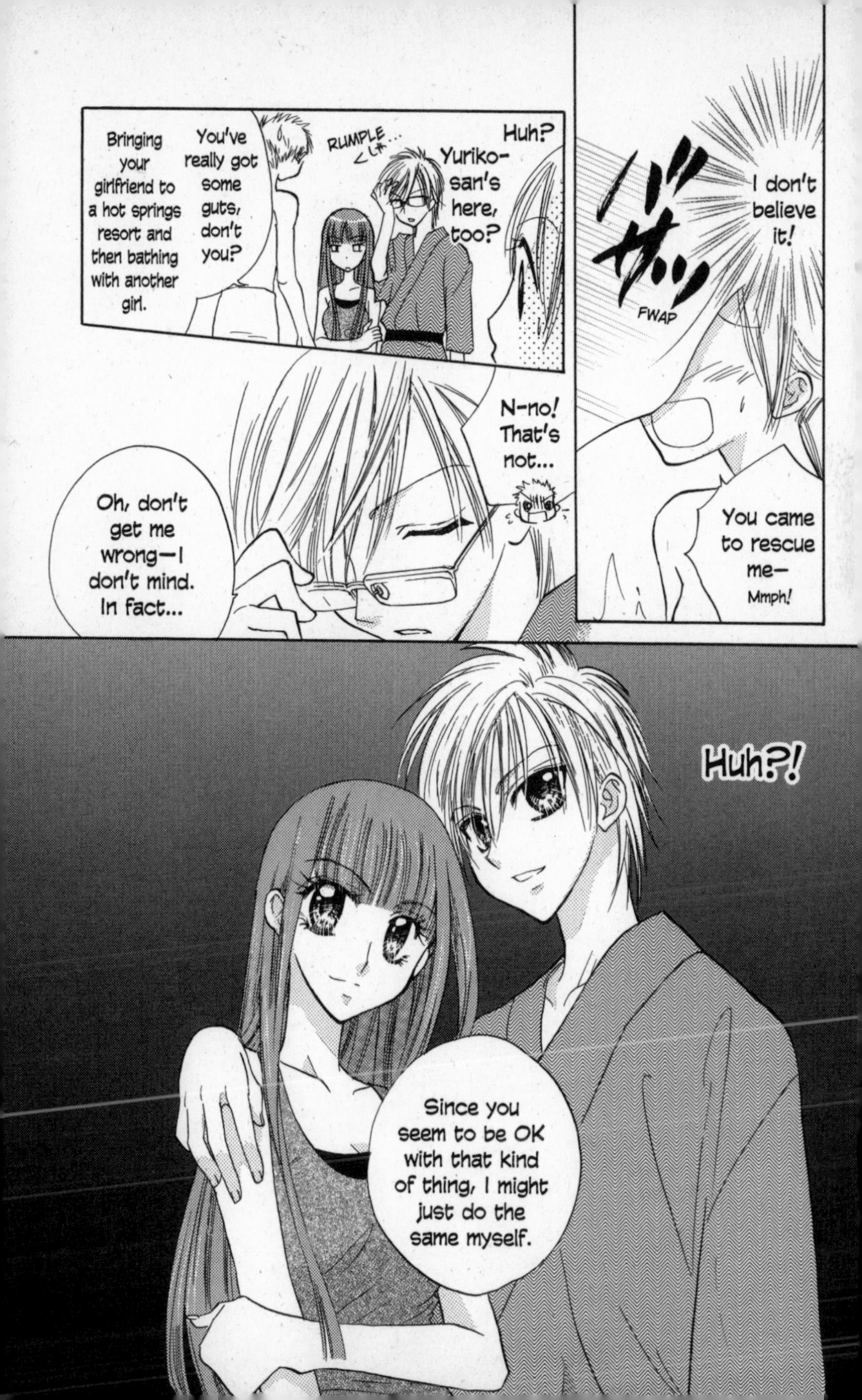

I don't believe it!
バサッ
FWAP
You came to rescue me—
Mmph!
Huh? Yuriko-san's here, too?
RUMPLE
くしゃ
You've really got some guts, don't you?
Bringing your girlfriend to a hot springs resort and then bathing with another girl.
N-no! That's not...
Oh, don't get me wrong—I don't mind. In fact...
Huh?!
Since you seem to be OK with that kind of thing, I might just do the same myself.

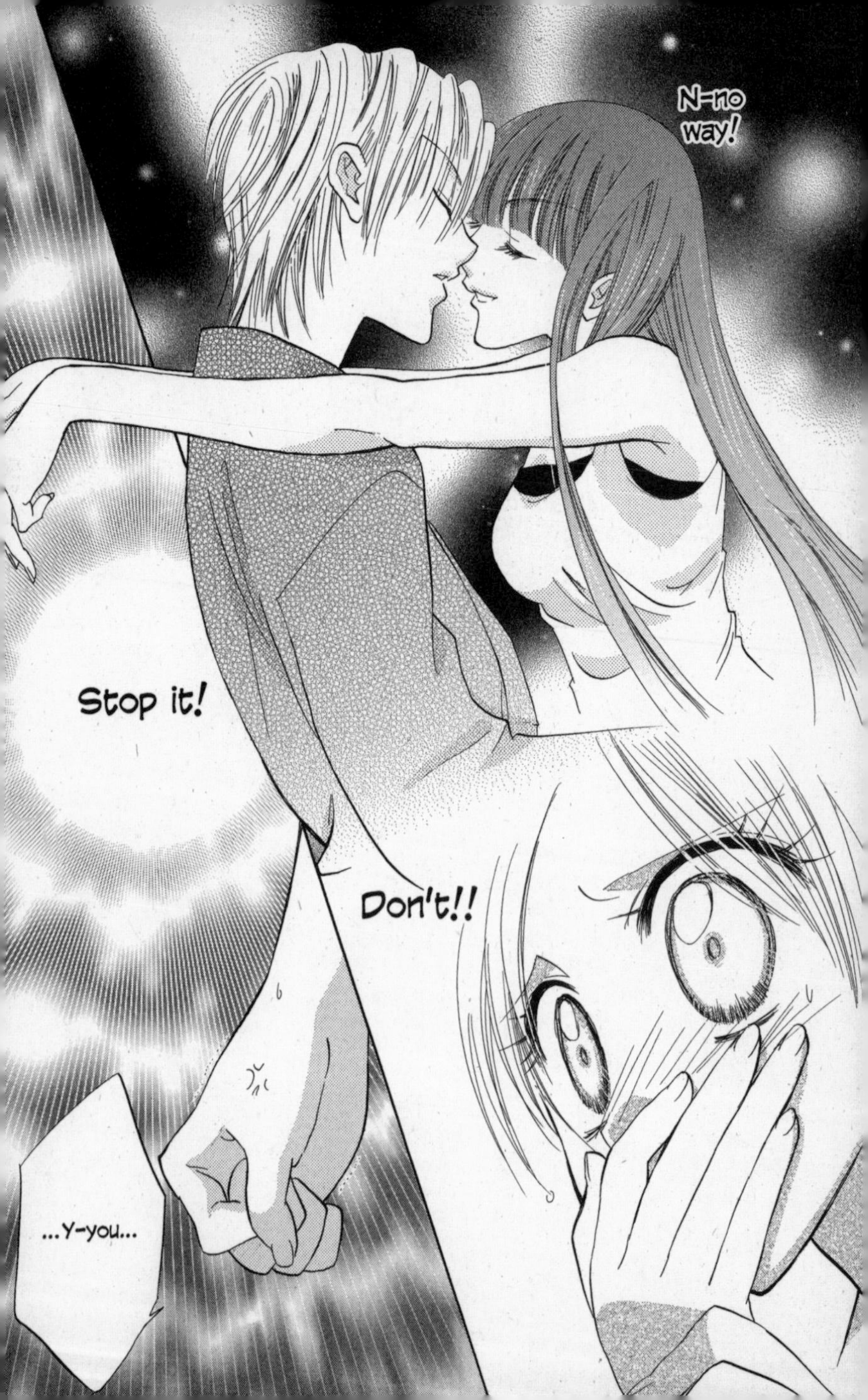
N-no way!
Stop it!
Don't!!
...Y-you...

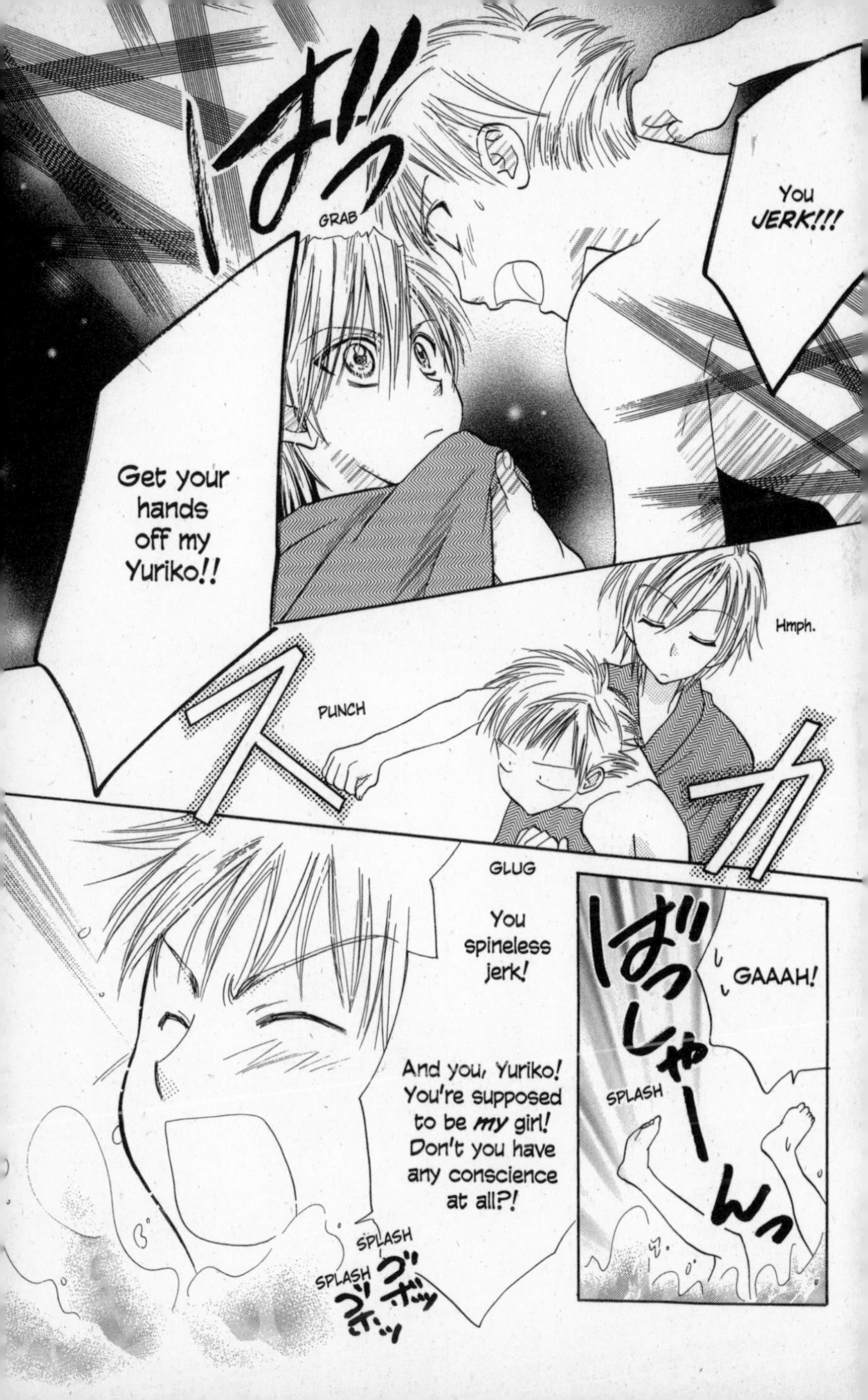
You JERK!!!
ぱっ
GRAB
Get your hands off my Yuriko!!
Hmph.
スカ
PUNCH
ばっしゃーんっ
SPLASH
GAAAH!
GLUG
You spineless jerk!
And you, Yuriko! You're supposed to be *my* girl! Don't you have any conscience at all?!
ごぽっ
SPLASH
ごぽっ
SPLASH

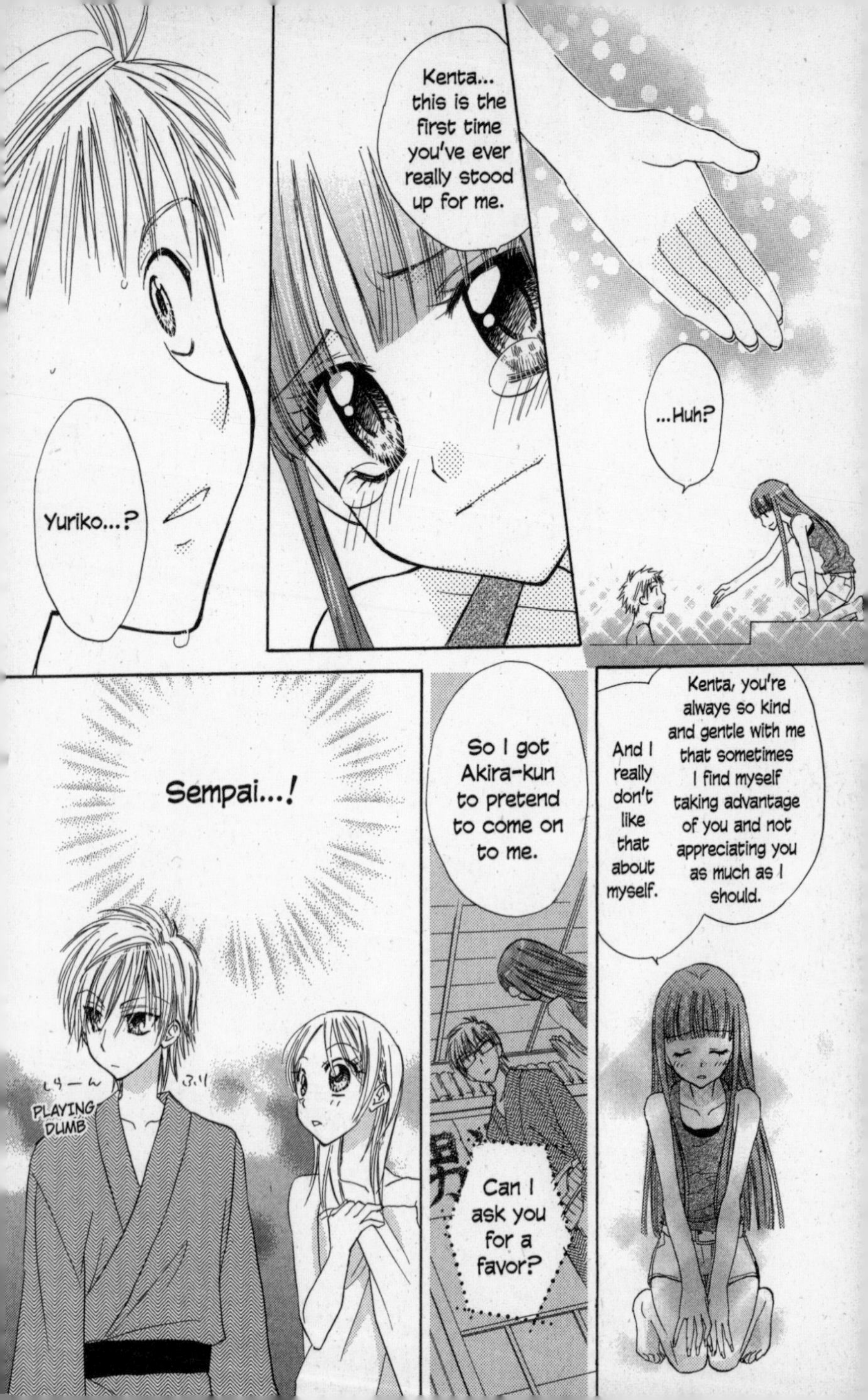

...Huh?
Kenta... this is the first time you've ever really stood up for me.
Yuriko...?
Kenta, you're always so kind and gentle with me that sometimes I find myself taking advantage of you and not appreciating you as much as I should.
And I really don't like that about myself.
So I got Akira-kun to pretend to come on to me.
Can I ask you for a favor?
Sempai...!
PLAYING DUMB

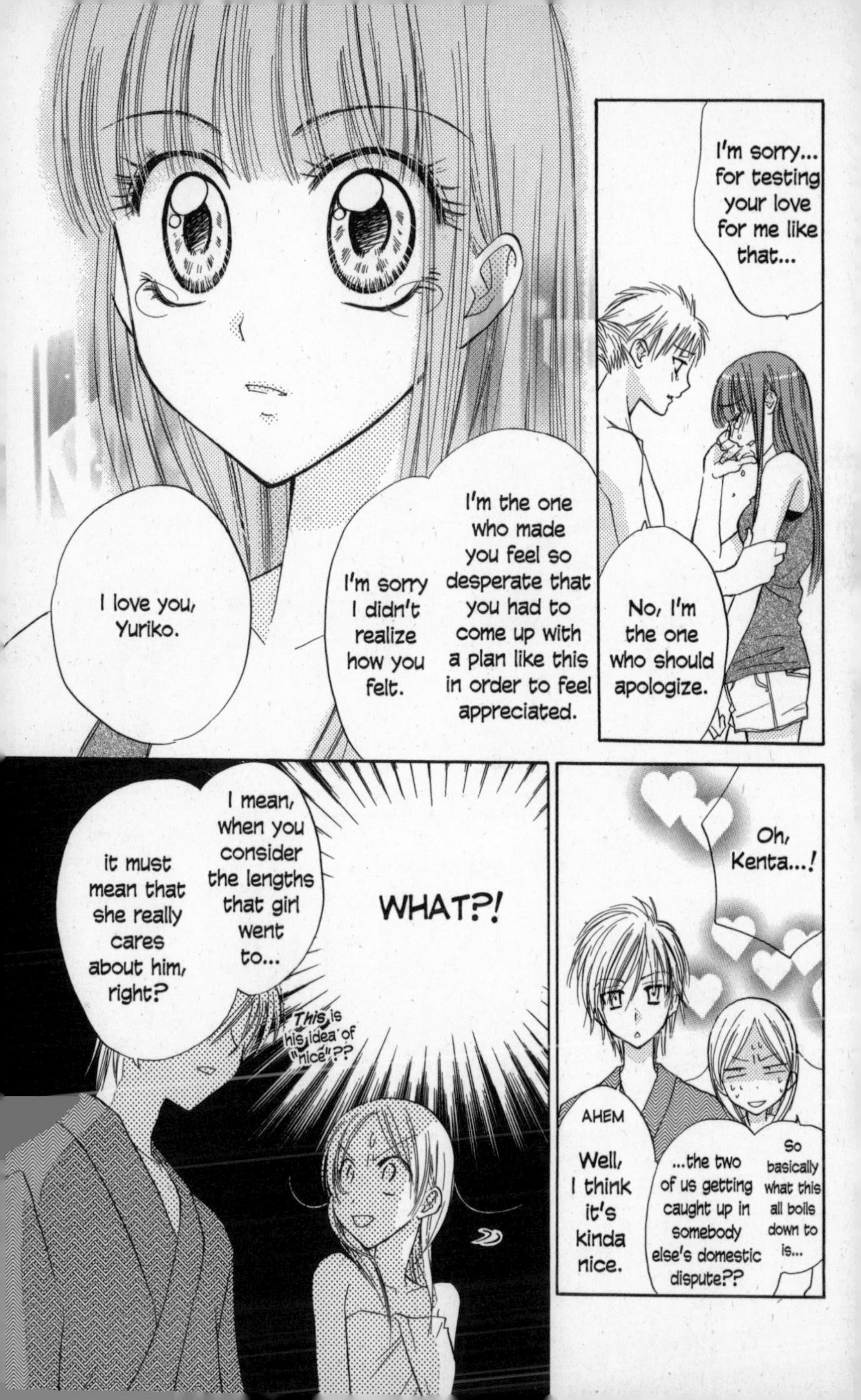

I'm sorry... for testing your love for me like that...
No, I'm the one who should apologize.
I'm the one who made you feel so desperate that you had to come up with a plan like this in order to feel appreciated.
I'm sorry I didn't realize how you felt.
I love you, Yuriko.
Oh, Kenta...!
So basically what this all boils down to is...
...the two of us getting caught up in somebody else's domestic dispute??
AHEM
Well, I think it's kinda nice.
WHAT?!
I mean, when you consider the lengths that girl went to...
it must mean that she really cares about him, right?
This is his idea of "nice"??

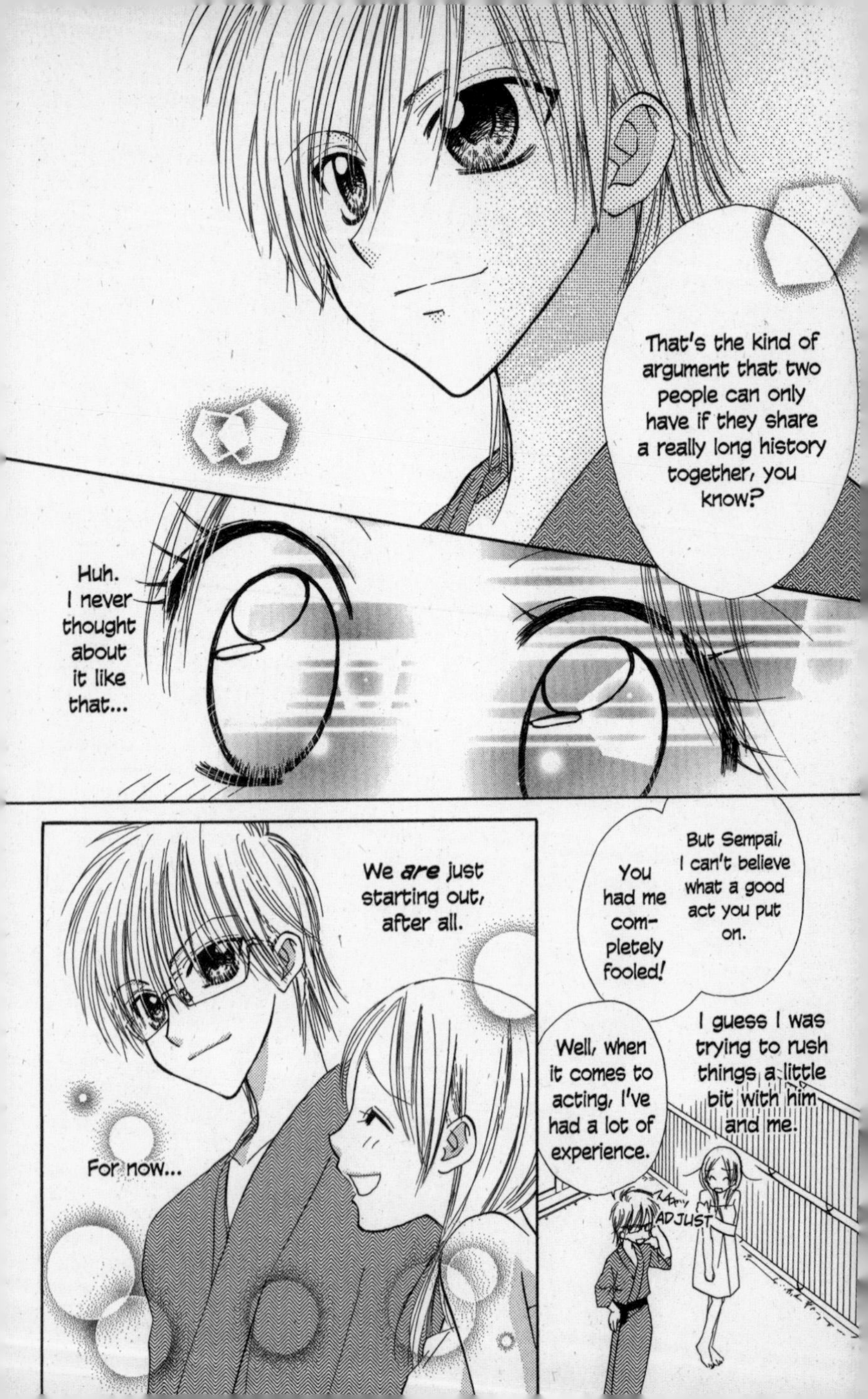
That's the kind of argument that two people can only have if they share a really long history together, you know?
Huh. I never thought about it like that...
But Sempai, I can't believe what a good act you put on.
You had me completely fooled!
I guess I was trying to rush things a little bit with him and me.
Well, when it comes to acting, I've had a lot of experience.
ADJUST
We *are* just starting out, after all.
For now...

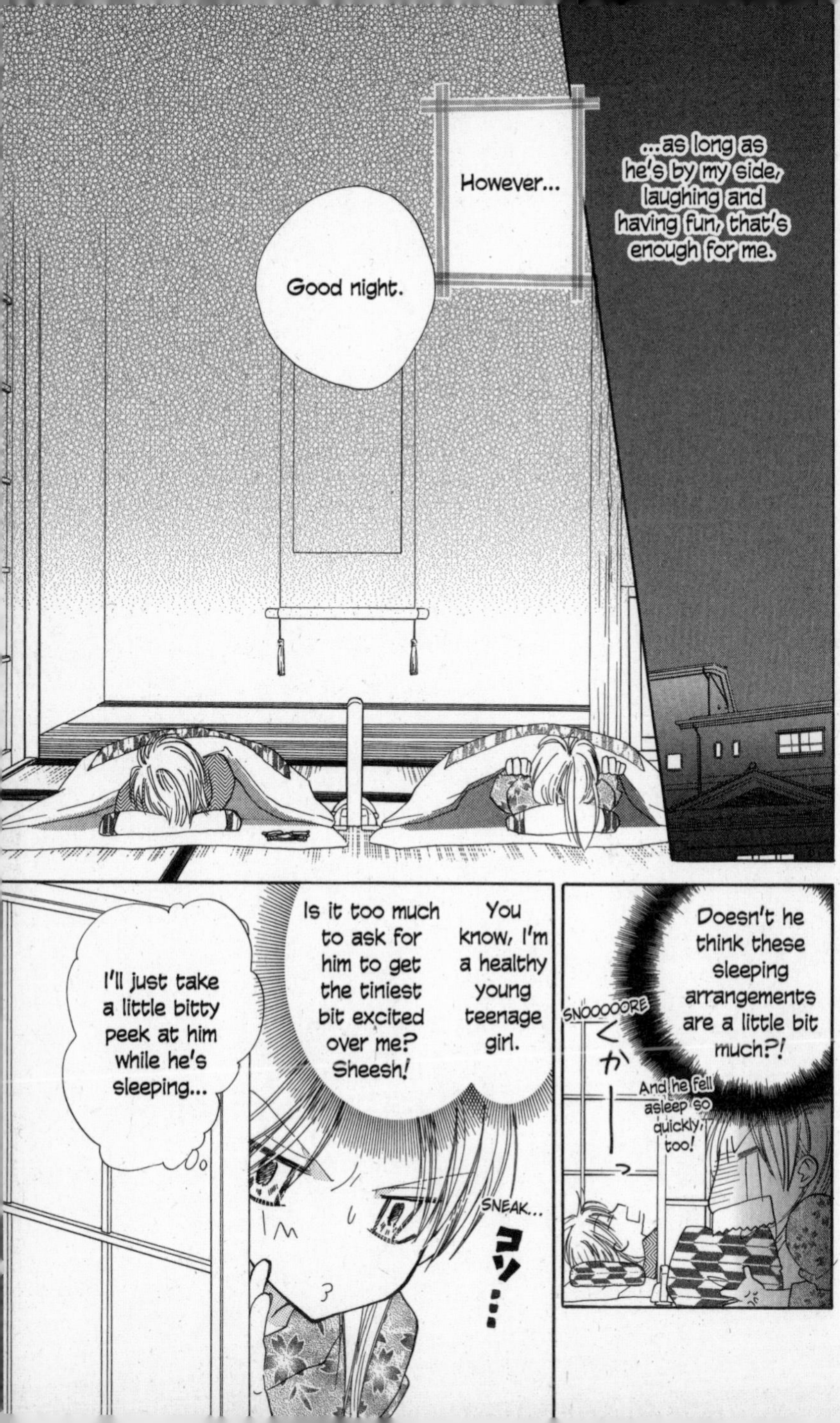
However...
...as long as he's by my side, laughing and having fun, that's enough for me.
Good night.
Doesn't he think these sleeping arrangements are a little bit much?!
SNOOOOORE
And he fell asleep so quickly, too!
You know, I'm a healthy young teenage girl.
Is it too much to ask for him to get the tiniest bit excited over me? Sheesh!
I'll just take a little bitty peek at him while he's sleeping...
SNEAK...

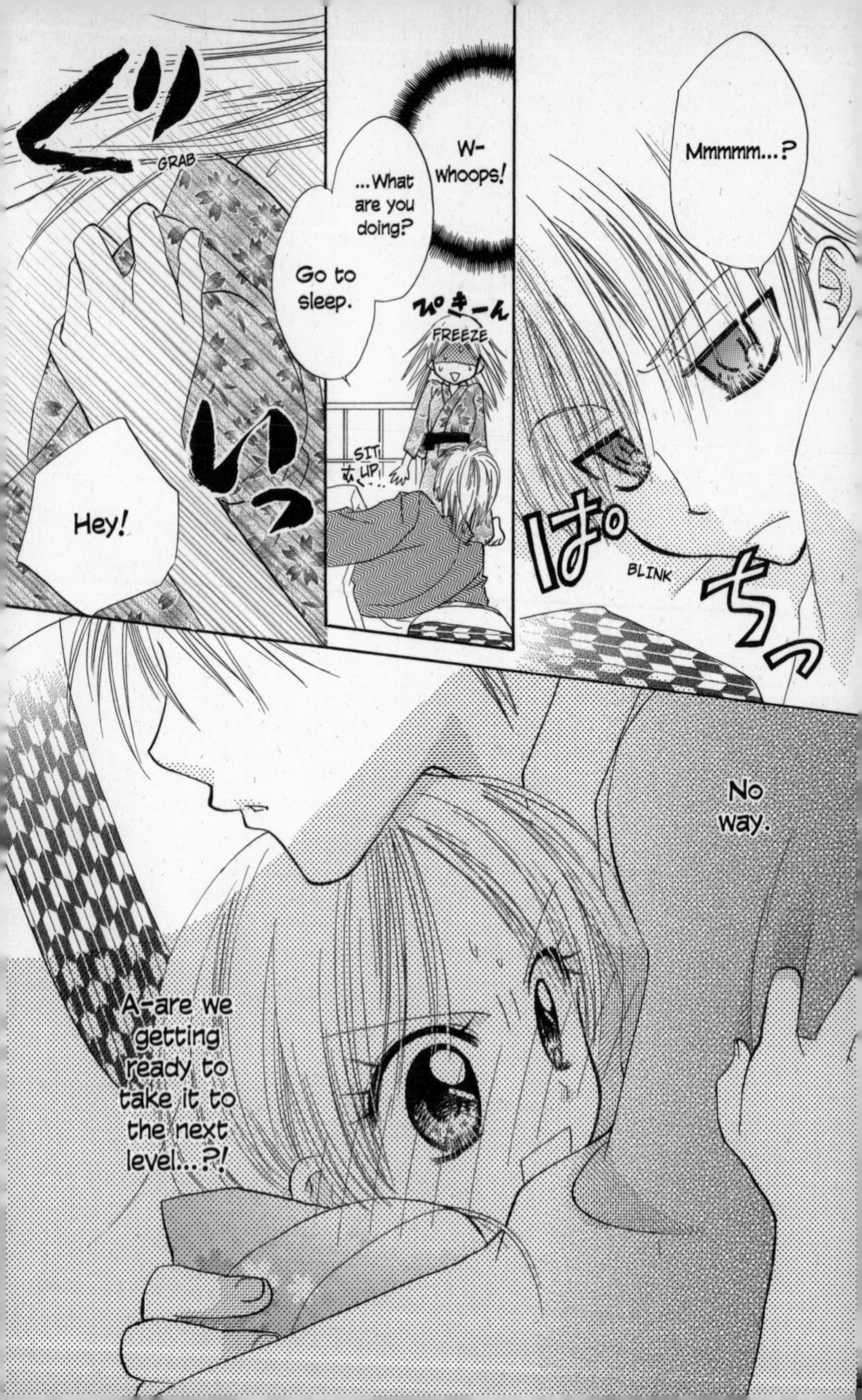
Mmmmm...?
はっ
BLINK
W-whoops!
...What are you doing?
Go to sleep.
ぴきーん
FREEZE
SIT UP
GRAB
Hey!
No way.
A-are we getting ready to take it to the next level...?!

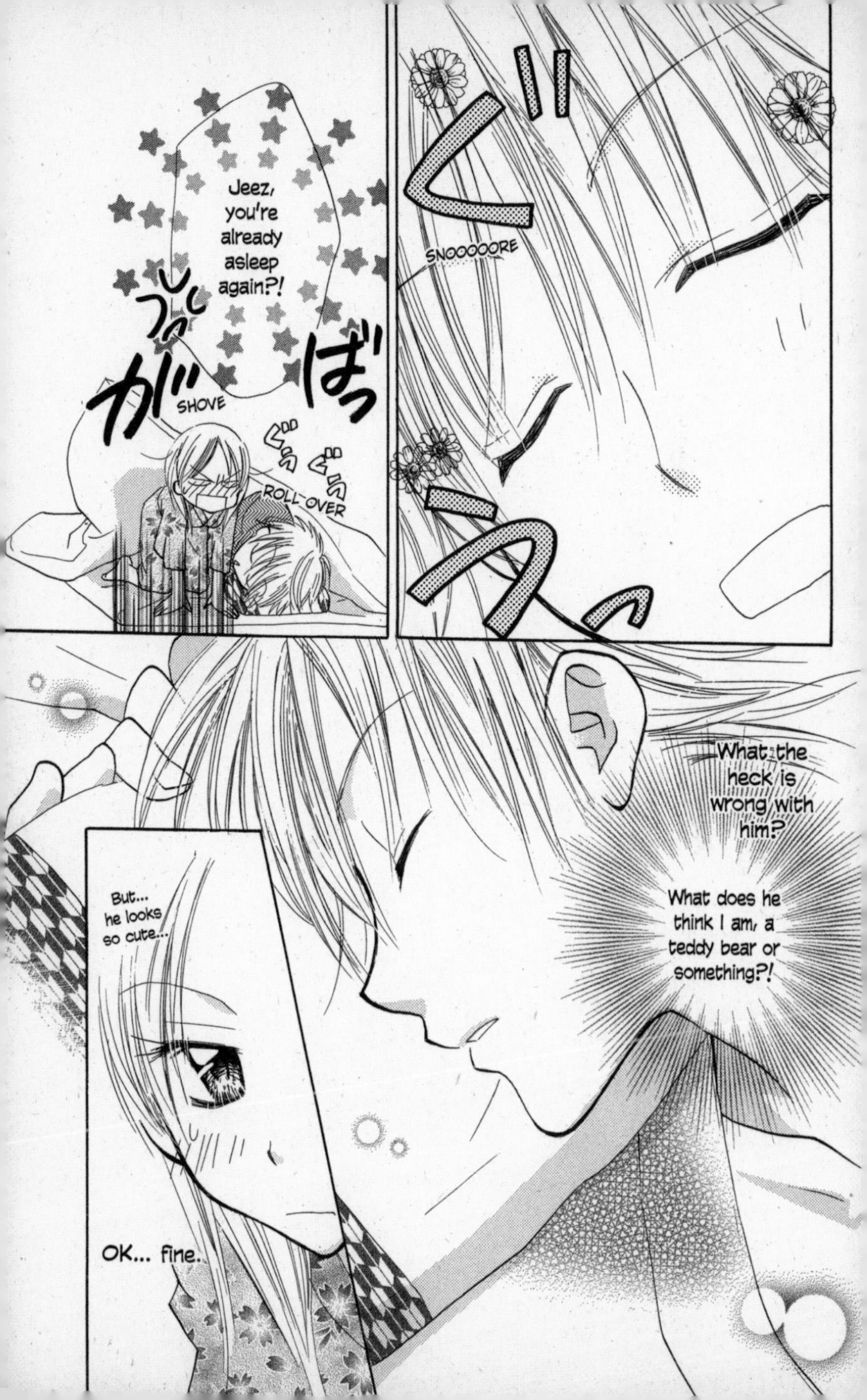
SNOOOOORE
Jeez, you're already asleep again?!
SHOVE
ROLL-OVER
What the heck is wrong with him?
What does he think I am, a teddy bear or something?!
But... he looks so cute...
OK... fine.

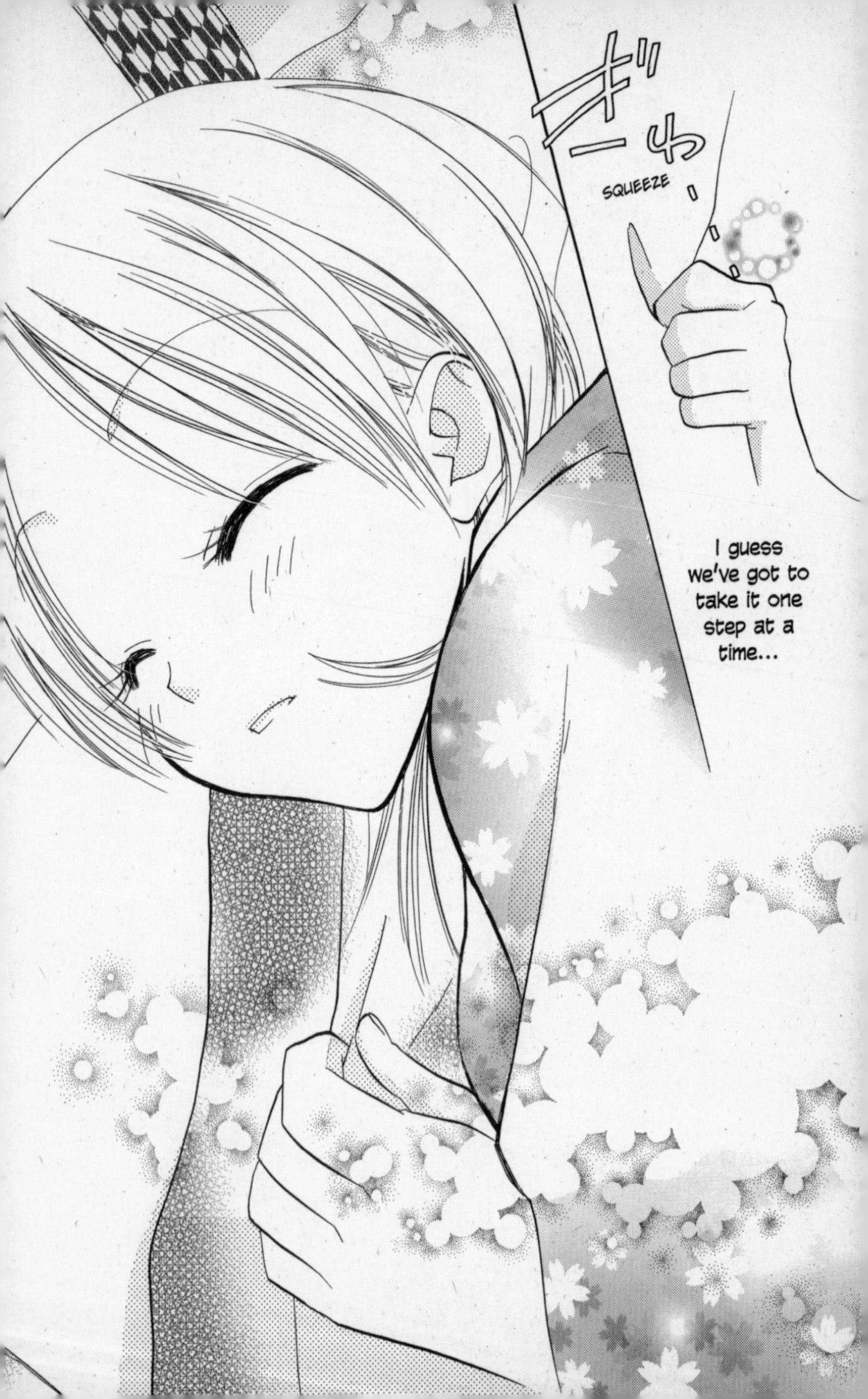
ぎゅ
SQUEEZE
I guess we've got to take it one step at a time...

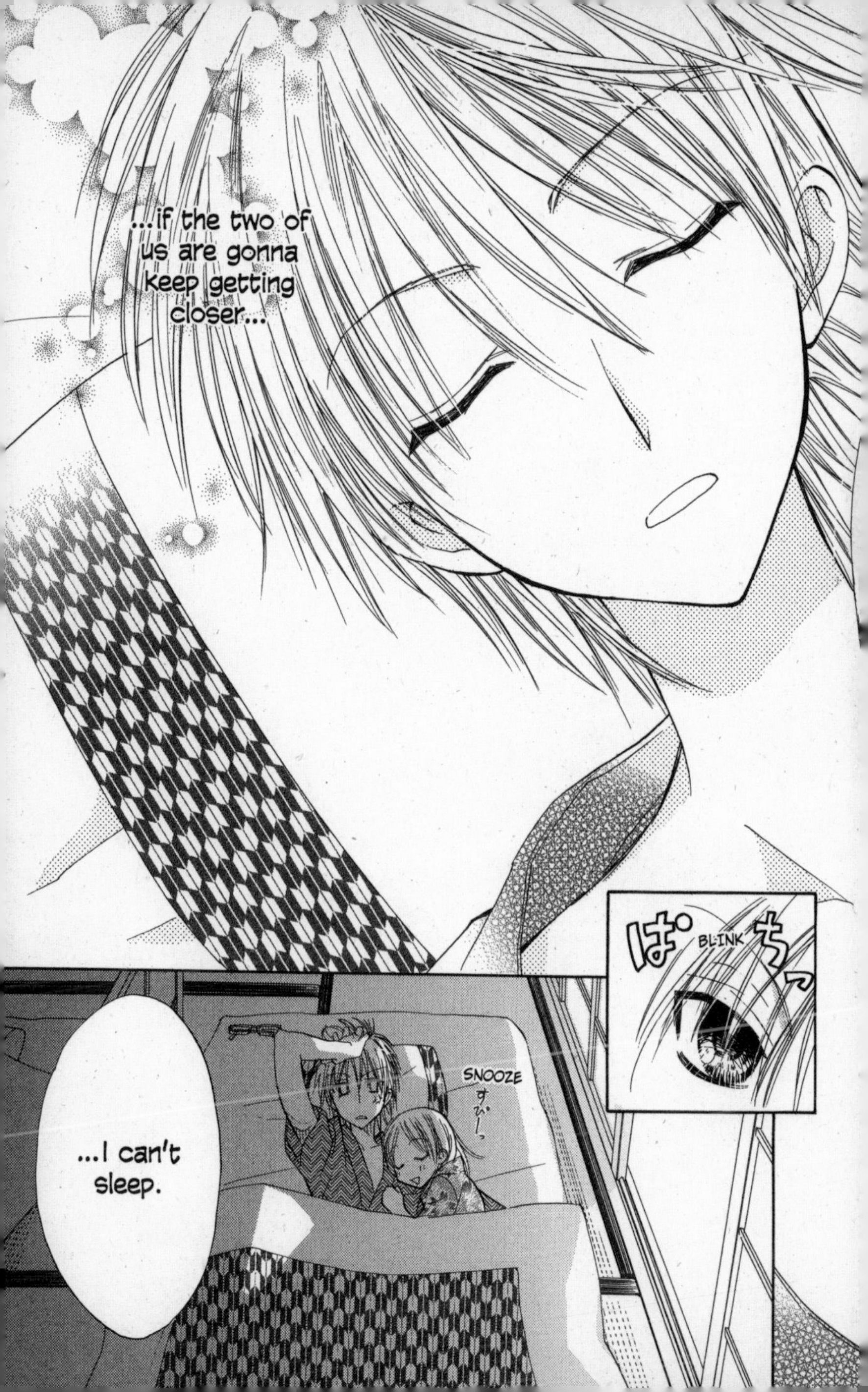
...if the two of us are gonna keep getting closer...
ぱちっ
BLINK
SNOOZE
すぴーっ
...I can't sleep.

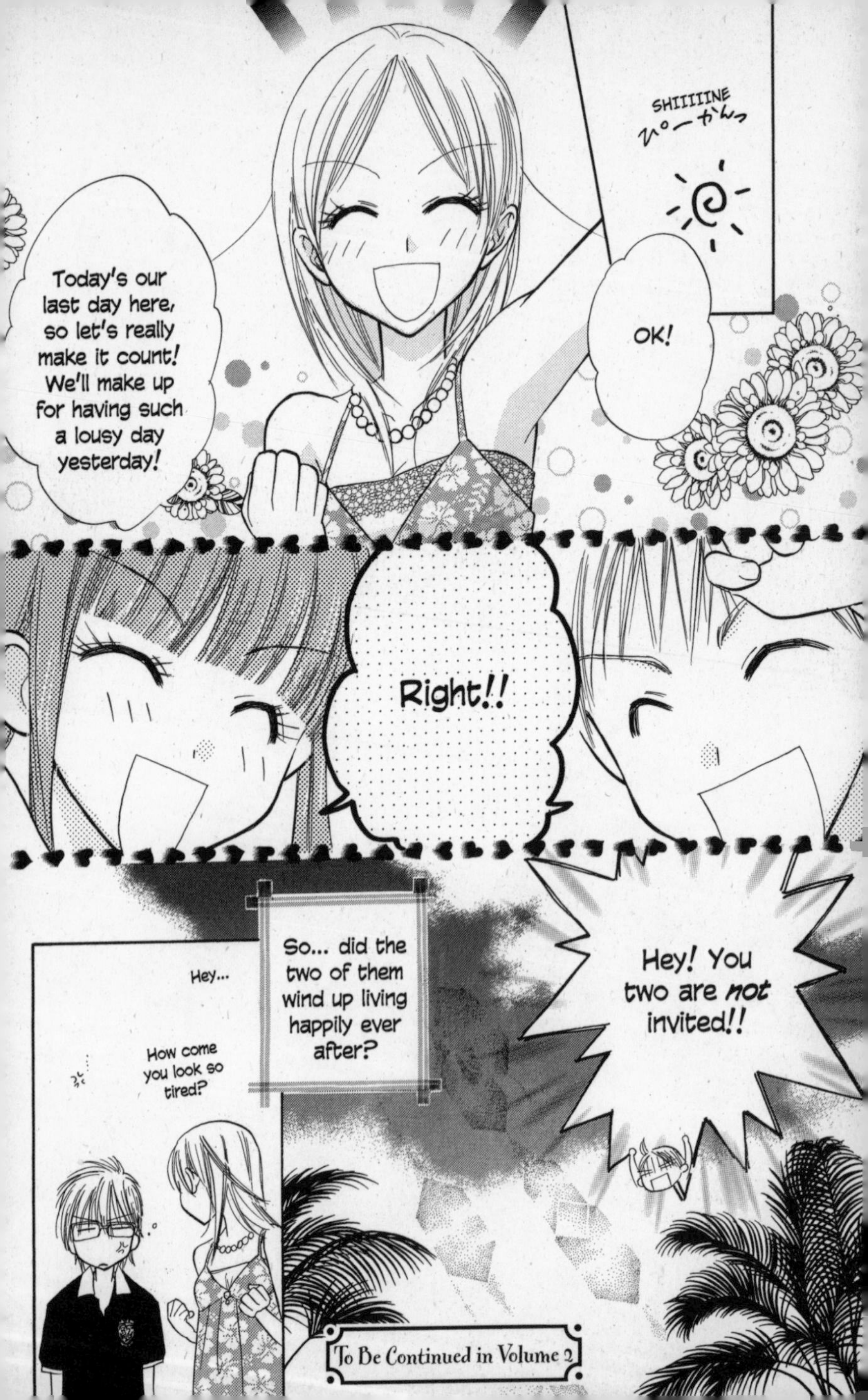
SHIIIIINE
ぴーかんっ
OK!
Today's our last day here, so let's really make it count! We'll make up for having such a lousy day yesterday!
Right!!
Hey! You two are *not* invited!!
So... did the two of them wind up living happily ever after?
Hey...
How come you look so tired?
To Be Continued in Volume 2

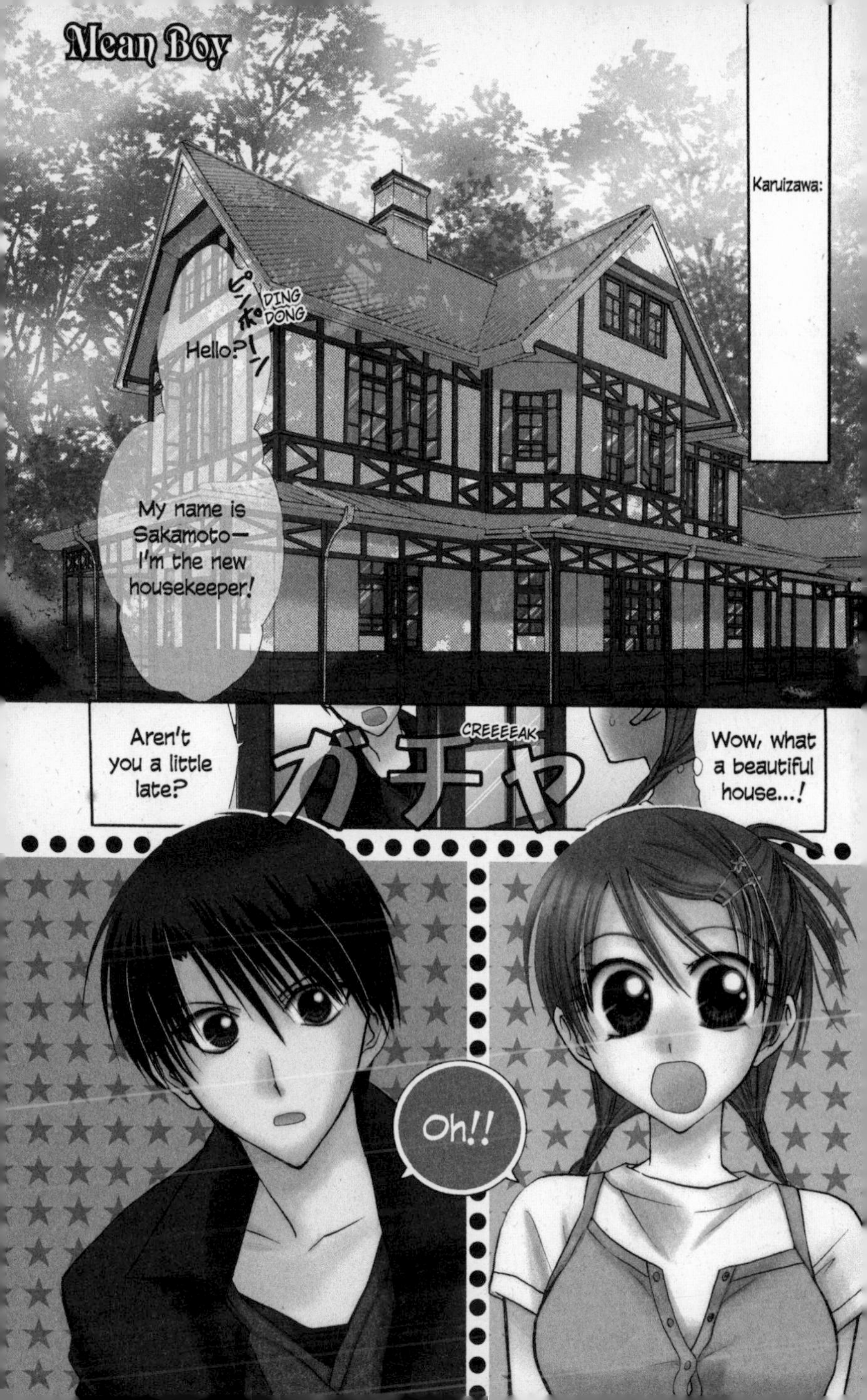
Karuizawa:
DING DONG
Hello?!
My name is Sakamoto—I'm the new housekeeper!
Wow, what a beautiful house...!
CREEEEAK
Aren't you a little late?
Oh!!

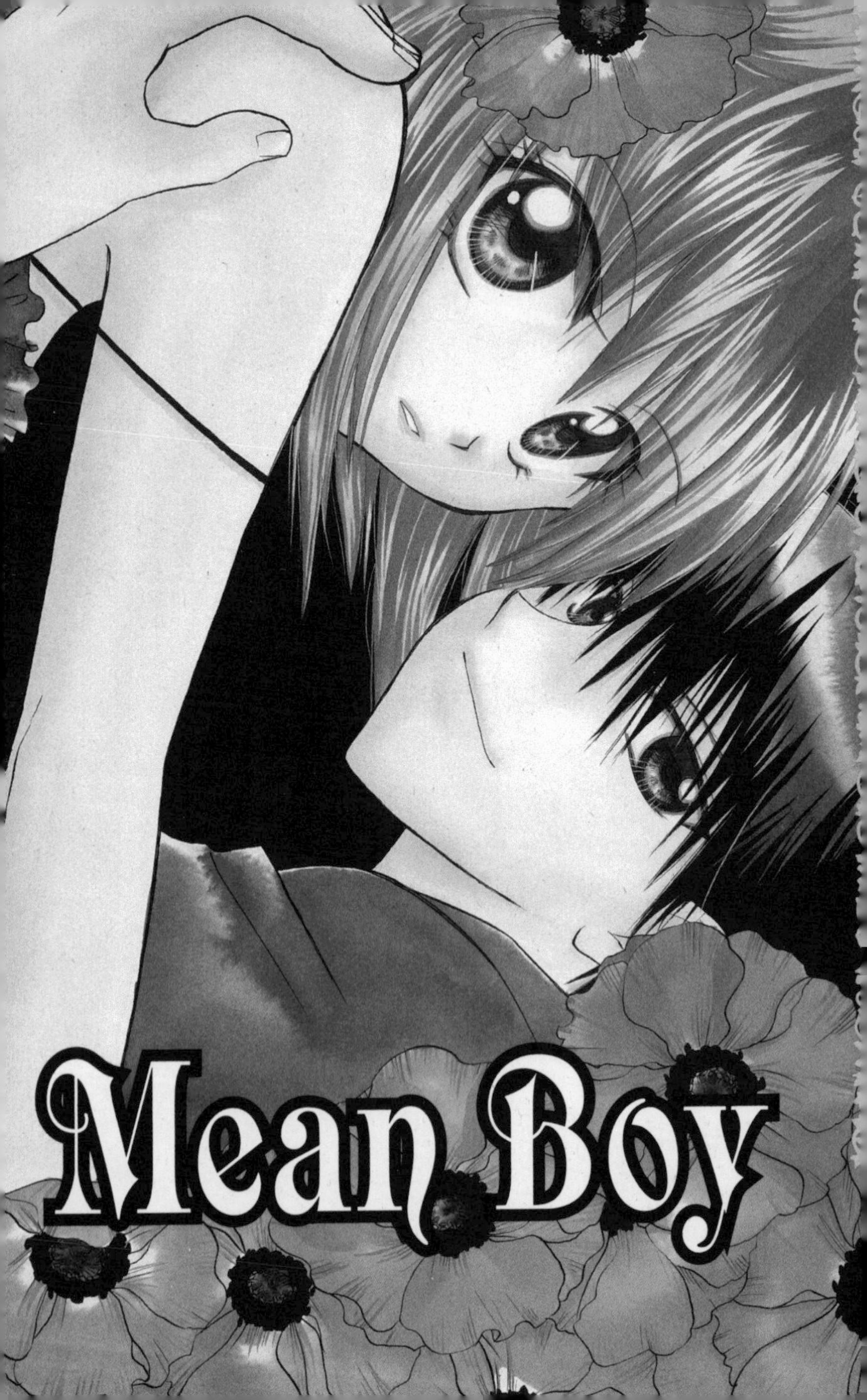
Mean Boy

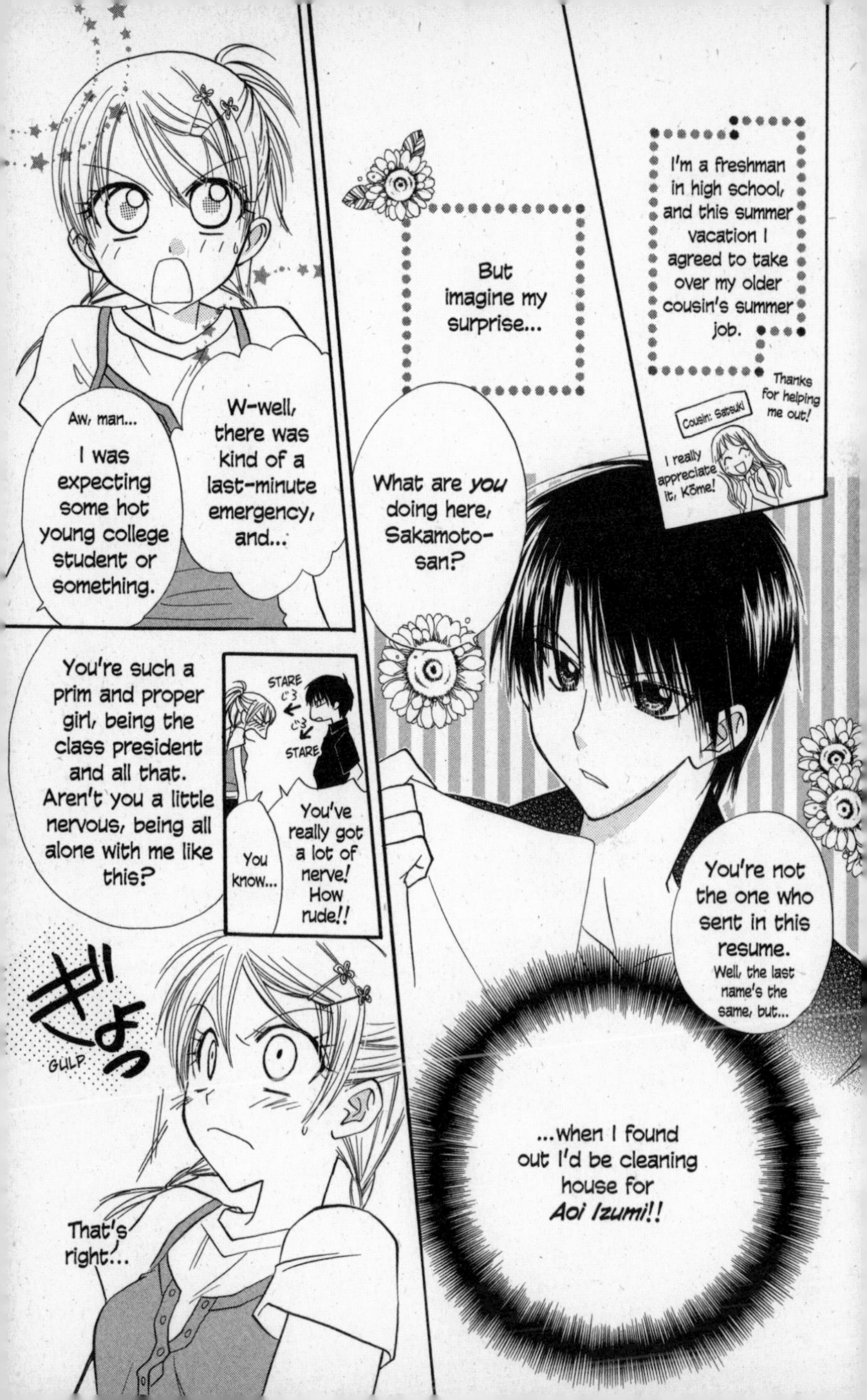
I'm a freshman in high school, and this summer vacation I agreed to take over my older cousin's summer job.
Thanks for helping me out!
Cousin: Satsuki
I really appreciate it, Kōme!
But imagine my surprise...
What are *you* doing here, Sakamoto-san?
You're not the one who sent in this resume.
Well, the last name's the same, but...
...when I found out I'd be cleaning house for *Aoi Izumi!!*
W-well, there was kind of a last-minute emergency, and...
Aw, man...
I was expecting some hot young college student or something.
You're such a prim and proper girl, being the class president and all that. Aren't you a little nervous, being all alone with me like this?
STARE
STARE
You've really got a lot of nerve! How rude!!
You know...
GULP
That's right...

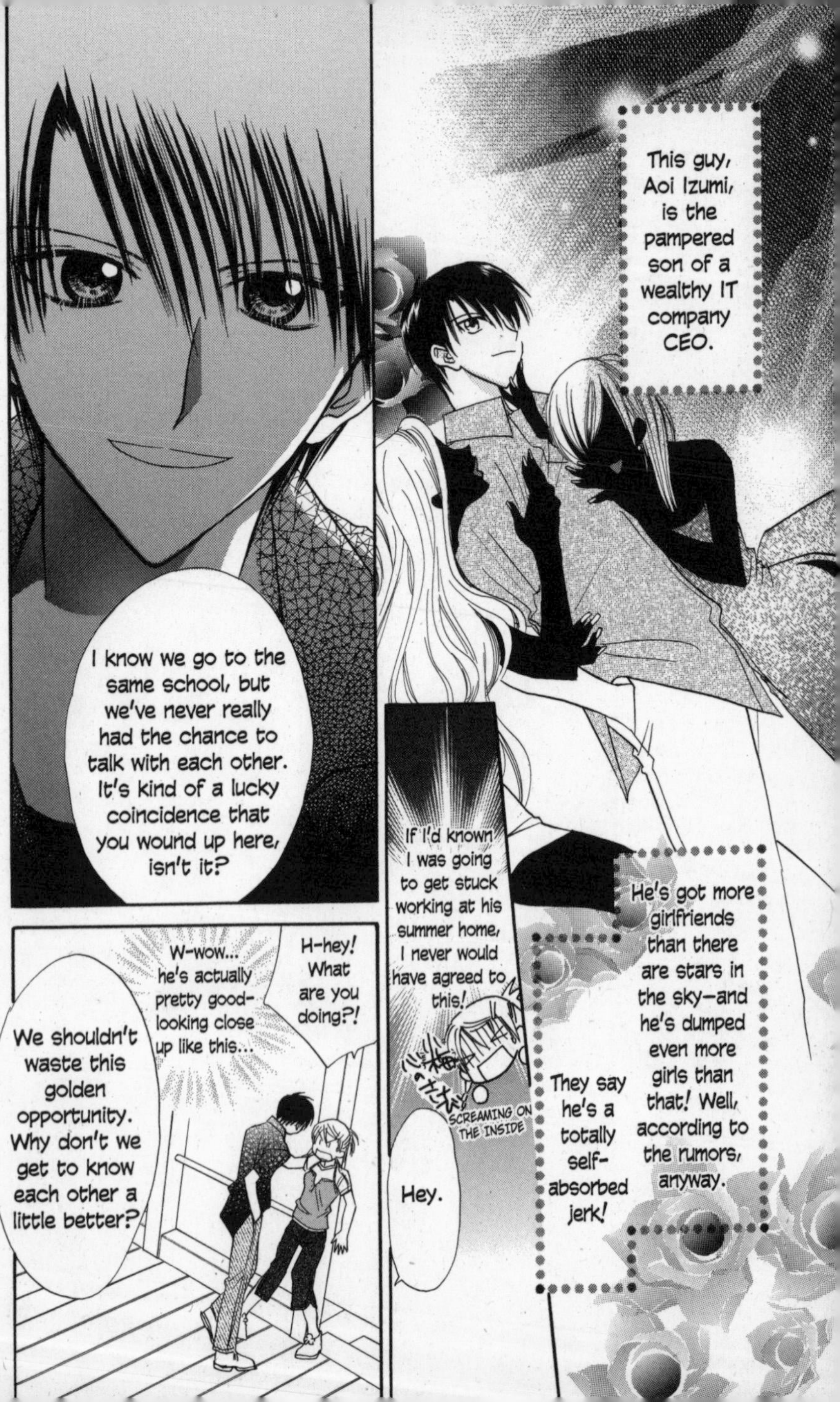
This guy, Aoi Izumi, is the pampered son of a wealthy IT company CEO.
He's got more girlfriends than there are stars in the sky—and he's dumped even more girls than that! Well, according to the rumors, anyway.
They say he's a totally self-absorbed jerk!
If I'd known I was going to get stuck working at his summer home, I never would have agreed to this!
SCREAMING ON THE INSIDE
Hey.
I know we go to the same school, but we've never really had the chance to talk with each other. It's kind of a lucky coincidence that you wound up here, isn't it?
H-hey! What are you doing?!
W-wow... he's actually pretty good-looking close up like this...
We shouldn't waste this golden opportunity. Why don't we get to know each other a little better?

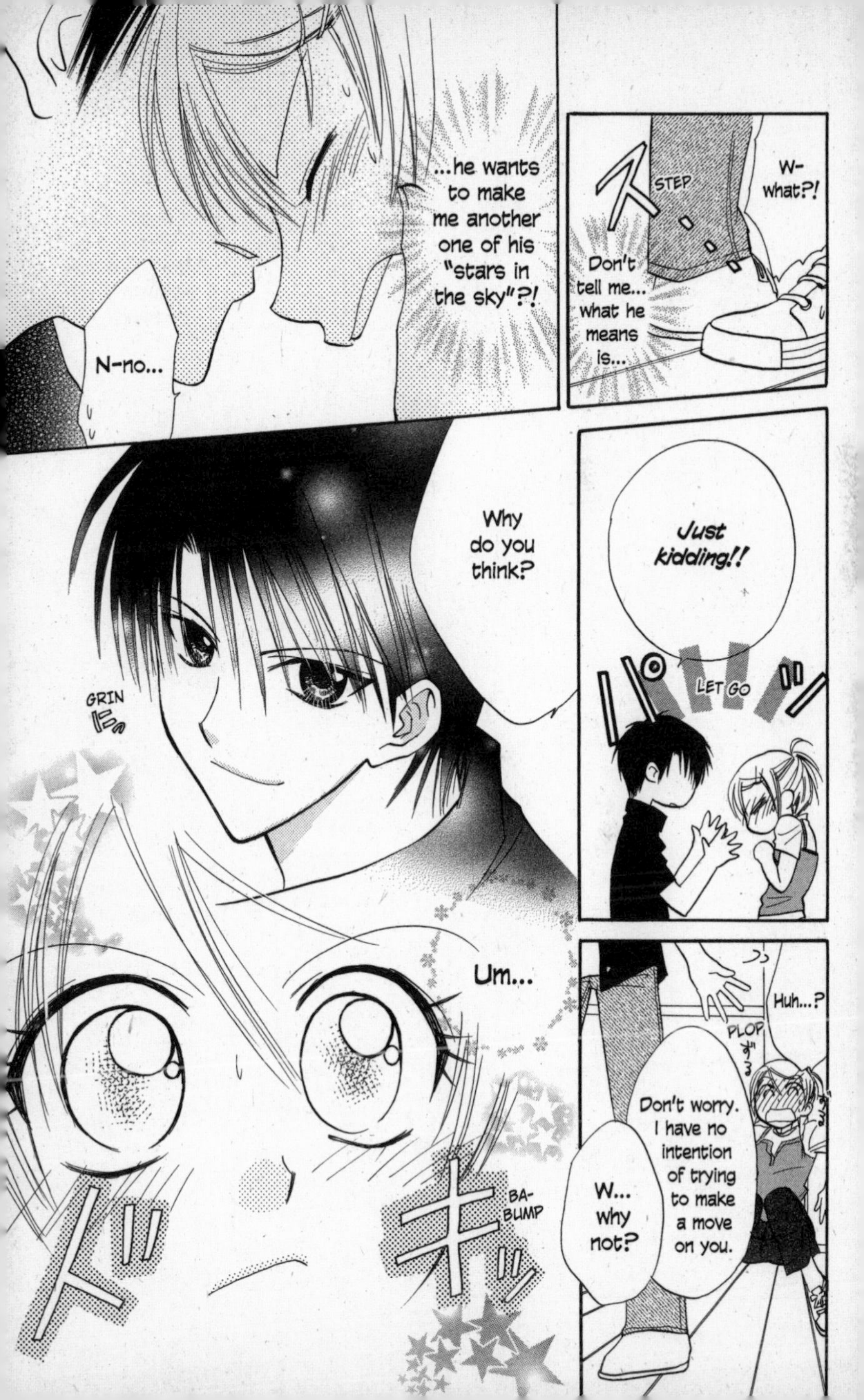
W-what?!
STEP
Don't tell me... what he means is...
...he wants to make me another one of his "stars in the sky"?!
N-no...
Just kidding!!
LET GO
Huh...?
PLOP
Don't worry. I have no intention of trying to make a move on you.
W... why not?
Why do you think?
GRIN
Um...
BA-BUMP

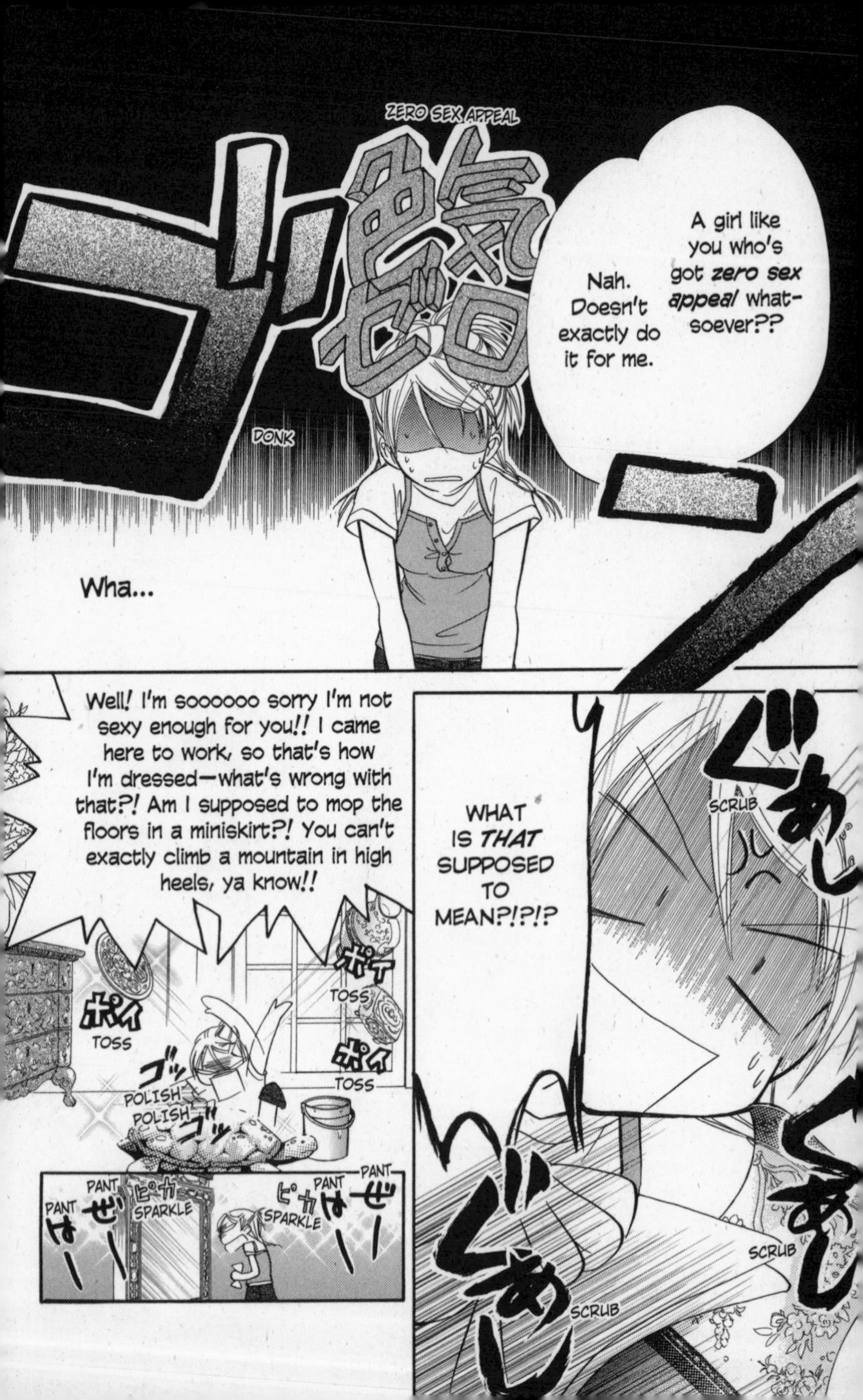

A girl like you who's got *zero sex appeal* whatsoever??
Nah. Doesn't exactly do it for me.
色気ゼロ
ZERO SEX APPEAL
DONK
Wha...
WHAT IS *THAT* SUPPOSED TO MEAN?!?!?
SCRUB
SCRUB
SCRUB
Well! I'm soooooo sorry I'm not sexy enough for you!! I came here to work, so that's how I'm dressed—what's wrong with that?! Am I supposed to mop the floors in a miniskirt?! You can't exactly climb a mountain in high heels, ya know!!
TOSS
TOSS
TOSS
POLISH POLISH
PANT PANT
SPARKLE
SPARKLE
PANT PANT

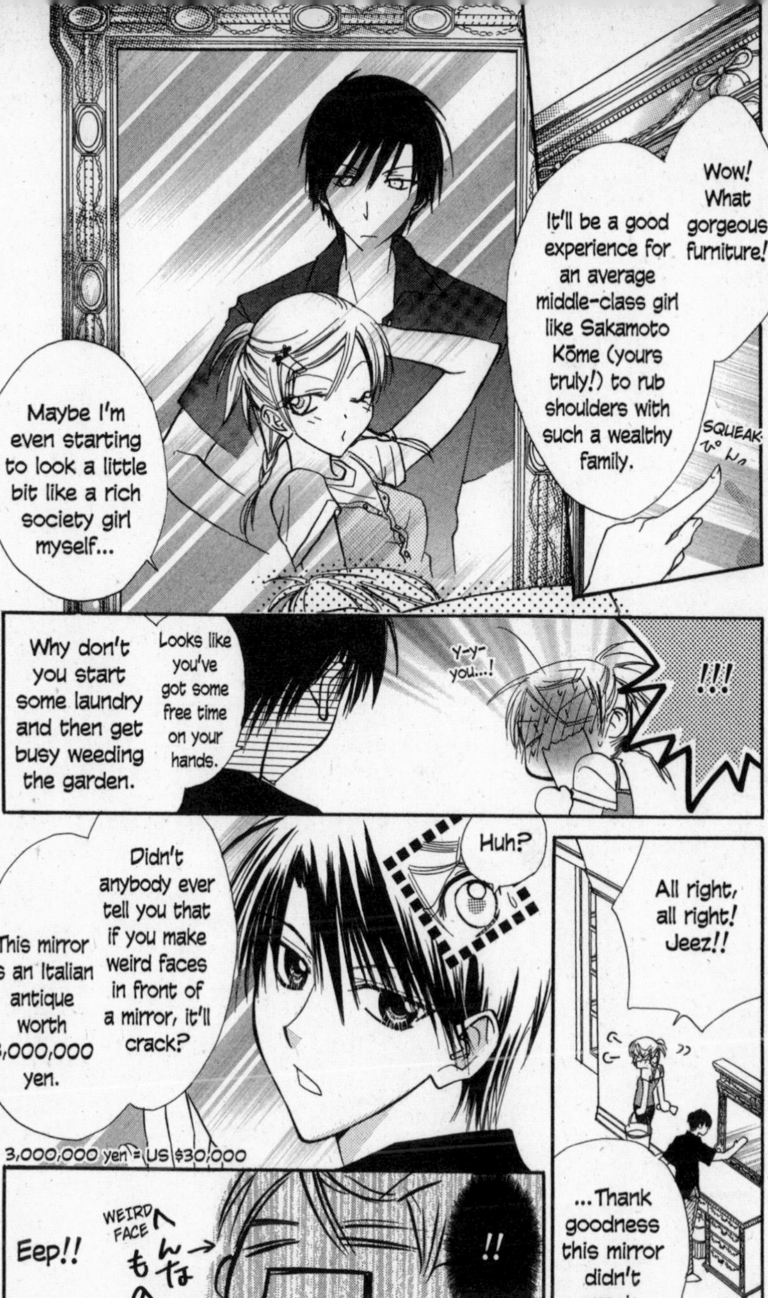
Wow! What gorgeous furniture!
It'll be a good experience for an average middle-class girl like Sakamoto Kōme (yours truly!) to rub shoulders with such a wealthy family.
SQUEAK
ぴん
Maybe I'm even starting to look a little bit like a rich society girl myself...
!!!
Y-y-you...!
Looks like you've got some free time on your hands.
Why don't you start some laundry and then get busy weeding the garden.
All right, all right! Jeez!!
...Thank goodness this mirror didn't crack.
Huh?
Didn't anybody ever tell you that if you make weird faces in front of a mirror, it'll crack?
This mirror is an Italian antique worth 3,000,000 yen.
3,000,000 yen = US $30,000
!!
WEIRD FACE
へんなもの
Eep!!

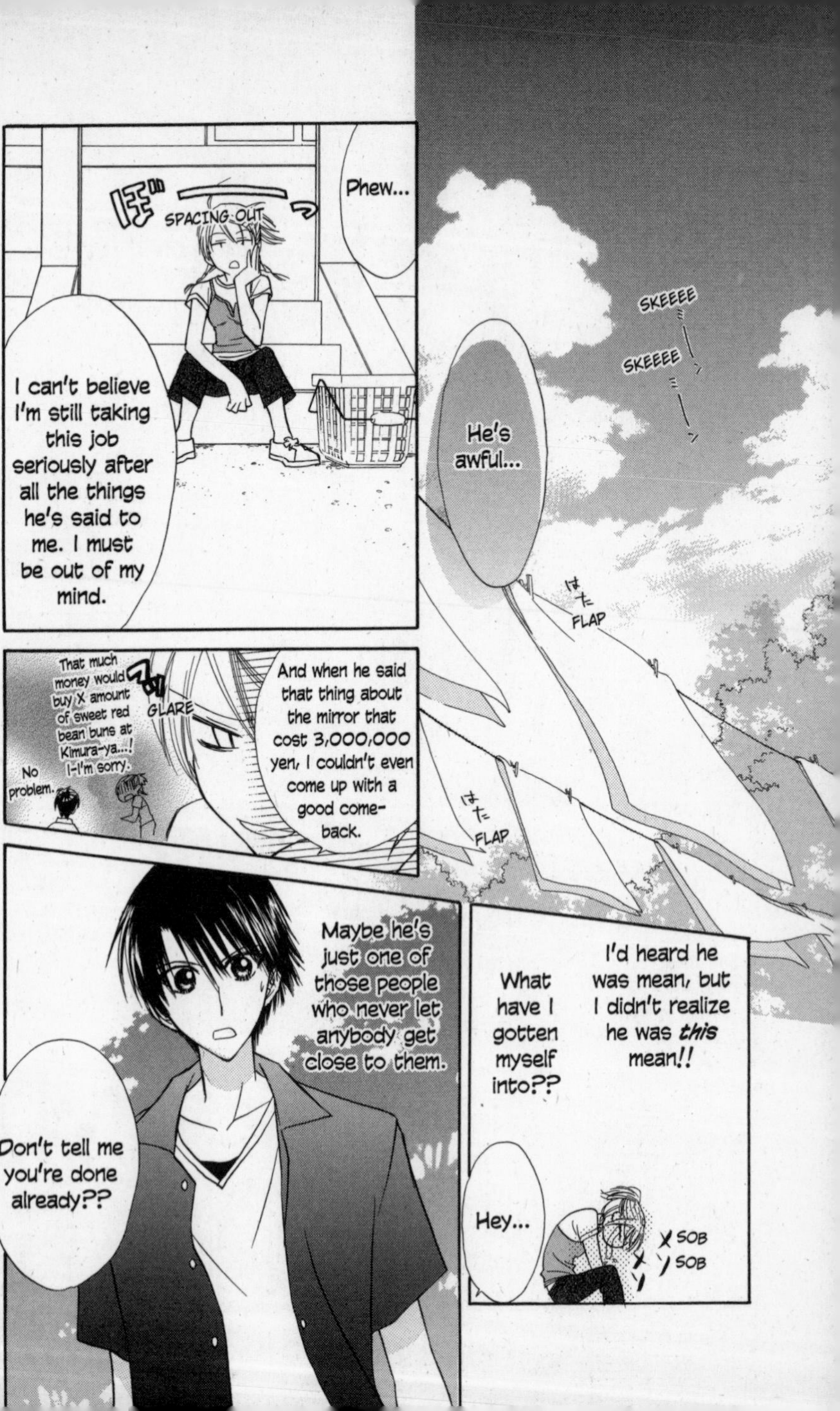

SKEEEE
SKEEEE
He's awful...
はた
FLAP
はた
FLAP
Phew...
SPACING OUT
I can't believe I'm still taking this job seriously after all the things he's said to me. I must be out of my mind.
And when he said that thing about the mirror that cost 3,000,000 yen, I couldn't even come up with a good come-back.
GLARE
That much money would buy X amount of sweet red bean buns at Kimura-ya...!
I-I'm sorry.
No problem.
I'd heard he was mean, but I didn't realize he was *this* mean!!
What have I gotten myself into??
Hey...
SOB
SOB
Maybe he's just one of those people who never let anybody get close to them.
Don't tell me you're done already??

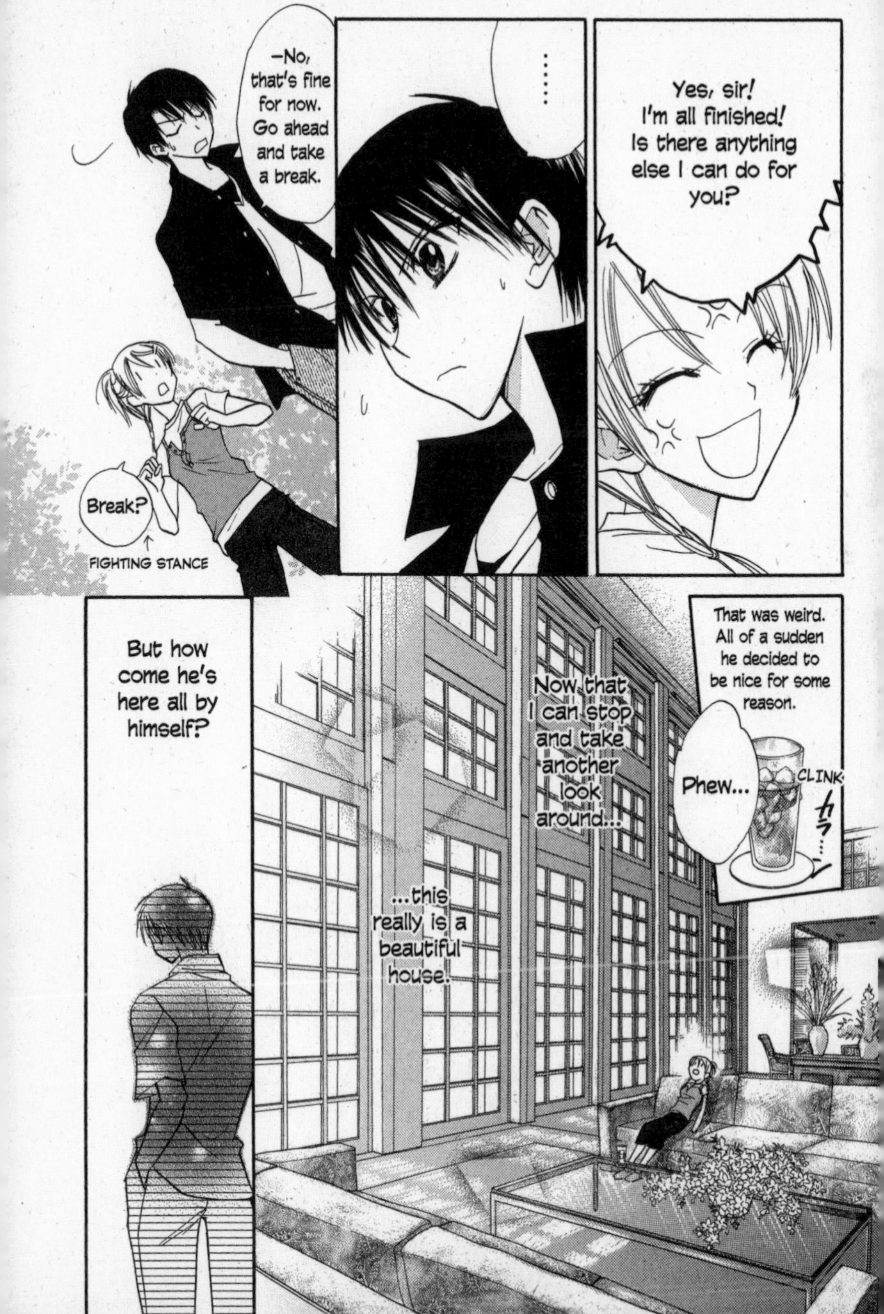
Yes, sir! I'm all finished! Is there anything else I can do for you?
......
—No, that's fine for now. Go ahead and take a break.
Break?
FIGHTING STANCE
That was weird. All of a sudden he decided to be nice for some reason.
Phew...
CLINK
Now that I can stop and take another look around...
...this really is a beautiful house.
But how come he's here all by himself?

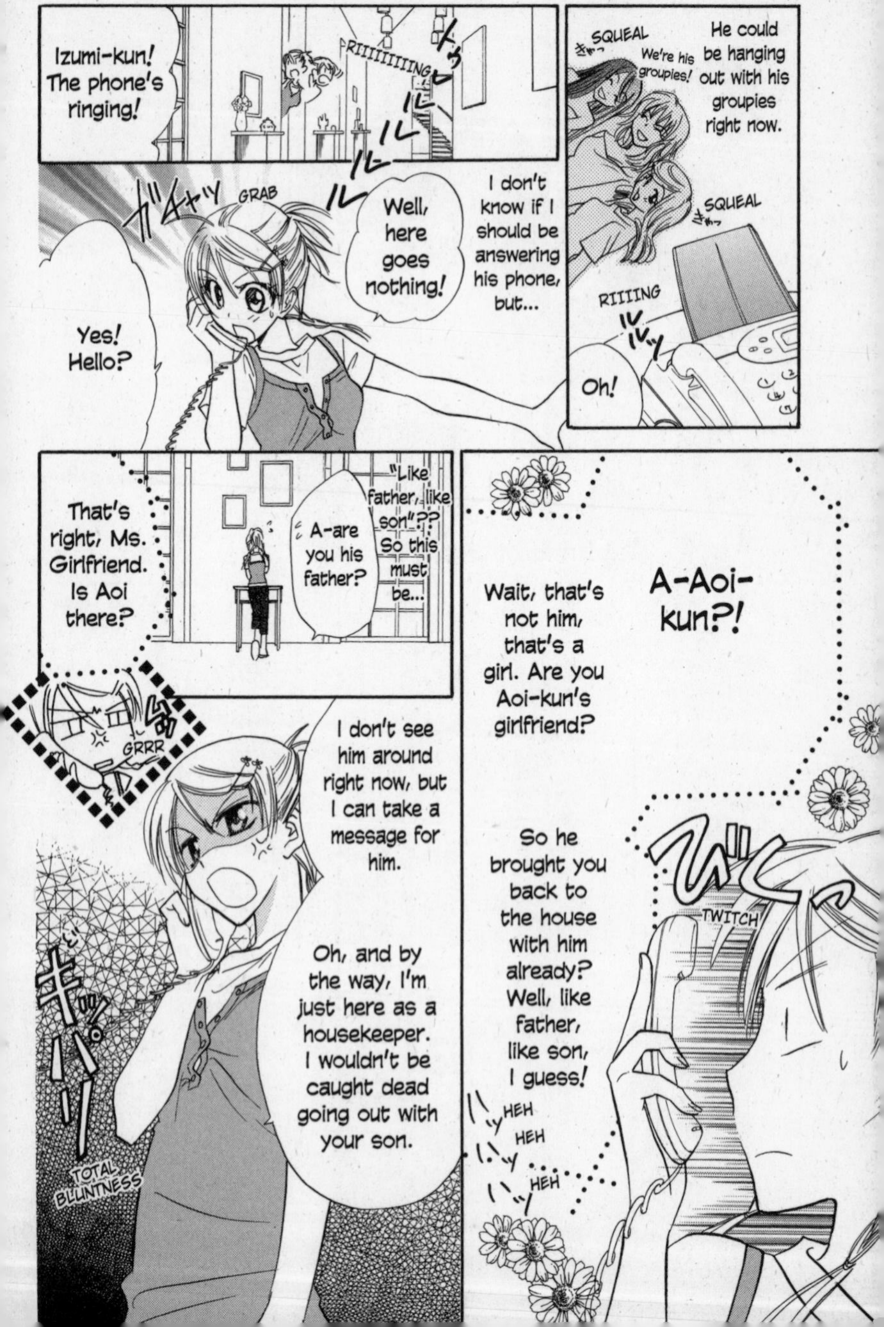
He could be hanging out with his groupies right now.
We're his groupies!
SQUEAL
SQUEAL
RIIIING
Oh!
Izumi-kun! The phone's ringing!
PRIIIIIIIING
I don't know if I should be answering his phone, but...
Well, here goes nothing!
GRAB
Yes! Hello?
A-Aoi-kun?!
Wait, that's not him, that's a girl. Are you Aoi-kun's girlfriend?
So he brought you back to the house with him already? Well, like father, like son, I guess!
HEH
HEH
HEH
TWITCH
"Like father, like son"?? So this must be...
A-are you his father?
That's right, Ms. Girlfriend. Is Aoi there?
GRRR
I don't see him around right now, but I can take a message for him.
Oh, and by the way, I'm just here as a housekeeper. I wouldn't be caught dead going out with your son.
TOTAL BLUNTNESS

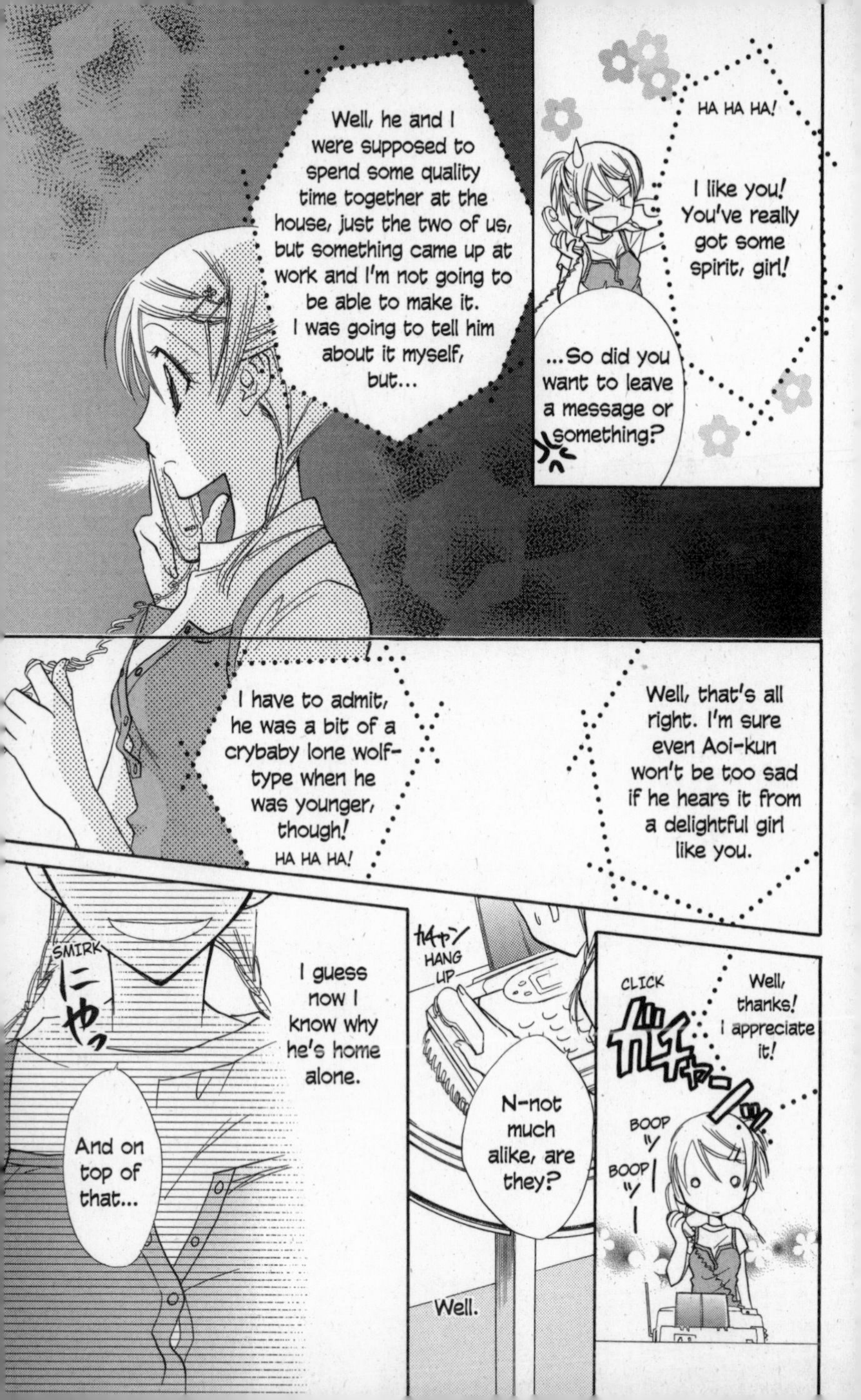
HA HA HA!
I like you! You've really got some spirit, girl!
...So did you want to leave a message or something?
Well, he and I were supposed to spend some quality time together at the house, just the two of us, but something came up at work and I'm not going to be able to make it. I was going to tell him about it myself, but...
Well, that's all right. I'm sure even Aoi-kun won't be too sad if he hears it from a delightful girl like you.
I have to admit, he was a bit of a crybaby lone wolf-type when he was younger, though!
HA HA HA!
Well, thanks! I appreciate it!
CLICK
BOOP
BOOP
HANG UP
N-not much alike, are they?
Well.
SMIRK
I guess now I know why he's home alone.
And on top of that...

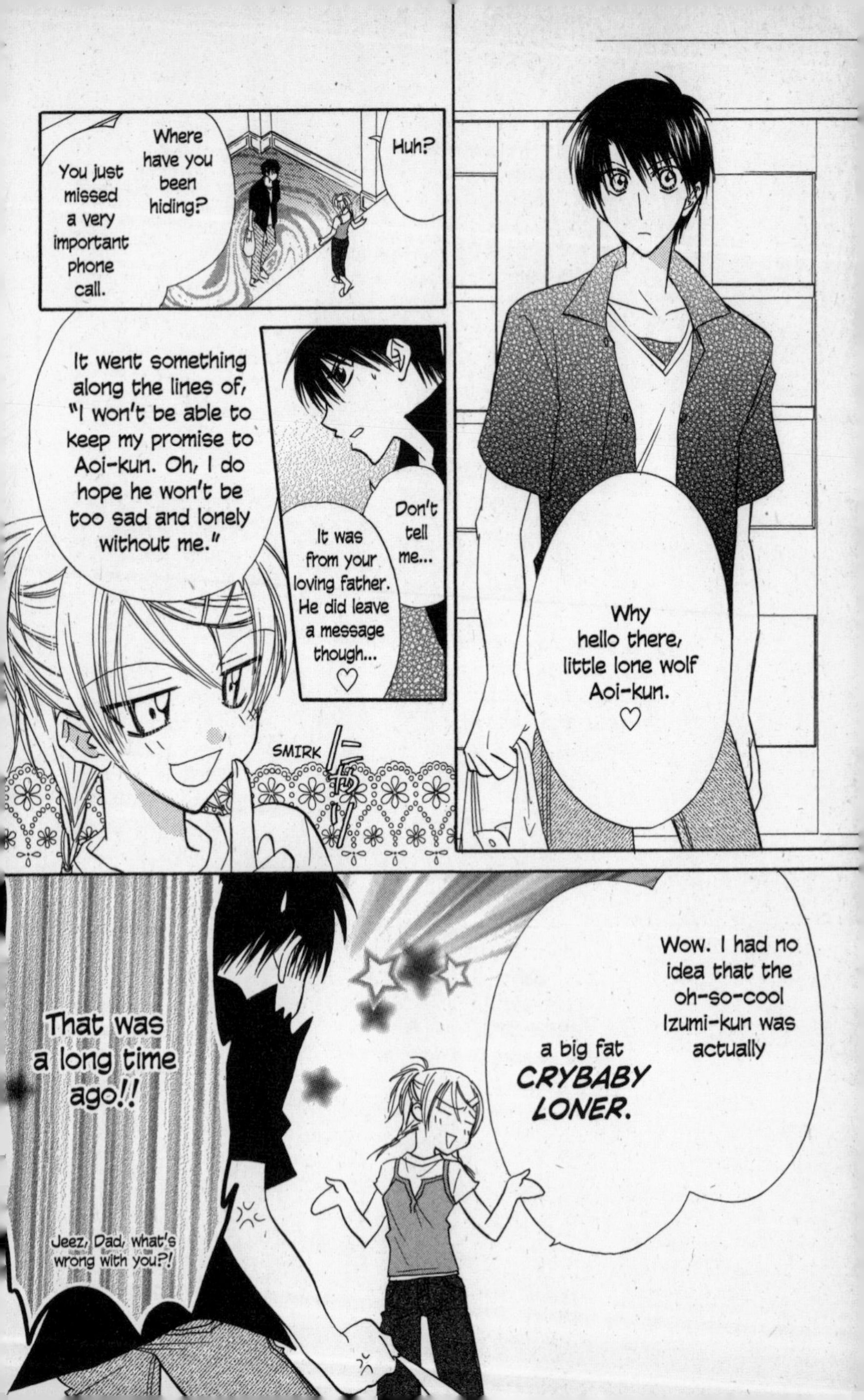

Why hello there, little lone wolf Aoi-kun. ♡
Huh?
Where have you been hiding?
You just missed a very important phone call.
Don't tell me...
It was from your loving father. He did leave a message though... ♡
It went something along the lines of, "I won't be able to keep my promise to Aoi-kun. Oh, I do hope he won't be too sad and lonely without me."
SMIRK
Wow. I had no idea that the oh-so-cool Izumi-kun was actually
a big fat CRYBABY LONER.
That was a long time ago!!
Jeez, Dad, what's wrong with you?!

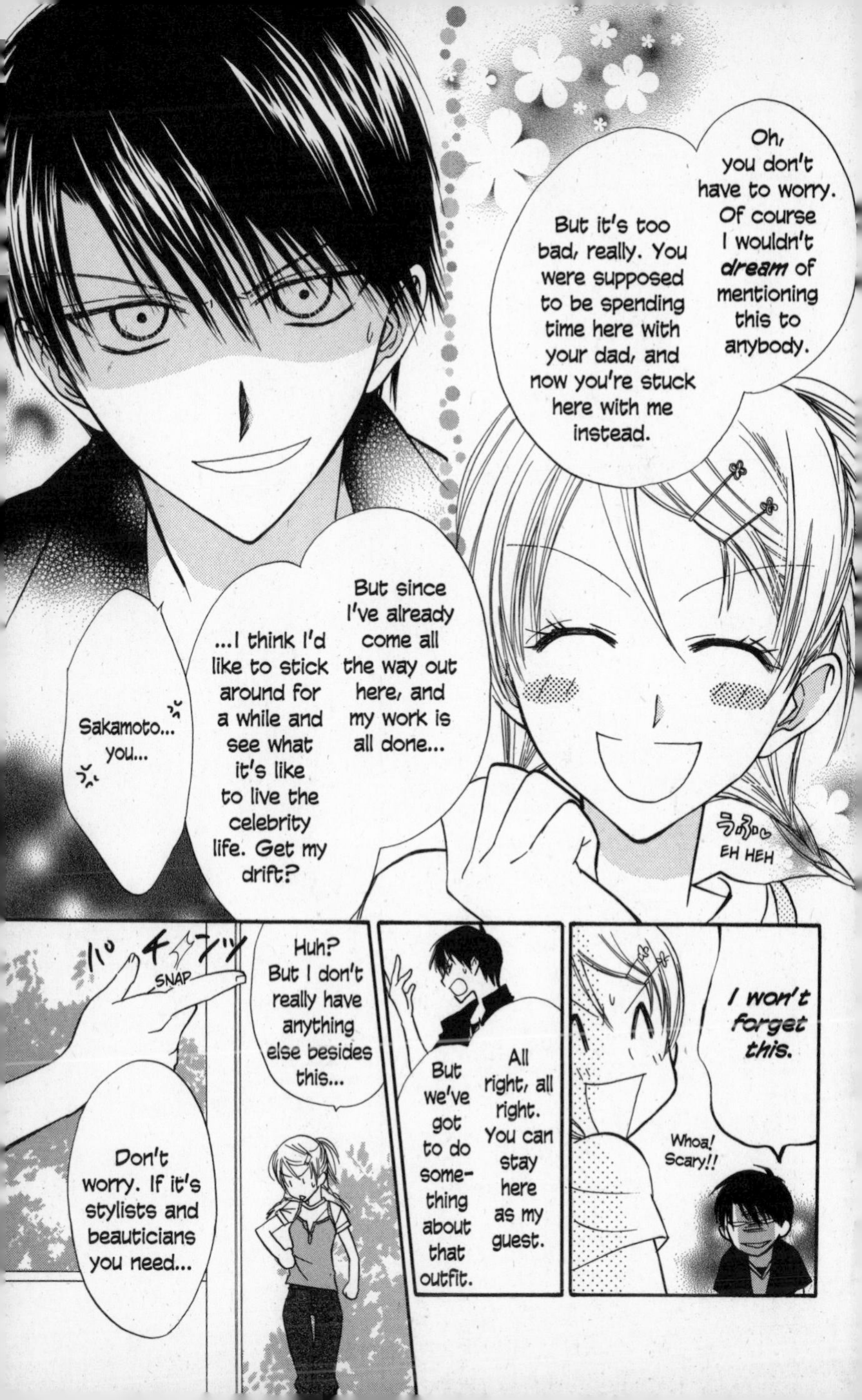
Oh, you don't have to worry. Of course I wouldn't *dream* of mentioning this to anybody.
But it's too bad, really. You were supposed to be spending time here with your dad, and now you're stuck here with me instead.
うふ♡
EH HEH
But since I've already come all the way out here, and my work is all done...
...I think I'd like to stick around for a while and see what it's like to live the celebrity life. Get my drift?
Sakamoto... you...
*I won't forget this.*
Whoa! Scary!!
All right, all right. You can stay here as my guest.
But we've got to do some-thing about that outfit.
Huh? But I don't really have anything else besides this...
パチンッ
SNAP
Don't worry. If it's stylists and beauticians you need...

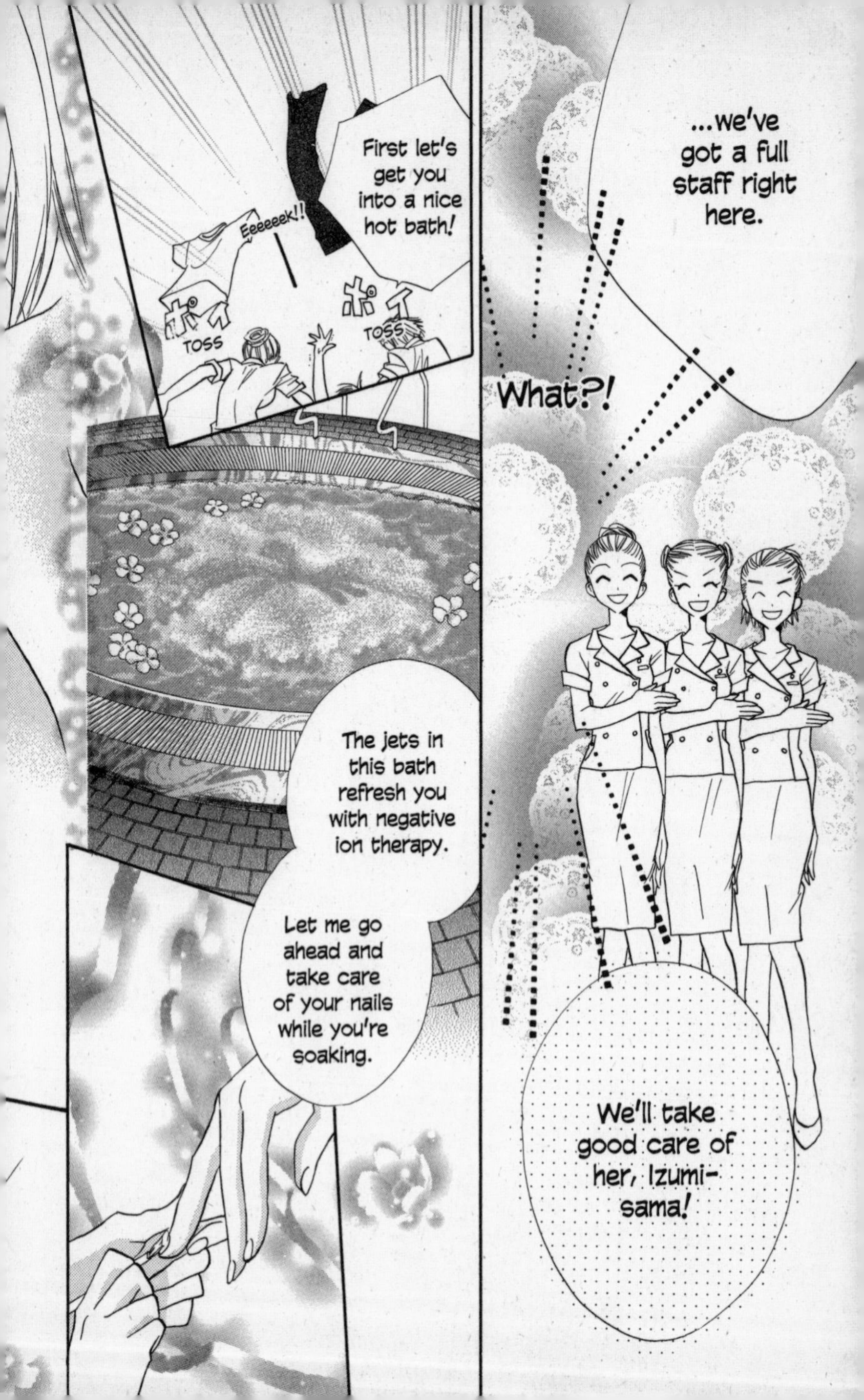
...we've got a full staff right here.
What?!
We'll take good care of her, Izumi-sama!
First let's get you into a nice hot bath!
Eeeeeek!!
ポイ
TOSS
ポイ
TOSS
The jets in this bath refresh you with negative ion therapy.
Let me go ahead and take care of your nails while you're soaking.

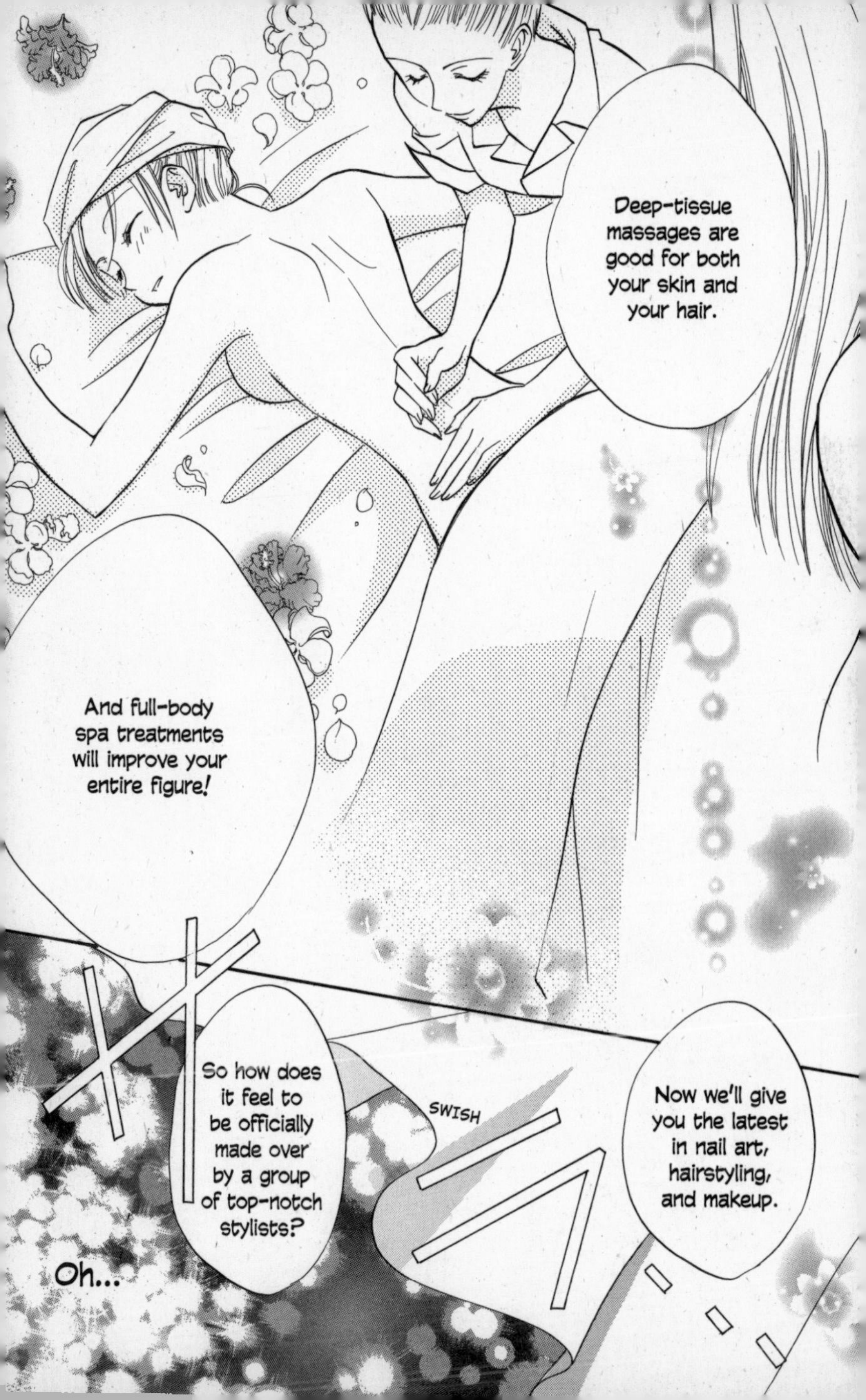
Deep-tissue massages are good for both your skin and your hair.
And full-body spa treatments will improve your entire figure!
Now we'll give you the latest in nail art, hairstyling, and makeup.
SWISH
So how does it feel to be officially made over by a group of top-notch stylists?
Oh...

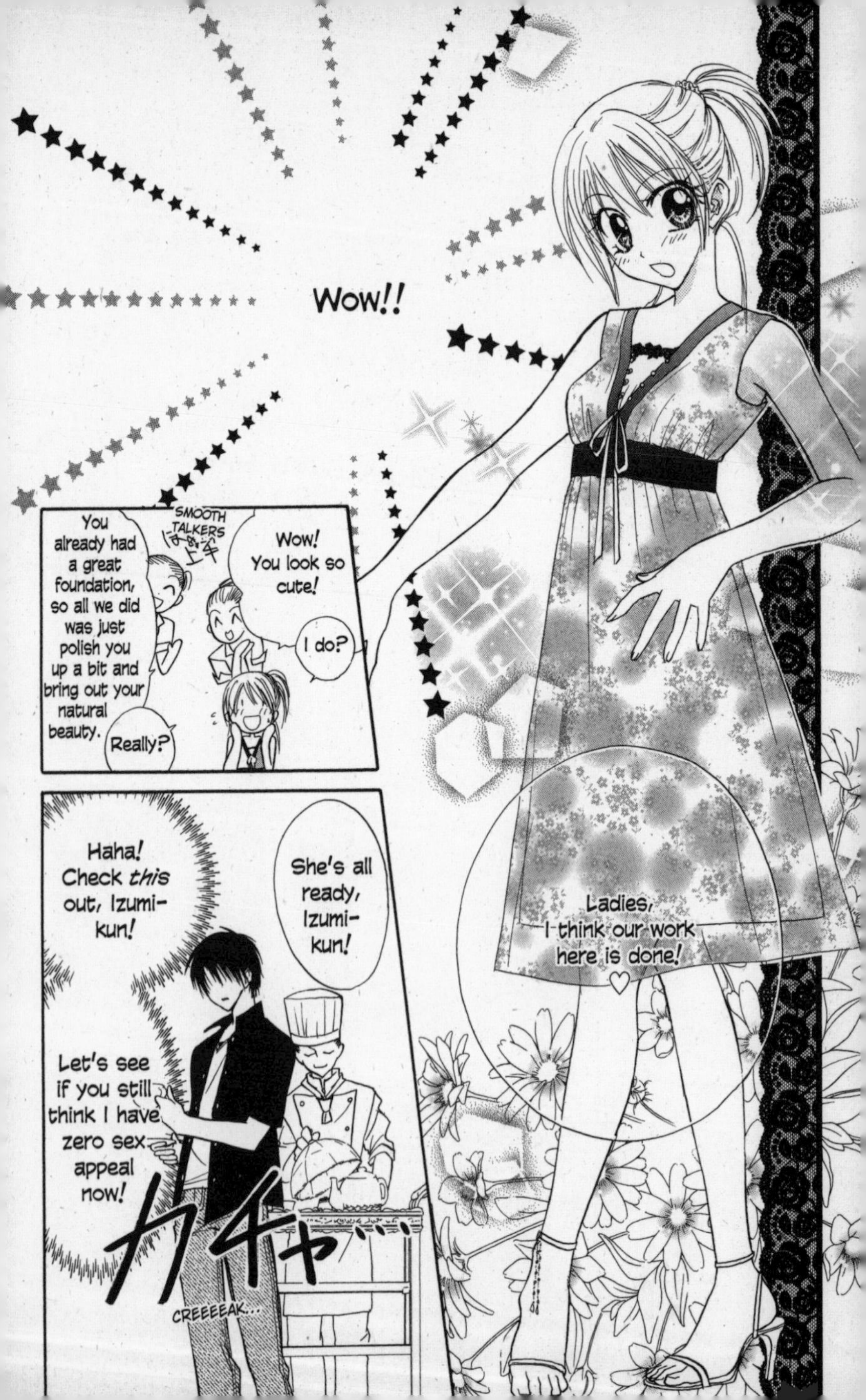
Wow!!
Ladies, I think our work here is done! ♡
Wow! You look so cute!
I do?
SMOOTH TALKERS
You already had a great foundation, so all we did was just polish you up a bit and bring out your natural beauty.
Really?
She's all ready, Izumi-kun!
Haha! Check *this* out, Izumi-kun!
Let's see if you still think I have zero sex appeal now!
CREEEEAK...

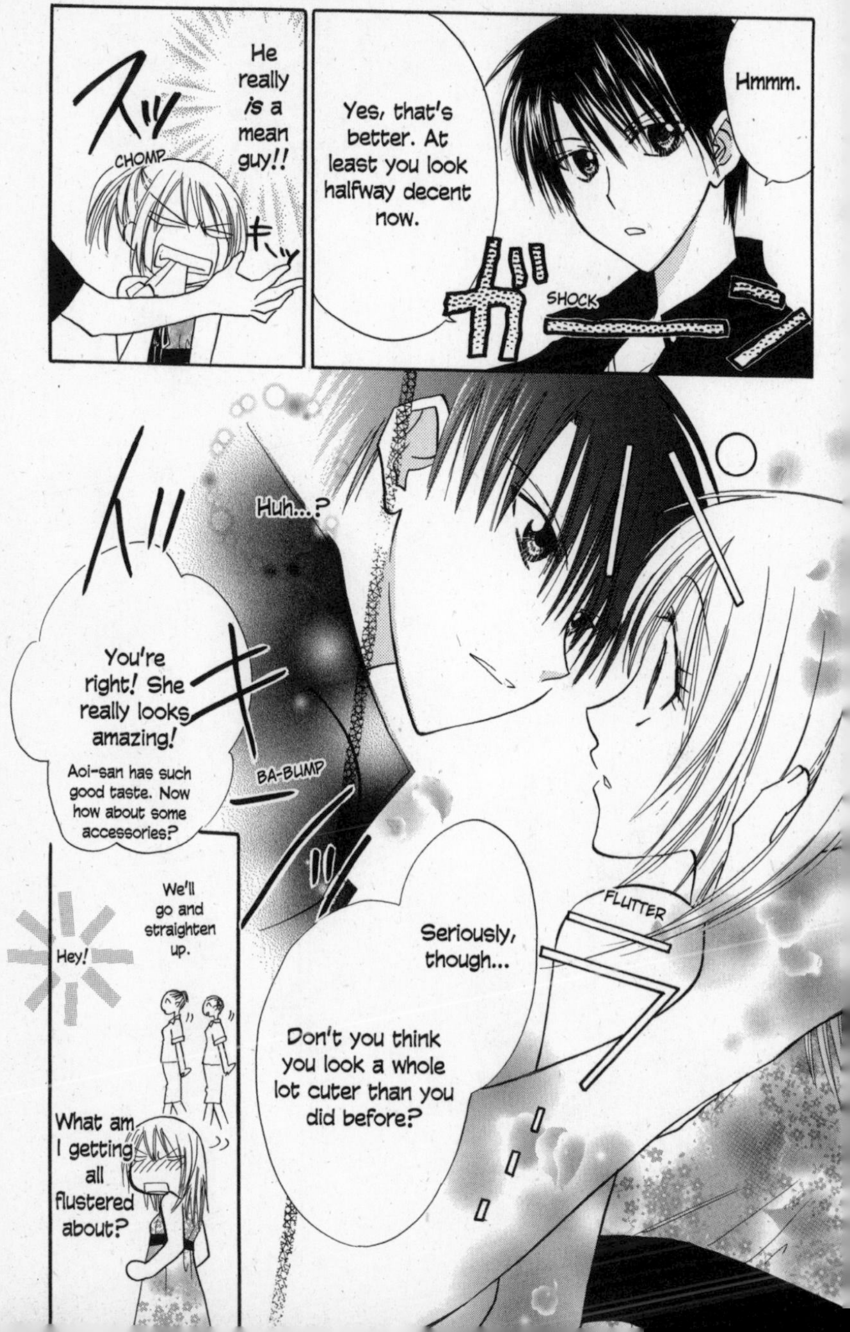
Hmmm.
Yes, that's better. At least you look halfway decent now.
SHOCK
He really is a mean guy!!
CHOMP
Huh...?
FLUTTER
Seriously, though...
Don't you think you look a whole lot cuter than you did before?
BA-BUMP
You're right! She really looks amazing!
Aoi-san has such good taste. Now how about some accessories?
We'll go and straighten up.
Hey!
What am I getting all flustered about?

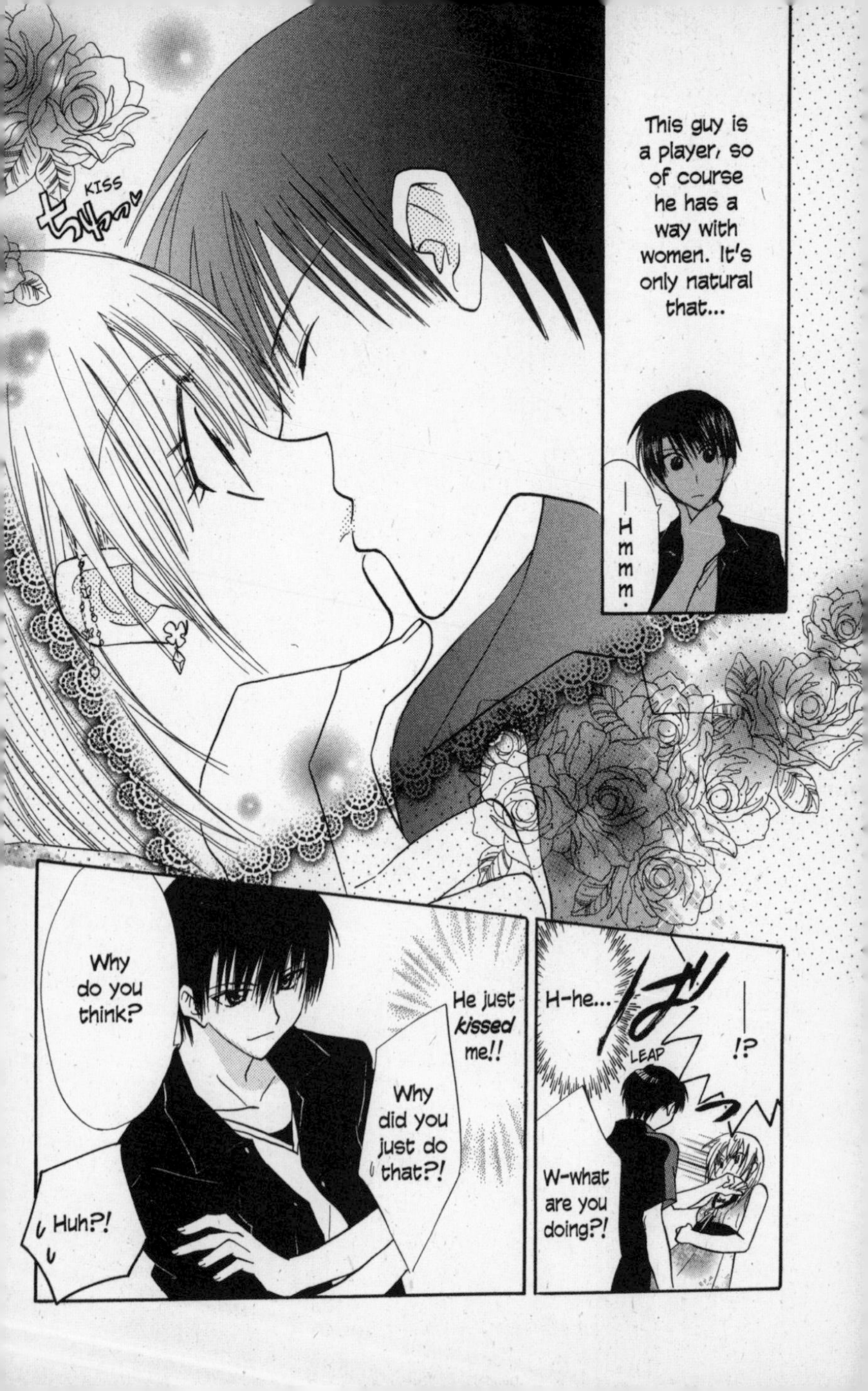

This guy is a player, so of course he has a way with women. It's only natural that...
—Hmmm.
KISS
—!?
H-he...
LEAP
W-what are you doing?!
He just *kissed* me!!
Why did you just do that?!
Why do you think?
Huh?!

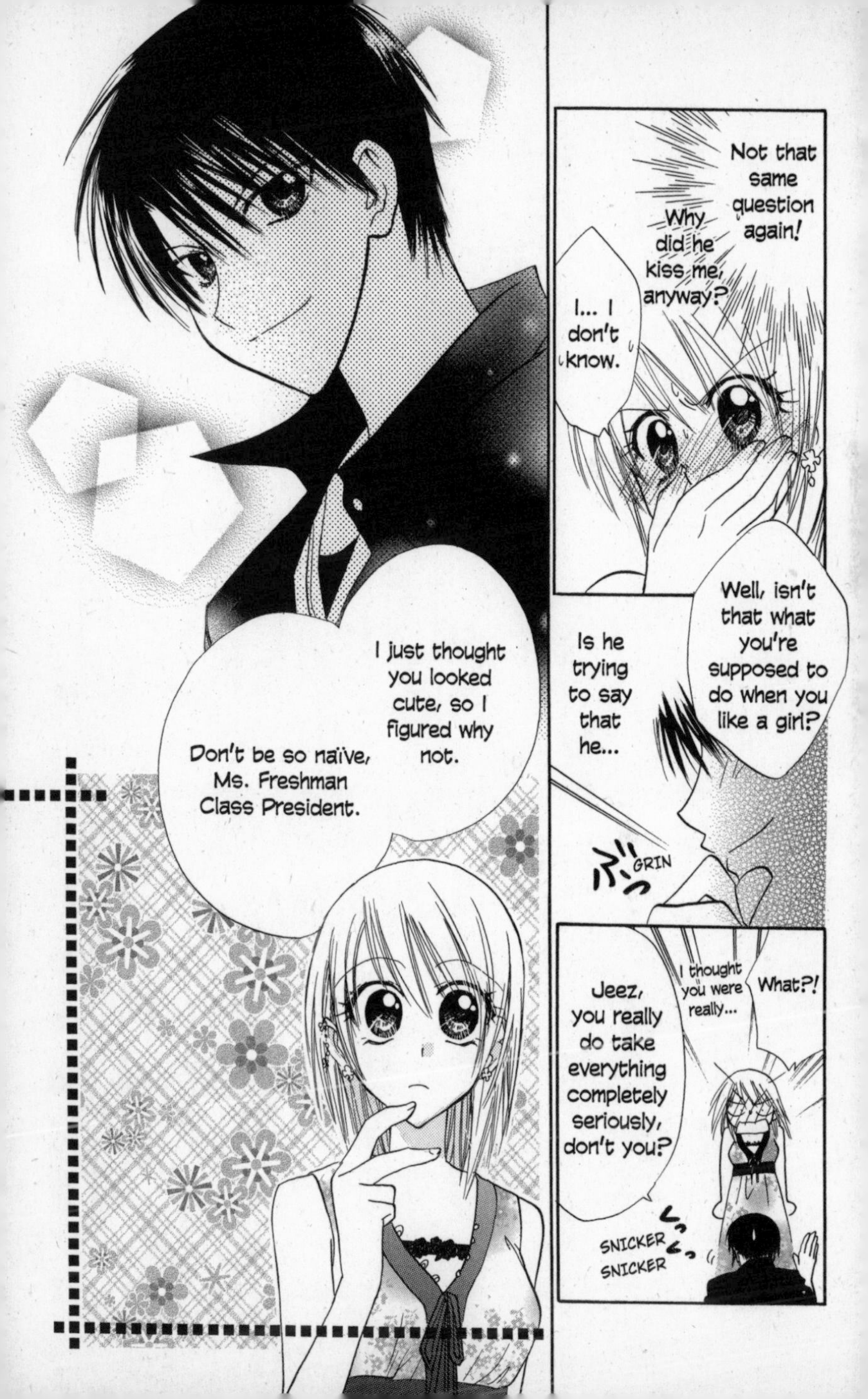
Not that same question again!
Why did he kiss me, anyway?
I... I don't know.
Well, isn't that what you're supposed to do when you like a girl?
Is he trying to say that he...
GRIN
What?!
I thought you were really...
Jeez, you really do take everything completely seriously, don't you?
SNICKER SNICKER
I just thought you looked cute, so I figured why not.
Don't be so naïve, Ms. Freshman Class President.

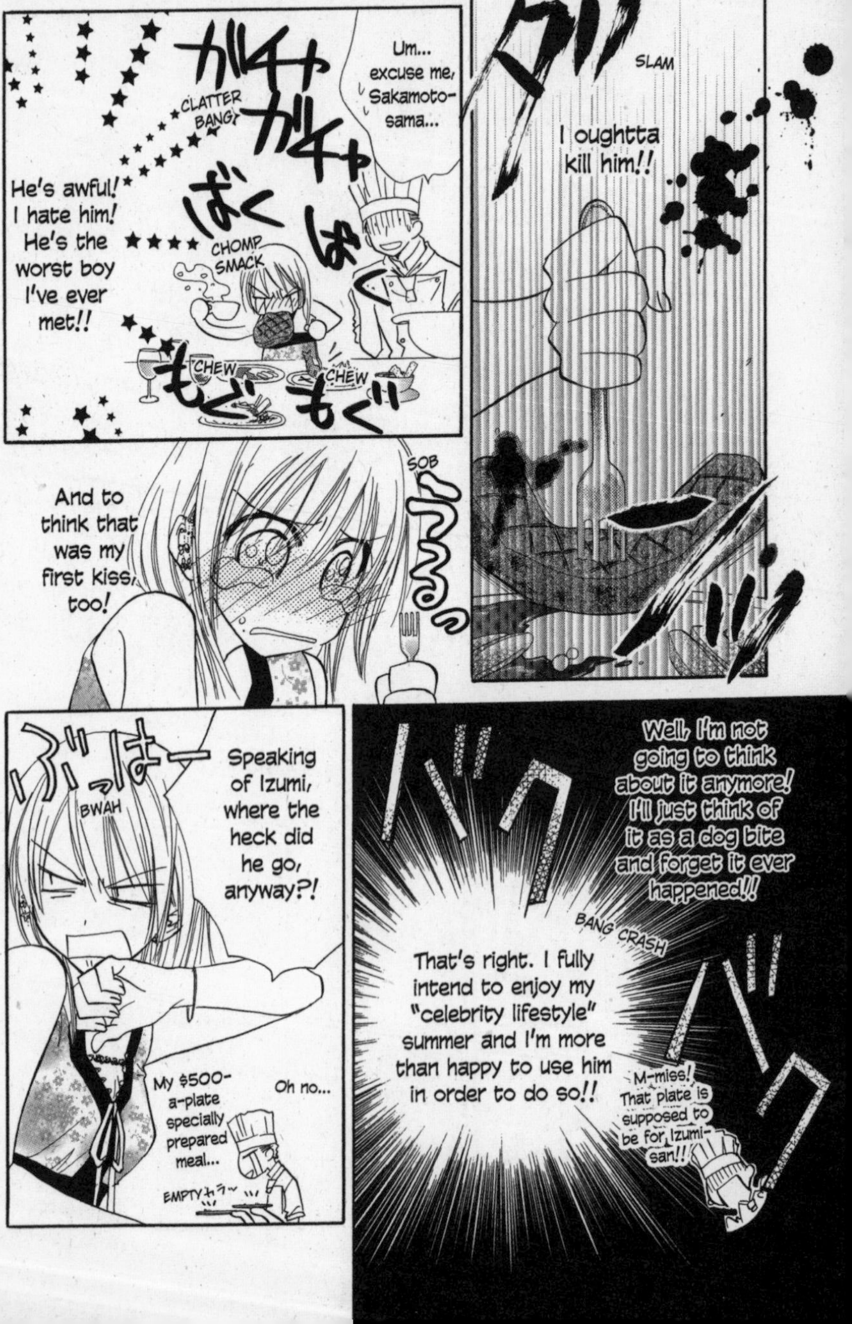
SLAM
I oughtta kill him!!
Um... excuse me, Sakamoto-sama...
CLATTER BANG
He's awful! I hate him! He's the worst boy I've ever met!!
CHOMP SMACK
CHEW
CHEW
SOB
And to think that was my first kiss, too!
Well, I'm not going to think about it anymore! I'll just think of it as a dog bite and forget it ever happened!!
BANG CRASH
That's right. I fully intend to enjoy my "celebrity lifestyle" summer and I'm more than happy to use him in order to do so!!
M-miss! That plate is supposed to be for Izumi-san!!
BWAH
Speaking of Izumi, where the heck did he go, anyway?!
Oh no...
My $500-a-plate specially prepared meal...
EMPTY

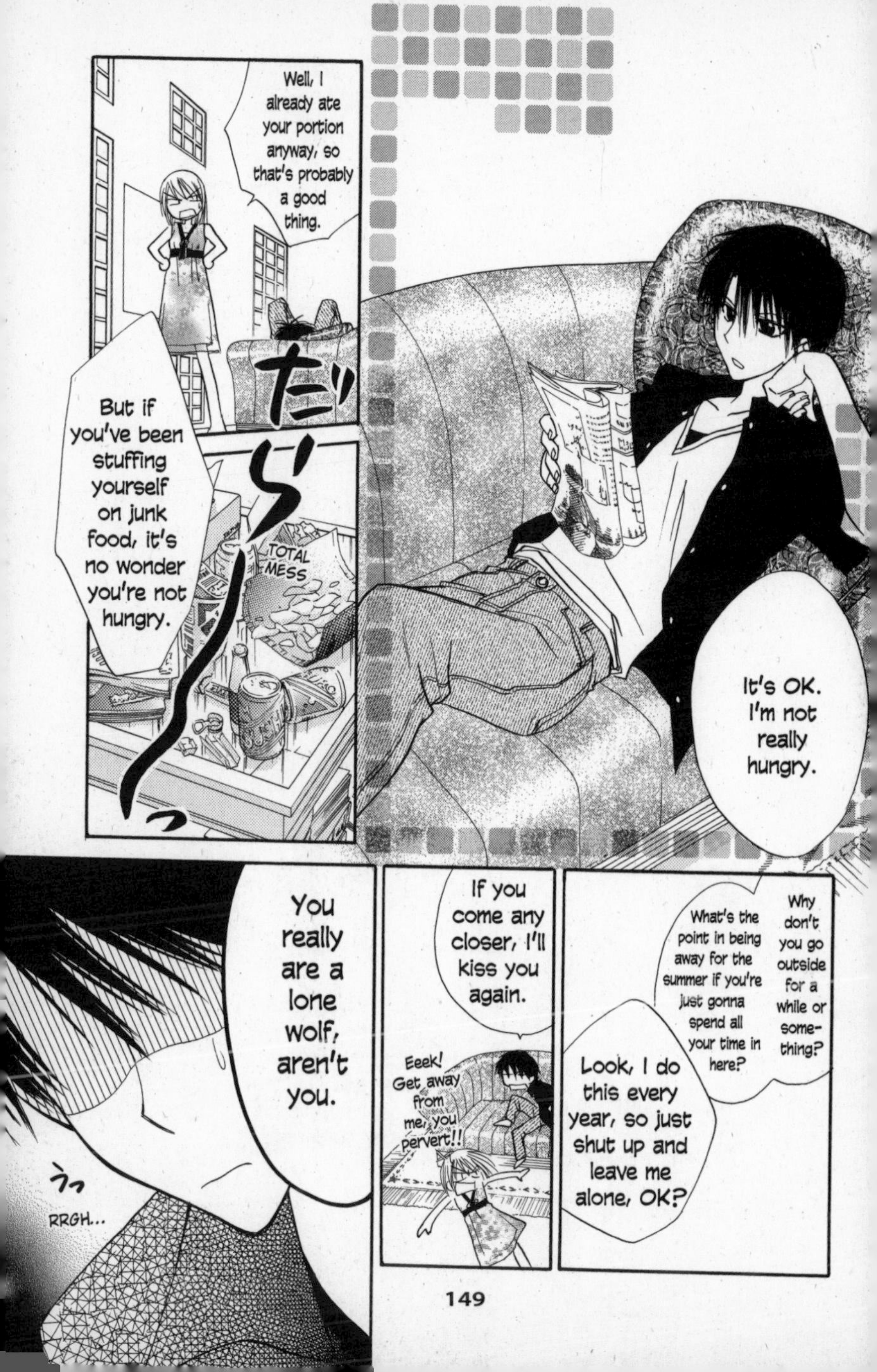
It's OK. I'm not really hungry.
Well, I already ate your portion anyway, so that's probably a good thing.
But if you've been stuffing yourself on junk food, it's no wonder you're not hungry.
TOTAL MESS
Why don't you go outside for a while or something?
What's the point in being away for the summer if you're just gonna spend all your time in here?
Look, I do this every year, so just shut up and leave me alone, OK?
If you come any closer, I'll kiss you again.
Eeek! Get away from me, you pervert!!
You really are a lone wolf, aren't you.
RRGH...

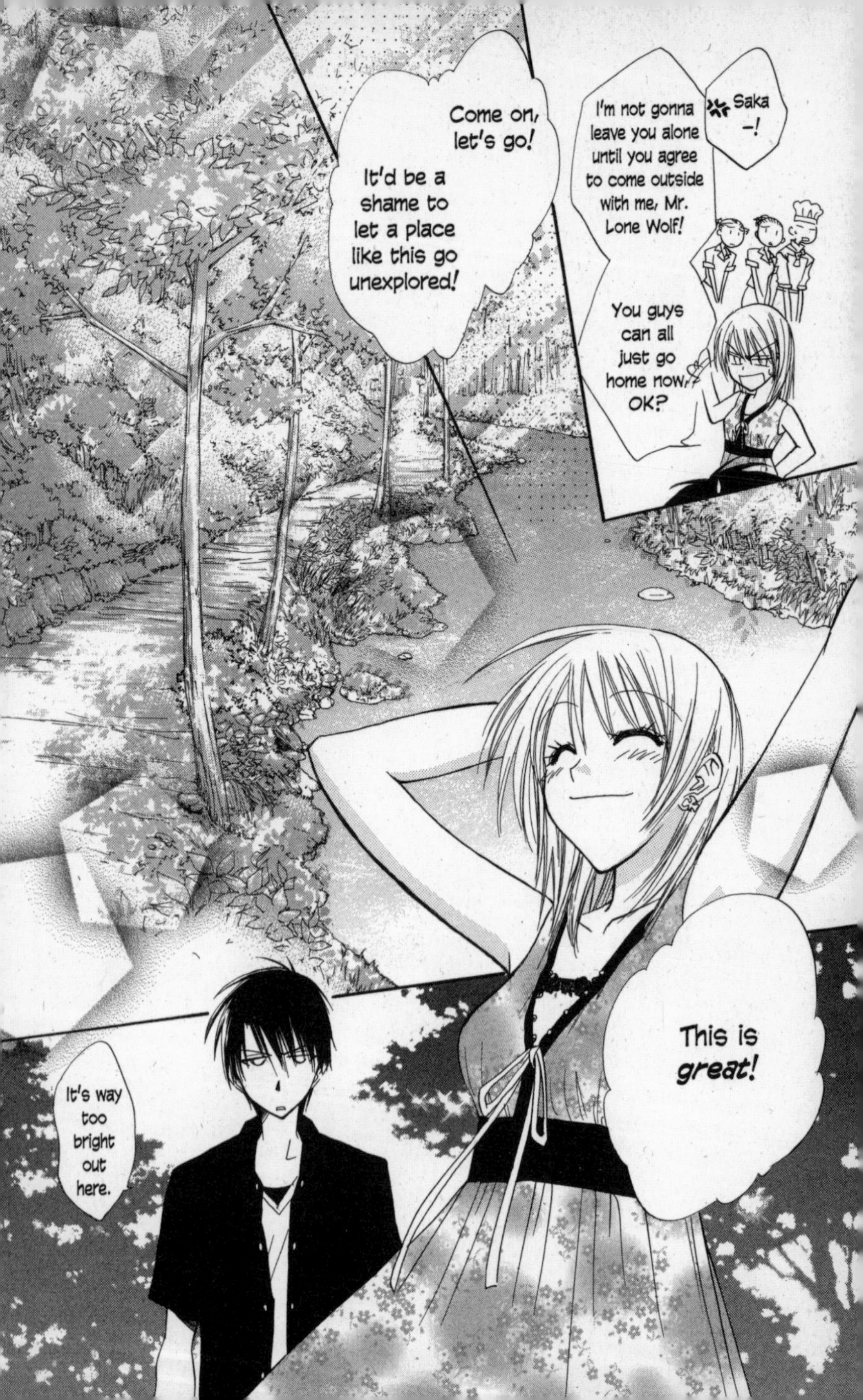
Saka—!
I'm not gonna leave you alone until you agree to come outside with me, Mr. Lone Wolf!
You guys can all just go home now, OK?
Come on, let's go!
It'd be a shame to let a place like this go unexplored!
This is *great!*
It's way too bright out here.

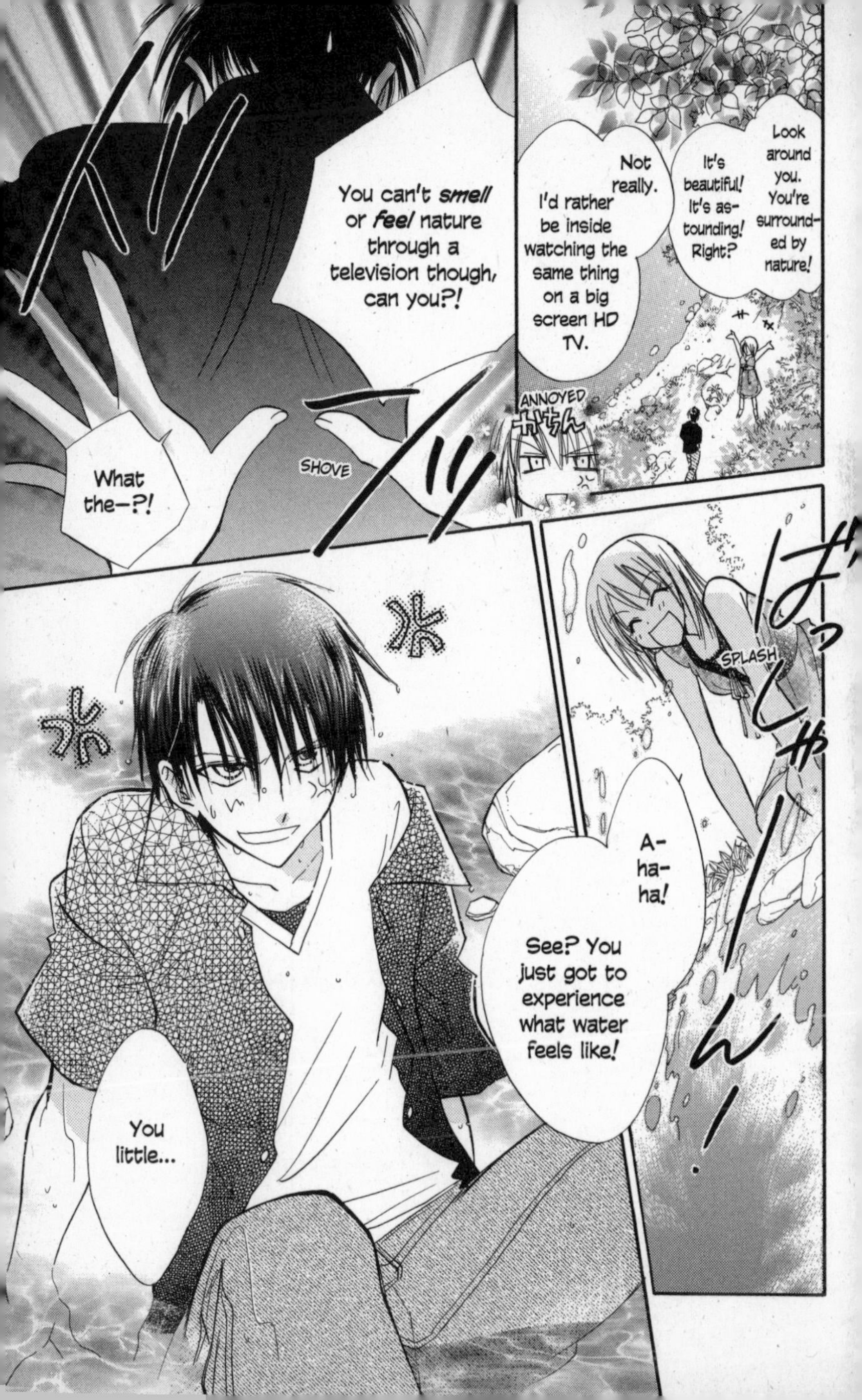
Look around you. You're surrounded by nature!
It's beautiful! It's astounding! Right?
Not really.
I'd rather be inside watching the same thing on a big screen HD TV.
ANNOYED
You can't *smell* or *feel* nature through a television though, can you?!
SHOVE
What the-?!
SPLASH
A-ha-ha!
See? You just got to experience what water feels like!
You little...

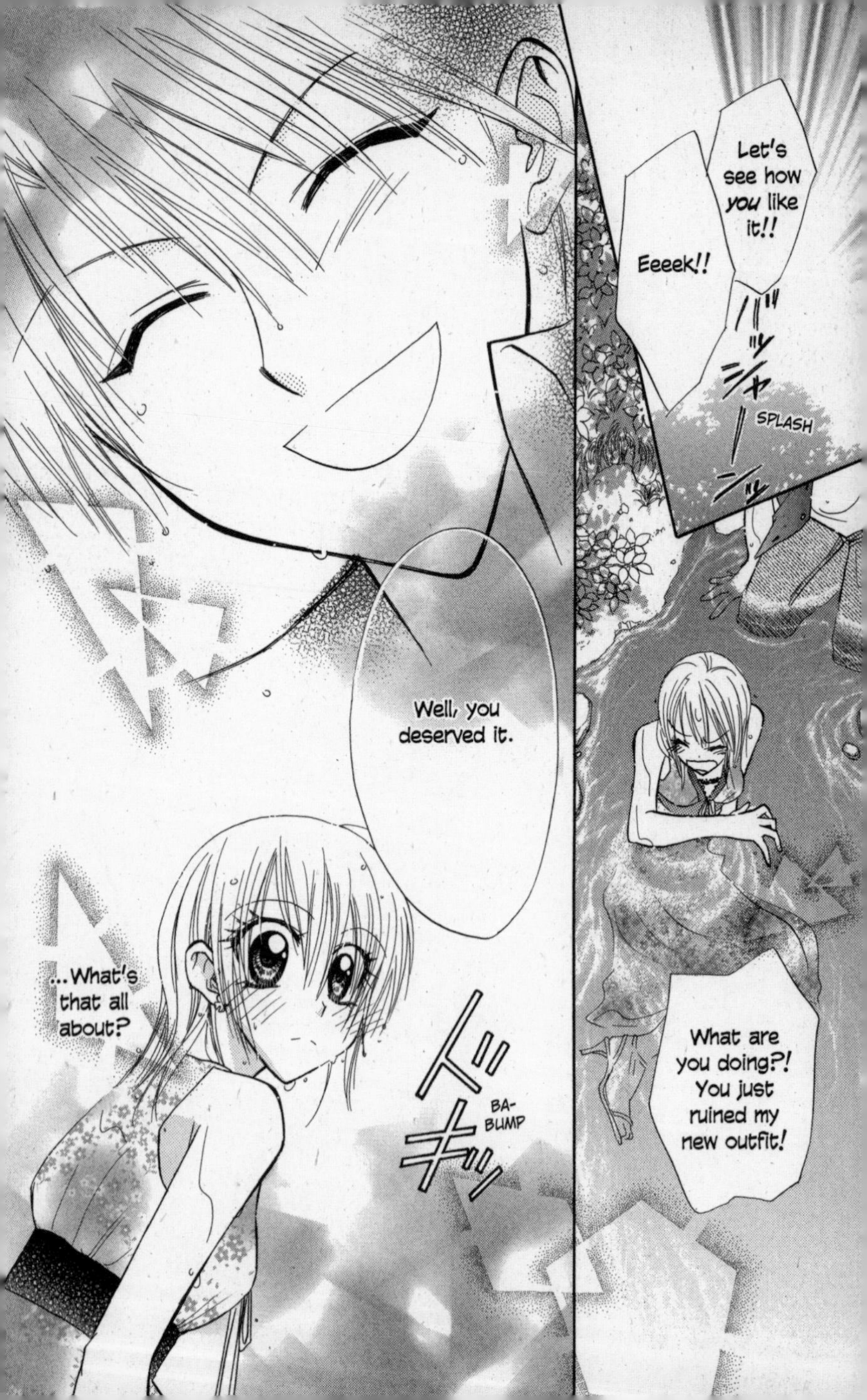

Let's see how *you* like it!!
Eeeek!!
バッシャーンッ
SPLASH
What are you doing?! You just ruined my new outfit!
Well, you deserved it.
ドキッ
BA-BUMP
...What's that all about?

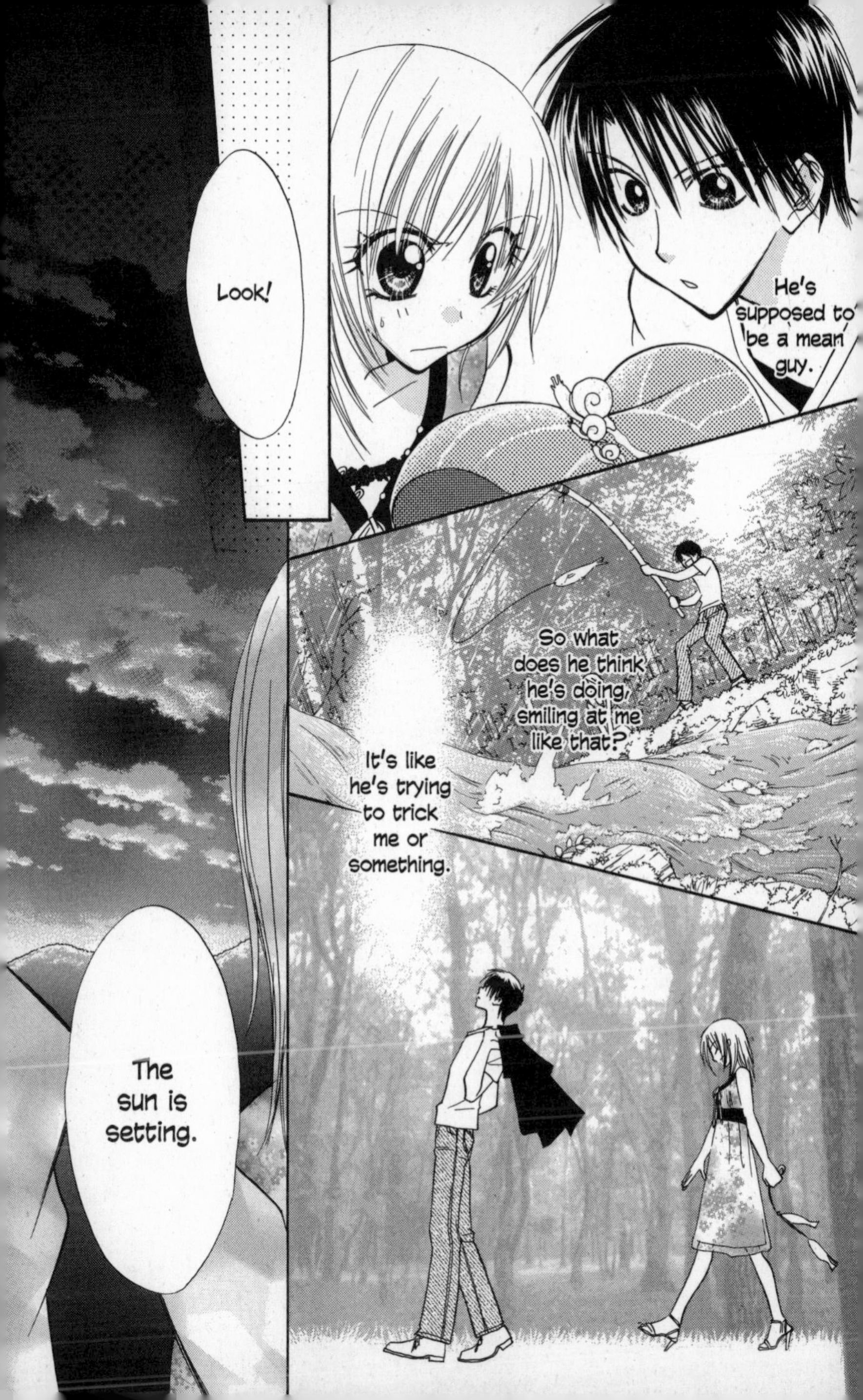
He's supposed to be a mean guy.
Look!
So what does he think he's doing, smiling at me like that?
It's like he's trying to trick me or something.
The sun is setting.

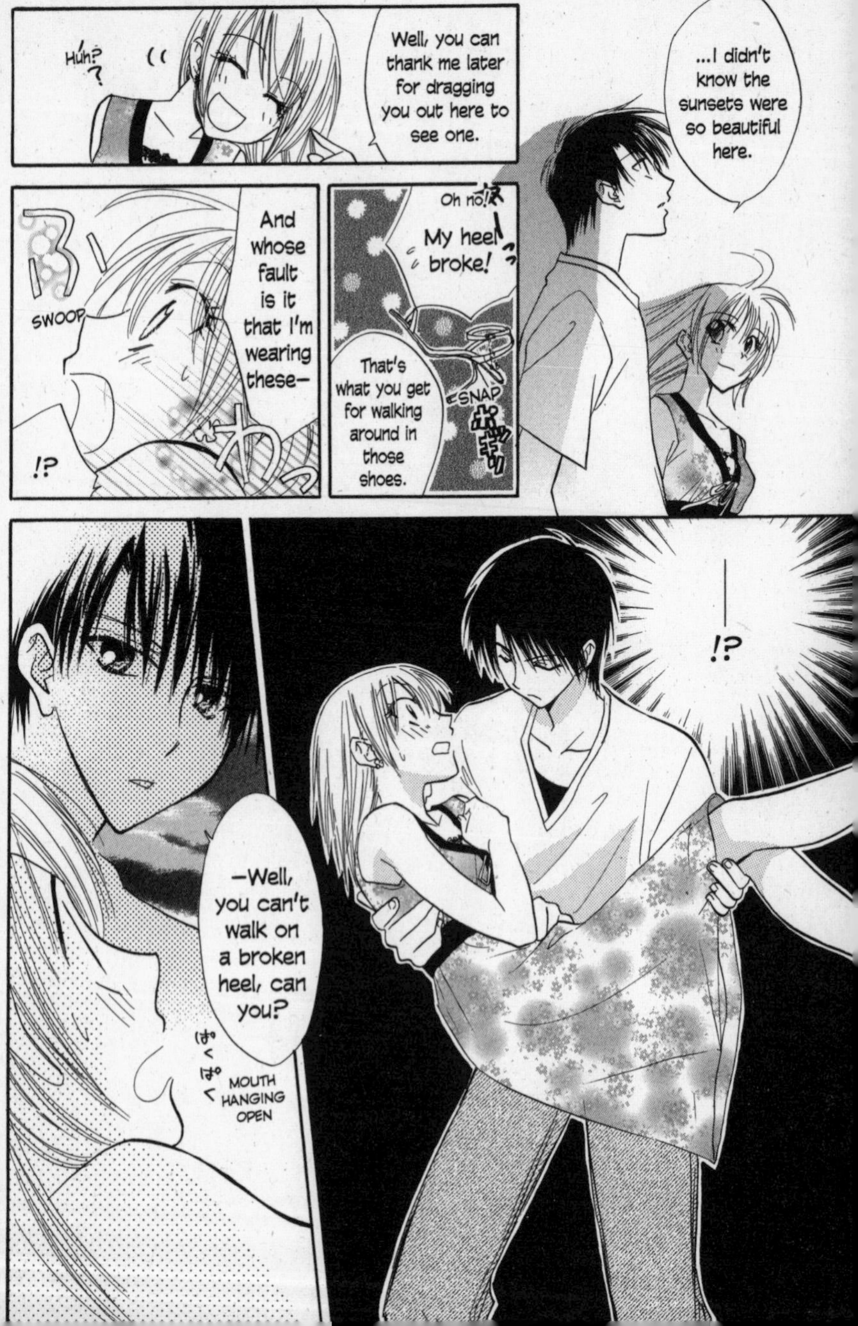
...I didn't know the sunsets were so beautiful here.
Well, you can thank me later for dragging you out here to see one.
Huh??
Oh no!
My heel broke!
SNAP
That's what you get for walking around in those shoes.
And whose fault is it that I'm wearing these—
SWOOP
!?
!?
—Well, you can't walk on a broken heel, can you?
MOUTH HANGING OPEN

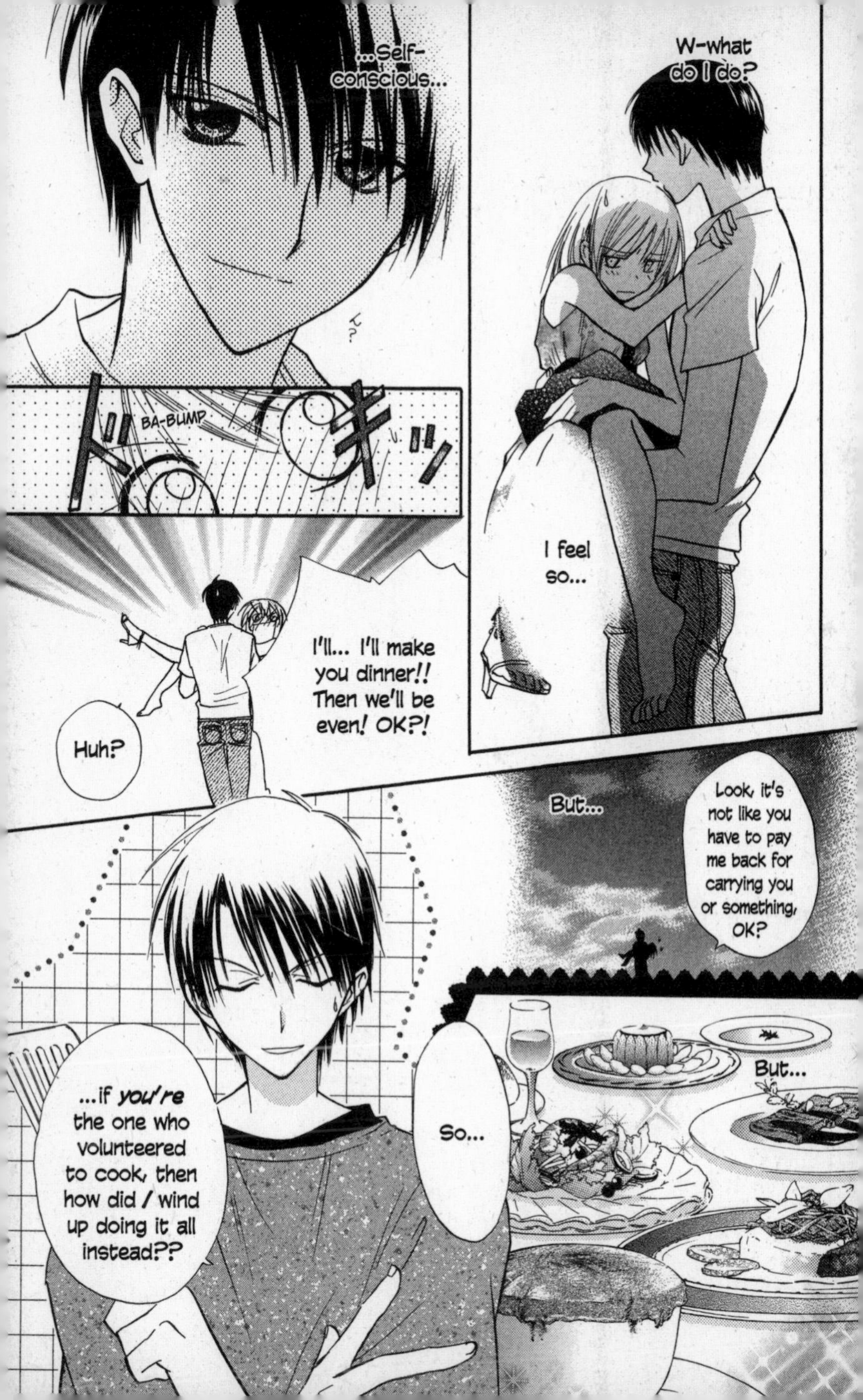
W-what do I do?
I feel so...
...Self-conscious...
BA-BUMP
I'll... I'll make you dinner!! Then we'll be even! OK?!
Huh?
Look, it's not like you have to pay me back for carrying you or something, OK?
But...
But...
So...
...if *you're* the one who volunteered to cook, then how did *I* wind up doing it all instead??

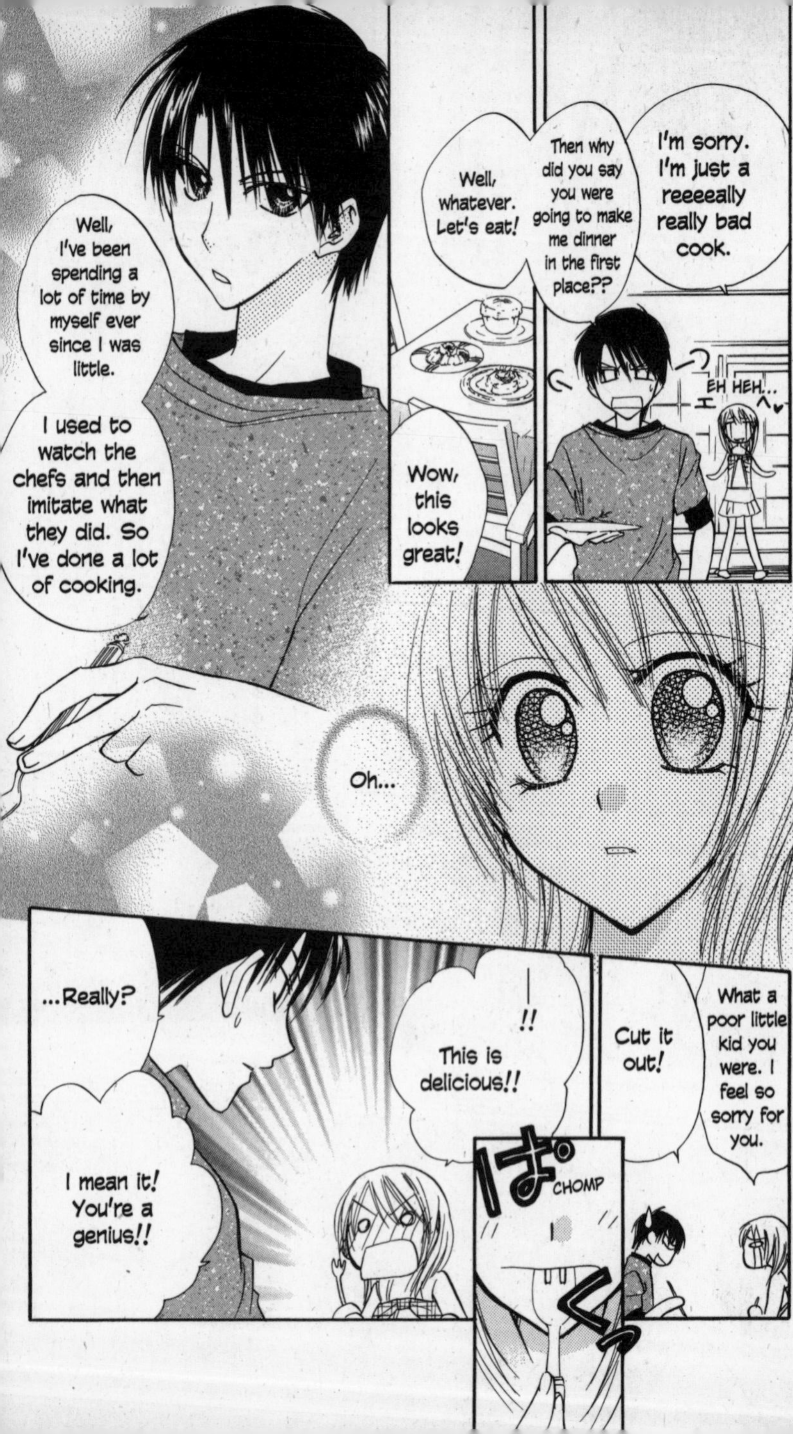
I'm sorry. I'm just a reeeeally really bad cook.
EH HEH...
Then why did you say you were going to make me dinner in the first place??
Well, whatever. Let's eat!
Wow, this looks great!
Well, I've been spending a lot of time by myself ever since I was little.
I used to watch the chefs and then imitate what they did. So I've done a lot of cooking.
Oh...
What a poor little kid you were. I feel so sorry for you.
Cut it out!
CHOMP
!!
This is delicious!!
...Really?
I mean it! You're a genius!!

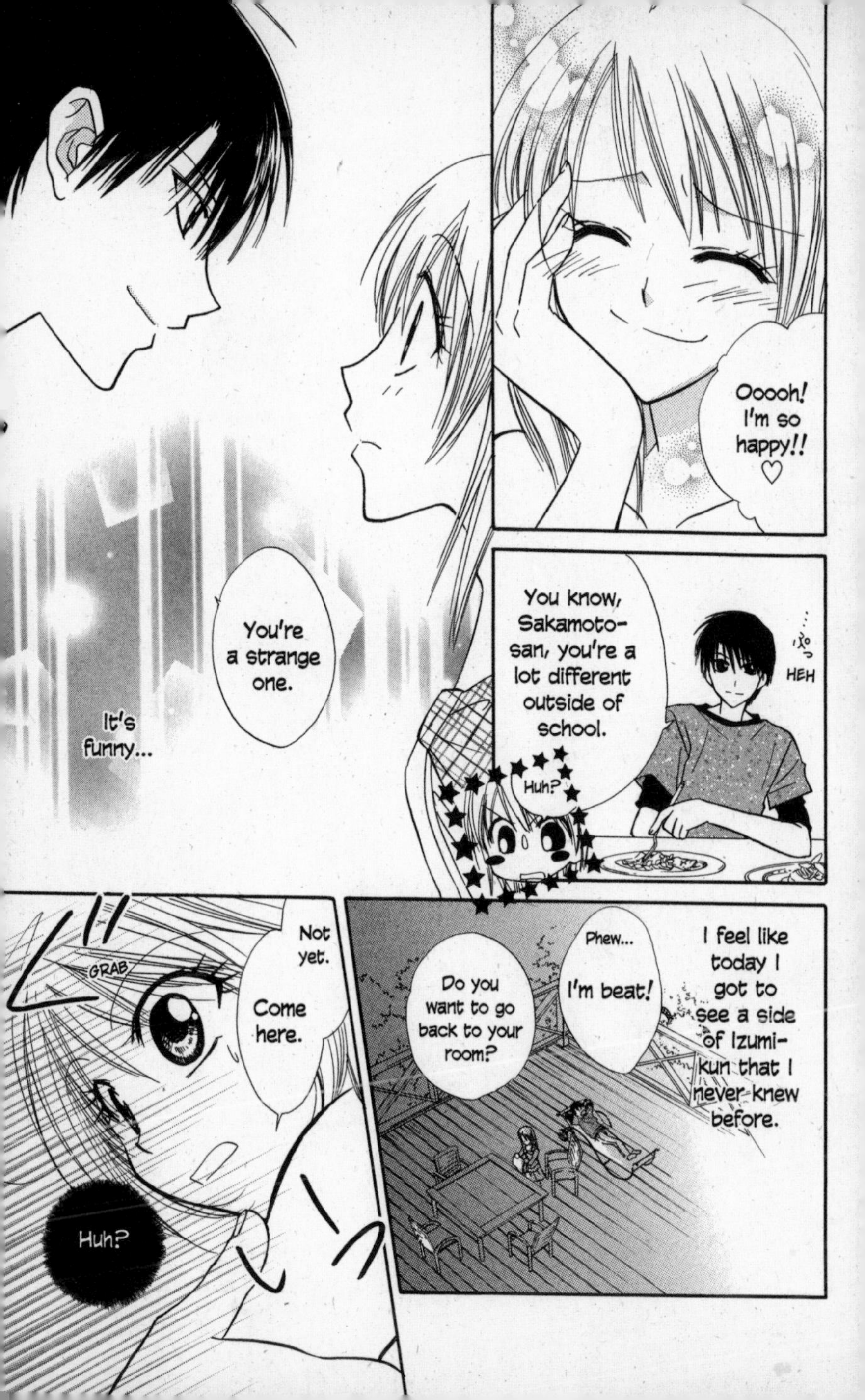
Ooooh! I'm so happy!! ♡
You know, Sakamoto-san, you're a lot different outside of school.
HEH
Huh?
You're a strange one.
It's funny...
I feel like today I got to see a side of Izumi-kun that I never knew before.
Phew...
I'm beat!
Do you want to go back to your room?
Not yet.
Come here.
GRAB
Huh?

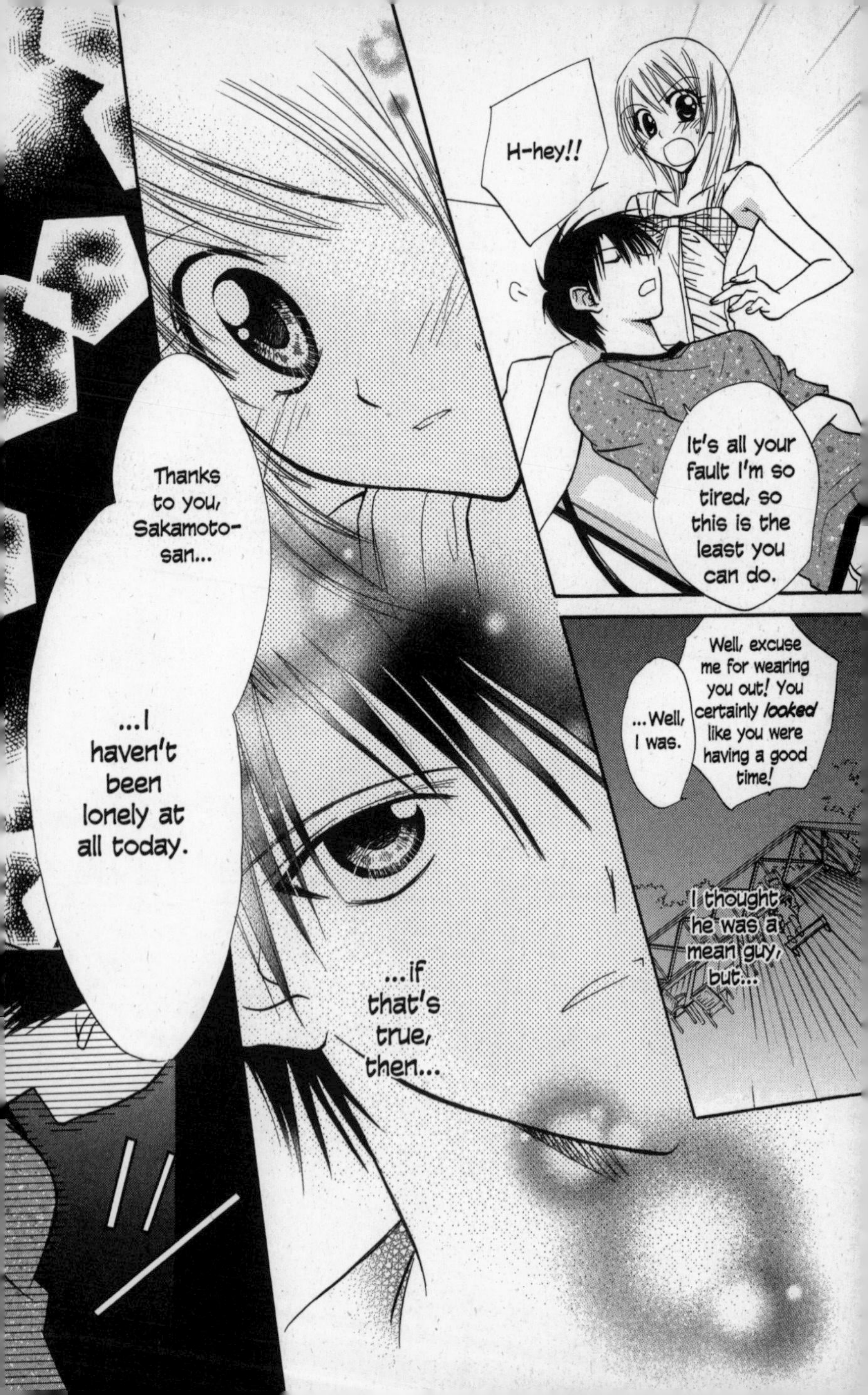
H-hey!!
It's all your fault I'm so tired, so this is the least you can do.
Well, excuse me for wearing you out! You certainly *looked* like you were having a good time!
...Well, I was.
I thought he was a mean guy, but...
Thanks to you, Sakamoto-san...
...I haven't been lonely at all today.
...if that's true, then...

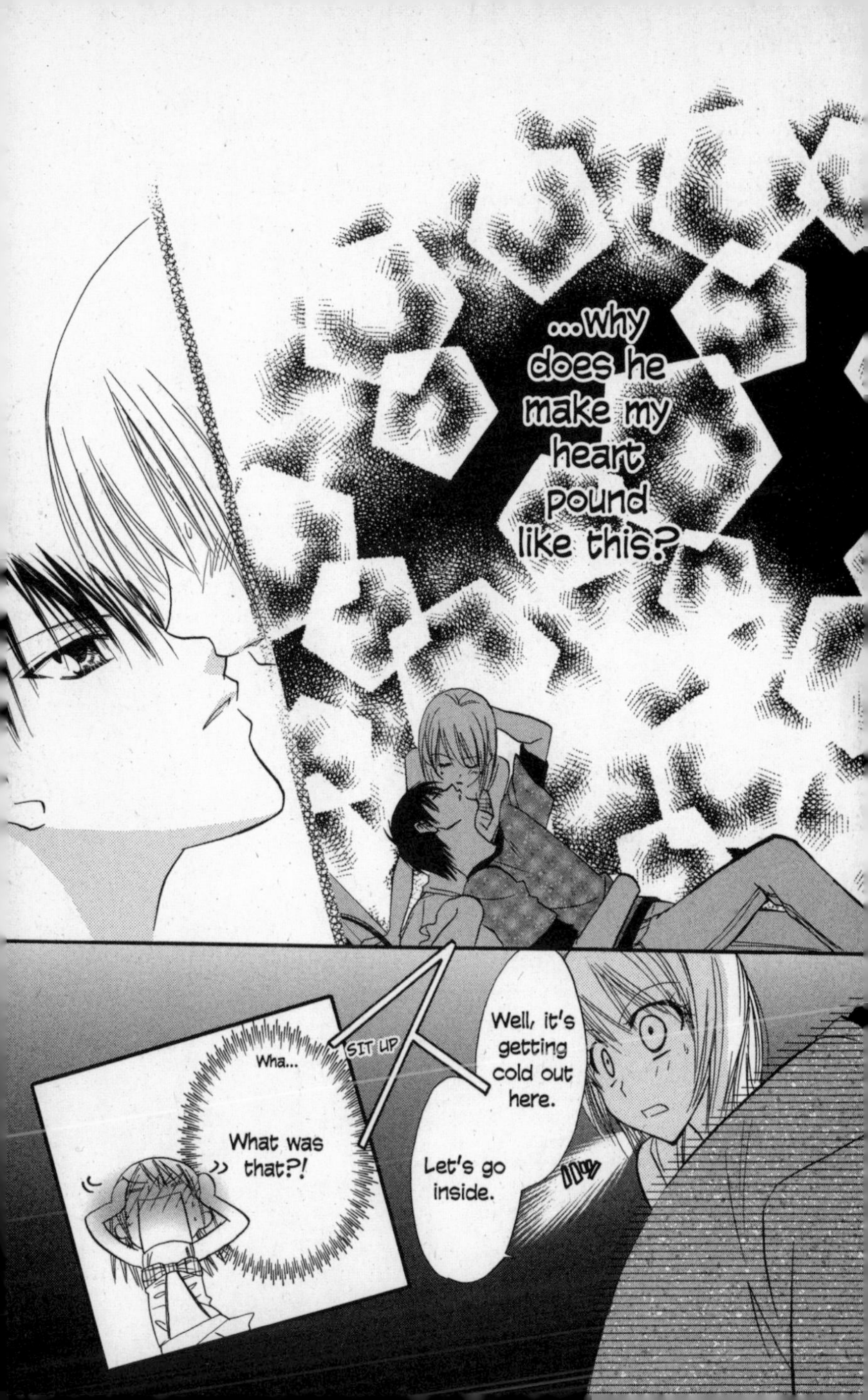
...why does he make my heart pound like this?
Well, it's getting cold out here.
Let's go inside.
SIT UP
Wha...
What was that?!

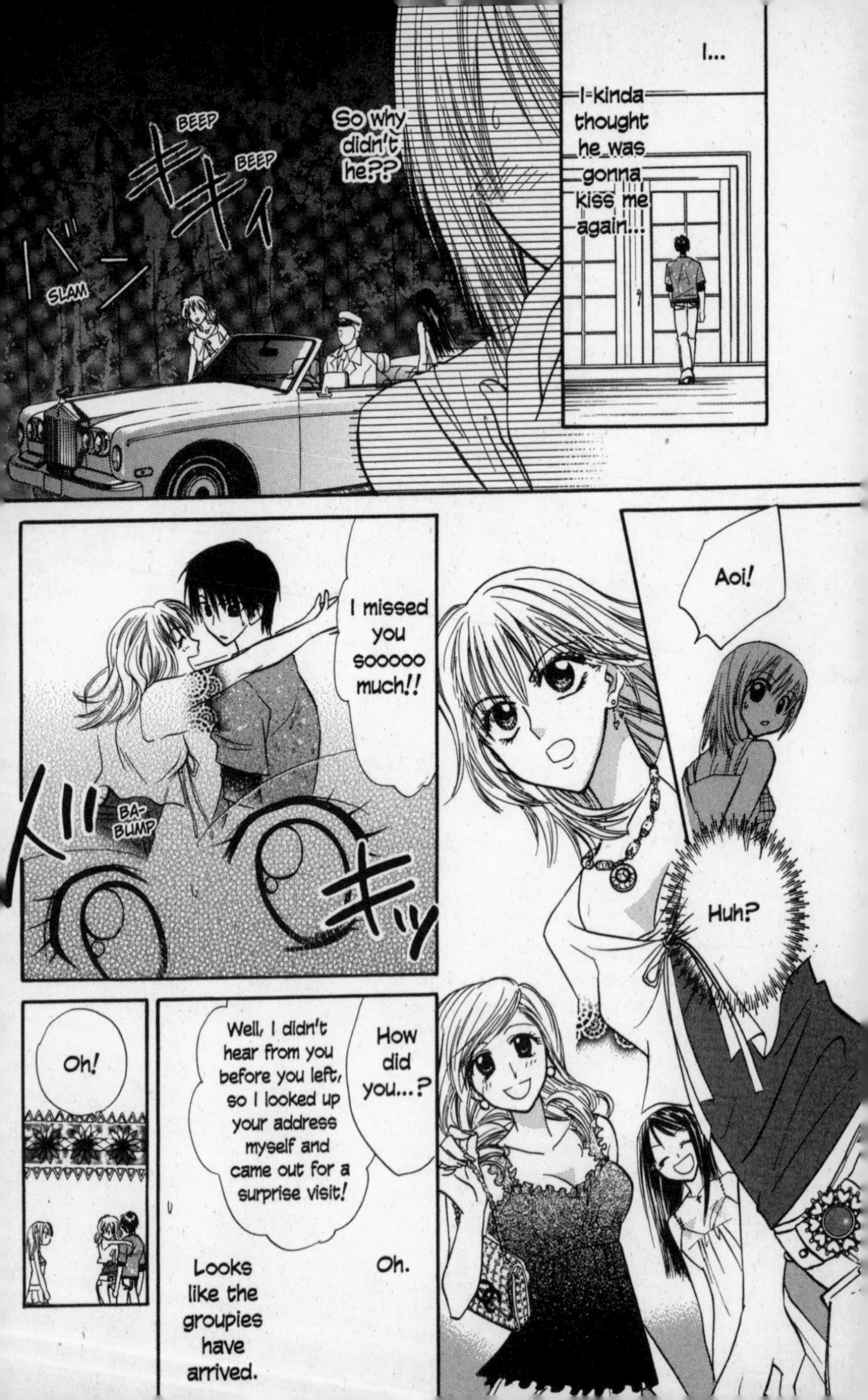
I...
I-kinda thought he was gonna kiss me again...
So why didn't he??
BEEP
BEEP
SLAM
Aoi!
Huh?
I missed you sooooo much!!
BA-BUMP
How did you...?
Well, I didn't hear from you before you left, so I looked up your address myself and came out for a surprise visit!
Oh.
Looks like the groupies have arrived.
Oh!

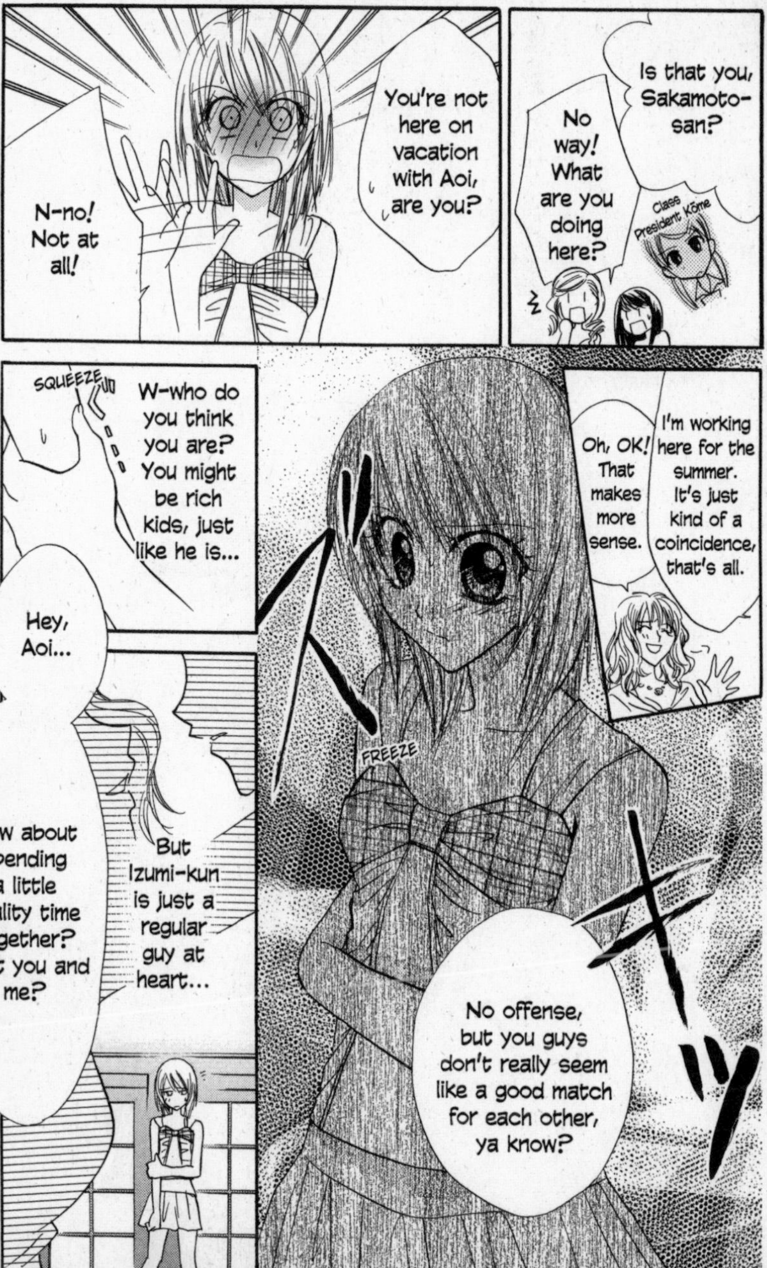
Is that you, Sakamoto-san?
No way! What are you doing here?
Class President Kōme
You're not here on vacation with Aoi, are you?
N-no! Not at all!
I'm working here for the summer. It's just kind of a coincidence, that's all.
Oh, OK! That makes more sense.
FREEZE
No offense, but you guys don't really seem like a good match for each other, ya know?
SQUEEZE
W-who do you think you are? You might be rich kids, just like he is...
But Izumi-kun is just a regular guy at heart...
Hey, Aoi...
How about spending a little quality time together? Just you and me?

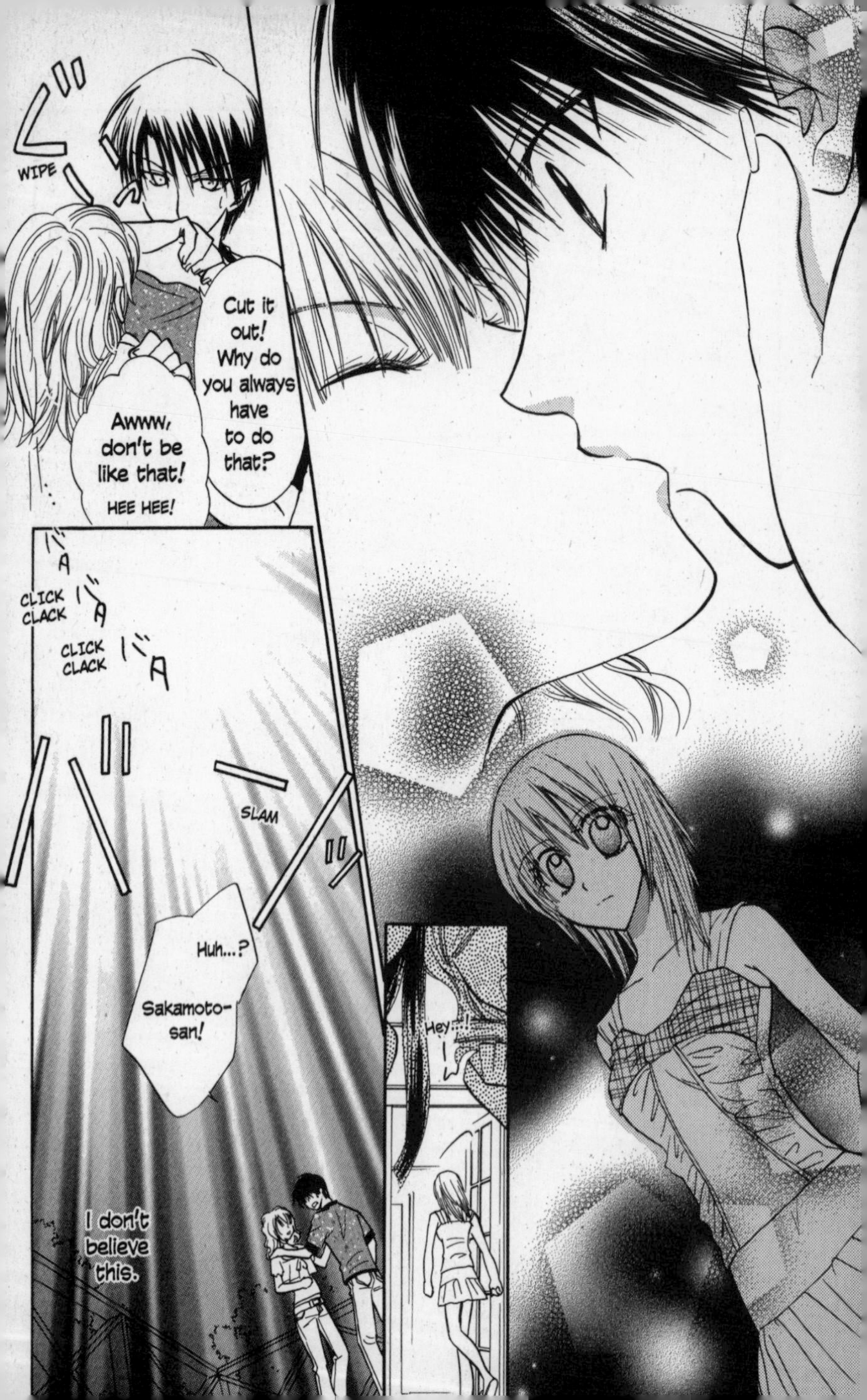
WIPE
Cut it out! Why do you always have to do that?
Awww, don't be like that!
HEE HEE!
Hey...!
CLICK CLACK
CLICK CLACK
SLAM
Huh...?
Sakamoto-san!
I don't believe this.

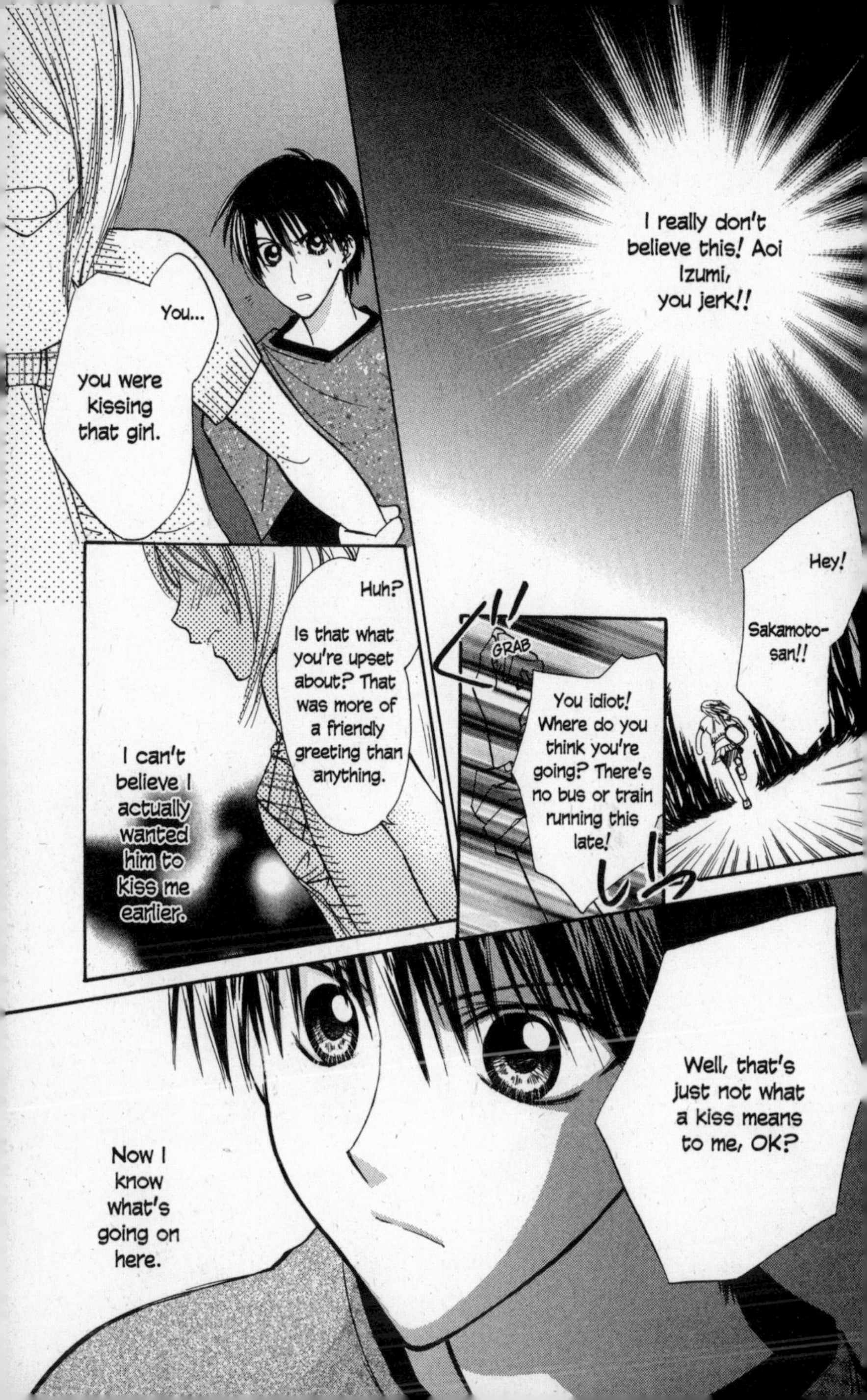
You...
you were kissing that girl.
Huh?
Is that what you're upset about? That was more of a friendly greeting than anything.
I can't believe I actually wanted him to kiss me earlier.
I really don't believe this! Aoi Izumi, you jerk!!
Hey!
Sakamoto-san!!
GRAB
You idiot! Where do you think you're going? There's no bus or train running this late!
Well, that's just not what a kiss means to me, OK?
Now I know what's going on here.

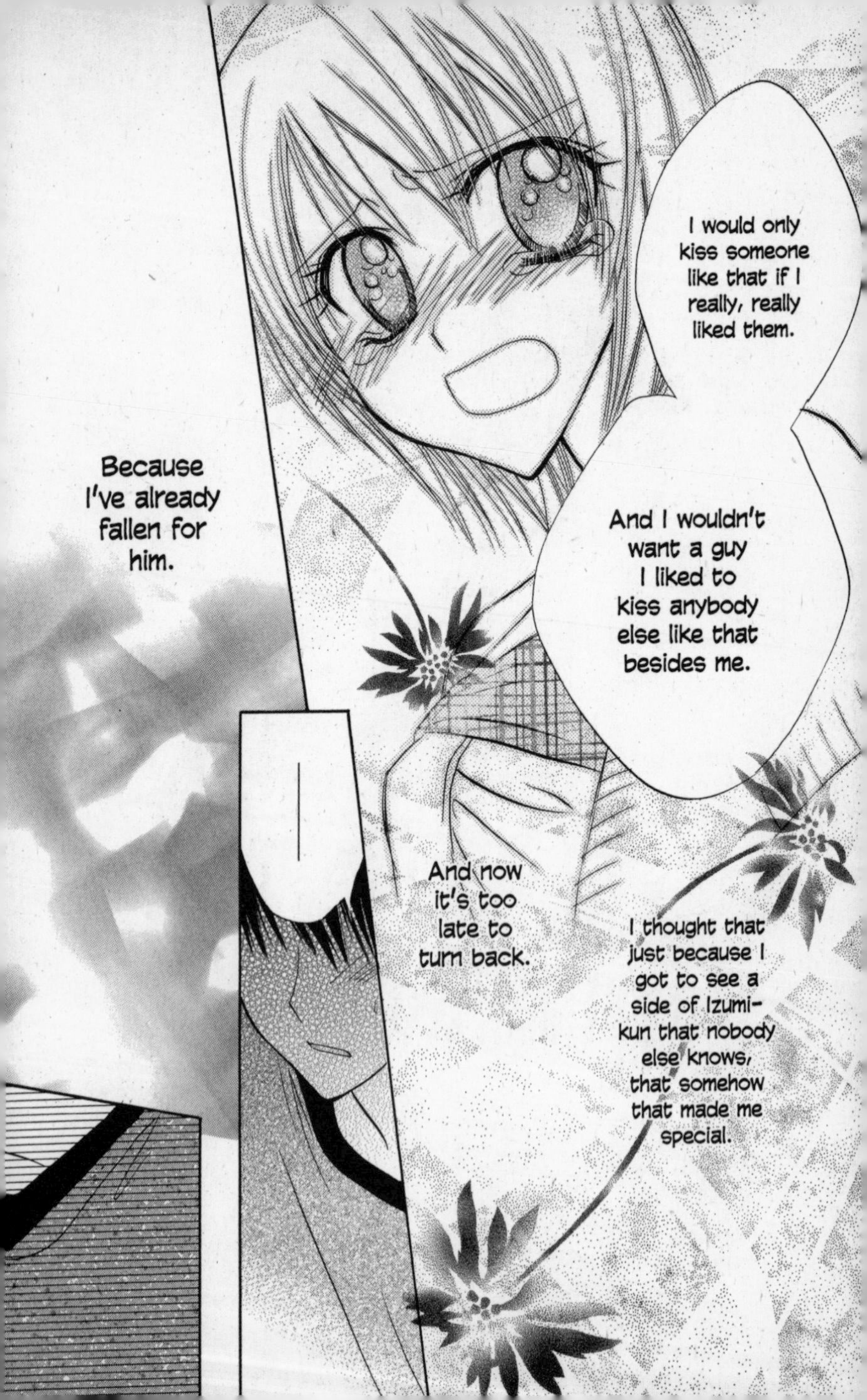
I would only kiss someone like that if I really, really liked them.
And I wouldn't want a guy I liked to kiss anybody else like that besides me.
I thought that just because I got to see a side of Izumi-kun that nobody else knows, that somehow that made me special.
And now it's too late to turn back.
Because I've already fallen for him.

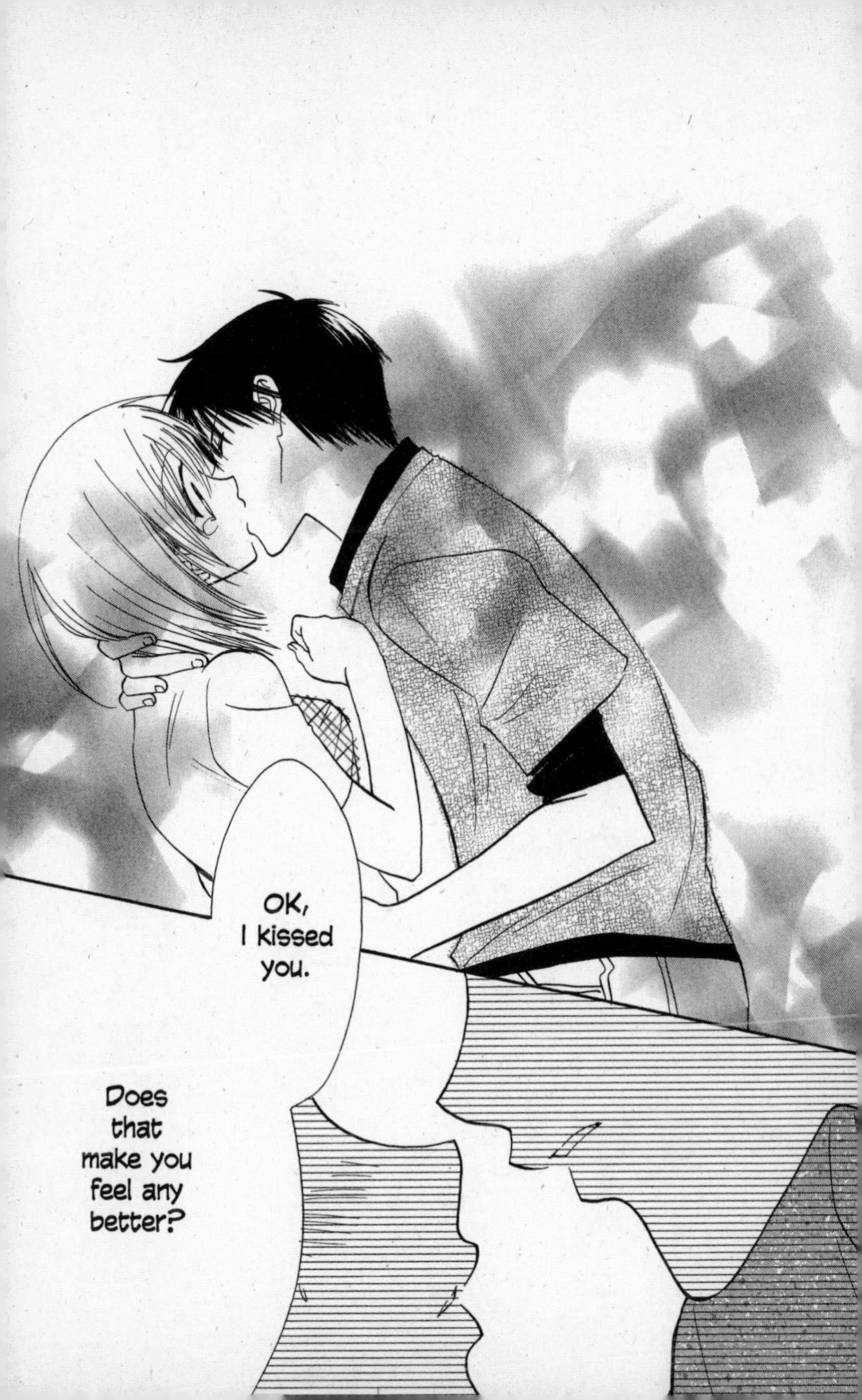
OK, I kissed you.
Does that make you feel any better?

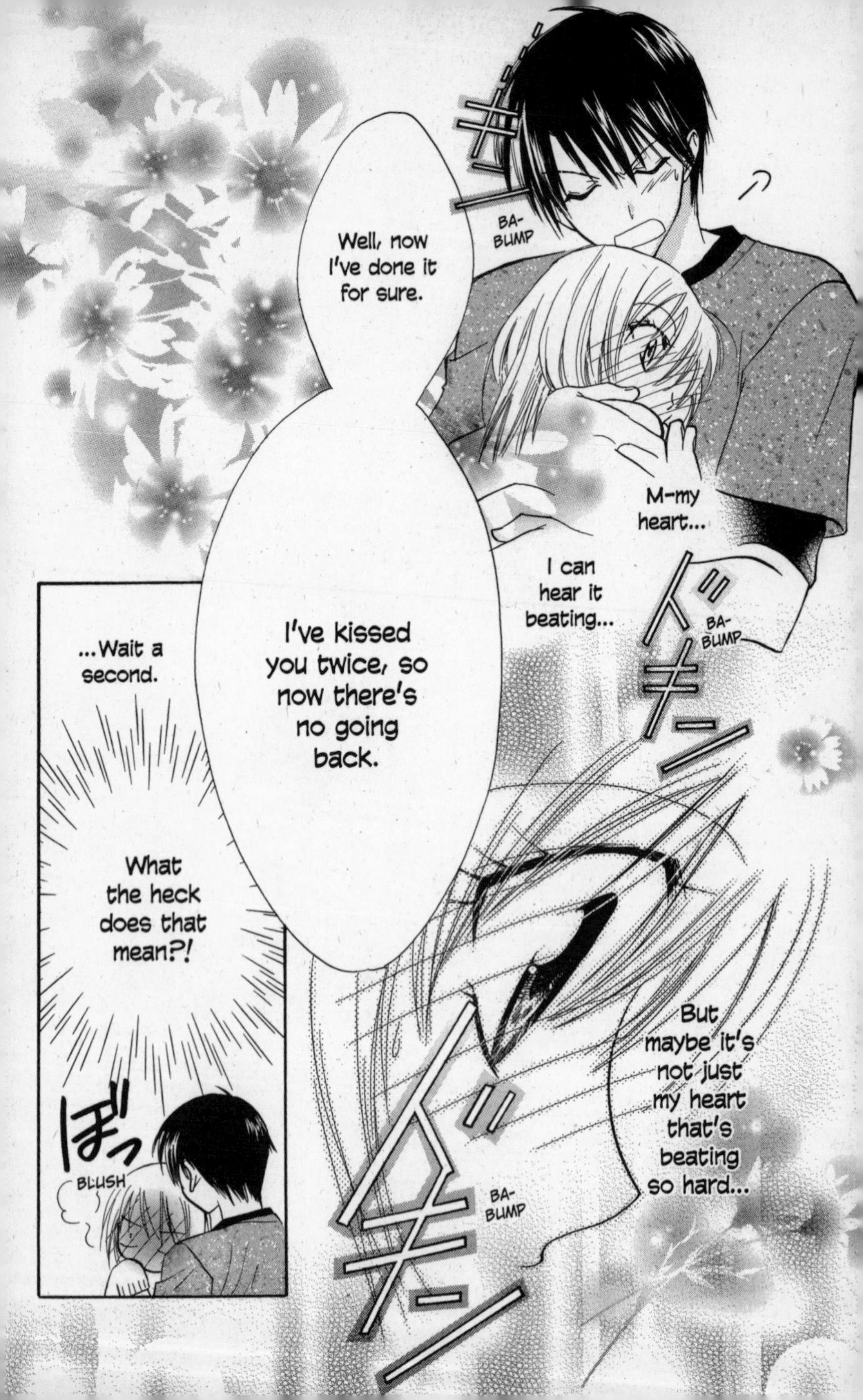
BA-BUMP
Well, now I've done it for sure.
M-my heart...
I can hear it beating...
ドキーン
BA-BUMP
I've kissed you twice, so now there's no going back.
But maybe it's not just my heart that's beating so hard...
ドキーン
BA-BUMP
...Wait a second.
What the heck does that mean?!
ぼっ
BLUSH

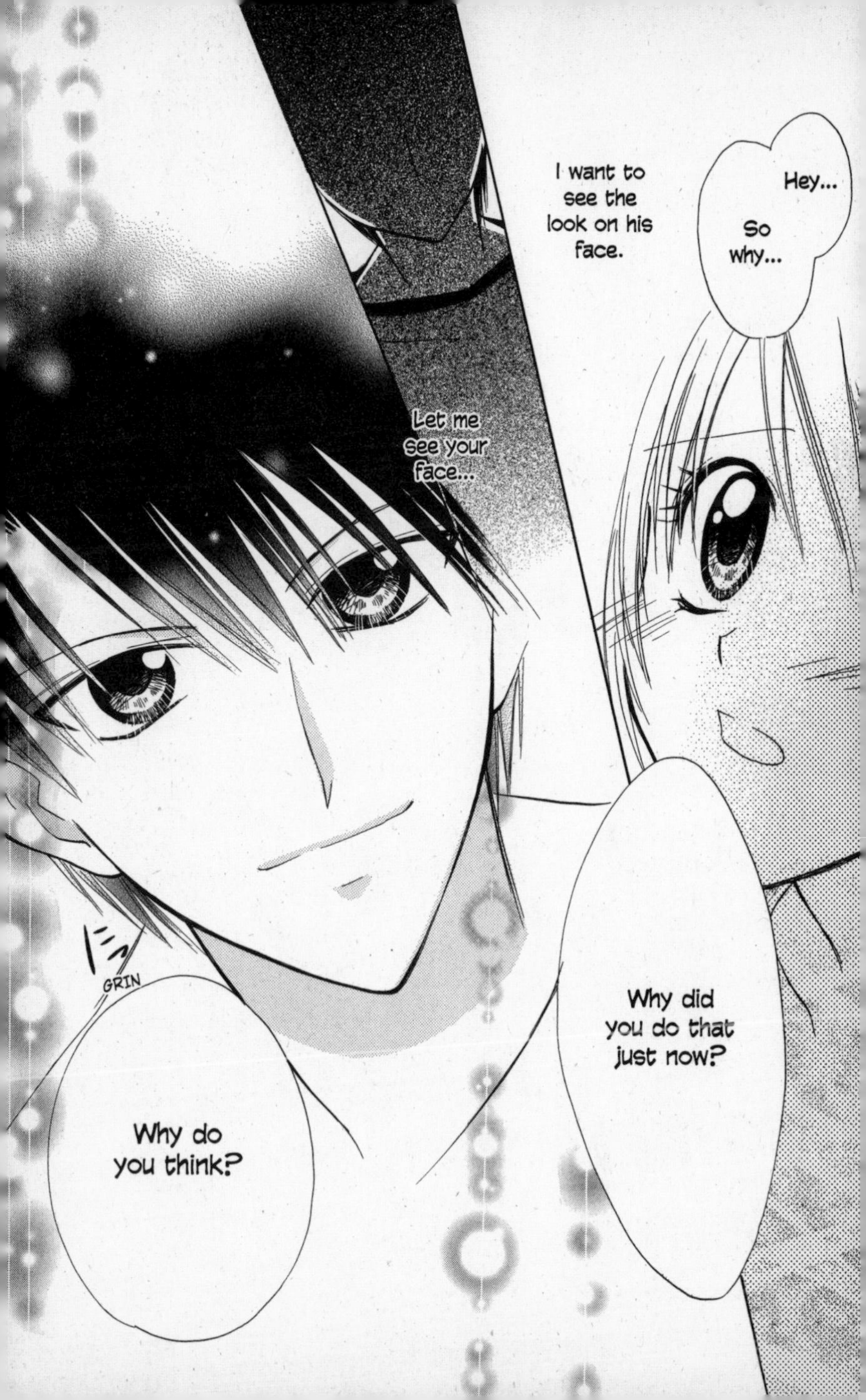
Hey...
So why...
I want to see the look on his face.
Let me see your face...
Why did you do that just now?
GRIN
Why do you think?

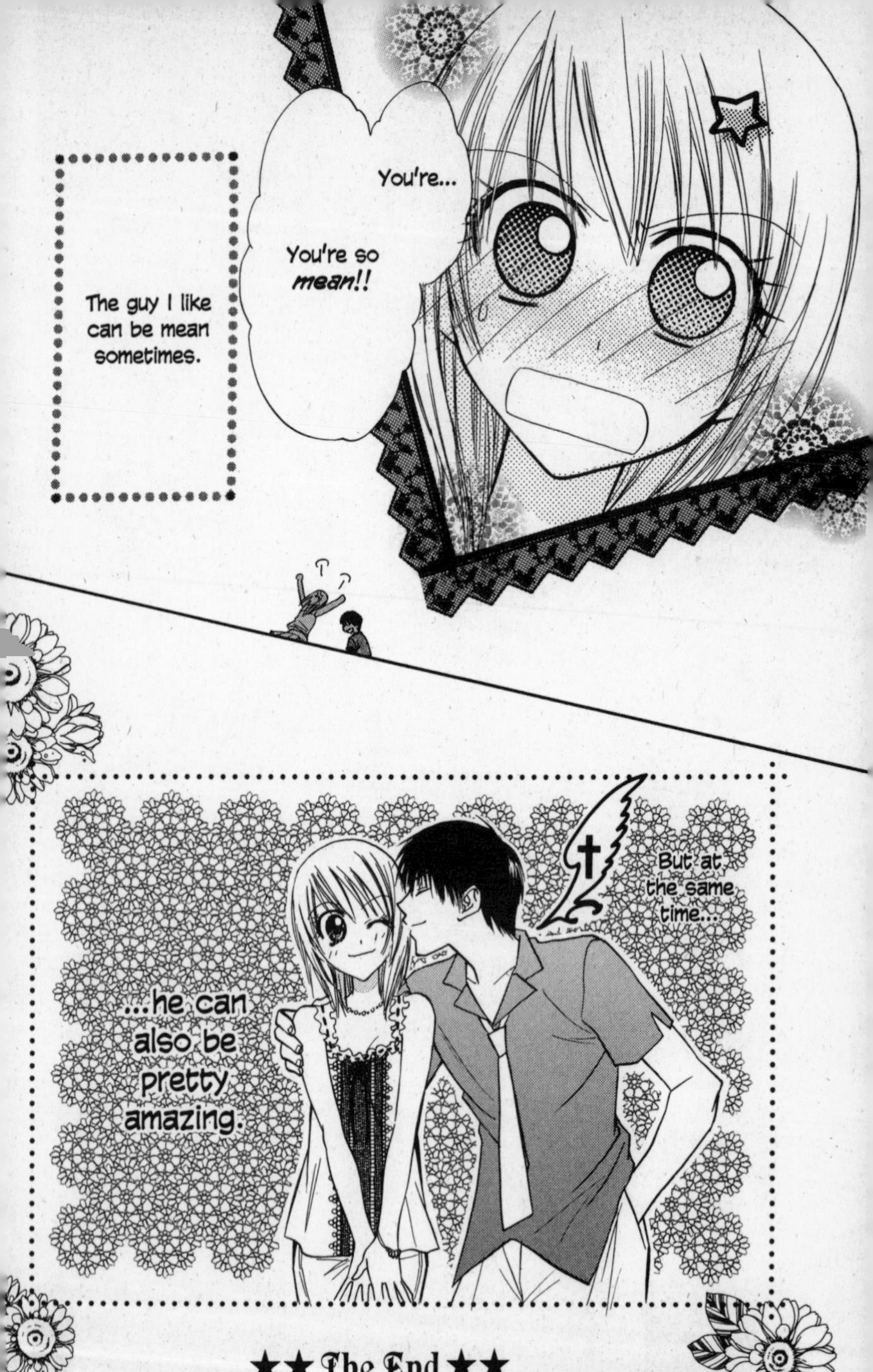
You're...
You're so *mean*!!
The guy I like can be mean sometimes.
But at the same time...
...he can also be pretty amazing.

★★ The End ★★

Glasses News Website: http://megane-ouji.cocolog-nifty.com/blog

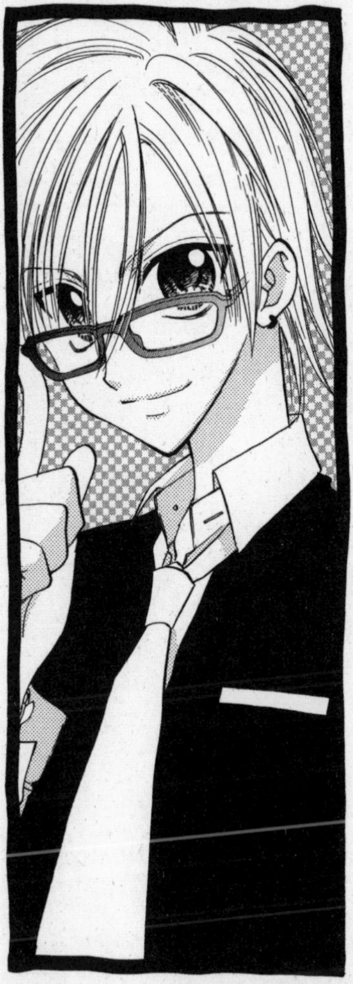

To all my first-time readers as well as the long-time readers, I'd like to say a great big "Glasses"! (It's my special greeting!) This is Mizukami. As the end of 2006 was drawing near, a chance word from my Supervisor, S-san—

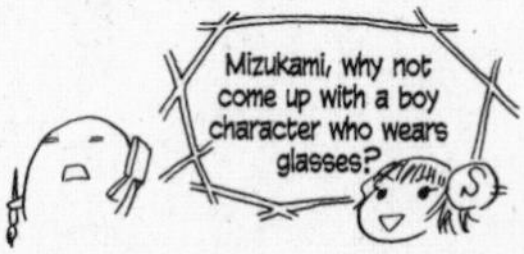

Mizukami, why not come up with a boy character who wears glasses?
S


—caused this manga to be born. What's that you say? This is supposed to be a manga about glasses, but there weren't enough scenes with glasses in them? If you're one of the people who thinks so, then by all means, be sure to read the next volume! I promise to up the percentage of scenes featuring glasses by 200%.

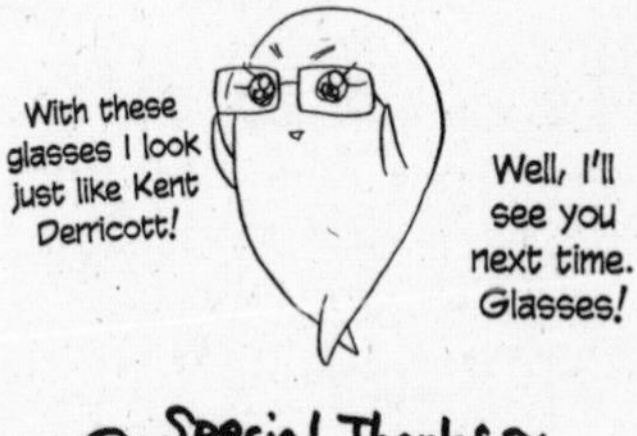

With these glasses I look just like Kent Derricott!
Well, I'll see you next time. Glasses!



~ Special Thanks ~

Ichiri Hashiba * Miki Fujimori
Naho Yamada * Hiromi Hiraiwa * Megumu Ara
&
Editor S & N * my Family * my friends
&
You!!

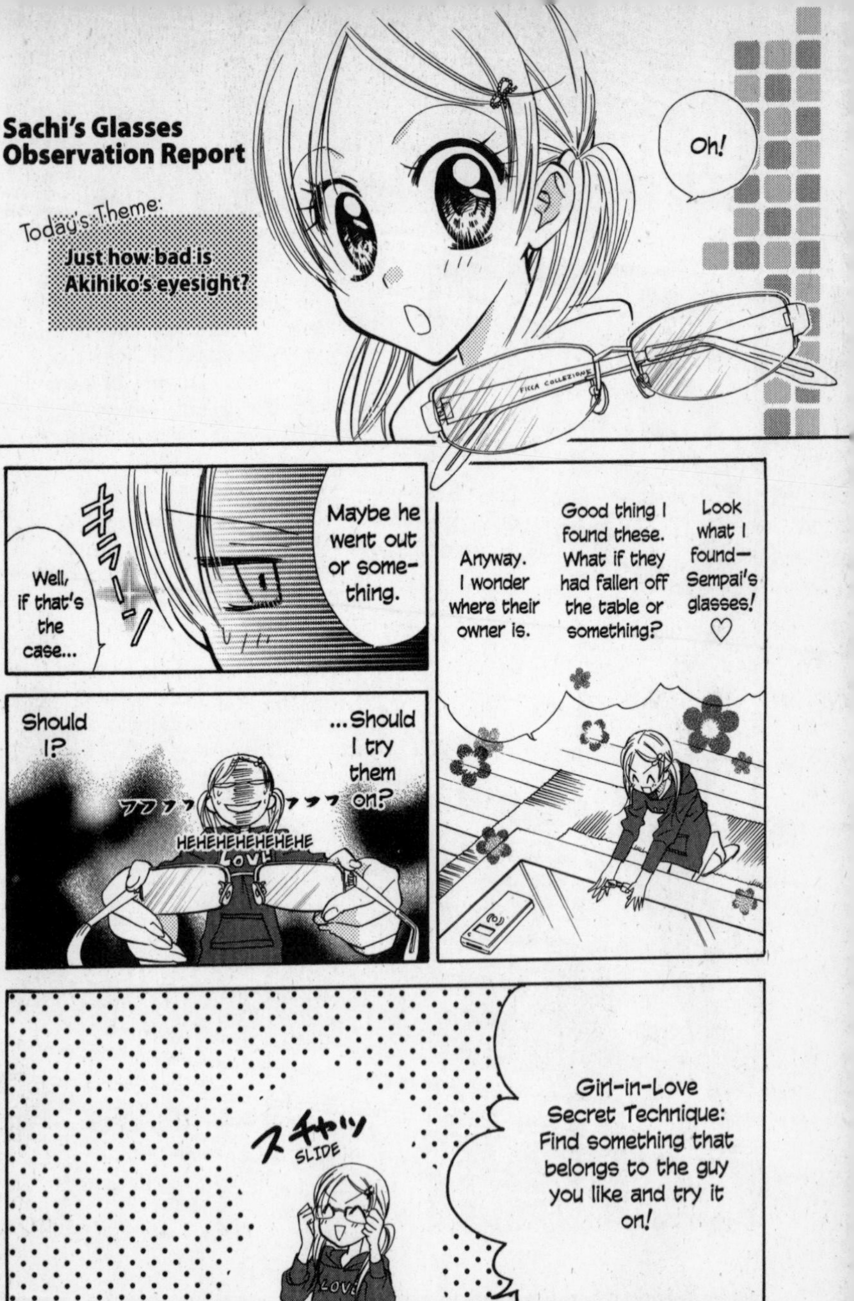
Sachi's Glasses Observation Report
Oh!
Today's Theme:
Just how bad is Akihiko's eyesight?
Look what I found—Sempai's glasses! ♡
Good thing I found these. What if they had fallen off the table or something?
Anyway. I wonder where their owner is.
Maybe he went out or something.
Well, if that's the case...
...Should I try them on?
Should I?
HEHEHEHEHEHEHE
Girl-in-Love Secret Technique: Find something that belongs to the guy you like and try it on!
SLIDE

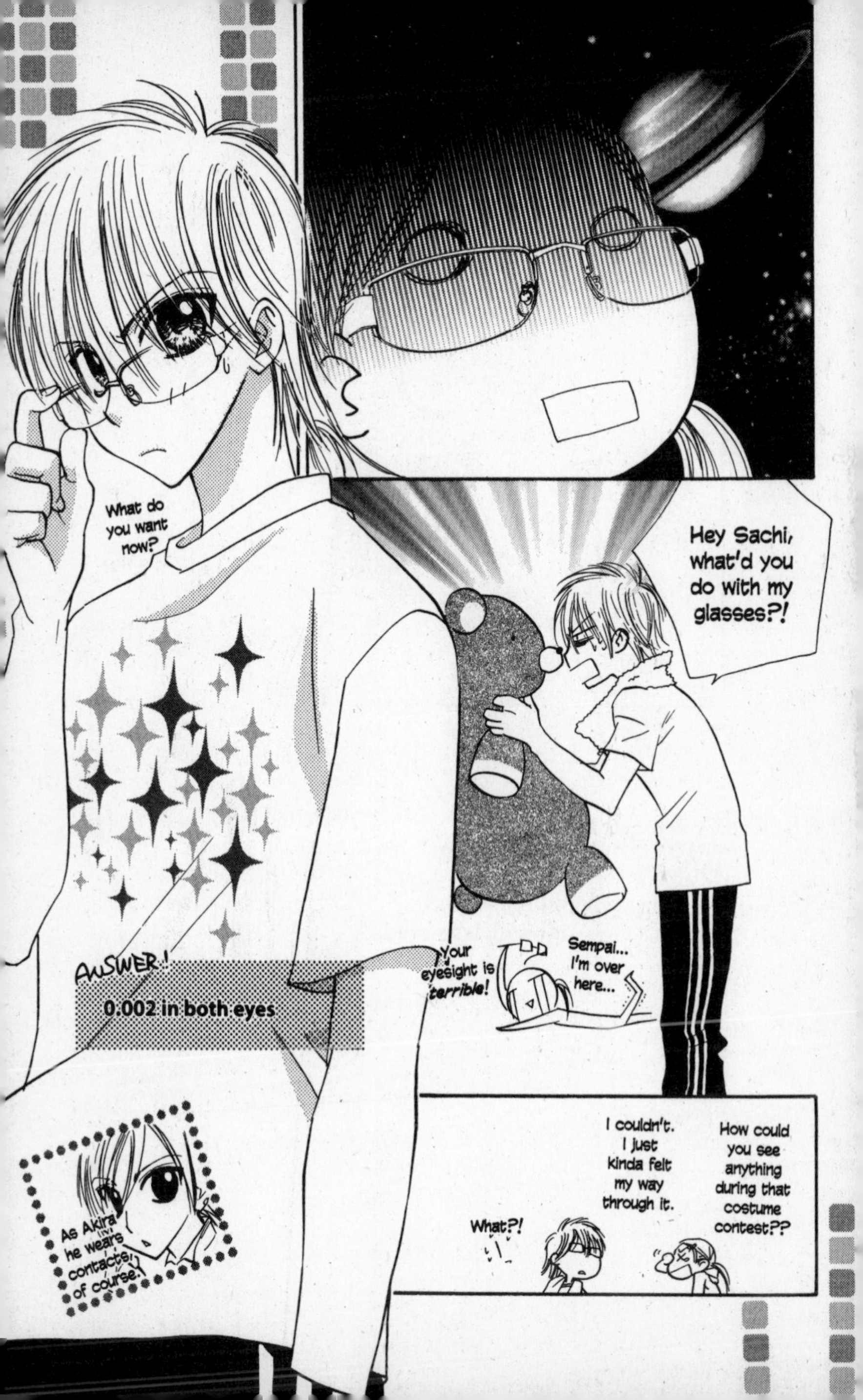

Hey Sachi, what'd you do with my glasses?!
Sempai... I'm over here...
Your eyesight is *terrible*!
How could you see anything during that costume contest??
I couldn't. I just kinda felt my way through it.
What?!
What do you want now?
ANSWER!
0.002 in both eyes
As Akira he wears contacts, of course.

Wataru Mizukami

Birthplace: Tokyo. Birthday: August 25. Debuted in 1995 with the Nakayoshi Manga Newcomer award-winning work *Never Give Up!* Best-known manga: *Let's Get Married!* Hobbies: tennis, driving, and shopping. Lately she's been planning to move to a new house.

# Translation Notes

Japanese is a tricky language for most Westerners, and translation is often more art than science. For your edification and reading pleasure, here are notes on some of the places where we could have gone in a different direction, or where a Japanese cultural reference is used.

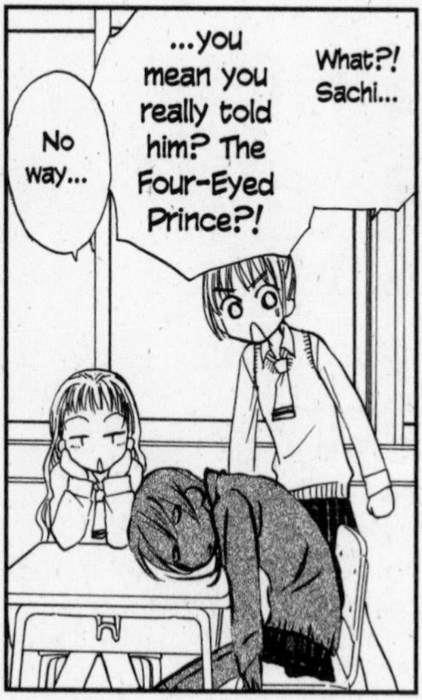
What?! Sachi...
...you mean you really told him? The Four-Eyed Prince?!
No way...

**Sachi, page 7**

"Sachi" is a nickname for the main character, Sachiko. The name "Sachiko" means "happy," so from that you can tell that Sachiko tends to have a bright and positive personality.

***Megane*, page 7, 169**

*Megane* is the Japanese word for "glasses." Since part of the reason for Sachiko's crush on her sempai is the fact that he wears glasses, it's safe to say that glasses (or *megane*) are a significant part of the story of *Four-Eyed Prince*.

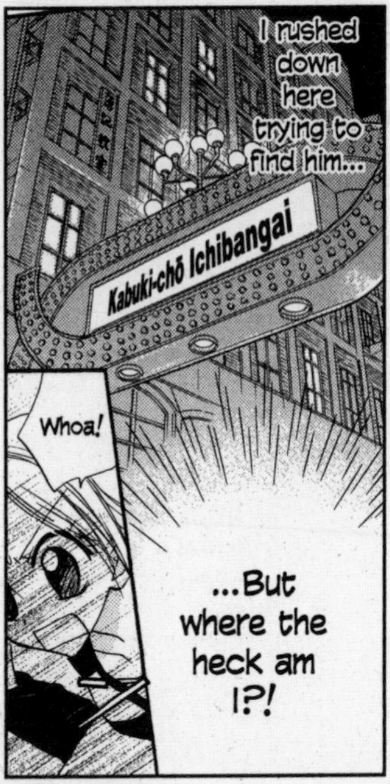
I rushed down here trying to find him...
Kabuki-chō Ichibangai
Whoa!
...But where the heck am I?!

**Kabuki-chō Ichibangai, page 19**

Kabuki-chō Ichibangai is the main street of the Kabuki-chō entertainment and red-light district in Tokyo. The neighborhood is called Kabuki-chō because at one point there was a plan to build a kabuki theater in that area, which was formerly known as Tsunohazu. The theater was never constructed, but the name Kabuki-chō stuck.

**Master, page 20**

In Japan, a bartender is generally referred to as "Master."

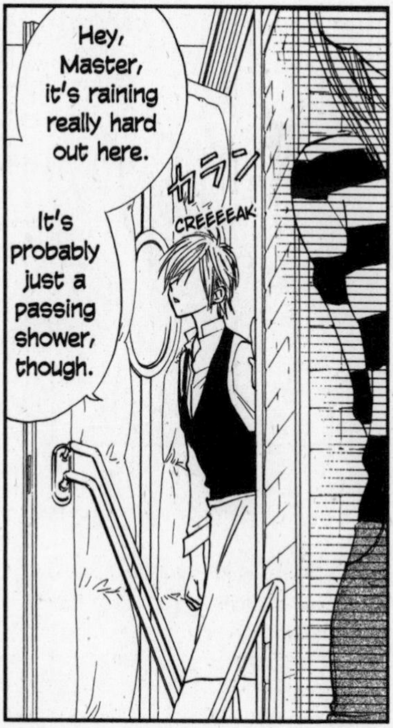
Hey, Master, it's raining really hard out here.
カラン
CREEEEAK
It's probably just a passing shower, though.

If you win, you get a free trip to a hot spring!

A hot spring...?

### Trip to a hot spring, page 56

Taking a trip to a natural hot spring, or *onsen*, is a typical cultural activity in Japan. Friends, couples, or families travel to a town located near a hot spring and stay at an inn that has bathing facilities that are fed from the naturally heated spring waters. *Onsen* group bathing is a favorite way to relax and rejuvenate the body.

### Kent Derricott, page 169

Kent Derricott, originally from Canada, gained fame as a television personality in Japan. He originally moved to Japan in 1983 to expand his import business, and subsequently became an actor and celebrity after a chance appearance on a Japanese variety show. Of course, he also wears glasses, just like the Four-Eyed Prince.

# PREVIEW OF VOLUME 2

We're pleased to be able to present you a preview from Volume 2. Please check our website (www.delreymanga.com) to see when this volume will be available in English. For now you'll have to make do with Japanese.

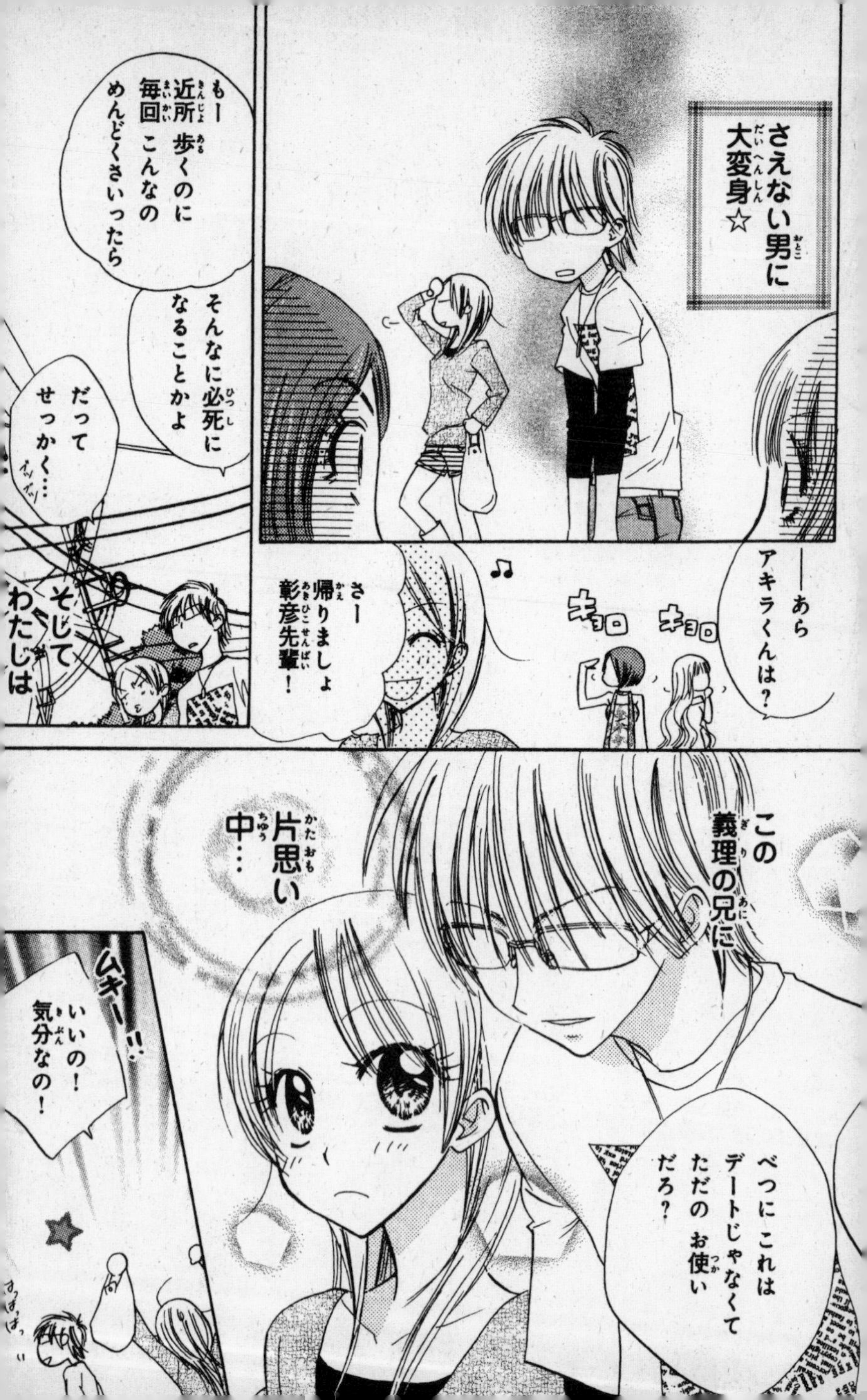
さえない男に大変身☆
キョロ キョロ
ーあら アキラくんは?
さー 帰りましょ 彰彦先輩！
もー 近所歩くのに 毎回 こんなの めんどくさいったら
そんなに必死に なることかよ
だって せっかく…
そして わたしは
この義理の兄に
片思い中…
べつにこれは デートじゃなくて ただの お使い だろ?
ムキー!!
いいの! 気分なの!

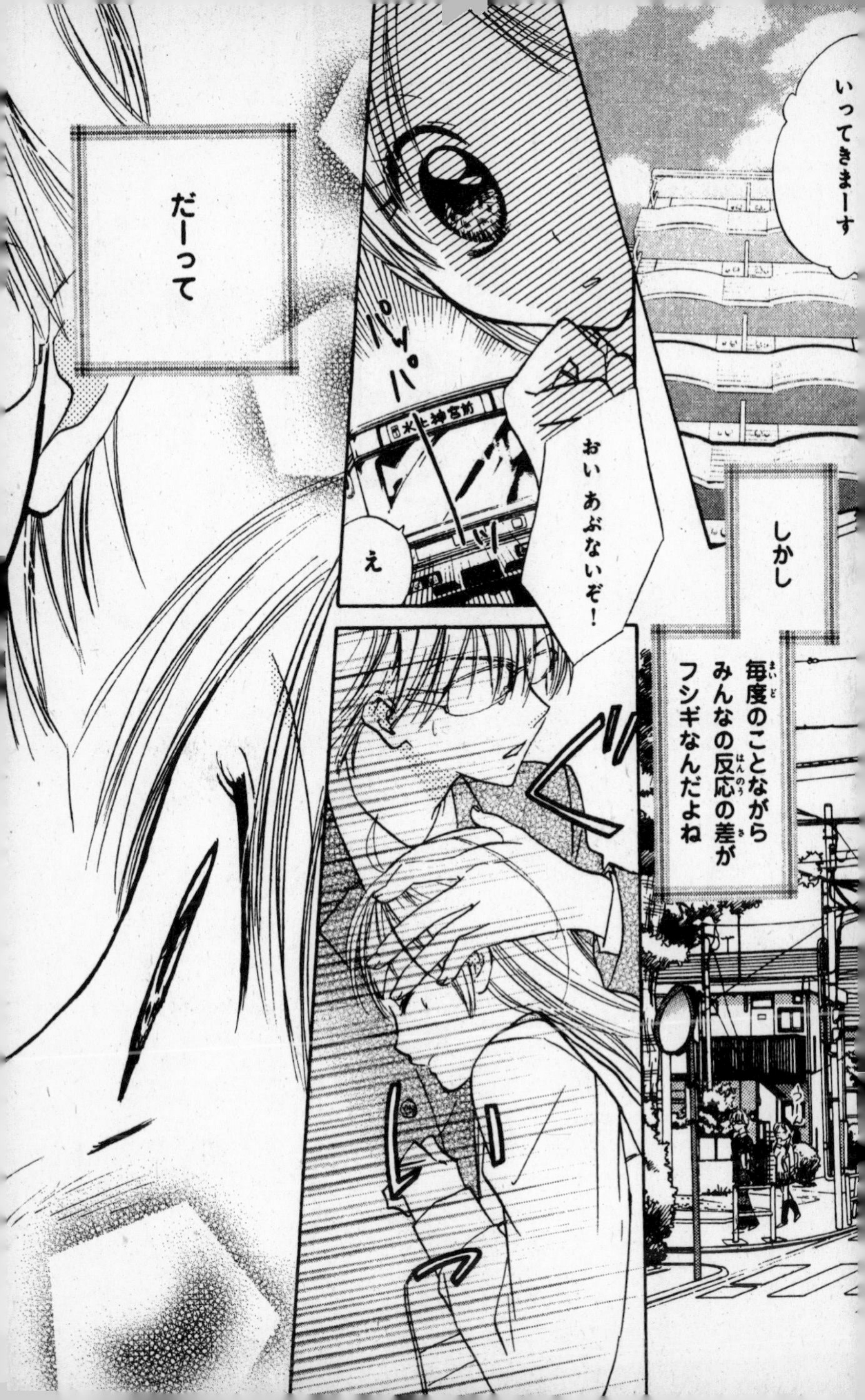

いってきまーす
しかし
毎度のことながら
みんなの反応の差が
フシギなんだよね
パッパ
おい あぶないぞ!
え
だーって

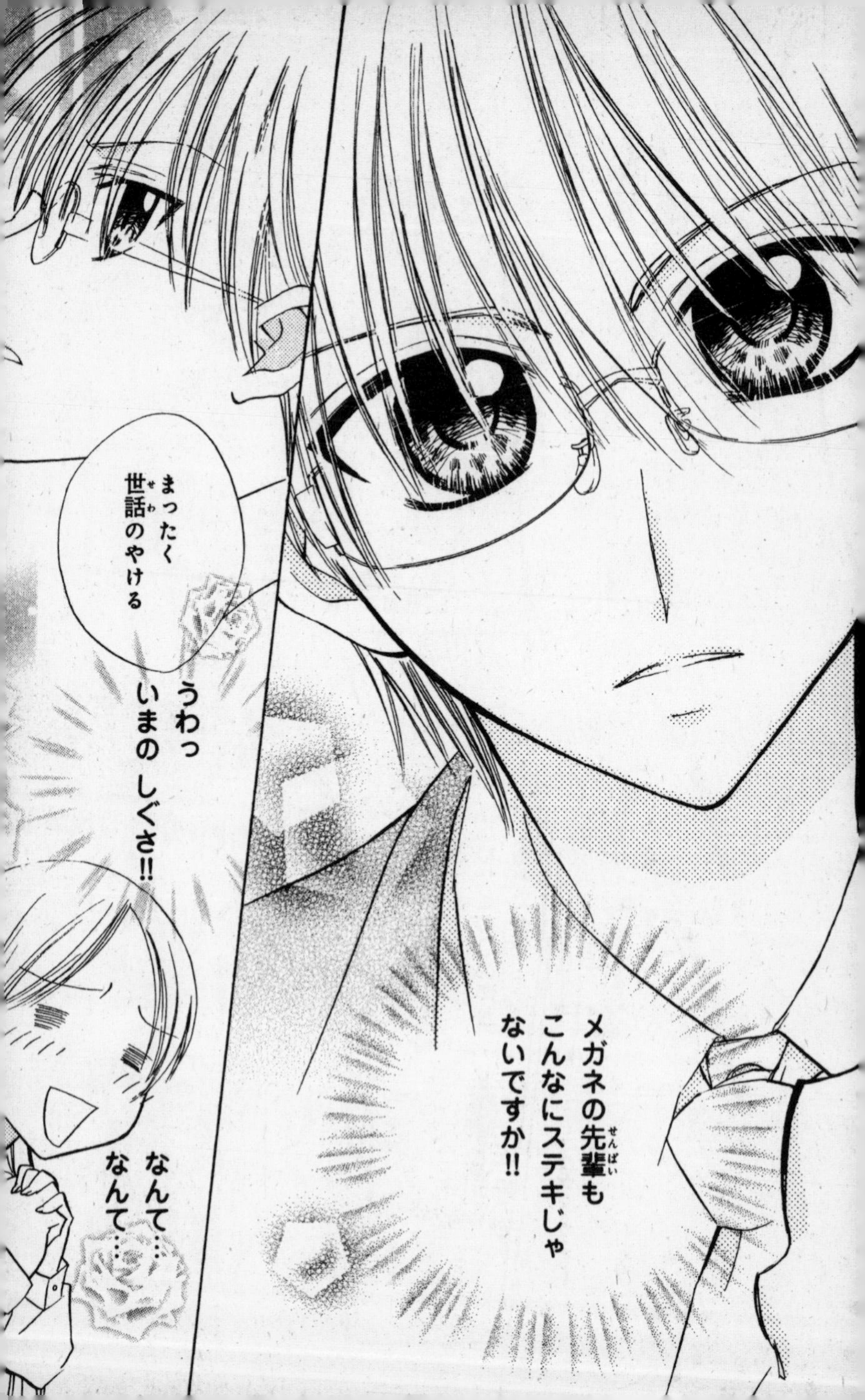
メガネの先輩もこんなにステキじゃないですか!!
まったく世話のやける
うわっ いまの しぐさ!!
なんて… なんて…

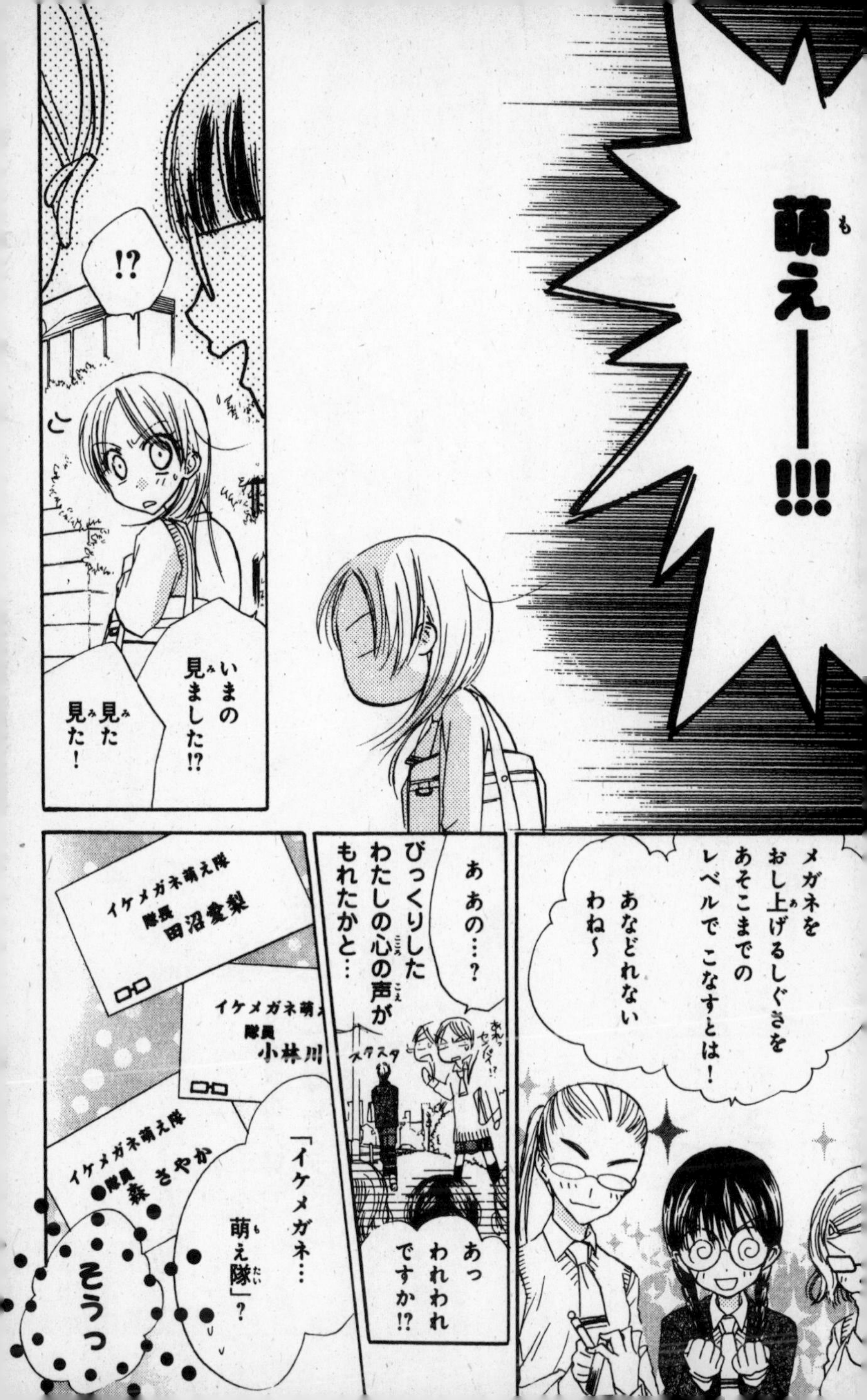
萌えー!!!
!?
いまの見ました!?
見た見た!
メガネをおし上げるしぐさをあそこまでのレベルでこなすとは!
あなどれないわね～
ああの…?
びっくりしたわたしの心の声がもれたかと…
スタスタ
あれっセンパイ!?
あっわれわれですか!?
イケメガネ萌え隊 隊長 田沼愛梨
イケメガネ萌え
隊員 小林川
イケメガネ萌え隊 隊員 森さやか
「イケメガネ…萌え隊」?
そうっ

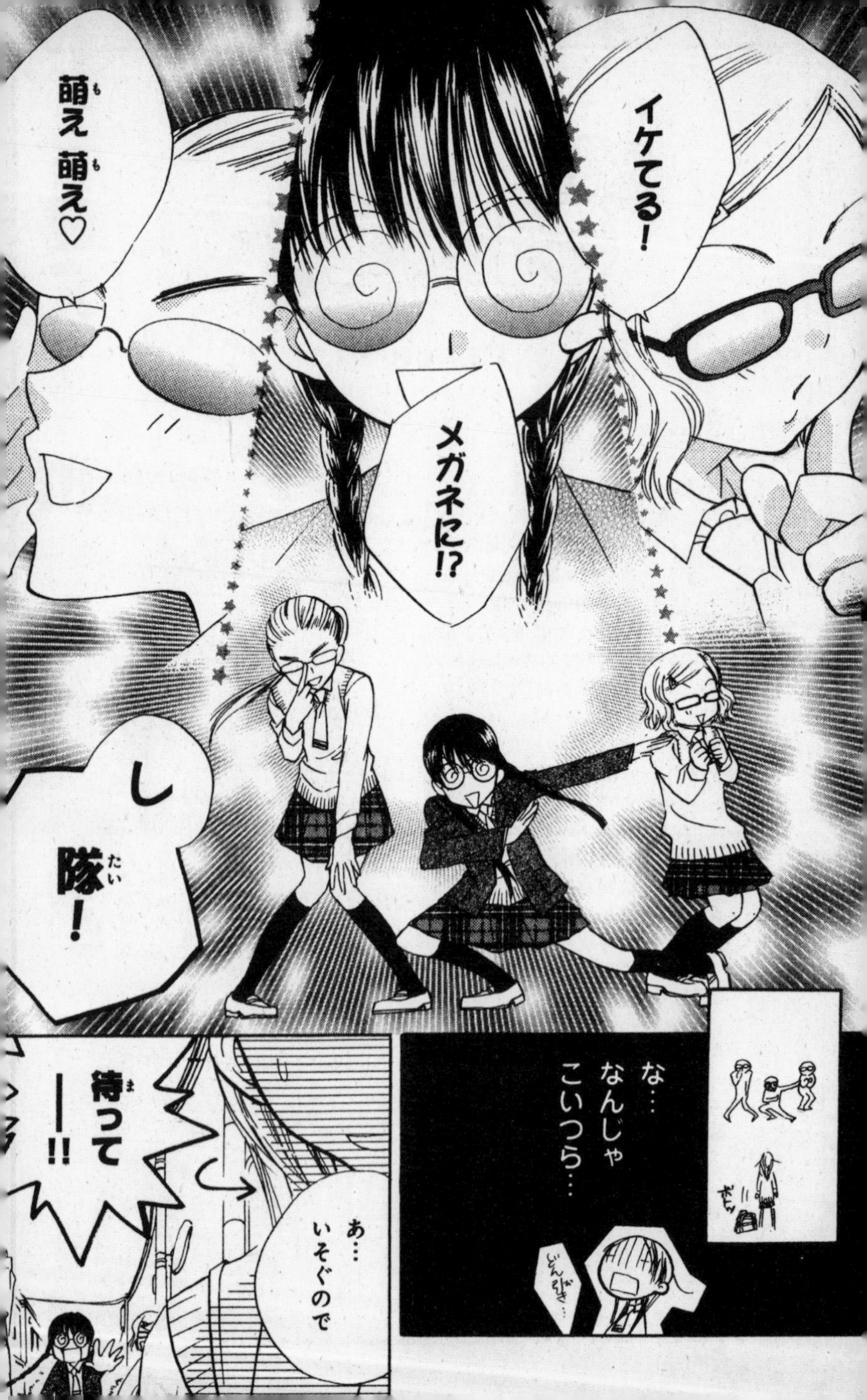
イケてる！
メガネに!?
萌え萌え♡
し隊！
ボトッ
な…
なんじゃ
こいつら…
どん引き…
あ…
いそぐので
待って
——!!

# SHUGO CHARA!

## PEACH-PIT

### Creators of *Dears* and *Rozen Maiden*

Everybody at Seiyo Elementary thinks that stylish and super-cool Amu has it all. But nobody knows the *real* Amu, a shy girl who wishes she had the courage to truly be herself. Changing Amu's life is going to take more than wishes and dreams—it's going to take a little magic! One morning, Amu finds a surprise in her bed: three strange little eggs. Each egg contains a Guardian Character, an angel-like being who can give her the power to be someone new. With the help of her Guardian Characters, Amu is about to discover that her true self is even more amazing than she ever dreamed.

## Special extras in each volume! Read them all!

# TOMARE!

## [STOP!]

## You're going the wrong way!

## Manga is a completely different type of reading experience.

## To start at the *beginning,* go to the end!

That's right! Authentic manga is read the traditional Japanese way—from right to left. Exactly the opposite of how American books are read. It's easy to follow: Just go to the other end of the book, and read each page—and each panel—from right side to left side, starting at the top right. Now you're experiencing manga as it was meant to be!